The Selma of the North

The Selma of the North

*Civil Rights Insurgency
in Milwaukee*

Patrick D. Jones

Harvard University Press

Cambridge, Massachusetts

London, England

2009

Library of Congress Cataloging-in-Publication Data

Jones, Patrick D.

The Selma of the North : civil rights insurgency in Milwaukee / Patrick D. Jones.

p.   cm.

Includes bibliographical references and index.

ISBN 978-0-674-03135-7 (alk. paper)

1. African Americans—Civil rights—Wisconsin—Milwaukee—History—20th century.
2. Civil rights movements—Wisconsin—Milwaukee—History—20th century.
3. Insurgency—Wisconsin—Milwaukee—History—20th century.
4. Community life—Wisconsin—Milwaukee—History—20th century.
5. African Americans—Wisconsin—Milwaukee—Politics and government—20th century.
6. Milwaukee (Wis.)—Race relations—History—20th century.
7. Milwaukee (Wis.)—Politics and government—20th century.
8. Milwaukee (Wis.)—Social conditions—20th century.   I. Title.

F589.M69N45   2009

323.1196'07307759509046—dc22   2008024142

To Raymond C. and Elizabeth L. Jones

Contents

Illustrations follow page 142.

Abbreviations

EC	Eagles Club
KKK	Ku Klux Klan
MBPP	Milwaukee Black Panther Party
MCCR	Milwaukee Commission on Community Relations
MCEO	Milwaukee Committee on Equal Opportunity
MCORE	Milwaukee Congress of Racial Equality
MNAACP	Milwaukee National Association for the Advancement of Colored People
MNALC	Milwaukee Negro American Labor Council
MPS	Milwaukee Public Schools
MUSIC	Milwaukee United School Integration Committee
NALC	Negro American Labor Council
SCLC	Southern Christian Leadership Conference
SDC	Social Development Commission
SNCC	Student Nonviolent Coordinating Committee
UE	United Electrical, Radio and Machine Workers of America
YC	Milwaukee NAACP Youth Council

Milwaukee Civil Rights Landmarks

Hampton Ave

Capitol Dr

Fond du Lac Ave

Locust St

Lisbon Ave

North Ave

76 th St

35 th St

27 th St

6 th St

Holton St

Oakland Ave

Lake Dr

Prospect Ave

Walnut St

Wisconsin Ave

Menomonee River

16 th St

Viaduct

National Ave

Greenfield Ave

16 th St

Kosciuszko Park

Lincoln Ave

Kinnickinnic River

Oklahoma Ave

Lake Michigan

Milwaukee River

African American Inner Core:

◼ 1940
▨ 1960

⬚ Kosciuszko Park
⌂ Freedom House I
✹ Freedom House II
✝ St. Boniface Church
● Eagles Club
▲ Home of Judge Robert Cannon
★ City Hall

0   0.5   1
Miles

Milwaukee County Inset

INSET

Created by Kenny French

The Selma of the North

Introduction

Two hundred civil rights marchers gathered in Milwaukee at the north end of the Sixteenth Street Viaduct on Tuesday, August 29, 1967.[1] The bridge, crossing the Menomonee River Valley, the city's equivalent of the Mason-Dixon Line, linked and divided the largely African American North Side from the predominantly white, working-class South Side. Some joked that the viaduct was the longest bridge in the world because it connected "Africa to Poland." The marchers held a city permit to conduct an open housing rally at Kosciuszko Park, located a few blocks from the hall where three years earlier hundreds of local people enthusiastically welcomed Alabama governor George Wallace during the Democratic presidential primary. The mood was tense as the demonstrators began their half-mile journey over the factories, smokestacks, coal piles, loading cranes, and railroad yards that made up Milwaukee's industrial base. The previous evening, more than 5,000 white spectators had pelted civil rights supporters on a similar trek with rocks, debris, and obscenities. On this night, members of the local NAACP Youth Council (YC), along with their advisor, a young white Catholic priest named James Groppi, sang freedom songs and chanted Black Power slogans to try to steel their supporters against what lay ahead. Thirty white Milwaukee police officers flanked the demonstrators, while eleven cars, one police wagon, reporters, and television camera crews from the three major national networks trailed closely behind. A line of young African American men clad in fatigues and gray sweatshirts emblazoned with the words "NAACP Commando" walked in formation between the marchers and the police. As the group neared the other side of the bridge, they could hear a low, growling clamor rise ahead of them.

1

The first thing the civil rights activists passed when they entered the South Side was Crazy Jim's used auto lot. Several hundred young white toughs had gathered there, and rock and roll blared from loudspeakers. An effigy of a white priest, defaced with a swastika, swung by the neck from a rope. The crowd leered at the passersby and hurled threats, jeers, and obscenities. Two of the counter-protesters held up a Confederate flag, while others waved signs that stated "White Power," "Bring Back Slavery," "Trained Nigger," "I Like Niggers: Everybody Should Own a Few," and "Work Don't March." A detachment of police rushed forward to head off trouble. With the national and local media nervously watching and recording, the marchers passed the raucous throng at Crazy Jim's without major incident.

Beyond the auto lot upwards of 13,000 angry white spectators lined the sidewalks opposite the marchers and filled the blocks around the park. Some wore stickers that said, "Wallace: Stand Up for America." Bottles, eggs, rocks, wood, firecrackers, urine, and spit began to fly. Shouts of "Get yourself a nigger," "We want slaves," "E-I-E-I-E-I-O, Father Groppi's got to go," and "Kill . . . kill . . . kill . . . kill" could be heard. Police commanders quickly passed out shotguns, rifles, and gas masks to the officers protecting the marchers. The demonstrators defiantly moved forward, working their way through the menacing crowds, protected by both well-armed police and unarmed Commandos. Father Groppi told the young marchers, "Keep cool. Walk fast. Girls in the middle. Don't be afraid. If we were afraid to die we wouldn't be good Christians." Police shoved their way through crowds of white spectators at every intersection. At the nearby Police Safety Building, local law enforcement officials conferred with leaders of the Wisconsin National Guard about a possible call-up of troops. Civil order seemed to dance on edge.

As the demonstrators continued toward their destination, a convertible with tags from Crazy Jim's and loaded with taunting kids holding signs and the swinging effigy slowly passed by the marchers; the white spectators erupted in cheers. Then, in the passion of the moment, more than 1,000 whites poured out into the intersection of Eleventh and Lincoln Streets, rushing the open housing advocates. The surge caught the police off guard. The mob swarmed over marchers, newsmen, and officers. Rampaging whites beat huddled and fleeing civil rights supporters—many of them children and women—and battled openly with the Commandos, who had stepped forward to meet the attack. Several angry young whites rocked a police car, while others threw objects and used their fists. Bedlam had broken out on the South Side of the Sixteenth Street Viaduct in a scene eerily reminiscent of the racial violence at the foot of the Edmund Pettus Bridge in Selma, Alabama, two years earlier.

Riot-clad police moved quickly to regroup and quell the racial disturbance by pumping shotgun blast after shotgun blast into the air above the crowd. Other officers lobbed tear gas into the mob, then moved in to disperse them. Most of the whites scattered, and police corralled the civil rights demonstrators onto a side street. Officers tried in vain to convince the marchers to call off their rally. Instead, Groppi defiantly declared, "We won't move out of our shell. We'll stay here until the National Guard comes and we can march like free American citizens." Someone then broke into the Movement standard, "Ain't Gonna Let Nobody Turn Me Around," and suddenly the whole crowd was moving again. Without legal power to challenge the activists, police scrambled to surround the marchers and escort them down the middle of the street to the park.[2]

When the group reached Kosciuszko Park, white spectators reassembled and closed in around police and demonstrators. Groppi rose and told the marchers who had made it to the picnic area, "You've shown you're willing to die for freedom." He encouraged them not to hate the angry white spectators but to "feel sorry for them." Just as he said, "Jesus Christ died for brotherhood," a small explosion injured three civil rights supporters. Responding to the danger, Groppi and the YC led the marchers in a hasty and haphazard retreat toward the viaduct. Feeding on the air of panic, a core of 600 frenzied whites continued to pursue and attack the battered activists as they scurried toward safety. The marchers endured one last vicious barrage of bottles and debris as they passed by the crowd at Crazy Jim's.

Tear gas still hung in the air when the open housing advocates finally reached the Sixteenth Street Viaduct. Journalist Frank Aukofer, who witnessed the scene, thought the marchers looked like "refugees from a battle." Signs of combat were everywhere: wounded demonstrators carried home by dazed comrades, a seminarian with blood streaming down his face, dozens nursing bumps and cuts and bruises, and a pervasive sense of bewildered fright. As these beleaguered civil rights foot soldiers slowly regrouped and made their way back across the viaduct, police continued to grapple with angry whites at the entryway to the South Side behind them.

Once the marchers reached the north side of the viaduct, they were escorted by eight police officers to the YC's Freedom House a few blocks away. As they got off the dilapidated bus that Groppi drove to demonstrations, several protesters shouted that the police had not given them sufficient protection. A large crowd from the neighborhood gathered, and soon the taunts turned into a hail of bottles and rocks upon the outnumbered police. Amid the turmoil, some officers claimed they heard gunshot from a nearby house. Police shot tear gas into the crowd in an attempt to regain control. Suddenly, dozens of young people came pouring out of the Freedom House with flames at their backs. Groppi rushed inside to see whether any others remained. A Commando, Prentice McKinney, used his body to shield some of the younger kids. Police claimed that someone in a passing car had thrown a firebomb into the civil rights headquarters, and they refused to allow firemen near the blaze because of the reported sniper in a nearby abandoned house. YC members and their advisor believed that a tear gas canister shot deliberately into the house by police caused the fire and that this was a further attempt by city officials to disrupt their quest for freedom.[3] By the time the police permitted firefighters to battle the blaze, the YC Freedom House was engulfed in flames and there was little hope of saving the structure from total ruin.

The story of Milwaukee's open housing campaign does not fit with the popular narrative of the modern civil rights era. What do we make of a white Catholic priest leading a band of young African American activists in a militant Black Power campaign in Wisconsin? How should we understand the massive resistance of thousands of white Milwaukeeans to aggressive nonviolent protest? And what about those unarmed Commandos who stepped forth to repel the vicious attacks of violent white residents and police? The traditional account of this period does not provide a framework within which we might answer these and other questions to make sense of this dramatic and important episode in American history.

Over the past two decades, there has been a revolution in the way we understand the southern struggle for racial justice.[4] Historians and other scholars pushed back the beginnings of the Movement at least as far as the New Deal and World War II.[5] They made clear that beyond the well-known leaders, national organizations, and television cameras, local circumstances drove campaigns for racial equality.[6] Other studies underscored the central, but often overlooked, role of women in the southern Movement[7] and linked the domestic struggle to broader national and international trends.[8] Still others reconfigured Black Power as an enduring concept with roots stretching back decades before it became a popular slogan during the mid-1960s and demonstrated the way nonviolent direct action and armed self-defense worked "in tension and in tandem" throughout the South.[9] And a steady stream of civil rights memoirs and biographies has consistently enriched our view of the southern Movement with intimate personal stories.[10]

Despite these exciting advances in the literature, scholars have not yet forged a comparable body of work on civil rights activism outside the South, although a small but growing number of historians have begun to take up the challenge. The signal shot came in 2003 when Jeanne Theoharis and Komozi Woodard published *Freedom North,* a collection of essays by a new generation of scholars focusing on black freedom struggles outside the South between 1940 and 1980. "Foregrounding the South has constricted popular understandings of race and racism in the United States during and after WWII," argued Theoharis in an introductory essay that read as a scholarly call to arms. She suggested that this narrow perspective on civil rights activism made it seem

> as if the South was the only part of the country that needed a movement, as if blacks in the rest of the country only became energized to fight after their Southern brothers and sisters did, as if Southern racism was more malignant than the strains found in the rest of the country, as if social activism produced substantive change only in the South.

The eleven essays included in *Freedom North* displayed the great array of black activism in the North, Midwest, and West. Woodard and Theoharis followed up this landmark work in 2005 with another volume of cutting-edge civil rights historiography, titled *Groundwork.*[11]

It is clear that when we look in new ways at old topics, we often see new things. The Movement in the North shared a consciousness with those who struggled in the South, but it took place within and responded to a distinctive context. The industrial base of the economy, with its strong labor movement; the presence of white ethnic groups; the dominance of the Catholic Church; the strong link between race, ethnicity, and urban geography; the relatively secure African American right to vote; and the diffuse nature of discrimination—all of which set the region apart from the South—critically affected the development of race relations and civil rights activism in Milwaukee and other northern industrial locales. Although previous scholars have highlighted the way large-scale forces shaped the racial contours of American cities, they have not placed civil rights activism within this framework in an attempt to figure out how social change occurred and how the North's racial caste system persists.

Books that explore race relations and black freedom movements outside of the Deep South have been slowly emerging. Robert Self's award-winning *American Babylon* explored the complex interactions among civil rights, Black Power, and suburbanization in Oakland. Peter Levy challenged many of the standard conceptions of civil rights activism in *Civil War on Race Street*, his fascinating study of Gloria Richardson and the struggle for racial justice in Cambridge, Maryland. Similarly, Martha Biondi's *To Stand and Fight* powerfully illustrated that the roots of northern freedom movements stretch back before the well-known early milestones of the southern Movement in the mid-1950s. Biondi's work emphasized radical influences on the Movement in New York City and made clear that activists embraced a mix of goals, tactics, and strategies that cut across easy distinctions between civil rights and Black Power. Most recently, Matthew Countryman published a fine book, *Up South*, which traced two generations of black activists in Philadelphia and strongly suggested that Black Power was less a sharp break from the past than a natural evolution out of the frustrations and failures of racial liberalism in the postwar period. Collectively, these historians have begun the hard work of unearthing the many unexplored stories of civil rights insurgency in the urban North.[12]

Even so, we have only just begun this important new subfield of civil rights history. In effect, we are in the "archeological" stage of northern Movement historiography, still early in the process of excavating the terrain outside of the South. This book seeks to add another tile to the mosaic, another local story to the emerging literature, focusing on the civil rights insurgency in Milwaukee. By civil rights insurgency I mean, in the most general sense, the era of direct action, when marches, picketing, sit-ins, and other forms of protest politics played a central role in civil rights activism. More specifically, I use the phrase to capture the sense that these grassroots challenges most often came from outside established institutions of power; sought to confront, and maybe topple, traditional authority; and often contained an element of rebelliousness.

In Milwaukee from the late 1950s through the 1960s, a distinctive movement for racial justice emerged from unique local circumstances. A series of indigenous leaders led a growing number of local people in campaigns against employment and housing discrimination, segregated public schools, the membership of public officials in discriminatory private organizations, police brutality, and cuts in social welfare funding. Although Milwaukee activists espoused many of the tenets of "Black Power"—years before that slogan echoed across the Mississippi Delta—its most prominent leader was a white Catholic priest, Father James Groppi. In campaigns that were morally complex, politically realistic, and sometimes effective, local activists, like many of their counterparts in the South, professed peace but provoked violence. Employing nonviolent direct action, they confronted racial inequality, pushed it into the public spotlight, and forced the entire city to respond. Their provocative tactics aroused a violent reaction from many local whites and helped spur reform at both the municipal and federal levels. At its height during the open housing campaign, many viewed the Milwaukee struggle as a last stand for an interracial, nonviolent, and church-based Movement. The story of civil rights insurgency in what many called "the Selma of the North" is as compelling—and remains as revealing—as any in the nation. Even so, it has been largely forgotten in the popular narrative of the era.[13]

The Selma of the North demonstrates the importance of local stories to the civil rights movement and highlights the links between national events and local campaigns. This research delineates the interconnections between northern and southern movements for racial justice and extends the findings of recent scholarship on Black Power. Moreover, it builds on new work that has reconfigured the relationship between nonviolent direct action and armed self-defense, introduced gender as an important analytic lens for civil rights scholars, and uncovered the often hidden origins of the urban crisis and white backlash.[14] Though it is rooted in a careful sifting of a complex history, *The Selma of the North* speaks directly to contemporary racial and urban dilemmas: Milwaukee continues to be one of the most segregated cities in the country.[15]

The failure of the Movement in Milwaukee, if it can be fairly called a failure, is part of the larger and continuing inability of this nation to come to grips with its enduring chasm of race and caste in urban America. Betty Martin, a YC member for most of the 1960s, remembered the walk across the Sixteenth Street Viaduct in late August 1967 as one of "the most frightening experiences" of her life. "[To] not know if you are going to get out alive or not because you had never experienced anger like you had experienced it by going across that viaduct," she recalled, "and then to be pinned down with fire going over your head. With [police] actually shooting over your head at the Freedom House and then to be bombed, and then the house catching on fire . . ." But as fearful as local activists were of what they might find on the other side, Betty Martin and thousands of other courageous Milwaukeeans, along with allies from across the country, ultimately made the long journey across that bridge with the hope of creating a more just and equitable community. Similarly, today, as difficult and frightening as it may seem, we also need to cross that bridge, to confront our collective history, and to broach the persistent tragedy of race in American society. It is my hope that this history might speak to that desire by helping readers to better understand the recent roots of the urban crisis.

— 1 —

Ethnic Milwaukee and the
Black Community

On the evening of July 27, 1922, thirty-six African American workers from Chicago relaxed after a long day of work on the Milwaukee railroad. In the midst of a nationwide strike, Chicago Northwestern Rail Road and Milwaukee Railway had imported black laborers to replace unionized white workers as pitmen, clerks, waiters, cooks, and general laborers. The company housed the African American workers and other strikebreakers in a series of boxcars at the rail yard in New Butler, Wisconsin, a small community just outside of Milwaukee. As many of the men tried to sleep, Jack Wilson, a chef, sat in the cook car reading the newspaper. A few unarmed company guards patrolled the area outside. Several hundred yards away, a crew of white foremen and white gang bosses slept in another set of boxcars.[1]

A few miles away, at the New Butler headquarters of the Fraternal Order of Eagles, striking white ethnic union workers held a meeting. The laborers were angry that the railway company had recently decided to import black strikebreakers from Chicago despite the pleas of Daniel Hoan, Milwaukee's Socialist mayor. After the meeting ended at 9:00 p.m., dozens of armed strikers made their way toward the enclave of the resting replacement workers. A half hour later, the men emerged from a wheat field that ran along the northeast side of the tracks, shouting and shooting hundreds of rounds of ammunition into the boxcars where the black workers slept. The first shots penetrated the cook car, missing Jack Wilson's head by inches before embedding in the ceiling and wall. Immediately, dozens of half-clad men flooded out of the boxcars and disappeared into the nearby woods. Wilson claimed to have heard "100 to 150 shots" and "could see Negroes jumping out of windows and doors and crawling under the cars for protection." According to William Washington, a black porter, "[It] seemed like a million men yelling. Then I heard shots fired. I knew there was target practice going on somewhere. It was too close for me. I up and beat it. Everybody else done the same thing at the same time. We all had just one idea, to get away from there." As the African American workers escaped, the marauding white terrorists rushed through the boxcars, overturning tables, smashing dishes, destroying beds, shredding clothes, and spoiling the next day's rations. Outgunned company guards were helpless against the mob. By the time the police arrived, the rail yard stood eerily quiet once again. One black worker sustained serious injuries in the attack when he fell from a boxcar window, and nearly thirty others received glass cuts and other moderate injuries. Curiously, nearby white strikebreakers were left untargeted and unharmed in the violent outburst. The police failed to make any arrests in connection with the incident.

Local reaction to the attack at New Butler was swift. Newspaper accounts and local law enforcement officers played down the seriousness of the attack. Union officials blamed the violence on the company for importing black strikebreakers. Chicago and Northwestern executives, in turn, blamed the violence on the striking workers and offered a $50 reward for information leading to the arrest of strikers or sympathizers. The company also rushed "156 special agents, 155 riot guns, and 75 revolvers" to the New Butler rail yard as a hedge against further assaults. The day before the incident, Mayor Hoan, who had consistently opposed the introduction of black "scab" workers in the city,[2] reminded W. H. Finley, the president of the railway company, that "the importation of colored laborers in time of strikes as in St. Louis, Kansas City, New Orleans, and dozens of other American cities brought about bitter race hatred and led to disgraceful race riots which has blackened the names of those cities everywhere." Hoan begged Finley not to contribute to local racial animosities and warned him that the city of Milwaukee "will feel compelled to hold your company personally responsible as accessory to any race riots which may result."

The mob violence at New Butler outraged Milwaukee's small black community. Writing on behalf of the Milwaukee chapter of Marcus Garvey's Universal Negro Improvement Association (UNIA), the African Communities League, the City Federation of Colored Women's Clubs, the Milwaukee NAACP (MNAACP), the Milwaukee Urban League, and the Sixth Ward Political Club, John Alexander, president of the local UNIA, told Mayor Hoan, "We, the colored citizens of Milwaukee are seriously opposed to the Milwaukee and Northwestern railroads importing Negroes from Chicago and other cities to fill strikers' positions" and criticized the rail companies for "using us for a tool to further their cause." At the yard, eighteen African American strikebreakers failed to report for work the following Monday. Shortly thereafter, on August 2, 1922, striking workers accepted a settlement proposal from President Warren Harding and headed back to work, effectively rendering all protest moot.

It would be decades before large numbers of African Americans made Milwaukee their home, but many of the same tensions and conflicts that would animate race relations in the city during the civil rights era already existed in 1922. Milwaukee at this time, as it would be after World War II, was a white working-class city where the infusion of a new African American population easily provoked fear, reaction, and even violence from the majority.

Years later, when Father Groppi, the NAACP Youth Council (YC), and the Commandos made their stand on the south side of the Sixteenth Street Viaduct, their actions and those of their opponents were tapping into a deeper legacy of racial struggle in Milwaukee. To better understand the open housing campaign and the modern struggle for racial justice in Milwaukee, it is necessary to situate those prominent efforts within the broader history of African American experience and race relations in the city. This chapter is aimed at providing that context.

Early Black Settlement and Community Development

From its beginnings, the settlement that is today called Milwaukee was pluralistic, its character significantly forged by the competition, cooperation, and conflict of distinct groups living along the western shore of Lake Michigan near the confluence of the Menomonee, Kinnickinnic, and Milwaukee rivers. An 1817 British census of the community found a cosmopolitan mix of roughly 300 inhabitants from the Potawatomi, Ho-Chunk (Winnebago), Mascouten, Ottawa, Chippewa, Sac, and Fox tribes. By this time, European and American missionaries, fur traders, and land speculators had also made their way into the area. In 1832, growing conflict between the native inhabitants and European settlers over property claims culminated in the Blackhawk War in northern Illinois and southern Wisconsin. In the war's wake, whites drove out most Indians from Milwaukee to make way for economic development. By the late 1830s, the three rival "founding fathers" of the city—the French Canadian Solomon Juneau, the Connecticut-born Yankee

Byron Kilbourn, and the Virginia-born fur trader and land speculator George Walker—had established a presence on contending sides of the Milwaukee River, each struggling to attract investment and inhabitants to their "town." The competition eventually led to the Milwaukee Bridge War of 1845, which in turn brought about the consolidation of the competing areas into a unified City of Milwaukee on January 31, 1846.[3]

It was during this early, formative period that Milwaukee's first African American inhabitants arrived. Most historical accounts of the city credit Joe Oliver, who in 1835 became the cook for Solomon Juneau's family, as the city's first black resident, but at least one study gives the distinction to Henry and Georgiana Anderson, who moved from Green Bay to Milwaukee during the same period.[4] Regardless, by 1850 the black population of Milwaukee had grown to 100, out of a total population of 20,000. According to William Vollmar, this early African American community was, overall, self-reliant and relatively prosperous. Most of these black pioneers were free people of color or former slaves who had purchased their freedom or escaped. The majority were literate, and most men possessed marketable skills that translated into economic opportunities as artisans, barbers, cooks, waiters, store owners, clerks, and skilled mechanics. Some of Milwaukee's early African American residents owned property on good land alongside prominent white neighbors. Vollmar counted five interracial marriages and concluded that the city enjoyed "exceptionally good race relations."[5]

Over the next two decades, racial antagonisms in Milwaukee sharpened as sectional tensions in the nation increased. The Fugitive Slave Act of 1850 extended the reach of the slave catcher nationwide, including such areas as Southeast Wisconsin, which contained strong pockets of abolitionist sentiments and had been viewed as a safe haven for escaped slaves. The prospect of federally sanctioned kidnapping placed Milwaukee's black population on precarious footing, prompting many African Americans to move to Canada and deeply dividing white residents. Yet, although the act empowered slave owners and local bounty hunters, it also spurred political organizing among African Americans and their abolitionist allies. For example, in 1854, a mob of white abolitionists and a few black allies, led by abolitionist newspaper editor Sherman Booth, broke down the door to the Milwaukee jail to liberate Joshua Glover, an escaped slave who had been living in Racine until his recapture by his master and the U.S. Marshals. The case ultimately resulted in a Wisconsin Supreme Court decision that declared the Fugitive Slave Act unconstitutional. The Glover rescue was the most dramatic incident in a series of local conflicts over the kidnapping of black residents.[6]

During this same period, voting rights were another point of contest in Milwaukee's struggle for racial justice. Wisconsin residents had debated statehood and a new constitution for much of the mid- and late 1840s, giving their approval to a second draft of the document in 1848. The state constitution left the question of voting rights for African Americans to local and state officials. Beginning in 1849, white voters failed to provide the requisite support for several measures ensuring African American voting rights. In 1865, Ezekial Gillespie, a railroad employee and emancipated slave with support in the local abolitionist community, attempted to register to vote but was turned away due to his "mixed African blood." Gillespie's lawyer, Byron Payne, who had gained notoriety in 1854 when he argued successfully against the Fugitive Slave Act in Joshua Glover's case, sued election inspectors, setting off another historic legal battle. The following year, in *Gillespie v. Palmer,* the Wisconsin Supreme Court unanimously ruled in favor of African American voting rights.[7]

However, despite occasional victories like those in the Glover and Gillespie cases, other trends did not bode well for the long-term prospects of African Americans in Milwaukee. According to historian Joseph Ranney, the "pattern of weak racial liberalism," established by white civic leaders in the 1840s, continued through the civil rights era of the 1960s. "Wisconsin never countenanced de jure discrimination," he explains, "but de facto segregation and discrimination were common [throughout this period]." In addition, the influx of thousands of German and Irish immigrants to the city during the middle part of the nineteenth century signaled greater job competition for black workers and a rise in interracial tensions. A startling illustration of the explosive potential of these ethnic and racial conflicts occurred in 1861 when a fight between two Irishmen and two African American men resulted in the stabbing death of one of the Irishmen and the public lynching of one of the black men by a white mob. Furthermore, in 1863, several petitions were introduced in the state legislature to prohibit African American migration into the state. "The accumulation of events like these made a dramatic change in Milwaukee's Black population," writes historian Jack Dougherty. "Most of the early settlers had either died or moved away. In their place came a newer, less established Black community with lower literacy rates, fewer skilled jobs, reduced property holdings, and decreased interracial marriages."[8]

With the collapse of Reconstruction, federal authority retreated from racial equality nationally, leaving local communities across the country to debate the status and rights of their black residents. In Wisconsin, despite strong, widespread Union support by whites during the war, most were not sympathetic to the struggles of African Americans afterward. "Black Milwaukeeans of this era began facing a different kind of racism," Dougherty explains, "induced by more direct economic competition with white immigrants, and rising opposition to interracial marriages." By the 1880s, both formal and informal mechanisms—including laws, court decisions, social customs, and tradition—had evolved to regulate the color line. New disputes emerged over public accommodations.[9]

Black residents continued to press for full equality. In 1889, when an African American railroad porter named Owen Howell was refused seating on the main floor of the Bijou Opera House, he sued and won. Importantly, Howell won his case by appealing more to standards of middle-class respectability than to racial justice. Milwaukee attorney William Green led a more direct political effort to secure passage of the 1895 state Civil Rights Act, which banned discrimination in restaurants, hotels, theaters, and other public establishments in Wisconsin. He and his allies also helped thwart several attempts by white lawmakers to pass anti-miscegenation laws at the turn of the century.[10]

A City of Nations

The late nineteenth and early twentieth century was a period of dynamic growth and change in Milwaukee, spurred by industrial expansion and massive immigration. By the second half of the nineteenth century, Milwaukee boasted the world's largest primary wheat market and the world's largest tanning center, and enjoyed an international reputation as the U.S. beer capital. Milling, tanning, meatpacking, brewing, and iron production anchored the local economy, and each continued to expand through the turn of the century. Universal Foods, Kohls, Roundys, Sentry, and Usingers filled the bellies of generations of Milwaukeeans while the Miller, Pabst, and Schlitz breweries topped off thousands of mugs nationwide. During the first decades of the 1900s, metal fabrication added a powerful new industry to Milwaukee's economic mix. Dozens of machine shops, foundries, and forges turned out everything from bicycles to buckets to state-of-the-art machinery, earning the city the nickname "Machine Shop of the World."

Allis-Chalmers, Bucyris Erie, Harley-Davidson, Harnischfeger, A. O. Smith, and OMC Evinrude worked with iron and other metals to make machinery parts, engines, motorcycles, and other large manufactured goods. Allen-Bradley, Johnson Controls, and Square D. Corporation specialized in electrical manufacturing.

As industry flourished, Milwaukee's population mushroomed from roughly 20,000 residents in 1850 to more than 285,000 in 1900 and upwards of 587,000 in 1940. Most of the increase came from European immigrants seeking economic opportunity and improved lives. During the 1840s and 1850s, more than 1,000 Germans arrived in the city every week, and by the early twentieth century, a majority of the population was of German descent. By 1890, Milwaukee Germans had created a distinct subculture with separate schools, churches, social clubs, fraternal organizations, political groups, and breweries. The German imprint on the city was so strong that many referred to Milwaukee as the "German Athens of America." The second largest immigrant group during this early period, and the main rival to the Germans in jobs and politics, were the Irish, who accounted for about 15 percent of the city's population in 1850. Smaller numbers of Czech, Austrian, Dutch, Norwegian, British, and European Jewish immigrants also came to Milwaukee in the mid-nineteenth century.[11]

Beginning in the 1880s, wave after wave of new immigrants, this time from southern and eastern Europe—Poles, Italians, Greeks, Serbs, Slovenes, Croats, and Eastern European Jews—flooded Milwaukee in search of a better life. In fact, by 1890, immigrants and their children comprised a stunning 86.4 percent of the city's total population, marking Milwaukee as the "most foreign" city in the United States. By 1910, Russians, Ukrainians, Lithuanians, and other working-class migrants from Eastern Europe further contributed to the city's ethnic stew. That year, the proportion of foreign residents totaled 78.6 percent, still enough to tie Milwaukee with New York as most foreign city. Almost all who came were white, though not all white ethnics were equal. As was the case elsewhere, the earlier immigrant groups, particularly in Milwaukee the Germans, secured their positions in the social and economic hierarchies at the expense of the newer groups. Many spoke languages other than English and strove to preserve Old World heritage and a traditional way of life. For good reason, then, Milwaukee earned a new title, the "City of Nations." Well into the twentieth century, the primary lines of tension and division in Milwaukee revolved around ethnicity, religion, and class, not race.[12]

Milwaukee's cultural diversity was stamped into its physical geography as a patchwork of tight-knit, white ethnic neighborhoods. First Germans, then Jews, lived in what would later be called "the inner core." Poles and other working-class central Europeans dominated the area south of the Menomonee River. American-born whites of English ancestry shared the East Side with still more Germans. Italians settled along Brady Street and replaced the Irish in the Third Ward when the latter group moved to the western suburbs. Greeks lived along the northern edge of downtown, Serbians in Walker's Point, and Croatians on the near North Side under the shadow of the Schlitz brewery. Concentrations of other groups could also be found scattered across the city. In part, ethnic identity was rooted directly in this sense of place—in physical space, or "turf," a specific number of blocks controlled by a particular group. Ethnic neighborhoods were a source of pride for their residents. They were to be tended and defended, as necessary. But as historian John Gurda is quick to point out, "Although the broad ethnic patterns were obvious even to casual observers, few sections of Milwaukee belonged exclusively, or even largely, to members of a single group." A certain degree of fluidity and ethnic complexity existed in virtually every neighborhood, ensuring a constant process of formation and reformation and a unique blend of conflict and cooperation.

Milwaukee's immigrant neighborhoods revolved around a particular sense of community. At the center most often stood a church, a pivotal institution because it served the social, spiritual, economic, and even political needs of the community. The Catholic Church dominated the religious life of most new immigrants, but the Lutheran Church was also strong in the city among Germans and others. Small but significant numbers of Jews, Orthodox Christians, and mainstream Protestants worshiped throughout the city, too. In general, immigrant communities tended to embrace an ethos rooted in family, authority, and patriotism, adhering to a strict Christian morality, though perhaps more Old Testament in judgment than New Testament in grace.

Ethnic neighborhoods were also working-class neighborhoods, intimately tied to the industrial economy. During the early twentieth century, Milwaukee ranked second among the twenty largest U.S. cities in the percentage of its workforce in manufacturing. Several early suburban communities, such as Cudahy and West Allis, were established as company towns before ultimately being annexed by the city. For many immigrants, work in a plant or mill was grueling and underpaid, but it also created opportunities to get a foothold on economic security. One of the key markers of that security was homeownership, which in turn reinforced the bonds among identity, economic class, and physical space. According to Gurda, "The newest groups get the oldest houses. The majority of Milwaukee's newcomers lived within a mile of downtown, in hand-me-down neighborhoods left behind as earlier residents moved out to greener pastures."[13]

Not surprisingly, perhaps, given the dominance of industry in the city, the labor movement and white progressive left enjoyed strong support and real political power in Milwaukee during the first half of the twentieth century. Like many urban, industrial centers, Milwaukee was stricken by labor unrest during the late nineteenth century. The most famous incident occurred on May 5, 1886, just two days after police in Chicago fired on a crowd of strikers at the McCormick Harvester plant, killing four, and one day after a bomb ripped through a labor rally in Chicago's Haymarket Square, killing eight. The Wisconsin state militia in Bay View, under the direction of Governor Jeremiah Rusk, fired on 1,500 peaceful union members, most from the city's Polish South Side. Seven workers were killed as they marched in favor of an eight-hour workday outside the Bay View Rolling Mills plant. But by the first decade of the 1900s, the combined power of an invigorated local labor movement, "Fightin' Bob" LaFollette's Progressives, and the Milwaukee Socialist Party led to a series of labor reforms. With the election of Daniel Hoan in 1910, Milwaukee became the only major American city ever to elect a Socialist mayor. The Socialists advocated a platform of clean municipal government, an expansion of city services, and strong support of organized labor. Their pragmatic approach to city government earned them the nickname "the Sewer Socialists." With the exception of a brief stint during the Depression and World War II, when a sequence of Progressive Party and liberal Democratic Party candidates won office, the Socialists maintained the mayoral seat until 1960, although their influence in the Common Council began to wane much earlier. In 1958, *Fortune* magazine, commenting largely on the administration of the city's last Socialist mayor, Frank Zeidler, voted Milwaukee the second-best-run city in the country; Daniel Hoan had received similar accolades three decades before.[14]

Because class was their primary mode of analysis, the Socialists did not have a significant or sustained program to address the discrimination and inequality faced by Milwaukee's small black population. In fact, as in the New Butler strike in 1922, Socialist politicians colluded with organized labor throughout the early twentieth century to maintain a citywide ban on the importation of foreign black strikebreakers by local industries. At its base, Socialist opposition to strikebreakers—white or black—was a form of support for labor unions. But it was also an attempt to avoid the massive racial violence visited on other industrial centers during this period. Beyond that, the Socialist Party failed to push labor unions or employers to eliminate discrimination against black workers.[15]

Despite Milwaukee's progressive and even radical traditions, local politics was tempered by a pervasive cultural conservatism. Traditional values and a strong sense of family dominated the city's self-perception. Until the 1960s, Milwaukee had a comparatively low crime rate and few incidents of urban unrest; there was even a healthy amount of civic chauvinism as politicians, business leaders, and citizens proudly repeated over and over, "We're not like other cities." Milwaukeeans, often viewed as provincial by outsiders, were proud of their tradition of civic engagement and retained a faith in established institutions as the proper mechanisms for change. Milwaukeeans preferred a slow, studied approach to municipal problems over protest politics. "Since the era of the early progressives at the turn of the century," state historian William Thompson noted, "the people of Wisconsin had come to believe in the power of legislation and in the idea that good laws enforced by honest and vigorous public servants could resolve virtually any problem involving discrimination and the exploitation of one group by another."[16] This cautious institutional approach to change would frustrate local African Americans during the civil rights era as they sought full equality and "Freedom Now!"

The Creation of the "Inner Core"

Even though white working-class immigrants and their descendants dominated Milwaukee at the turn of the century, the black community continued to struggle to define its own destiny and find its place in the "City of Nations." Prior to 1910, fewer than 1,000 African Americans lived in the city. The need for labor during World War I, which spurred hundreds of thousands of African Americans to migrate to Chicago, Detroit, and Cleveland, among other northern industrial locales, also fueled a much slower rate of expansion in Milwaukee's black community. In 1910, 980 African Americans, or roughly one-fourth of 1 percent of the city's total population, lived in Milwaukee. By 1920, the number had more than doubled to 2,229, and then it tripled between 1920 and 1930 to 7,501. Yet, African Americans still accounted for less than one and one-half percent of the city's total population. During the Depression and war years of the 1930s and early 1940s, Milwaukee's black community grew more slowly, adding only 1,000 more inhabitants. Following World War II, the local African American community skyrocketed.[17]

Between 1890 and 1915, the growth of Milwaukee's black community coincided with increasing racial concentration, supporting Gilbert Osofsky's "ghettoization model" of urban African American development. For the first time, through a mixture of choice, economic necessity, restrictive housing covenants, discriminatory real estate and loan practices, and overt racism, an identifiable thirty-five-block "black district," referred to variously as "Little Africa," "Bronzeville," or, later, "the inner core," emerged on the near North Side, an area also known for its brothels, liquor joints, and gambling dens. By 1940, the inner core had expanded to a seventy-five-block area and housed more than 90 percent of Milwaukee's black population. White Milwaukeeans outside of the inner core staunchly resisted the encroachment of black people into their neighborhoods, and real estate agents, banks, and local, state, and federal authorities also worked to maintain the racial status quo in housing. Historian Thomas Buchanan concludes, "The benevolent paternalism and street-nodding familiarity that had once seemed to characterize relations between blacks and whites in the city had given way to a cold and formalized pattern of race relations."[18]

The area known as the inner core, in fact, was originally an extension of Milwaukee's "Gold Coast." As wealthy people left the area, their large homes were sold and subdivided into rooming houses or one- and two-bedroom apartments. Germans and Jews occupied the area prior to the influx of African Americans during World War I. In 1940, the inner core remained roughly half white, but it had already become known as a "Negro district." When affluent whites moved, they either rented the properties themselves or sold them to loan associations, realtors, and other "slum investors."

Residential segregation also meant inferior housing for the vast majority of Milwaukee blacks. Roughly 3 percent of local African Americans owned their homes, while most of the remaining 97 percent rented homes or apartments from landlords—almost always white—inside the inner core. Housing in the core was among the oldest in the city, often absentee-owned, neglected, and deteriorating. A disproportionate number of black families lived in overcrowded, dilapidated dwellings that violated building codes.

Broken stairwells, bad wiring, out-of-date plumbing, and leaking roofs were common. A Works Progress Administration survey of Milwaukee housing in 1939 found that only 7 percent of inner core homes were in good physical condition while more than three-fourths were substandard. "A city that prided itself on tidy streets, swept stoops, and a high rate of homeownership," historian Henry Louis Suggs explains, "Milwaukee's [inner core] was an anomaly of aged housing abandoned by absentee landlords." Poor African Americans could afford only the worst housing in the segregated area, while middle-class blacks were thwarted in their efforts to find higher quality housing inside and outside the core. It was this inability to move to other areas of the city if they chose or could afford to do so that set black Milwaukeeans apart from white immigrants, giving lie to the idea that African Americans were simply another immigrant group in a city filled with migrants.[19]

Social life in Milwaukee was also historically segregated. As historian Joe Trotter has detailed, although a vibrant black community thrived along Walnut Street—with restaurants, nightclubs, theaters, offices, and stores—African Americans faced blatant forms of discrimination in restaurants, theaters, health services, recreational facilities, and hotels outside of the inner core. Many businesses used harassment, refusal of service, poor service, and overcharging as mechanisms to discourage black patronage. Interracial couples claimed frequent harassment and discrimination. Racial bias could also be detected at insurance companies, banks, real estate agencies, public utilities, social welfare organizations, and in law enforcement. Newspaper coverage regularly included stereotyped depictions of African Americans that both mirrored and reaffirmed discriminatory treatment of black people.[20]

Despite the industrial base of the city, most Milwaukee African Americans worked in the unskilled manual labor and service segments of the economy prior to World War II. Blacks labored as household workers, janitors, porters, launderers, cooks, elevator operators, waiters, cleaning women, bootblacks, and in other similar occupations. Whites in Milwaukee held many personal service jobs usually deemed "Negro jobs" in other cities. Hiring discrimination by employers, membership restrictions in labor unions, and widespread competitive fears among white workers kept blacks out of all but the most menial or dangerous industrial jobs. During World War I, less than a dozen of the city's 2,000 manufacturing companies employed black men. In 1941, as Milwaukee industries geared up for World War II, over one-third of all local black workers were unemployed, compared with only 2 percent of the white population. In short, most African Americans in Milwaukee occupied low-paying jobs that were extremely vulnerable to economic downturns.[21]

Even so, black residents worked hard to create a livable community within the walls of segregation. Faced with liberal neglect and pervasive white racism, African Americans banded together to form self-help organizations for racial uplift. Churches, social clubs, and literary societies were established, and many adopted the racial ideologies of Booker T. Washington. A flourishing policy game[22] attracted those who were more attuned to the profane than to the sacred. Black bands on the Midwest "chitlin' circuit" played at inner core clubs, such as the Metropole, the Flame, and Moon Glow. In 1916, an African American newspaper, the *Milwaukee Blade,* began publication under the leadership of writer-editor J. Anthony Josey, a tireless champion of the Milwaukee African American community. In 1919, Josey challenged racially biased coverage of crime in the *Milwaukee Journal* and won, earning a front-page correction in the city's main daily. A small middle class emerged, including a tight circle of clergymen, dentists, doctors, lawyers, attorneys, shopkeepers, tavern owners, cafe operators, barbers, and beauticians who all owed their livelihood to the segregated black community that they served or to the tenuous relationships they cultivated among prominent whites. In 1924, Ardie and Wilbur Halyard established the Columbia Savings & Loan Association, the city's first black-owned bank. A few Milwaukee African Americans held minor administrative positions in the educational and academic system. Some worked for voluntary associations concerned with poverty and minority groups. A handful received appointments to government boards or commissions, but none held political office. In large measure, white leaders preferred African American leaders that they knew and felt were "acceptable" to the status quo.[23]

A variety of black organizations, clubs, and church groups attempted to address the numerous challenges facing the growing African American community in Milwaukee. As in other northern cities, the local NAACP (established in 1915) and Urban League (established in 1919) were central to these efforts, though in Milwaukee the Urban League played a more significant role between the 1920s and 1940s. Middle-class and professional black leaders worked through these institutions to provide recreational activities for young people, better medical and public health services, and improved housing conditions and jobs for unemployed blacks. These groups relied on community contacts, behind-the-scenes negotiation, and a faith in established institutions, particularly the courts, to achieve their goals. Although these organizations aided many black Milwaukeeans, neither the NAACP nor the Urban League seriously challenged racial discrimination or the white power structure in Milwaukee prior to World War II.[24]

The reality of this "institutional ghetto," as historian Alan Spear called it, should not obscure the fact that the black community was not monolithic or that there were sharp class divisions within the inner core. As Joe Trotter made clear in his trailblazing study of "Black Milwaukee" between 1915 and 1945, "ghettoization" was not the only transformation taking place during the pre–World War II period. In addition, African American workers underwent a process of "proletarianization," whereby they transitioned from agricultural, domestic, and personal service laborers to an urban industrial working class. A by-product of this segregated proletarian community was the rise of the "black bourgeoisie." Dependent on the working class for their livelihoods and caught in a mutual struggle against racial inequality, the African American middle class often attempted to simultaneously defend the black community, as a whole, while distancing themselves from the poor. Divergent class interests often complicated matters in the inner core. For example, when Columbia Savings & Loan helped middle-class African Americans move to better neighborhoods in transitional areas along the edge of the expanding inner core, it was also helping to create a distinct middle-class district apart from working-class sections of the community. In addition, when black residents went to church on Sunday, they chose between working-class churches and middle-class churches. Class divisions often stymied efforts at racial unity.[25]

The confluence of these factors ensured that the black community in Milwaukee remained politically powerless, economically impotent, largely ignored, and completely marginalized through the 1950s. African Americans did not possess the numbers to command political power or to make politicians responsive to their needs. Likewise, black businessmen did not husband enough resources to bargain from a position of strength with other economic players. Nor did African American workers occupy any significant positions within the powerful labor movement. In fact, the quality of life of most Milwaukee African Americans in the period before World War II was severely limited. A 1946 Citizens' Governmental Research Bureau study of Milwaukee's black population found that relative to whites, Milwaukee African Americans suffered from dramatically higher rates of infant mortality, poverty, welfare dependence, and criminal convictions and from lower rates of employment, homeownership, and educational attainment.[26]

Arsenal of Democracy?

The Depression hit Milwaukee's black community hard. Half of the city's African American workers were unemployed, three times the rate for white workers and twice the rate for black workers in Chicago and New York. One-third of Milwaukee's black population received government relief, compared with 2 percent of the white population. Many of Milwaukee's largest employers continued to discriminate against black workers. For instance, two major breweries, Schlitz and Pabst, refused to hire black workers at the peak of the Depression in 1933. Similarly, despite the city's strong labor movement, no black–white working-class alliance materialized as it did in other major industrial cities at the time. In fact, the era is dotted with examples of white union violence against black workers. Compounding the economic turmoil facing African Americans in Milwaukee was the fact that the black community remained politically weak. James Dorsey, a prominent black attorney and head of the MNAACP, refused to call meetings or raise funds for the chapter during the 1930s because he did not believe that the local community could support both the NAACP and the Urban League. For its part, the Urban League continued to focus narrowly on negotiation and compromise with white employers as its major strategy for change.[27]

During World War II and the years that followed, Milwaukee's racial dynamics changed dramatically. During the war, the city became a major site in the U.S. "Arsenal of Democracy," Franklin Roosevelt's effort to mobilize the industrial economy for the war effort. The increased need for labor created by wartime demand attracted thousands of African Americans, poor Appalachian whites, and displaced rural workers to the city. Following the ebb in black migration during the Depression-era 1930s, 13,000 African Americans relocated to Milwaukee during the 1940s, an increase of 146 percent. During the 1950s, the African American population again nearly tripled to 62,458, and by 1970, 105,088 black people lived in Milwaukee. By 1960, African Americans made up roughly 8.5 percent of Milwaukee's total population and topped 10 percent of the total in 1965. Altogether, the black community grew over 700 percent in twenty-five years, rising from less than 2 percent of the population in 1945 to nearly 15 percent in 1970. The majority of these new migrants were under the age of thirty, and birth rates remained comparatively high, ensuring a disproportionately young population. Tensions were perhaps inevitable, but white Milwaukee, with its ethnic pride, moral traditionalism, and tendency toward xenophobia, was dramatically unprepared to deal with this large and rapid influx of African Americans.[28]

The impact of this rise in population on the inner core was equally striking, intensifying racial segregation and fueling the deterioration of housing, health, and urban education. The most immediate problem was overcrowding in an already severely stressed and deteriorating housing market. While white homeowners, realtors, banks, and government officials continued to conspire against African American renters and homeowners to maintain strict racial boundaries, the inner core steadily pushed north and west from its original location. Neighborhoods on the frontiers of this expansion changed rapidly as more affluent whites abandoned them for the suburbs. By 1960, the inner core claimed an area six times larger than the square-mile space it had occupied in 1950. Inside that area, well over 75 percent of the black population lived on blocks that were more than one-half non-white. In effect, the level of segregation in Milwaukee equaled Birmingham, Atlanta, and other southern cities.[29]

The inner core showed numerous signs of stress and strain in the postwar period. Though the urban crisis had been developing for many decades, the rapid influx of African American migrants after World War II overwhelmed Milwaukee's inner core and accelerated urban decay. Often, what had been a "respectable neighborhood" was slowly gobbled up by blight. Unemployment and chronic underemployment led to increased poverty and rising crime rates. Housing conditions continued to be overcrowded and grossly substandard. The inner core's aging structures and a general lack of resources for needed improvements caused entire neighborhoods to decay. Many white residents joked that so many inner core houses were becoming decrepit in the 1950s that there was getting to be a shortage of blacks to live in them. With high unemployment and poverty rates on top of poor housing conditions, social problems in the inner core blossomed. Milwaukee lacked a sufficient African American population to have created institutions capable of successfully dealing with its explosive growth. Economic, social, and spiritual decay spread; crime rates and drug use escalated; the presence of the police grew; and confrontation simmered.

The construction of Highways 43 and 94 between 1960 and 1967, connecting suburban residents with downtown businesses and cultural institutions, exacerbated these trends by cutting a swath through the heart of the inner core. During that period, 14,219 inner core housing units were razed for the construction of a six-lane highway without equal provisions enacted to relocate this disproportionately poor and black population. More than one-half of the families displaced by freeway construction in the 1960s were African American. Social scientist Frederick Olson has noted that freeway construction resulted in the growth of suburbs at a rate three times faster than the growth of the city.[30]

The need for labor combined with pressure from the Federal Employment Practices Commission in the late 1940s and early 1950s to finally open up the industrial segment of the economy to African Americans. Black pioneers also found employment for the first time as trolley operators, police officers, brewery workers, teachers, nurses, and downtown salespeople. Overall, advancement was slow, and black workers continued to suffer from hiring discrimination, union restrictions, and unequal wages and benefits.[31] A 1952 survey in Milwaukee revealed that of the more than 4,700 black people employed in Milwaukee, only 10 were professional workers, 47 held clerical positions, and 345 were skilled laborers.[32] The pace of change could not keep up with the sheer volume of young, new migrants looking for work. Young African Americans faced a particularly rough labor market and disproportionately high unemployment rates. Each year, community leaders looked for new ways to battle chronic youth unemployment during the summer months.

Politically, the growth of Milwaukee's black population in the postwar years and their concentration in a small geographic area held the promise of greater political power, as had been the case in other northern cities.[33] By the 1950s, Milwaukee's Tenth and Twelfth wards, which covered large areas of the inner core, had become known as "Negro districts." In 1946, LeRoy Simmons, an African American Democrat, won an assembly seat representing the Sixth District and ultimately served four terms. The district quickly became a "safe" seat for both Democrats and African Americans, with Isaac Coggs and later Lloyd Barbee succeeding Simmons as the only African American in the state legislature. Coggs served six terms in the state assembly and later moved on to the county board. Barbee spearheaded the school desegregation campaign in Milwaukee before entering the legislature in 1964. But election to the city's Common Council and county board proved much more difficult than capturing one seat in the state assembly. In 1956, Vel Phillips became the first African American and the first woman to sit on the Common Council, but it took twelve more years before another African American joined her. Voter registration rates remained chronically low among Milwaukee African Americans, and black electoral power in the city and state continued to lag well into the 1960s and beyond, despite rising population figures. Phillips suggested that the migrants' refusal to register and vote resulted from the violence and repression they had faced in the South when trying to exercise the franchise. She also suggested that because most new migrants lacked formal education, many felt intimidated by the registration and voting process. Without a well-organized and mobilized black electoral presence, African American candidates faced significant obstacles to political office. At the same time, white elected officials could feel secure that no political cost would result from neglecting African American concerns and inner core problems.[34]

Leadership dynamics in the black community did not change much from the prewar era. A small group of middle-class black professionals continued to speak for the community and curry favor from prominent whites. The NAACP and Urban League still preferred quiet negotiation, mild political pressure, and acculturation. But as a new national civil rights consciousness emerged during the mid- and late 1950s, the clamor for change, particularly among young people and new migrants, grew. Internal fissures emerged between young people and old, between new migrants and those who had been born in Milwaukee, and between those that thought change was coming at a sufficient pace and those that thought the pace should quicken. Frustration with the slow rate of change gave rise to calls for new leadership, new tactics, and new strategies. The circumstances were increasingly ripe for the emergence of a fresh, militant style of black leadership in Milwaukee.

At the same time as the influx of African Americans transformed the inner core, the flight of more affluent white residents to suburban areas outside the city's grasp further fueled Milwaukee's changing racial dynamics. Some whites left traditional urban neighborhoods for the "crabgrass frontier" in search of larger homes, more green spaces, and greater safety for their growing families. Others sought to escape declining property values, faltering urban public schools, rising crime rates, poverty, and blight. Many were simply unwilling to live near a rapidly growing population of African Americans, a group they often associated with urban decline and plummeting property values. Highway construction and federal home and business loan policies supported this move and magnified its effects.

The impact of this "white flight" was disastrous for those residents and low-income neighborhoods that were left behind. Suburbanization exacerbated racial segregation in Milwaukee through the creation of an "iron ring" of eighteen overwhelmingly white communities safely outside the geographic grasp of city leaders. With little affordable housing, scant public transportation, and a variety of formal and informal discriminatory real estate practices, suburban mobility remained out of range for most poor, working-class African American Milwaukeeans. Milwaukee businesses increasingly followed white residents to the outskirts of the city. Between 1960 and 1970, central city jobs in Milwaukee declined by 10 percent, while the number outside the central city grew at a rate of 75 percent. Although this downturn affected all areas of the inner city, it translated into particularly difficult job prospects for black workers. Research by Charles O'Reilly found that during this period African American men in the inner core were three times more likely to be unemployed than male workers who lived in other parts of the city.[35] Taken together, the exodus of affluent whites and the loss of many businesses undermined Milwaukee's tax base at precisely the time that the city needed more resources to deal with the influx of a large, impoverished population. The shortfall, in turn, resulted in underfunded social services, rising crime rates, the deterioration of public schools, and a growing number of boarded-up homes and vacant lots in the inner core. In short, suburbanization left a legacy of enormous social problems for Milwaukee, including hypersegregation and large concentrations of poverty and inequality. Though this historical arc had several aspects that were unique to Milwaukee, in many respects these changes trace the postwar history of urban America.

These demographic and economic changes sharply altered life in traditional white, working-class neighborhoods in Milwaukee. Economic forces prevented many poor and working-class whites from following their more affluent neighbors to the suburbs. And some blue-collar residents, particularly on Milwaukee's South Side, opted to remain in traditional neighborhoods. Catholic parishes, neighborhood schools, and the corresponding cultural life revolved around a unique sense of community that was intimately tied to geography. The residents of these one-time stable neighborhoods now found themselves in an increasingly imperiled situation. They held jobs and union membership and perhaps even owned a small home, but many of the economic, social, and cultural markers that had anchored their way of life seemed to be increasingly unmoored during the postwar era. New migrants with dark skin and unfamiliar cultural traditions and a deteriorating urban infrastructure, increasing crime rates, social and religious liberalization, rising taxes, automation, and economic uncertainty all encroached upon their lives. To these Milwaukeeans, the rapid influx of poor and working-class African Americans who were beginning to talk about civil rights and who were calling attention to their own struggles seemed like a threat to their homes, their jobs, their unions, their schools, and to their traditional way of life. Many white Milwaukeeans, like most white Americans of their time, fell prey to stereotypical and discriminatory ideas about African Americans and race relations. The lack of direct experience that most white Milwaukeeans had with black people compounded misinformation and spread fear. Rather than seeing African Americans as the victims of economic transformations and widespread racial discrimination, many inner-city whites chose to see black migrants as the cause of the urban decay and social disintegration that appeared to follow them.[36]

By the late 1950s, Milwaukee contained the necessary preconditions for significant racial conflict. More affluent second- and third-generation white ethnics, along with a growing number of businesses, had left the city limits and taken their much needed tax dollars with them. Inner core and working-class white neighborhoods within city boundaries continued to deteriorate as a host of economic and social forces preyed upon them. African Americans sought to break through the web of discrimination that maintained the inner core and racial inequality, while working-class whites got ready to defend their old neighborhoods, their jobs, and their schools. Within this cacophony of demographic and economic transformation and pervasive social tension, Milwaukee city leaders struggled to find new solutions to a deepening urban crisis.

A clear indication of the divisive power of these new racial politics came during the 1956 mayoral campaign between Frank Zeidler, long-time incumbent and Social Democrat, and Milton McGuire, conservative Democrat and president of the Common Council. Throughout the 1950s, Zeidler had challenged Milwaukeeans to absorb the latest wave of immigrants, proposing among other things an ambitious new public housing project. Many white Milwaukeeans had come to associate public housing with the influx of new black residents and urban decline and so opposed the project. Real estate brokers exploited these fears by circulating rumors that Mayor Zeidler planned to import African Americans into their neighborhoods. During the campaign, McGuire revived these old rumors and added new ones. One smear claimed that Zeidler's oldest daughter was married to a black man, a taboo among most Milwaukee whites. Another accused Zeidler of posting billboards throughout the South that invited black people to move to Milwaukee. Even after an investigation by the Milwaukee Federated Trade Councils found no evidence of these signs, Zeidler campaign supporters were still jeered at as being "nigger lovers." During a debate on public housing, McGuire—whose campaign used the slogan "Milwaukee needs an honest white man for mayor"—opposed building more low-income housing units, stating, "I will call a spade a spade. If there is more housing, more people will move into Milwaukee. The only thing that has kept . . . Negroes from coming up here is the lack of housing." Even *Time* magazine, no friend of the Socialists, defended Zeidler against the charges, calling McGuire's campaign "The Shame of Milwaukee." Zeidler won reelection by a slim margin but decided not to run again in 1960, citing the bitter racial acrimony engendered throughout the city during the 1956 campaign. Zeidler's successor, business Democrat Henry Maier, staked out a "go slow" approach on civil rights and urban renewal.[37]

It was rare for race to play such a prominent role in Milwaukee politics during the 1950s. Although most city leaders acknowledged a generalized problem with urban decay and blight and some spoke of a growing migrant "invasion" or "crisis," few, if any, focused special attention on the unique challenges facing African Americans in the inner core. Many sought comfort in the fact that Milwaukee's urban ills paled in scope to those of other large northern cities. When public officials did discuss the inner core or African Americans, they invariably explained away inequality as a problem of "acculturation." This view held that new African American migrants did not possess the basic skills and cultural knowledge necessary to succeed in the urban North. The acculturation model, which was in line with the dominant thinking of social scientists at the time and which was embraced by the bulk of the black middle class as well as by whites, emphasized the physical, cultural, and familial bases of the inner core's problems, implying that they emanated solely from within its bounds and could be dealt with through compensatory measures limited to that area. By focusing exclusively on internal factors, the acculturation model failed to assign any responsibility for racial inequality to white Milwaukeeans. It also minimized the large-scale changes that were ravaging inner-city neighborhoods and

ignored racial discrimination as a significant cause of African American inequality. In short, the acculturation model argued that inner core problems
could be cured without any disruption to the ways in which most Milwaukeeans and city institutions then worked. Given this consensus, it is not surprising that little significant change came to the inner core during the
1950s, particularly through existing institutions.

Nevertheless, there were signs of change. Emboldened by A. Philip Randolph's successful March on Washington movement in 1941, which resulted
in Executive Order 8802, outlawing racial discrimination in the war industries, William Kelly and James Dorsey, two prominent middle-class black
leaders, led 350 Milwaukee African Americans in a march through downtown to protest job discrimination. Kelly, Dorsey, and others also pressed
the Milwaukee school board to hire more black teachers and to end the
board's policy that restricted African American teachers to teaching in segregated black schools. In 1951, Vel Phillips became the first African American woman to earn a law degree from the University of Wisconsin–Madison.
Afterward, she and her husband, Dale, also a lawyer, served on the board of
the MNAACP, and Vel worked for the League of Women Voters. In 1956, she
became the first African American and the first woman to win election to
Milwaukee's Common Council. Lloyd Barbee also finished his law degree in
Madison and worked as president of the Wisconsin State NAACP and as an
advisor to the Governor's Commission on Human Rights. Following the
Brown v. Board of Education decision of 1954, he began to formulate a legal
strategy to extend the promise of integration to public schools in the urban
North. Calvin Sherard came home from the military, settled in Milwaukee
as an industrial worker at American Motors Company, and began to talk to
his co-workers about the unfair employment practices of inner core businesses. Father James Groppi and dozens of other young white Catholic seminarians learned firsthand about the struggles of African Americans in the
inner core by working with children at St. Martin's summer day camp. At
the same time, a cross-section of liberal white Milwaukee clergymen began
to pay more attention to the problems of the inner core and lay the foundation for an organization called the Greater Milwaukee Conference on Religion and Race. These individuals and others would form the backbone of
Milwaukee's civil rights insurgency during the 1960s.

But change would not come easily in Milwaukee. The deterioration of the
urban landscape had no easy or swift solutions. The factors that caused
these shifts would provide the backdrop against which racial politics in the

city would play out over the next decade. These factors set the stage for a dramatic and confrontational new chapter in the history of race relations in Milwaukee, a history that speaks to the larger transformation of American life during this period. White and black residents were deeply divided by geography, history, experience, perception, and self-interest. Beginning in 1958, a movement for racial justice swelled in Milwaukee. Slow to catch fire initially, the growing civil rights insurgency ultimately compelled thousands of local residents, black and white, as well as their allies from across the country, to take to the streets for equality and freedom. Like the black migrants at the new Butler rail yard in 1922, the protesters were met by white mob violence. Thousands of local whites moved to stop this movement or at least to slow the rate of change. The result was a tumultuous and often violent decade of race relations and civil rights activism in Milwaukee. The story reveals much about the black freedom movement in the urban North and the unfinished business of racial justice in American cities today.

— 2 —

Early Protest Politics

Sunday, February 2, 1958, was a typically wintry day in Milwaukee.[1] Snow covered the ground, and temperatures dipped below zero as people went about their business. At about 8:30 p.m., Thomas Grady and Louis Krause, two white uniformed motorcycle patrolmen, stood smoking and talking at the corner of Wright and Seventh Streets, in the heart of the inner core. Grady told Krause that he was headed to some vacant homes to "arrest some niggers" in order to beef up his arrest rate.[2] As they spoke, Daniel Bell, a twenty-two-year old African American man, passed through the intersection on his way home. Grady noticed that one of Bell's taillights was dark and gave pursuit.

We do not know what Daniel Bell was thinking as he drove home that night. He might have been smiling as his mind wandered back over the birthday party his family and friends threw for him the previous night—the food, the cake, the laughing, and the singing. Or, if he found himself in a more pensive mood, maybe he pondered the difficult journey he and his siblings had made from rural Louisiana to urban Milwaukee several years before. Perhaps, once he saw the lights in his rearview mirror, Daniel got nervous, his mind racing through the many stories that circulated in the community about police brutality and late-night clashes between white police officers and young black residents. We will never know, of course, what thoughts filled Daniel Bell's head, but we do know what happened next.

Bell pulled to the curb, then jumped out of his car and ran. Grady and Krause followed on foot, shouting "Halt!" and firing several warning shots into the air. Unable to catch up to Bell, Krause commandeered a passing car, picked up Grady, and continued the chase. The driver stopped just ahead of Bell, and the patrolmen scrambled out of the car with their guns drawn. Bell hopped a snow bank and darted between two homes. Grady, sprinting ahead of Krause, mounted the snow heap while shouting for Bell to stop running. As he closed in on the young man from behind, Grady extended his right arm and, with the tip of the muzzle touching the fabric of Bell's jacket, fired a single shot into his upper back. The bullet traveled upward, broke Daniel Bell's neck and entered his head. Grady stopped, holstered his firearm, took off his gloves, and felt Daniel Bell's outstretched wrist for a pulse. "I think he's dead," he said to his partner. Krause removed his glove, felt Bell's jugular vein, and agreed. Grady sloughed it off: "He's just a damn nigger kid anyhow."[3]

What happened next compounded the initial tragedy of Bell's death with the injustice of a cover-up. Krause walked to a nearby house, where he called the district station to report the incident. Back at the scene, Grady removed a small pocketknife from his jacket and placed it in Bell's right hand, but Krause warned him that it was too small. Grady closed the knife, returned it to his coat, and produced a larger one, again laying it in Bell's right hand. The two patrolmen then "dealt with the story they would tell people in charge, officials, on what happened." Police officers and detectives soon arrived and went about the business of documenting what they found at the scene.[4]

According to the lie the two officers concocted, Bell fled his vehicle with knife in hand, yelling the curiously self-incriminating "You won't catch me, I'm a hold-up man!" Grady said that he believed that Bell fit the description of a man listed on a recent police bulletin for a string of armed robberies and that he had thus shot him as a "fleeing felon," a critical distinction that, if true, justified the use of deadly force. Later, Grady claimed that Bell had lunged at him with the knife. These fictions, repeated and amplified in police reports and news stories over the next several days, became the official version of events.[5]

Almost immediately, Daniel's brothers and sister questioned the circumstances surrounding his death. Newspaper accounts emphasized Daniel's criminal record, but according to his sister Sylvia, he was "a really good child . . . [not] a wild boy, or a drunken boy. He had lots of friends, black and white. He let things roll off his back." Television reports claimed that Daniel had had a knife, yet he left his own pocketknife at home on the sink in the bathroom. And Grady claimed that Bell had attacked him with his right hand, but, in fact, Daniel was left-handed. The Bells offered a much simpler explanation for Daniel's decision to run from officers Grady and

Krause, one that did not trade on deep-seated stereotypes of black male criminality. They explained that none of the Bell brothers could read or write well, a legacy of Jim Crow schools in the South and substandard inner core schools in Milwaukee. This made it difficult to ride the bus, fill out job applications, and read newspapers or unfamiliar place names. It also precluded the Bell brothers from getting driver's licenses in Wisconsin because the state required a written exam as well as a road test. Even though the Bells could all handle a vehicle safely, they could not pass the written portion of the test. As a result, the Bell brothers had received numerous citations from the Milwaukee police for driving without a license. In fact, most of Daniel Bell's criminal record consisted of citations for this offense. Given this, Bell's brothers and sister believed the situation was clear: Daniel ran to avoid another ticket, hardly an offense that warranted lethal force. Yet, when the family raised these issues at the police station the night of the murder, the exchange degenerated into a shouting match. Frustrated and angry, one of the Bell brothers was heard to say, "Oh, you think it's open season, like on rabbits? We are going to start shooting a few of you cops." The sergeant on duty allegedly responded, "You can't tell you niggers nothing. Get out of here or I will throw you in jail."[6]

Internally, the case was also falling apart. Serious discrepancies in the physical evidence at the scene and inconsistencies in the officers' own accounts emerged, calling into question the veracity of their claims. Two African American witnesses came forth to challenge the officers' story, and none of the victims of recent inner core robberies identified Daniel as the perpetrator. Even so, the district attorney and an all-white inquest panel cleared Patrolman Grady of wrongdoing, stating that he "had justifiably shot and killed" Daniel Bell in "the reasonable execution of his duty as an officer making a lawful arrest, and in self-defense." The inquest verdict was a devastating blow to the Bell family and an outrage to many in the black community.[7]

The gunshot that killed Daniel Bell was the signal shot for the black freedom movement in Milwaukee. As the coming decade unfolded, the dozens who marched downtown to protest his killing would later turn into a group of thousands who would follow Father James Groppi and the NAACP Youth Concil (YC) across the Sixteenth Street Viaduct into the brick-throwing mobs from the Polish South Side. With the advantage of several decades' hindsight, Officer Grady's assessment—"He's just a damn nigger kid anyhow"— mirrored the sentiments of vast numbers of white citizens in Milwaukee.

The white people who read about the killing in the news pages of the *Milwaukee Journal* and the *Milwaukee Sentinel* the next day did not throw urine, chant "send the cannibals back to Africa," or firebomb the NAACP office, as would happen in the years to come. But the Bell killing—and the official indifference and popular complacency that confronted those who protested it—pointed to issues that would remain salient in the city.

This chapter focuses on a series of discreet protest campaigns that took place between the Daniel Bell murder in 1958 and 1963 to see what they reveal about the roots of civil rights insurgency in Milwaukee. Although no unified movement for racial justice emerged during this early phase, and differences over goals, tactics, and strategies remained near the surface, it was a time of experimentation and growth for civil rights activists. The percolating protests of this transitional period highlighted enduring issues of racial inequality and official inaction by city leaders as activists settled on an approach to social change that combined grievance with nonviolent direct action. In addition, southern civil rights events dramatically altered the national context within which these campaigns evolved. Faced with a more assertive effort to achieve African American freedom in Milwaukee, as well as with increased national pressure to act, some white city leaders began to pay attention to the inner core and to the struggles of black people even as they continued to avoid significant action to ameliorate these conditions. Often overshadowed by the more dramatic displays of protest and white reaction in the city a few years later, these early protest campaigns laid the groundwork for a mass movement for racial justice and served as the bricks and mortar in the local Movement foundation.

Organizing Community Protest in the Wake of the Daniel Bell Murder

The Bell case was but one, albeit the most tragic, in an increasingly contentious string of incidents between inner core residents and the Milwaukee police during the second half of the 1950s. Most of these episodes played out in sensationalized ways in the local media, heightening white fear of black migrant crime, reinforcing stereotypes about the criminality of African Americans, and fueling racial tensions throughout the community. In 1955, the *Journal* reported that a "mob" of angry inner core residents had attacked white police officers when they arrested a young black woman. However, according to several prominent members of the NAACP, the group was attempting to "rescue" the woman from what they viewed as an unjust detention. The following summer, the arrest of a young black man incited more than 400 African American teens to surround two policemen and pelt their car with stones. Again, media coverage focused solely on the plight of the two white officers, although according to an African American minister at the scene, the incident was an example of police misconduct. And in 1957, following an inner core crime wave that included attacks on four white women, overheated media reports of a "gang of Negro rapists" prompted a police dragnet that resulted in the indiscriminate arrest of more than 260 inner core black men—both middle class and poor, new migrant and old—and "pitched an otherwise calm community into turmoil." The incident, which must have reminded many inner core black migrants of southern lynch law, made clear that most white Milwaukeeans did not make subtle distinctions of class or status in their judgments of black people.[8]

Following the inquest verdict in the Bell case and fruitless negotiations between the Milwaukee NAACP (MNAACP) and police officials, an array of local leaders and inner core residents attempted to mobilize a community response. Those organizing efforts quickly fragmented after an initial mass meeting attracted 450 people. One group formed around the conservative leadership of Reverend T. T. Lovelace, pastor of Mount Zion Church. Lovelace had initially called Bell's fatal shooting a "dastardly attack" and stated that "something should be done . . . not just as a matter of vengeance, but justice." However, he laid the bulk of the blame for police–community conflict at the feet of unruly African American migrants, not on systematic discrimination or individual racism. Lovelace exhorted his followers to "improve the general behavior of the Negro community" through an "ounce of prevention" and a healthier respect for law and order. He claimed that black migrants "created in the general populous disgust, shame and fear" and encouraged all black Milwaukeeans to "quit rioting among ourselves" and "stop slashing each other to pieces." At a February 25 meeting, an estimated 300 inner core residents—many of them members of Mount Zion—agreed to establish the Institute for Social Adjustment to deal with problems facing African Americans in Milwaukee. According to Reverend Lovelace, the institute would help rehabilitate black people who had violated the law; would orient rural and immigrant blacks to the "standards and customs" of a large city; would try to get at least 5,000 African Americans to join so that the group could make an impact on local politics; and would form a "tavern committee" to deal with black people who became "problem cases" while drinking. In addition, the group drafted and sent to the Milwaukee police a resolution that suggested that any officer who took the life of a person in a "questionable shooting" should receive a reprimand not less than a form of suspension. The resolution also praised the department for a tradition of "impartial law enforcement." Reverend Lovelace unexpectedly passed away from a heart attack on April 14, 1958. With his death, the Institute for Social Adjustment fizzled, although the sentiments he espoused continued to play a significant role in community politics, particularly among older residents and the black middle class.[9]

Several moderate black leaders, along with a few liberal white political figures, spoke out through the Lapham-Garfield Neighborhood Council. In 1957, representatives of sixty-two local civic, fraternal, social, and religious organizations, representing a collective membership of over 5,000, founded an umbrella organization as an outgrowth of concern over the mass arrest of African American youth during a North Side crime wave that year. Grant and Lucinda Gordon, mainstays of Milwaukee's black establishment, headed the council. At the group's first public gathering on February 28, 1958, Grant Gordon cited Bell's death as an impetus to action. "If there had been more understanding and trust between our community and the community at large," he said, "Daniel Bell would be alive today." Gordon added, "We cannot bring Daniel Bell back to life, but we can improve our relationships so that this type of incident will not happen again." He called for increased educational, recreational, and employment opportunities for Milwaukee's black population and said that the group would aim to develop more adult leadership to work with youth in the area, to secure better housing, and to obtain representation in city governmental bodies. Mayor Zeidler also spoke at the gathering and urged greater "mutual trust" as the foundation for improved race relations in the city.[10]

Elsewhere, a group of activists and working-class inner core residents joined together around the leadership of Assemblyman Coggs; Reverend R. L. Lathan, pastor at New Hope Baptist Church; and Calvin Sherard, a local metal finisher at American Motors Company and the founder of the Citizen Committee to Protest the Case of Daniel Bell. At the initial mass meeting, Coggs and attorney George Brawley suggested that the best way to address their grievances was at the ballot box. "We talk about the poor Negro in the South who doesn't have the opportunity to vote," Brawley said. "What about the poor Negroes in the North? Do you get out and vote when the opportunity comes? If you don't vote to protect yourselves, you have no right to attend this protest meeting or any other meeting to protest anything." Sherard argued that the Milwaukee police had shown a consistent pattern of prejudice in enforcing the law and encouraged local people to organize a march or a demonstration in response. On March 17, Reverend Lathan announced plans for a "prayer protest" the following Sunday at MacArthur Square in front of the courthouse. Participants were to meet in the afternoon and then march a short distance to the square to pray for "justice and the good of all mankind." Organizers hoped to attract 2,000–3,000 community members to the event and stressed that the "pilgrimage" was not restricted to African Americans but rather was open to "anyone who believes in justice." Assemblyman Coggs endorsed the "prayer protest," stating, "There is no difference between shooting Dan Bell in the back than killing Emmett Till in Mississippi." Following a burst of applause, he added, "and there wasn't much difference in the picking of the [inquest] jury either." "Hats off to Ike Coggs for not pussyfooting," one local resident wrote in a letter to the *Milwaukee Defender*. "Almost everyone is saying it was 'down right murder.'"[11]

The New Hope contingent's proposed "prayer protest" elicited alarm from traditional black leaders who felt uncomfortable with the group's strident rhetoric and confrontational style. Vel Phillips voiced middle-class unease when she warned that "lawless elements" might infiltrate a protest march, a claim repeated by a number of African American leaders. Three prominent black ministers—Reverend Melvin Battle, pastor of Calvary Baptist Church; Reverend E. B. Phillips, pastor of Galilee Baptists Church; and Reverend Cecil Fisher, chair of the Milwaukee Housing Authority— also paid Reverend Lathan a private visit in an attempt to dissuade him from going forward with the demonstration. The ministers urged Lathan to preserve the dignity of the clergy by confining prayer to its "proper place" within a church and again warned that there might be unfavorable repercussions if the crowd of poor and working-class migrants could not be handled. Following the meeting, Lathan relented and called off the march "in the best interest of both Negroes and Whites" because he feared that they might be "smeared" as subversive if they went ahead with the planned protest. Later that spring, after the emotion and energy of the Bell shooting had died down, Sherard and Lathan held another public meeting at New Hope, this featuring Reverend Fred Shuttlesworth, a Birmingham civil rights minister, charter member of the Southern Christian Leadership Conference, and cousin of Reverend Lathan. After Shuttlesworth encouraged the crowd to continue their push for racial justice in the urban North, he led a group of fifty to seventy-five people, including Daniel Bell's sister Sylvia, on a short protest march down Walnut Street.[12]

A new round of after-hours clashes in 1959 again focused public attention on the inner core and the need to develop more effective means to cope with the struggles and stresses of Milwaukeeans living in that area. In response, Mayor Zeidler appointed a committee to study and make recommendations on the "social problems" of the inner core. At the initial meeting, Zeidler told community leaders that he had "long felt that the problems in the core of the city are growing and need faster and greater action than the community has given them." More than 100 public officials, community leaders, specialists, and authorities worked together on the report. The mayor's Study Committee on the Social Problems in the Inner Core Area of the City issued its final report, complete with fifty-nine recommendations, on April 15, 1960. The Zeidler Report, as it came to be known, represented the largest official study of the city's African American community in Milwaukee's history and indicated a greater awareness of the area than had previously been acknowledged by the white power structure.[13]

The Zeidler Report relied on statistical data culled mainly from city agencies to make its analysis and mirrored the dominant social scientific thinking of the day. Historian William Thompson has pointed out that the report emphasized the physical and family bases of the core's problems, implying that the root causes "emanated from the Core alone and could be dealt with by measures limited to the Core." It failed to seriously address much more nettlesome external causes, like white supremacy and institutional discrimination. Instead, the Zeidler Report argued that "Physical rebuilding of the area and acculturation of many of its citizens are the key problems." In addition to bricks and mortar, the authors urged city leaders to inaugurate a variety of programs to help assist Milwaukee's African Americans to better make the transition to urban life. In this way, the Zeidler Report embraced the immigration model of ethnic succession put forth the previous year by Harvard historian Oscar Handlin in *The Newcomers—Negroes and Puerto Ricans in a Changing Metropolis.* Handlin argued that, similar to earlier waves of European immigrants, African American and Puerto Rican migrants to large northern cities would ultimately adjust to the demands of urban living and escape the ghetto. As Jack Dougherty has pointed out, Handlin's analysis "did not fully consider the powerful economic and political forces that contained black Milwaukeeans within the inner city; it simply sought to adjust the migrants to them."[14]

On those issues black people considered most pressing, the Zeidler Report offered only vague and cautious recommendations. For instance, on education, the committee asserted, "there is adequate educational opportunity available to the residents of the core area. But there is a need to increase the motivation of individuals to avail themselves of the existing opportunity." The report remained silent on the pattern of segregation in Milwaukee's public schools. On employment, the report put forth only a vague statement about ending discrimination but provided no details about how that might be achieved. Instead, the authors emphasized job training, education, and part-time summer employment for high school students as the primary remedies for the economic struggles of core residents. Finally, on housing, although the report did implicitly acknowledge racial discrimination in real estate and lending practices, it failed to call for an open housing ordinance. As an alternative, the authors proposed the "Covenant of Open Occupancy," a voluntary agreement by property owners prohibiting racial discrimination in the renting or sale of housing and prohibiting panic selling.[15]

Almost as soon as Zeidler received the report, his tenure in office ended. His successor, Henry Maier, inherited the problems of the inner core but showed little inclination to aggressively attack them. A pro-business, pro-growth Democrat in the Kennedy mold, Maier had spent the previous decade in the state senate before taking over the reins at city hall. Later, while under fire for his handling of race relations in Milwaukee, Maier would claim that he had been a leader in civil rights during his days in the senate. Early in his mayoralty, however, he showed little interest in African Americans or in the city's pervasive racial inequality.[16]

A savvy politician and rising star within the nationwide ranks of Democratic mayors, Maier may have ignored issues of race in Milwaukee because of politics. African Americans did not make up a significant proportion of the new mayor's base. In fact, although Maier had easily defeated Congressman Henry Reuss in the 1960 election, those wards with the largest number of black voters had given him his weakest support. Given the widespread racial prejudice and stereotyped thinking among white Milwaukeeans, it stands to reason that the new mayor might not have been willing to aggressively address the needs of African Americans for fear of alienating key components of his electoral coalition.[17]

If the Bell case and its aftermath alerted Milwaukee to the crisis of the inner core, it also revealed the limits of direct action in Milwaukee during the late 1950s. Those advocating more forceful and aggressive action to achieve racial justice in the city remained a relatively small group. Organizing efforts following the inquest verdict brought to light not only the shallow pool of popular support for direct action but also the serious divisions among new and old black leaders over goals, tactics, and strategy. The immigration-acculturation model, so prevalent among whites, also continued to be popular among traditional African American leaders. If the Zeidler Report reflected a myopic complacency, and if the new mayor was no firebrand for racial reform, they still mirrored much of Milwaukee. Although most black Milwaukeeans readily acknowledged the presence of racial problems in the city, many continued to hold fast to the hopeful idea that steady progress through negotiation and accommodation was preferable to confrontation and demand. All of that, however, would change in the early 1960s.

Calvin Sherard and the Politics of Economic Protest

Out of the fractious organizing campaign that followed the coroner's inquest in the Bell case, a small group of African American industrial workers coalesced around the leadership of Calvin Sherard. Sherard was born in Atlanta, Georgia, the son of a Baptist minister. At the age of twelve, he read a book about the African American labor and civil rights leader A. Philip Randolph and was deeply impressed. "It was his fight for jobs and economics," Sherard remembered. "I felt that that was the foundation [for racial equality], jobs and economics." Following high school graduation, Sherard moved to Cleveland, Ohio, to live with his brother. There he got "a good job" with American Motors and became active in the labor movement. After a stint in the military during the mid-1950s, Sherard settled in Milwaukee, attracted by the strong industrial economy and labor movement.[18]

The old guard's halting, fragmented, and ultimately failed efforts to organize a response to the Bell shooting frustrated Sherard and his supporters. Tom Jacobson, a white lawyer who represented Sherard and his organizations during the early 1960s, recalled, "Sherard had some guys and they wanted to go down in flames [after the Bell incident]. They were totally upset by the way blacks were deserting and selling out to whites and undercutting them." Jacobson claimed that the group was particularly embittered that prominent black ministers talked what they called "Negro talk," emphasizing "cleaning ourselves up instead of going out and demonstrating." According to Sherard, "There was no [African American] leadership. When an issue came up where there should've been a response from the Afro-American community, there was no response." He and about a dozen of his co-workers set about creating a new organization, the Crusaders Civic and Social League, to focus on employment discrimination and police community relations. Although the organization accepted white members, positions of power were reserved for African Americans.[19]

The Crusaders believed that expanded black business ownership and increased African American employment in white-owned businesses were the keys to black success in Milwaukee. They noted that most businesses operating in the inner core were white-owned and rarely employed black workers. The Crusaders argued that all businesses located in the inner core ought to hire from within the local community. By employing African Americans, businesses would be putting resources back into the community from which they drew the bulk of their profits.

Sherard and his men first targeted a popular ice cream parlor on North Avenue, in the heart of the black community. About a dozen Crusaders, fortified by a group of local churchgoers, picketed outside the store. The owner quickly relented and agreed to hire more African Americans. In May 1960, the Crusaders organized sympathy pickets outside Milwaukee Woolworth stores to support the southern student sit-in movement. That same year, Sherard began negotiations with the inner core's largest national grocery chain, A&P, to increase African American employment at three North Side stores.[20]

The Crusaders also continued to fight what they viewed as police brutality and the unjust treatment of black people by the legal system. In July 1960, three African American sisters appeared before Judge Frank Gregorski after a late-night disturbance. When one of the sisters testified about police brutality, Gregorski interrupted to cast doubt on her claims. As he did, laughter erupted in the gallery. Gregorski exploded and ordered the bailiff to bring "all the dark people" before the bench, where he promptly fined ten black spectators $100 each for contempt of court, whether they had laughed or not. Once again, all "dark people" in the courtroom paid the consequences for the behavior of a few individuals. The Crusaders supported an MNAACP media campaign against the judge and led picketers outside his office.[21]

That fall, a confrontation between Milwaukee police and more than 1,100 black youths outside an inner core rock concert degenerated into what the *Journal* called "a wild 40 minute fracas." In the end, a hail of rocks and bottles injured five officers and resulted in the arrest of seventeen black youths. Typically, conflicting stories emerged. Police claimed that the altercation began when Joseph Baker, a twenty-two-year-old African American man, cursed police, struck an officer, and then asked the crowd for help. Alvin Moorer, one of the young men arrested that night, disagreed, stating, "Police just cut loose and started beating on us." Robert Brill, the theater manager, blamed "all those Milwaukee policemen lined up in front of the theater." In a mass meeting organized by the Crusaders and held the night after the incident, three of the arrested African American youths shared their experiences. However, as with the Bell case, Sherard and his men were unable to attract the support of traditional black leaders or to mobilize a large number of inner core residents to the cause, despite widespread frustration at police brutality. In the end, the three men, along with one white youth, received sentences of up to two years in jail. No action was taken against any of the white officers involved.[22]

Frustrated by what appeared to be a pattern of inaction, the Crusaders called another public meeting at New Hope Baptist Church one month later to protest police brutality and criticize African American leadership. An estimated 200 local people sat inside as a small group of picketers stood outside holding signs that read "Commie Plot to Discredit Police Dept.," "Pro-Communist Meeting," "The Reds Want to Create Race Hatred," and "Calvin Sherard Go Back to New York City."[23] Ali Anwar, the Crusaders' field secretary, told the gathering, "In a crisis you can't find [traditional black leaders] anywhere" and asked, "What are they doing for you?" Sherard slammed police brutality and attacked black civic groups as "nothing but social clubs." He said that African American leaders used their "intellect to keep the lower Negro classes in hand," and he encouraged community members to "Get up off your knees." "There's a time for praying and a time not to pray," he urged them. "These folks out here are hurting us. Let's go march!" Sherard's call for a new organization in Milwaukee to hear African American complaints of injustice met with enthusiastic applause. The local NAACP, American Civil Liberties Union (ACLU), and Human Rights Commission, all dominated by more moderate leadership, rejected the Crusaders' charges, labeling the group "irresponsible" and "precipitous."[24] But behind the scenes, some NAACP leaders recognized the growing gap between the organization and the black community and suggested change. During a "very heated board meeting," traditional leaders prevailed and, according to

Jack Dougherty, further consolidated organizational leadership in the hands of a small black elite who contributed large sums to the group.[25]

In a bid to increase their effectiveness and legitimacy in the eyes of local black people, Sherard's group became affiliated with the newly created Negro American Labor Council (NALC) toward the end of 1960. The NALC was organized by A. Philip Randolph to pressure the labor movement to take a more active approach to civil rights. Like the original March on Washington movement in 1941, the NALC restricted membership to African Americans, sought to bar Communist infiltration, and vowed to use "pressure tactics" to combat racial inequality. Although at the national level the NALC focused on pressing the leadership of the American Federation of Labor–Congress of Industrial Organizations (AFL-CIO) to adopt a "racial code of conduct" for its unions, local chapters largely defined their own agenda within the broad parameters of the parent organization. "We thought that we would identify with that group to get national recognition," Sherard explained. "So, we changed the Crusaders into the Negro American Labor Council." A Milwaukee chapter of the NALC (MNALC) might even evolve into the new kind of civil rights organization Sherard and Anwar had suggested at the December mass meeting.[26]

The MNALC ratcheted up pressure on three inner core A&P grocery stores during the summer of 1962. Negotiations with the chain's management had proven fruitless, so MNALC members, including twelve inner core high school students, conducted a two-week picket of the stores. Police arrested Sherard and other picket leaders for "disorderly conduct" during the protest, the first civil rights–related arrests in Milwaukee. Three weeks later, representatives of the MNALC and A&P announced an agreement to increase the number of black clerks, to accept African Americans in the store's management training program, and to hire qualified black journeymen in the meat department. Soon after, the organization reached an agreement with another inner core grocery chain, Kroger-Kramble, to hire more black workers. In September, Sherard met with representatives of the Upper Third Street Businessmen's Association to discuss ways to increase black employment along the inner core's main shopping district. The MNALC also sponsored a forum with black businessmen to discuss ways to stimulate support for black-owned business. Sherard emphasized the need for African Americans to enter business on a much larger scale so as to stem the outflow of money from the community in the form of salaries and wages to white workers who neither lived in the core nor shopped in its stores.[27]

Meetings and rhetoric yielded minimal concrete results. The MNALC campaign had shined a light on employment discrimination in Milwaukee, but the actual employment numbers in targeted stores did not change fast enough, leading to charges of tokenism. In the end, despite small gains in employment for African Americans at a few inner core stores, the MNALC could not overcome the considerable obstacles in its path. In addition to business resistance, the local retail clerk union argued that the MNALC's demands threatened their members' seniority. Sherard countered, stating, "we are not here to do a wrong, but to correct a wrong. If you had employed Afro-Americans there would be some Afro-Americans with seniority . . . We are here to correct that."

Though many middle-class black leaders supported the goals of the MNALC, they also opposed their tactics, worried that a developing militancy among newer African Americans in the city might prove explosive. Corneff Taylor, the African American head of the Milwaukee Commission on Community Relations, told Sherard he agreed with the goal of increased black hiring in core businesses but preferred that the MNALC work with "established agencies" to increase employment. "If the Negro is to make progress," Sherard replied, "he must assume primary responsibility himself. No agency is going to do it for him." Reflecting years later, Sherard explained, "Afro-Americans at that time who considered themselves middle-class sometimes didn't identify [with working-class or poor black people]. They were fearful of the opposition they might get from their Caucasian counterparts so they didn't identify with the grassroots struggle."

There is also evidence that a broader debate within the local African American community over the philosophy and tactics of black nationalism, fueled by a spirited Nation of Islam membership drive, may have contributed to the MNALC's difficulties mobilizing local people. During the summer of 1963, as the MNALC's economic campaign peaked, the Nation of Islam began a statewide membership drive in Wisconsin, focused primarily on the large black population in Milwaukee's inner core. Dozens of members of the controversial group moved to the city from Chicago, held educational rallies, exhorted from street corners, sold copies of *Muhammad Speaks* at busy intersections, and reportedly converted "hundreds" of new adherents. The drive ignited an energetic debate within the local community about the group's philosophy and aggressive organizing style. The *Milwaukee Star*, the city's lone African American newspaper at the time, noted that most black residents "readily agree [with the Nation of Islam] that the Caucasian has taken them for all they're worth, hung their fathers and raped their mothers." Others appreciated the organization's attempt to build up African American economic power, their accent on race pride and self-defense, or their more militant style. One local paint sprayer told a reporter, "Muslims are doing more, materially, for the Negro than any other Negro supported organization." But others criticized the Nation of Islam as anti-Christian and violent, and for advocating a philosophy of racial superiority and separatism. "The Muslims are causing nothing but trouble," claimed an inner core housewife. "They preach race hatred. I am certain nothing ever born of hatred can flourish." While general opposition remained strong, many black Milwaukeeans seem to have held a more ambivalent view of the Nation of Islam. "Muslimism is a good idea," a local teacher argued. "Don't misunderstand. I am not a Muslim, and I am certain I never will be. However, at least they are making whites aware that the Negro has the potential for insurrection." Then she added, "The Muslims will never reach their true objectives. There are too many objectionable ideas in their laws." *Star* editorialists concurred, writing, "While most of us delight in the strides we as a race are making, we wish to continue as citizens of the United States regardless of our color, and not set ourselves up as something separate or better. Go out and fight for your rights and freedoms as individuals and as a race of people, but in the end, remain in the true fold of free men. Remain an American—a Negro American."[28]

According to Calvin Sherard, this debate intersected with the work of the MNALC. Ali Anwar, one of Sherard's main lieutenants in the group, was an outspoken adherent of Orthodox Islam. His name indicated his faith to the public in news articles and on television. Sherard stated that many black Milwaukeeans failed to make a distinction between Anwar's faith and that of the Nation of Islam blitzing the community. He recalled that those who criticized the MNALC often employed similar rhetoric as they did against the Nation, calling the group "separatist" and "anti-white." Ironically, the Nation of Islam complained that Sherard's group did not go far enough advocating black business ownership in the inner core.[29]

But the greatest obstacle to the group's success came not from white business leaders, unions, moderate black leaders, or even members of the Nation of Islam, but from working-class African Americans themselves who failed to honor picket lines. "Some of them didn't have transportation [to another store]," Sherard explained, "some of them didn't agree with us, and some of them just didn't want to drive." By November, an exasperated

Calvin Sherard publicly complained that black people were "committing financial suicide on their own community. It's disgusting to see black faces going through picket lines set up to get them jobs." Lola Bell Holmes, the national vice president of the NALC, visited Milwaukee in the fall to drum up local support, telling one audience, "If [traditional leaders] say [protest] is not the right way, ask them what is the right way. We have waited, knocked on doors and begged. Picketing is the only way. Top sit, wait, and pray like our parents did, expecting it to come to them, didn't work. The Negro must move in *masses*." Later, she underscored the link between economic empowerment and racial autonomy, "Give the Negro economic opportunities and you will see the end of the slums. We must have full employment in our neighborhoods so we can end ADC . . . We are tired of being degraded . . . When you get economic opportunities then everything else will fall into place." Holmes may have been speaking truth to power, but without grassroots support the MNALC faced a tough road to success.[30]

Sherard and his followers continued to picket local stores until 1965 and supported the school desegregation campaign spearheaded by Lloyd Barbee and the Milwaukee United School Integration Committee (MUSIC). Sherard left Milwaukee in late 1965 for Detroit. "[Local people] got satisfied with things by going into stores and seeing Afro-Americans working," he explained. "I guess they thought that was the whole show. I got disgusted and moved to Detroit." In Detroit, Sherard worked for Chrysler and continued to be active in the NALC through the United Auto Workers (UAW) Trade Union Leadership Conference.

For a short time, between 1960 and 1963, the Crusaders and the MNALC played a leading role in the city's emerging civil rights movement. Their story offers an important continuity with the fragmented community protest that followed Daniel Bell's death and provides further evidence of a rising activist spirit among some African Americans. This activism pressed the concerns of working-class black people living in the core into the public spotlight and stoked growing pressure on the city's white civic leaders. By appealing to young African Americans and involving them in their direct action campaign, the MNALC anticipated the explosive awakening of youth in the civil rights insurgency in Milwaukee. Calvin Sherard's leadership highlighted the interconnection between racial inequality and economic issues. The Crusaders and the MNALC made the case that employment and economic justice were central to the more general goal of racial equality. The history of the MNALC, though, also reaffirmed the tensions and schisms within Milwaukee's black leadership over direct action and black nationalism. Most important, perhaps, the MNALC's actions represented the first attempt at a sustained direct action campaign in Milwaukee. Those efforts showed that more militant tactics could be effective in generating media attention and at least modest results. They also made the point that black people in Milwaukee wielded collective economic power if they could stay unified; in 1962, that remained a pretty big "if." At the same time, the picketing and boycotting of the MNALC also revealed the limits of direct action in Milwaukee during the early 1960s. Resistance by white businessmen and union leaders, disinterest from local government officials, internal community opposition from conservative black leaders, and public apathy all proved potent obstacles.

To be sure, there were signs of growing anger and frustration within the black community over racial inequality. But in 1961 and 1962, these issues did not ignite the passions of local African Americans and move them to action. Perhaps employment discrimination did not inspire most black Milwaukeeans to take the personal risks necessary for a direct action campaign. Maybe more education on the issue was needed before rallying grassroots support. It is possible that the charges of Communism and separatism leveled at the national and local NALC deterred potential supporters. Many African Americans may have supported traditional community leaders who encouraged them to oppose the MNALC's tactics. It is also possible that black people in Milwaukee did not believe that racial inequality in the local economy was as dire as the MNALC portrayed it. No doubt many clung to the hope that although the economic situation in Milwaukee might not be great for black people, steady progress was being made and more change would come through the traditional mechanisms of hard work and negotiation. Whatever the reasons for their limited success, the MNALC marked a further step from the Bell activism. As Tom Jacobson put it, "[the MNALC] were really the first demonstrations here in Milwaukee where people really hit the streets and went to jail for their freedom."[31]

The Milwaukee Congress of Racial Equality
and the Fred Lins Protest

The year 1963 was pivotal for the black freedom movement across the nation. Martin Luther King Jr. called the racial upheavals of 1963 "revolutionary" and wrote that it was "the year that the American Negro, so long

ignored, so long written out of the pages of history books, tramped a declaration of freedom with his marching feet." In Milwaukee, although not
quite revolutionary, 1963 was also a transitional year for civil rights.[32]

On January 1, the 100th anniversary of the Emancipation Proclamation,
the Milwaukee Commission on Community Relations (MCCR), an organization made up of civic leaders founded to support the southern civil rights
movement and to address local racial issues, issued an optimistic report titled "The Negro in Milwaukee: Progress and Portent, 1863–1963." The report emphasized minor improvements in employment and housing but
failed to confront persistent racial inequality and discrimination in education, hiring, union membership, police–community relations, or the sale and
rental of property. By way of solutions, "Progress and Portent" stayed close to
the acculturation model but suggested only two programs to aid black
youths in their adjustment to urban living. Overall, "Progress and Portent"
reflected the views of prominent social scientists, like Nathan Glazer and
Daniel Patrick Moynihan, who diagnosed black migrant culture in pathological terms. "We must also realize that Negroes of low income, still unac-
customed to life in a Northern city, do not have a long heritage of culture
and an ethical tradition on which to build their lives," the report asserted.
"[Negroes] seem to lack a sense of family intimacy and interdependence; as
a result, their families often do not instill into children good behavior patterns and ideals. Not everybody is fortunate enough to be born into families
with these principles. In time, of course, Negroes will learn them."[33]

At the end of the month, the Ford Foundation rejected a $16 million
grant application from the city of Milwaukee aimed at attacking urban social problems, instead awarding funds to Oakland, New Haven, Boston, and
Philadelphia. The director of public affairs for the foundation, Paul Ylvisaker,
told the *Journal* that the grant had not been approved, in large measure, because Mayor Maier was not willing to "stand up and face the charge he is a
'nigger lover.'" In response, Maier denounced the piece as "the most vulgar
journalism I have ever seen" and claimed that the problem was not his unwillingness to take on home-grown racism but the lack of a unified "central
authority" to coordinate the project. Either way, the episode fueled the pervasive sentiment among local African Americans that the mayor was not
committed to racial justice.[34]

During the spring, events in Alabama catapulted the civil rights movement back into the media spotlight, making race relations the major national domestic concern. In May, newspaper and television reports filled

with images of Birmingham's fire hoses, cattle prods, and German shepherds, confronting whites and blacks outside the region with the uncomfortable reality of southern segregation and racial violence. The conflict in Alabama reached another crisis point on June 11, when Governor George Wallace defied federal authority to make his infamous stand in the schoolhouse door to block the integration of the University of Alabama. That night, in a historic speech, President Kennedy told Congress and the nation, "It is a time to act . . . Those who do nothing are inviting shame as well as violence. Those who act boldly are recognizing right as well as reality." The *Journal* called Kennedy's remarks "the most dramatic and moving condemnation of racial discrimination by anyone who ever occupied the White House." The *Star* said it was "one of the greatest speeches of all time," while *Sentinel* editors argued that "June 11, 1963, may well be marked as a day of climax in the Negro equality drive." Significantly, none of this passionate praise linked national events to local circumstances.[35]

As in 1960, when the student sit-in movement swept through the South, the national civil rights movement became suffused with new energy. The Birmingham demonstrations awakened black people to a sense of their own power and ignited their confidence in the potency of mass social action to overcome white intransigence. Not content with incremental change, activists moved away from "respectable" protest and embraced "Freedom Now!" as their slogan. Although still committed publicly to nonviolence, civil rights leaders increasingly warned of "explosive cities" and "long, hot summers." The dramatic images emanating from Birmingham added leverage to local movements for racial justice, gave courage to activists, and pushed established organizations toward greater militancy. At the same time, it scared some white officials (and more than a few cautious black leaders) into a heightened awareness of the political stakes of inaction. During the summer of 1963, civil rights activists initiated hundreds of direct action campaigns in every region of the nation. Milwaukeeans opened their newspapers daily to tense stories and powerful images of racial protest in such places as Danville, Virginia; Cambridge, Maryland; Chicago; Harlem; Los Angeles; and Detroit.

Milwaukee activists underscored their moral outrage at events in Alabama and across the South with a series of actions. An ad hoc coalition of groups, including the MNAACP, the MNALC, the YC, and the UAW joined a nationwide sympathy protest against Woolworth stores. Thirty African Americans and six whites marched from the safety building down Wisconsin

Avenue with signs that read, "Finish Medgar Evers' Work in Wisconsin" and "Medgar Evers Is Dead, Make Freedom Live Here." A few weeks later, an interracial group of more than 100 Milwaukeeans picketed in front of city hall in support of national civil rights legislation being debated in Congress. And throughout the summer, a variety of groups rallied local people to participate in the August March on Washington.[36]

Instead of seizing the moral authority conferred by recent events, Henry Maier stepped awkwardly into the fray. The same day that Kennedy urged the nation to action, Maier asked Milwaukeeans to "go slow" on civil rights. In a forty-five-minute speech to the MCCR, during which he frequently pounded the table, the mayor stressed a "step by step" approach and "long-term programming," warning against "precipitous" action.[37]

Local reaction to Maier's "go slow" speech was swift and mostly critical. The MCCR was cool toward the mayor's remarks. The *Journal* complained, "Milwaukee has never had adequate civil rights leadership from city hall. It lacks it completely now." The *Star* compared the Mayor's remarks to John C. Calhoun's defense of slavery and wrote, "For too long, our mayor has attempted to justify 'his' non-progressive action with appointments of 'fact finding boards,' and 'do committees' that take literally eight months (sometimes longer) to 'do' nothing." Vel Phillips, at a White House meeting for 300 Democratic leaders, accused Maier of being out of step with liberals all over the country and got into a bickering match with him during a follow-up meeting a few weeks later. The head of the MNAACP declared, "We are tired of approaches, period. We want results." Thirty-four prominent black doctors, clergymen, businessmen, educators, and attorneys placed a "Statement of Concern" in local newspapers to express "grave concern" with "the apparent negative reaction of official Milwaukee to the present rightful demands of this country's Negro population." Even Wesley Scott, the usually cautious leader of the Milwaukee Urban League predicted, "demonstrations will come [to Milwaukee] unless action is taken." Only the *Sentinel* supported the mayor, calling his critics "emotional, impatient, impractical and uninformed" and arguing that "there is no miracle of law or moral persuasion which can overnight achieve an ideal integration of the black and white races."[38]

In this political atmosphere, a group of Milwaukee activists formed a local branch of the Congress of Racial Equality (CORE) in early July 1963. Founded in 1942 by James Farmer and a group of Quaker pacifists, CORE aimed to eliminate racial inequality through "inter-racial, non-violent direct action." During the World War II era, CORE members participated in some of the first sit-ins and organized the 1947 Journey of Reconciliation. Later, CORE led the 1961 Freedom Rides. As the Movement mood migrated from moderation to militancy in 1963, many civil rights activists, particularly in the North, flocked to new and old CORE chapters. "If you were into the Movement, you knew about the [Freedom Ride] buses," explained John Givens, chairman of Milwaukee CORE (MCORE) from 1963 through 1965. "There was no CORE chapter here, so we started one." Like the MNALC a few years before, MCORE grew out of frustration with the cautious approach of traditional black leadership and the need to create an alternative vehicle for more aggressive activism. Givens put it plainly: "CORE was available and it was a more militant organization."[39]

Most charter members of the new MCORE chapter were "outsiders," either recent migrants to the city or younger Milwaukeeans beyond the traditional black leadership circles; almost all had previous activist experience. Tom Jacobson helped organize a fourteen-day sit-in at the state capitol in Madison, Wisconsin, to promote fair housing legislation in 1961. John Givens led the Milwaukee YC in an MNALC-style picket of three inner core restaurants in 1963. St. Louis police arrested Elner McCraty three times as a member of CORE while protesting employment discrimination in downtown restaurants during the early 1960s. And Willis Baker led successful CORE-sponsored campaigns to desegregate a bowling alley and to increase African American hiring at a supermarket chain in Cincinnati. For a few, military service was a crucial factor in their commitment to racial justice. Givens, who served in the U.S. Army in France from 1959 to 1961, said the experience gave him "a fresh concept, a new way of looking at [myself]." And at least two members cited a family history of race pride and self-assertion as an important explanation for their activism.[40]

The eager militants of MCORE did not have to wait long for an opportunity to act. On July 26, 1963, less than a week after the group had formed, public remarks made by a member of the Social Development Commission (SDC) ignited a controversy that led to an escalation in civil rights activism. The SDC was created to address the criticism Mayor Maier received following the rejection of the city's Ford Foundation grant proposal and embodied his "go slow" "step-by-step" approach to persistent urban problems. Maier called the metropolitan-wide organization an attempt to implement the Zeidler Report and hoped that it would be the vehicle by which the city would attract and distribute newly available federal funds for urban renewal. "[The SDC is] a new concept for the Milwaukee community," Meier told the press, "a joining together of hands, a marshaling of forces to bring to bear all available resources in an attack on urban social ailments wherever in the community they might exist, whether their victims were young or old, black or white." In framing the SDC in this manner, though, the mayor continued to resist the idea that there were unique problems confronting Milwaukee African Americans, implicitly rejecting race or racism as an important factor. Nevertheless, many local people looked to the new group with great hope.[41]

At the fledgling group's first meeting, Fred Lins, president of Lins-Hess Sausage, Inc., and a county appointee to the SDC, told a *Journal* reporter that some way should be found to keep the "ignorant poor" from migrating to Milwaukee. "If you could stop people who come in and immediately go on relief," he claimed, "it would save money for the taxpayer." Although Lins did point the finger at "Mexicans" and "poor whites," his primary concern was the danger he associated with impoverished black Milwaukeeans. "My business is in the core and my home is on the line. To the educated Negro, you can't feel hostile. It is the uneducated ones that cause the trouble. We have got to educate them." He continued, "The Negroes look so much alike that you can't identify the ones that committed the crime," and concluded, "An awful mess of them have an IQ of nothing."[42]

Lins's comments set off a political firestorm. To the members of MCORE and others in the civil rights community, Lins's statements reflected racist stereotypes and thus precluded him from serving on the SDC. Willis Baker, interim chairman of the group, called Lins's continued participation in the SDC "detrimental to the actual goals for which the commission was set up." A few days later, an interracial group of twenty-three MCORE members, including Wisconsin NAACP chairman Lloyd Barbee, began picketing outside the Lins-Hess Sausage factory, holding signs that read "MCORE Says Resign" and "No Bigots On Public Bodies." MCORE also sent two letters to county board chairman Eugene Grobschmidt, in which they expressed their outrage and demanded Lins's removal from the commission. A month later, Grobschmidt refused to remove Lins from the SDC and declared it a "closed matter." The county board chairman's willingness to see Lins's side of the issue without similar empathy for the civil rights activists' perspective confounded members of MCORE and fueled their militancy. "We were naïve," explained John Givens, "because we thought that in this great democracy, if you found this evil and you pointed it out, they would do something about it. So, we were really taken aback when [Grobschmidt] didn't get rid of [Lins]. And that is what led to the arrests."[43]

As more than 100 Milwaukee residents in five buses made their way to Washington, D.C., for the historic March on Washington for Jobs and Freedom, five white and four black MCORE members, each wearing a cardboard badge stating "Freedom Now!," launched Milwaukee's first sit-in outside Chairman Grobschmidt's office in the county courthouse; the act was a minor milestone in the city's civil rights drama. At the end of the day, police moved in to clear the room and arrested Willis Baker. The next day, as a quarter of a million American citizens stood in front of the Lincoln Memorial to hear Dr. King's soaring dream of a new society based in racial justice, MCORE members returned to Grobschmidt's anteroom, again resulting in arrests. Outside, Willis Baker, who had recently been released from jail, told a group of picketers, "Mayor Maier declared August 28 as Freedom Day in Milwaukee. If that was Freedom Day, I'd rather be a slave."[44]

Two days later, after "polite but tense" negotiations between four MCORE representatives and Grobschmidt ended without an agreement, six civil rights activists immediately resumed their protest, only to be carted out on dollies to a waiting paddy wagon. Over the next three weeks, MCORE and its allies continued to pressure local officials to act. The day after the Labor Day holiday, supporters of the group swamped the courthouse switchboard with a "phone-in." The same day, the national office of CORE declared Milwaukee "a civil rights disaster area." On Monday, September 16, the same day Milwaukeeans opened their newspapers to the horrific bombing of the Sixteenth Street Baptist Church in Birmingham, Alabama, fourteen MCORE members began a two-week sit-in at Mayor Maier's office. After negotiations failed to resolve the issue, a frustrated Givins told reporters, "The reaction of the mayor and Grobschmidt shows where their allegiance really lies . . . certainly not with minority groups, but with the absentee landlords and biased employers who have benefited from and contributed to the impoverishment of minority groups." Maier countered by calling MCORE's tactics "authoritarian." In the end, police arrested twenty-four civil rights activists; Lins remained on the commission.[45]

Unlike in the Bell case and the MNALC economic boycotts, middle-class black leaders were quick to line up behind MCORE's activism. Traditional community leaders had always counseled faith in established institutions and negotiation with white leaders, but the Lins controversy undercut that position by making clear that white politicians would not yield to black leaders' entreaties. As a result, Attorney Clarence Parrish, who had sided with Reverend Lovelace after the murder of Daniel Bell and who opposed direct action tactics in most circumstances, organized a group of fourteen lawyers to provide free legal aid to arrested protesters. Similarly, the MNAACP, the ACLU, and the newly formed Equal Rights Defense Fund, a group of affluent, liberal, white North Shore residents, raised funds to cover bail. And in an unusual public display of unity, five prominent black leaders—Councilwoman Phillips, MNAACP chairman Ed Smyth, MCORE leader John Givins, MNALC head Calvin Sherard, and Assemblyman Isaac Coggs—stood in succession at an August 31 mass meeting to denounce Lins's remarks and demand his removal.[46]

Broader public reaction to the Lins controversy was split. In an editorial titled "Fred Lins Must Go . . . Yesterday," the *Star* argued, "Lins could probably win hands down any political office in the South with his bigoted ideas. Milwaukeeans, however, will not stand for it." Local television news station 6, WITI, asked, "Where is our leadership in this community?" Many white residents did not agree with Lins's remarks but were equally opposed to MCORE's direct action tactics. The *Journal* reported "mostly mildly hostile comments" from white onlookers at the picketing site outside the courthouse. Privately, MCORE activists received more than 400 pieces of hate mail from local people, the Ku Klux Klan, and even the Nazi Party. The mail included letters, postcards, pamphlets, periodicals, and sheets bearing pasted pictures of monkeys with racist captions. One threatening missive stated, "Nigger—if you don't like it here—get out. Go back to the jungle and swing by your tail. This is just beginning—from here on it gets worse."[47]

The Lins controversy climaxed with more of a whimper than the bang many activists expected. At a scheduled SDC hearing on the issue, commissioners skirted a potential showdown with civil rights leaders by referring the conflict to the MCCR for further review. The night's sole drama came when thirteen prominent African American leaders, representing every major civil rights group in the city, stood one by one to condemn Lins and the inaction of the city's white political leadership. The next day, MCORE announced an end to its direct action campaign.[48]

The Lins controversy highlighted a fundamental racial impasse in Milwaukee. Members of MCORE and their allies believed that they had made a reasonable demand of public institutions in the face of what they perceived as an obvious injustice. Furthermore, they thought that they had made a good faith effort to pursue their goal, at least initially, through respectable means: letters, negotiation, and pickets. City officials likewise believed in the fundamental reasonableness of their position. They saw in Lins one of their own, a respected white businessman and community leader who had, admittedly, made some unfortunate statements, but who was essentially decent at heart. They believed they had risen above the early passions unleashed by the remarks to arrive at a more accurate assessment of the situation. Neither side in the conflict was willing to compromise. Each, in turn, viewed the other's obstinacy as the chief obstacle to solving the impasse.

Though ultimately unsuccessful, the Lins campaign demonstrated that a sustained protest could be mounted with broad community support in Milwaukee. The controversy had, for the moment, unified African American leaders and rallied grassroots support. Differences over class, generation, tactics, and strategy, which had been so divisive in earlier campaigns, were papered over by the immediacy of the Lins situation and the unwillingness of white civic leaders to budge. Yet, the limits of working within the system were also clear. Civil disobedience had not compelled city officials to remove Lins from the commission. It was clear that many white Milwaukeeans would not accept racial change without a fight.

To a significant percentage of white Milwaukeeans in 1958, African Americans were largely invisible. Most whites did not live near black people, nor did the two groups often work alongside one another. When white residents did turn their attention to African Americans, it was usually through a distorted lens, viewing them as a menace or a nuisance. African Americans came to signify for many white people all of the problems facing a rapidly changing industrial city like Milwaukee. The two groups had little mutual experience and seemingly no common history. It is not hard, then, in this context, to understand how white Milwaukeeans developed stereotypical views about African Americans and why, when confronted with their presence, they often rallied around the one thing that most distinguished the two groups: skin color.

Similarly, traditional African American leadership remained cautious well into the 1960s. Enmeshed with the white power structure, many took an optimistic view of African American prospects in Milwaukee. Moreover, the dramatic increase in the black population outstripped the ability of community institutions to respond effectively to the needs of new migrants. Although traditional leaders acknowledged that problems existed, they preferred quiet negotiation to confrontation, acculturation, and transformation. Many expressed righteous indignation over racial inequality in the South while ignoring or minimizing the equally abysmal plight of most African Americans in their own city. When they did focus on the problems of the inner core from their pulpits, commissions, and boards, all too often they blamed new migrants for their own struggles, rather than discrimination.

Beginning in the late 1950s, the city began a slow process by which Milwaukeeans, both black and white, became increasingly aware of the "problems of the inner core" and of the "civil rights crisis" in the city. Until then, most Milwaukeeans believed racial conflict "can't happen here." By the beginning of 1963, though, an increasing number of people worried that "it might happen here" if action was not taken to address the city's racial chasm. A series of protest campaigns—the Bell murder, the MNALC economic boycotts, and the Lins controversy, most significantly—forced public attention on the inner core, confronting civic and political leaders with the possibility that more dramatic demonstrations could take place. Clearly, frustration among inner core residents was mounting; a militant civil rights spirit was spreading; and a new, aggressive African American leadership group, committed to protest politics, was asserting itself in opposition to traditional community leaders. Official indifference from whites, even in the face of what most black Milwaukeeans viewed as blatant police brutality, obvious employment discrimination, and patent racial stereotyping, accelerated these trends, galvanized racial militancy, and progressively unified black leadership, at least publicly. More and more, civil rights organizers successfully drew on grassroots support, if not on mass participation, for their direct action efforts. Although the Bell and MNALC campaigns both wrecked on the shores of local opposition, both within and without the black community, the Lins case, though also unsuccessful in achieving its immediate goal, represented a breakthrough in the mobilization of community support for racial justice and set the stage for more dramatic, and successful, campaigns in the coming years.

At the end of 1963, the question was not whether racial strife and protest politics would come to Milwaukee; they had. The question was what would happen next. Could civil rights activists keep their momentum? Could they build on the successes of past campaigns, learn from their failures, and establish a vibrant movement to challenge racial inequality in Milwaukee by forcing city leaders to act? Could civil rights leaders find the right mix of formal and informal politics to give voice to the growing popular unrest throughout the inner core? Or would more cautious traditional black leadership move to temper the growing activist spirit? Would white civic leaders make concessions to stave off more dramatic change? Would pervasive frustrations among poor and working class outpace the ability of political action, even civil rights insurgency, to address the dire circumstances many local people faced? What issue, if any, could keep activists unified? Over the next five years, new possibilities to press for change would arise as the local and national context continued to evolve and as new leadership emerged. With these developments came answers to these and other pressing questions.

— 3 —

The Campaign to End
School Segregation

At 8:30 a.m. on Monday, May 24, 1965, thirty civil rights demonstrators arrived at the Brown Street Elementary School to protest racial segregation in Milwaukee public schools. As the protesters picketed and sang, three buses idled along the curb, waiting to transport African American pupils to the overwhelmingly white Hi-Mount and Hawley schools. Suddenly, a group of nine demonstrators, led by attorney Lloyd Barbee and a former nun, Marilyn Morheuser, broke ranks and scurried in front of the lead bus, where they linked arms and began to sing freedom songs. Milwaukee police promptly moved in and arrested the nine protestors in view of local news cameras. As officers closed the doors of the patrol wagon, two more women left the picket line and sat down in front of a second bus, blocking its exit. They too were arrested. A Milwaukee United School Integration Committee (MUSIC) press release called the new tactic "a human chain-in, designed to focus public attention and censure on this city's unique and flagrant abuse of Negro children's human rights." It went on to explain, "Intact busing of Negro children from overcrowded, inner core schools is worse than *de facto* segregation, which the Milwaukee School Board has refused to recognize and remedy. The policy . . . is a more blatant refusal to conform to the 1954 Supreme Court decision than any subterfuge yet attempted by Mississippi or Alabama." The civil rights coalition's release concluded with a threat: "Let the demonstration be a warning to the city that we will continue picketing, sit-ins, lay-ins, chain-ins, and any other kind of 'ins' until the intransigent school board caves in . . . Apparently, they won't do anything on their own initiative, so we will have to persuade them."[1]

Between May 24 and June 16, MUSIC members attempted to make their case against school segregation by continuing to block school buses with "human chains."[2] Activists showed a degree of mischievous sophistication in their approach. Journalist Frank Aukofer recalled that "MUSIC members, using automobiles like a civil rights Afrika Korps, kept police on the run by popping up at different schools without warning, then picketing or blocking school buses by forming human chains in front of them. Often reporters and television cameramen would be at the scene of a demonstration before the police arrived." In a further effort to dramatize the issue, some protesters bound themselves together with actual chains. On June 16, as eighty-five picketers looked on, fifty protesters completely encircled a school bus at Siefert Elementary School. The police arrested twenty persons, including fifteen women and five men. By then, MUSIC's "human chain-in" campaign had resulted in sixty-one arrests—Barbee, Morheuser, James Groppi, and several other clergymen among them—and a flurry of national media attention, including a feature on the Huntley-Brinkley television news program.[3]

During the mid-1960s, education emerged as a critical civil rights battleground in Milwaukee. The campaign against segregated public schools evolved from a one-man crusade into a large-scale grassroots campaign supported by several thousand local people. Activists attempted to ply city officials with reason and negotiation but quickly moved to legal action, confrontation, and civil disobedience. The school desegregation movement unified the African American community behind a sustained direct action campaign and focused disparate activist energies within the civil rights community on a single issue of racial injustice. The campaign propelled new leaders and new organizations to the forefront of Milwaukee's struggle for racial justice.

Lloyd Barbee's Fight

Even though the Milwaukee chapter of CORE grabbed most of the headlines in 1963, Lloyd Barbee quietly worked behind the scenes to put education reform at the forefront of the city's civil rights agenda. Born in Memphis, Tennessee, on August 17, 1925, Barbee grew up in relative prosperity amid the dire poverty afflicting many African Americans in the Depression-era South. Barbee's father, a union paint contractor, taught his sons about hardship, struggle, and race pride. He introduced them to the arts and literature, shared his love of oratory and debate, and always encouraged them to fight against injustice. "Be right, or get right," Barbee's father would say, "and when you are right, go ahead."[4]

Yet, Barbee also learned early the sting of racial inequality. As a boy, he walked past several all-white schools each day, aware of the qualitative differences between those institutions and his own destination. Strict formal segregation kept an inquisitive young Barbee from the books in the Memphis public library. In response, he joined the NAACP at age twelve. Five years later, Barbee felt "outrage" when local African American church leaders blocked A. Philip Randolph from speaking about war and civil rights for fear of the white reaction.[5]

From 1943 through 1946, Barbee served in the Navy, where his life aboard ship allowed him the opportunity to read books that helped make sense of the discrimination he had experienced growing up in Memphis. During shore leave visits to family in Milwaukee and Beloit, he observed firsthand the complicated racial dynamics of northern cities. Following his stint in the service, Barbee earned a bachelor of arts from LeMoyne College in 1949 and a law certificate from the University of Wisconsin–Madison in 1955, where he faced discrimination from classmates, teachers, and the local legal community. The "patronizing liberalism" of Madison gave the young lawyer "new insights into the many shades of discrimination" that existed outside the South. As he later recalled, "conscious racial discrimination was common, and unconscious racism among the educated was appallingly common." Nevertheless, Barbee built an impressive résumé during his time in the capital city, working as a legal consultant to the local and state commissions on human rights and serving as president of the Madison NAACP from 1955 to 1960 and as chairman of the Wisconsin State Conference of NAACP Branches from 1961 to 1964. In 1958, Barbee spurred the first serious study of housing discrimination in Madison. In 1961, he and Tom Jacobson organized a fourteen-day sit-in at the state capitol to force a fair housing bill out of committee; it was the first such protest since the Great Depression. The same year, Barbee spearheaded a successful effort to rename Nigger Heal Lake in northern Wisconsin Freedom Lake. By then, Barbee and Jacobson had also grown frustrated with Madison and, at the urging of Assemblyman Isaac Coggs, moved to Milwaukee to open a private law practice and continue their civil rights work.[6]

What made Barbee a unique and formidable leader was his combination of intellectualism, shrewd tactical judgment, and activist experience. Assessments of Barbee differed greatly throughout his career. Depending on the observer, he was described as fiery or bitter, elitist or intellectual, forceful or rigid, confrontational or courageous, but almost everyone acknowledged that Barbee was a maverick. According to Jacobson, "[Barbee] wasn't a grassroots leader like Father Groppi. He was more of an intellectual, a strategist with a vision." Although Barbee did not possess the personal charisma to turn out hundreds of local people for a demonstration, he knew how to create a network of community members who could plan, organize, and pull off such an event. "If people want justice," he said, "they are going to have to keep fighting for it."[7]

Following the Supreme Court's historic *Brown v. Board of Education* decision in 1954, Barbee joined a generation of lawyers and activists who debated whether the Court's ruling might be extended to the North. "If the *Brown* decision means anything," said Barbee, "it means that school segregation is unconstitutional wherever it exists, north or south." At first hesitant to wade into the more murky waters of de facto segregation, at the 1961 convention, the national NAACP passed a resolution encouraging local chapters to "ensure the end of segregated public education in fact or by law by all means possible." By 1963, the NAACP had filed eighteen legal suits against segregated urban school systems. The mounting legal challenges provided a seedbed for civil rights activism around the issue of education throughout the urban North and West during the mid-1960s. Taking his lead from the successful legal strategy employed in the 1961 *Taylor v. New Rochelle* Supreme Court decision, Barbee argued that segregated public schools in Milwaukee were not merely the result of housing patterns and economics, as most white school officials claimed. Rather, he pointed out that segregation was reinforced and extended by the way school officials drew boundaries, allocated resources, and enforced policy. Convinced he could win a lawsuit, Barbee consulted with Robert Carter, NAACP general counsel and one of the main assistants to Thurgood Marshall in the *Brown* case. Both Carter and NAACP chairman Roy Wilkins encouraged him to move to Milwaukee and to energize the more conservative local branch; if he could do this, they would support his case.[8]

Barbee's approach to what he viewed as a "long-haul fight" was methodical and deliberate. He realized that, ultimately, the issue would most likely be resolved in court and that over a period of years he would need to build and bring a case. In the meantime, he believed that school desegregation advocates had to work on other fronts to support the long-term goal of legal victory. To that end, Barbee sought to mobilize a coalition of community groups and sympathetic individuals in an escalating campaign of public pressure and protest politics.

Not surprisingly, Barbee faced initial resistance to his plan from Milwaukee NAACP (MNAACP) leaders. Clarence Parrish, president of the branch,
told Barbee that he did not believe that deliberate segregation existed in
Milwaukee public schools; Parrish maintained instead that conditions for
local African Americans were improving. A change in leadership in 1962
won Barbee a hearing before the executive board, whose members mostly
supported the overall goal of desegregation but were uncomfortable with
Barbee's confrontational style, preferring instead quiet, dignified negotiation and legal action. According to Barbee, board members feared that a direct public assault on segregated education might spoil race relations and
disrupt members' ties to the white power structure. In the end, Barbee received grudging support from a divided MNAACP.[9]

Rebuffed by the state superintendent of schools, Angus Rothwell, Barbee
and his allies turned their attention to the superintendent of Milwaukee
Public Schools (MPS), Harold Vincent. For many decades, local control and
a preference for neighborhood schools had been the guiding principles of
MPS. Vincent defended these policies but referred the issue to a special
committee for further review and recommendation. The Story Committee,
as it came to be known for its chairman, Harold Story, was split between
four conservative board members and three liberals. On December 10,
1963, Barbee presented the committee with a seventy-seven-page report
and petition representing the findings of a group of social scientists from
the University of Wisconsin–Milwaukee and Marquette University. In
essence, the report underscored the Supreme Court's ruling that segregated
schools were inherently inferior, regardless of whether the racial imbalance
was intentional or not. According to their 1963 data, one high school, two
junior high schools, and eleven elementary schools were more than 90 percent black. Four other elementary schools were 60–90 percent black, and
two high schools, one junior high school, and four elementary schools had
an African American enrollment of 50 percent and rising. "The problem is
obvious," Barbee said. "The time has come for solutions." Barbee offered a
number of concrete steps MPS might take to alleviate segregation: acknowledge the problem and establish a clear-cut policy to integrate the
schools; allow African American students to transfer into white schools; re-
zone districts to increase racial balance; select new school sites in locations
that would ensure greater diversity; and assign African American teachers,
administrators, and other school employees to schools throughout the system. The report referred committee members to seven plans already in use

in other cities as a guide for board action. Barbee also issued two deadlines to the committee. By January 30, 1964, the Milwaukee School Board of Directors was to establish a clear integration policy, allow African American students to transfer into white schools, and end a controversial busing policy. If MPS took these initial steps, the NAACP would give the school system until September to devise a more comprehensive plan for integrating the schools. If the board of directors failed to act, Barbee and his allies threatened a "direct action campaign," including demonstrations and legal action. Representatives of the Milwaukee Congress of Racial Equality (MCORE) and the Near Northside Non-Partisan Committee (NNPC) also appeared briefly before the special committee. Each supported Barbee's demands and presented their own findings and statements in favor of school desegregation. Story told the civil rights representatives that the report would have to be studied in detail before the special committee could respond to their demands. He invited the three groups to return on January 21 to answer questions from committee members. At that meeting, Barbee stormed out when committee members attempted to seat him away from other civil rights advocates; activists cheered this bold move, sang, and hoisted the lawyer onto their shoulders.[10]

Barbee's defiant stand signaled a break with school officials and energized the desegregation campaign. It also drew national attention. During a visit to Milwaukee, Martin Luther King Jr. gave the local effort another boost when he told reporters that residential segregation should not be used "as an excuse for perpetuating de facto segregation" in the schools and endorsed demonstrations to pressure school board officials into action.[11]

January 30 came and went with no significant attempt made by the Milwaukee school board to meet the coalition's demands. As education historian Robert Dahlk has explained, Barbee's ultimate goal was systemwide racial balance. He believed that the school board could be compelled to stake a public pro-desegregation stance and to take some modest steps to ameliorate the inequality. Barbee thought that the more difficult struggle would be to get the board to implement a full-scale, systemwide desegregation plan. In retrospect, he acknowledged that if the board had taken a compromise position short of systemwide racial balance that much of the community support for his campaign would have dissipated. As it was, MPS officials made scant effort to accommodate the coalition. Barbee believed that board conservatives viewed him as a "lightweight" and thought that the challenge would dissipate if they held fast to the neighborhood schools concept. After all, they understood that most white Milwaukeeans supported the current system. But the school board and special committee underestimated the depth of frustration within the African American community over segregated schools. Rather than defusing or demobilizing the situation, board inaction unified the civil rights coalition and galvanized community support for the desegregation campaign.[12]

Making MUSIC

During the first months of 1964, civil rights activists began planning a city-wide school boycott for May, a tactic employed by school desegregation activists in Boston, Chicago, New York, and elsewhere. At the same time, they picketed the school administration building and several schools associated with the intact busing policy. "Intact busing" referred to a practice whereby African American children at overcrowded schools or at schools undergoing construction were transported by bus to "white" schools, where they were kept "intact"—that is, separated from the classes and students at the receiving school. Previously, white students who were bused to other white schools had been integrated. In addition, black children were returned home for lunch even if the cafeteria at their receiving school was available. On top of this, because of the way MPS drew district lines to maintain racial segregation, a number of African American students lived closer to their white receiving school than to their official "neighborhood school." To those in the desegregation campaign, intact busing was the most flagrant example of the school board's determination to preserve the racial imbalance.[13]

In March, George Wallace's presidential campaign blew through Wisconsin like a tornado, churning white reaction and sharpening racial tension across the state. Facing Wisconsin governor John Reynolds as a stand-in for President Johnson, the contest quickly turned into a referendum on civil rights. Newspaper accounts framed the election as a choice between "liberalism" and "segregation." For four weeks, Wallace transfixed Wisconsinites as he traveled the state, peddling his politics of division, with the strong organizational backing of the John Birch Society. The pugnacious Alabama governor transformed the direct appeals to racial bigotry that he employed in the South into coded language tailored to the anxieties of various northern white constituencies. He warned blue-collar workers of the devastating impact the pending Civil Rights Act would have on trade union seniority. He told suburbanites that open housing measures would dramatically change their neighborhoods. And he argued that the Civil Rights Act would take away the rights of citizens to run their own schools. Wallace augmented these masked racial appeals with antigovernment rhetoric and red-baiting.[14]

An impressive array of liberal leaders, and even some Republicans, came out to condemn the Alabama governor and to encourage Wisconsin voters to reject his message at the polls. A closer look revealed a strong current of support for the segregationist. Wallace received warm and enthusiastic welcomes at appearances in La Crosse, Manitowoc, and Madison. At small-town luncheons and service clubs, local businessmen and professionals consistently applauded his remarks. The State Chamber of Commerce abetted Wallace's efforts by announcing its opposition to the Civil Rights Act. Below the desperate pleas of community officials, local voices sounded a supportive note for Wallace in the letters page of the *Milwaukee Journal*. "Gov. Wallace supports true Americanism," one writer explained. "Mr. Wallace is a Christian man. He hates no one but he is strongly opposed to the socialist welfare state."[15]

The most stunning moment of the campaign occurred on April 1, when the Alabama governor appeared before an overflowing crowd of more than 700 enthusiastic working-class white supporters at Serb Hall in the city's South Side. Bronko Gruber, an ex-Marine and Milwaukee tavern owner, arranged the appearance with the hope of giving Wallace "a fair hearing." Wallace entered the room to cheers and choruses of "Way Down upon the Swanee River" and "Dixie" sung in a mix of Polish and English. Racial friction started early when two African Americans refused to stand during the "Star Spangled Banner." Gruber pointed out the two men, and the audience quickly targeted them with boos, catcalls, and shouts of "Send them back to Africa." The men and about ten other civil rights advocates left the hall. As Gruber introduced Governor Wallace, Reverend Leo Champion, an African American minister at the small Jerusalem Baptist Church and a supporter of the school desegregation drive, stood and shouted "Get your dogs out!" several times. According to historian Dan Carter, at that point the mood turned "from threatening to near-homicidal." Faced with a jeering crowd, Champion and two associates fled Serb Hall as a smiling Wallace strode on stage and launched into his usual litany of attacks. The audience went wild, interrupting the governor's remarks thirty-four times with cheering and applause. Following the South Side gathering, which reporters called "the most enthusiastic" of any in the state, Wallace stated that if he ever had to leave Alabama, "I'd want to live on the South Side of Milwaukee."[16]

On election day, Wallace garnered 24.5 percent of the vote statewide and 31.3 percent of the tally in Milwaukee, a shocking result that catapulted the segregationist governor to national political prominence and signaled the rising tide of white racial backlash in the country. Wallace would go on to attain similar success in presidential primaries in Indiana and Maryland over the next several weeks. In Milwaukee, he received his strongest support from the predominately white working-class South Side as well as the more affluent white suburban communities along the North Shore and to the west of downtown. The large Wallace vote suggested deep-seated resistance to civil rights among many whites. A large number believed that liberal leaders had handled civil rights poorly and that racial change was moving too fast, the exact opposite conclusion of local civil rights leaders and a growing number of inner core residents.[17]

Even as the Wallace campaign cast Wisconsin's racial politics deeper into turmoil, Barbee and his allies went about the daunting task of organizing a citywide boycott of public schools. To aid this effort, civil rights leaders formalized their alliance by creating MUSIC as an umbrella organization. MUSIC members were both unaffiliated individuals and representatives of established organizations. Most were African Americans, at least early on. MUSIC membership never reached more than 100, but it could mobilize thousands of citizens when needed. Original organizers included leaders of the state and local NAACP, MCORE, NNPC, the Elks Civil Liberties Committee, and several working-class inner core churches. Later, the Milwaukee chapter of the Student Nonviolent Coordinating Committee (SNCC), the Milwaukee Negro American Labor Council, the Wisconsin Baptist Convention, the Milwaukee Citizens for Equal Opportunity, the Marquette Faculty Association for Interracial Justice, the Student Equality Fellowship (University of Wisconsin–Milwaukee), the Ninth Senatorial District Young Democrats, Americans for Democratic Action, Students United for Racial Equality (Marquette), and the Milwaukee Democrats for Freedom joined MUSIC.

The formation of an independent civil rights organization made sense on a variety of levels. First, it formalized the affiliation between various local civil rights organizations and presented a united front to school officials and in the inner core. In addition, MUSIC provided an effective vehicle, with lengthy tentacles into the community, through which mass action could be organized and mobilized. Last, a separate, independent organization helped moderate the tension between young militants and the more conservative old guard leadership and between the competing member organizations. As Barbee recalled, "We had to lay the groundwork of an umbrella organization to combat some of the weaker elements of the local NAACP . . . [and] because CORE wasn't going to knuckle under the NAACP and the NAACP wasn't going to let SNCC or CORE be in charge." MUSIC operated outside the control of any one organization and thus retained the freedom to operate as local conditions dictated, without the fear that any single group could veto mass action approved by the majority of its members.[18]

Although MUSIC membership remained fluid, a distinct leadership core, or "inner cabinet," shaped the organization and its decisions. Barbee was the most influential leader and the principal decision maker. Marilyn Morheuser served as the group's main organizer and administrator. Calvin Sherard worked as the MUSIC office manager until his departure from Milwaukee in 1965. Reverend B. S. Gregg served as treasurer. Tom Jacobson acted as MUSIC's legal tactician until his relationship with Barbee cooled after 1964. Other significant MUSIC leaders included Carole Malone, Leslie and Arlene Johnson, John Givens, Cecil Brown, Reverend Louis Beauchamp, Reverend Charles Luhn, and Reverend Henderson Davis. For important, broader decisions, MUSIC leadership sought community input and authorization. This usually meant a large, open rally at the MUSIC headquarters at Reverend Gregg's St. Matthew's CME Church. Discussion would be held and then a vote taken. Early on, during the direct action phase, weekly MUSIC meetings drew between ten and thirty people. After 1964, when the militancy of MUSIC escalated and the leadership wanted to keep its plans from the police, planning and decision making came from a deliberately small group.[19]

As important as Barbee's leadership and the strong organizational structure of MUSIC were, it was also true that different people came to the school desegregation campaign for different reasons. Jack Dougherty's important work on school reform makes clear that "While all became members of the same movement, there was not a universal ideology cohering their disparate views, experiences, and expectations." Juanita Adams and Arlene Johnson were drawn to MUSIC as staunch integrationists. Mildred Harpole was more concerned with quality education for all black students than with the broader goals of integration. Flo Seefeldt joined MUSIC as a way to secure more resources for African American children. And Vada Harris "internalized a positive black identity that bolstered her political commitment to integration rather than conflicted with it." Many joined MUSIC because it was the best available vehicle to press for change, while others—in particular, men—were involved in order to stick it to "the Man." Cecil Brown recalled, "It was wonderful, because it was the first time that the African American community and its supporters set up a new organization that The Man did not control, could not influence, could not intimidate, could not coerce." In this way, the school desegregation protests spoke to those currents in the community that preferred confrontation over negotiation, challenge to cooperation.[20]

As in other local campaigns throughout the civil rights era, women provided the organizational backbone to the school desegregation movement. Women served in important leadership roles in MUSIC, participated in every major demonstration, and were often arrested and jailed for their actions. Many MUSIC activists agree that Marilyn Morheuser deserves special attention for her role organizing the first boycott. According to Lloyd Barbee, Morheuser "probably did more 'nuts and bolts' administrative and organizing work than any other individual." Born in St. Louis, Morheuser had worked previously as a teaching nun, although she found her blossoming interest in civil rights too confined by the stricture of her vows. She moved to Milwaukee in 1962 and soon thereafter received a dispensation from the pope to leave her order. Morheuser lived in the inner core, became an editor of the *Milwaukee Star,* and plunged into civil rights. She served as MUSIC's first secretary as well as the chair of the Curriculum Committee for Freedom Schools. Some have described the former nun as authoritarian and patronizing. Others have called her courageous and proficient. Like Barbee, Morheuser possessed a single-mindedness and a crusading spirit. Regardless of what people thought of her personally, Morheuser, more than anyone else, directed the massive effort behind a large-scale school boycott.[21]

Even as MUSIC experienced overall success in its efforts to rally community support for the boycott, dissenting black voices did exist. For instance, at the initial organizing rally, Robert Taylor, an active Republican and Barry Goldwater supporter in 1964, opposed the boycott. Taylor, though, had little support within the community. E'Allyne Perkins, an MPS teacher and president of the Milwaukee Council of Negro Women, had urged MCORE to abandon the Lins protest and to concentrate instead on solving African Americans' problems, such as black students beating up white students, fights after high school football games, vandalism, juvenile delinquency, and parental apathy. Later, in a March 1965 letter to the *Star* about the boycott, she criticized emotional preachers, unqualified black leaders, and excessive drinking and pool playing by African American men. Even Reverend Gregg, who strongly supported the school desegregation effort and whose church was the primary meeting place for MUSIC, recalled that a sizable number of his church members were uncomfortable with the tactics and strategy of the campaign. Perhaps the most prominent African American opponent of MUSIC's boycott was James Dorsey, one of the first black attorneys in the city and an elder statesman of the traditional black leadership class. In a letter to the *Journal,* he argued that the proposed boycott stirred race hatred and lamented that the MNAACP had "slipped into the rut of emotional rabble rousers"; he later resigned from the MNAACP in protest. Dorsey's social status, age, his broad acceptance by whites, and his close ties with the Catholic hierarchy and white legal community help to explain his resistance to the boycott. Yet, the night before the boycott, Dorsey, Perkins, and Judge Christ Seraphim mustered only forty-six people for a rally, an indication that opposition to MUSIC's actions did not run deep within the community.[22]

Among white Milwaukeeans, most remained oblivious to the school issue. White civic leaders again focused on the tactics rather than issues; the boycott itself became the issue, not the segregation it protested. Many claimed that the boycott was illegal. Others argued that by keeping children out of school, civil rights leaders hurt the very people they claimed to be helping. Others simply thought that MUSIC leaders were "using" children and that they should be arrested and thrown in jail. Both the *Milwaukee Journal* and the *Milwaukee Sentinel* editorialized against the boycott. The mayor, who had remained aloof during the school controversy, now urged MUSIC to call off the boycott and offered to appoint an independent panel to mediate between MUSIC and MPS. MUSIC leaders agreed to mediation but not to call off the boycott. The board ultimately refused the offer by a vote of 9–6, along with a rather mild statement recognizing "the racial imbalance that exists in our core area schools." Other city officials made threats. The district attorney told parents and students they would be breaking the compulsory education law if they participated and suggested that poor parents might lose their Aid to Families with Dependent Children benefits if they took part. Superintendent Vincent told teachers who supported the boycott that they risked losing pay. In short, the full array of white civic leadership opposed the boycott, while none opposed the racial imbalance in the public schools with the same fervor.

Just prior to the boycott, on April 24, Harold Story seemed to slam the door on MUSIC's proposals. He announced that the only change that the school board could legally make was an "open enrollment policy." Currently, the board had a "free transfer policy" that allowed student transfers to schools with openings—for good reason. School officials did not deem a desire for integration as a "good reason," although they did accept white parents' desire to get their children out of a transitional or predominantly African American school as one. Civil rights organizations complained that white parents received transfers in far greater numbers than did black parents. Under an open enrollment policy, a transfer would be granted for any reason—space permitting. There was not nearly enough open space in other Milwaukee public schools to make an open transfer policy an effective means to desegregate the schools. In addition, as MUSIC officials later argued, it placed the primary burden for integrating schools on parents instead of on system administrators. Story called a policy statement favoring integration "only words" and ruled out all other integration proposals. He called the NAACP's plan a "complete violation of the law" and lectured, "It's almost sacred in our democratic concept of things that we do things without reference to race, religion and all the other things."[23]

On May 18, 1964, the day after the tenth anniversary of the Supreme Court's historic *Brown v. Board of Education* decision, the first MUSIC boycott took place, largely without a hitch. Barbee estimated that 15,000 elementary, junior high, and high school students withdrew from school and that about 11,000 attended one of thirty-three "freedom schools" set up mainly in small African American church basements and extra rooms throughout the inner core, though a few took place in grander confines, like the All Saints Chapel, the home parish of the Episcopal bishop of Milwaukee, Donald H. V. Hallock, a consistent supporter of racial equality. Harold Vincent put the withdrawal figures at 11,000. The freedom schools, which bore the names of famous African Americans, including Martin Luther King Jr., Crispus Attucks, Marian Anderson, and James Baldwin, emphasized four new concepts—freedom, brotherhood, justice, and equality—which temporarily replaced the traditional "three *R*s." Teachers and students explored African American history—often for the first time—the concept of the boycott, racial myths, human relations, nonviolent direct action, and the civil rights movement generally. Students wrote poems and journals, drew pictures, engaged in role-play, sang and danced, wrote letters, debated, and discussed. In all, roughly 320 college students and professors, businessmen, blue-collar workers, retired teachers, clergymen, professionals, and even a few public school teachers volunteered as freedom school instructors. MUSIC literature explained that teachers were to "help students understand that the withdrawal is not a rebellion against schools, teachers, principals or authority, but rather an organized, orderly, united effort to get better schools." Parents of boycotting students also pitched in, providing transportation, serving meals, and, in a few instances, teaching. Parents and activists also picketed at thirteen different sites on the day of the boycott. Dick Gregory returned to support the protest. He attended a freedom school, where he encouraged students to become active in the civil rights movement, then joined thirty-five people in a picket line at the school administration building. The day was capped with a "Freedom Day Hootenanny" to celebrate the boycott's success. Public reaction, despite previous opposition, was generally positive toward the well-run boycott, although it failed to budge the conservative MPS majority.[24]

Civil rights leaders reacted to the board's continued unwillingness to act with a mix of frustration, exasperation, and brewing outrage. Many MUSIC members felt that they had been hitting their heads against a brick wall; that their good faith efforts to reason, negotiate, and demonstrate had gone utterly unheeded. Ed Smyth of MNAACP told reporters that MPS inaction "gives substance and validity" to the belief that the board and its special committee held a "conservative, hostile and antagonistic attitude toward the idea of integrating schools in Milwaukee." June Shagaloff told a national NAACP gathering in Washington, D.C., that school segregation in Milwaukee was among "the worst in the nation" and that "Save Our Neighborhood Schools" meant "Save Our *White* Neighborhood Schools." Barbee ominously warned that the special committee had lost its chance to use "the last few ounces of prevention. Now it will take a pound of cure." Throughout the summer and fall of 1964, the mood changed within the MUSIC leadership. Confident that the Milwaukee School Board would make no concessions, the group was increasingly resigned to a protracted legal fight. The feeling that school officials simply did not understand segregation or care for African Americans also led to heightened militancy among desegregation activists.[25]

During the summer of 1964, MUSIC sponsored a series of "Freedom Camps" for students and "Freedom Institutes" for parents and organizers, but in the fall local civil rights leaders observed a nationwide moratorium on new protests during the national election. MUSIC took the opportunity to reassess its strategy and to plot its next move. Barbee ran for Isaac

Coggs's open assembly seat and won, giving the young lawyer a new base from which to attack segregation and inequality. His campaign literature stressed that the young attorney was a "Fighter on All Fronts."[26]

An Escalating Campaign of Civil Disobedience

In March 1965, the southern struggle for racial justice again briefly wrestled the nation's attention away from local events. The Selma voting rights campaign and the "Bloody Sunday" violence at the foot of the Edmund Pettus Bridge shocked the nation's conscience, sending a new jolt of energy through grassroots movements across the country, including Milwaukee. A number of white religious leaders, including Father Groppi, traveled south to bear witness to the racial brutality in Alabama and brought back a new commitment to action. MNAACP and MCORE voted to send Reverend Leo Champion to Selma as their emissary. The *Star* noted that a group of fourteen local African Americans had gone south, too, but criticized the conspicuous absence of black clergymen, who offered only "flimsy" excuses for their inaction. Foreshadowing controversies to come around the leadership of Father Groppi, *Star* editor Walter Jones complained, "The pathetic attitude of the Negro ministry here was made even more vivid by the participation of the local white clergy. Must the white clergy lead the Negro to freedom on their coattails?"[27]

Following the Selma campaign, another wave of school activism took place in cities across the North and West. June Shagaloff of the NAACP claimed that school desegregation campaigns were ongoing in twenty-four northern and western cities during the spring and summer of 1965. Nationally, Milwaukee officials gained a reputation for extreme inaction. A report by the NAACP failed to list Milwaukee among cities that had made gains in the northern school drive, instead placing it on the list of "do-nothing" cities. The report indicated that whereas other cities had taken effective steps to eliminate de facto segregation and other discriminatory practices in the previous few years, Milwaukee remained out of step with the rest of the nation.[28]

On May 15, the executive board of MUSIC voted to organize a second school boycott the following fall and approved a direct action program against the school board. Barbee told reporters, "We will have an all-summer long program of direct action. If the school board doesn't get off the dead center of inaction, we're going to see to it that Milwaukee has the kind of boycott this nation has never seen—in both scope and duration."

The following week, MUSIC began its three-week "human chain-in" campaign outside several inner core schools. Concurrently, members of a newly reinvigorated MCORE disrupted school board and Story Committee meetings, conducting two sit-ins outside Superintendent Vincent's office and a "sing-in" outside Harold Story's house.[29]

Official reaction to the heightened direct action campaign was mixed. Majorities on the school board and the Story Committee reiterated their belief that intact busing was necessary, temporary, and "educationally sound." Harold Vincent claimed that integrating classes at receiving schools was "administratively unfeasible," even though it had been successfully accomplished in several other cities. The board agreed, and most local whites assented without question. Judge Christ Seraphim, who presided over the cases of several civil rights demonstrators and had labeled the first boycott a "goofy stunt," told a group of protesters in court, "You can't get civil rights by doing civil wrongs." For his part, Mayor Maier, in an effort to defuse the situation, called for another broad "official" study of the school controversy by a group of experts. He suggested that an organization such as We-Milwaukeeans or the Conference on Religion and Race should take the initiative. The city's mainstream editorial writers tended to be of two minds on the renewed activism. In what had become, at this point, a familiar refrain, most criticized the confrontational tactics, even if they agreed with the overall school desegregation movement's goals. For instance, a *Journal* editorial, titled "Illegal Actions No Help in Settling School Problem," argued, "Throwing oneself in front of a school bus is a reckless, if dramatic, way of making a point. The civil rights demonstrators who engaged in this illegal action . . . have not advanced the cause they champion." Similarly, the *Journal*'s sister station on television, WTMJ-TV, called the human chains "ill-advised." Opinion makers, however, also criticized the school officials' continued inaction. Further down the column in the same *Journal* editorial, it stated, "The school board bears a good part of the blame for this. It has barely recognized that racial imbalance exists in the schools and, up to now, has refused to do anything about it." Many Milwaukeeans appeared to look on with increasing exasperation at the lack of progress between school board officials and civil rights leaders. WITI-TV editorial writers captured this sentiment in late June when they stated, "We're faced with this impossible impasse. So, where do we go from here? Well, how about a change . . . a change in personalities? Perhaps, we'd stand a chance of accomplishing something if there were different people to tackle the problem."[30]

On June 18, MUSIC leaders agreed to stop blocking buses. That same day, Lloyd Barbee filed suit in the U.S. District Court on behalf of forty-one students and their parents—African American and white—asking for a decree to end segregation in the Milwaukee public schools. The suit, one of twenty before courts nationwide at that time, charged that the school board had drawn boundaries along racial patterns in housing, that black teachers were assigned to predominantly black schools, that school transfers were made more easily available to white students, and that intact busing perpetuated segregation. A few weeks later, Milwaukee civil rights activists joined seven other cities when MUSIC sent a nine-page letter of complaint to the Department of Health, Education, and Welfare, detailing charges of discrimination and segregation and requesting the withdrawal of federal funds from MPS. Over the next year, the federal suit would consume more and more of MUSIC's energy, but the group still had work to do in the short-term.[31]

By the end of the summer, MUSIC was steaming ahead with plans for another student withdrawal on October 18, 1965, this time for three days. Supporters of the protest generally felt that it was regrettable but necessary, given the intractability of the school board. The stubborn recalcitrance of white officials even began to alienate moderate groups like the Milwaukee Commission on Equal Opportunity, the Milwaukee Committee on Community Relations, and the Milwaukee Urban League, who had long counseled negotiation with white leaders as an alternative to direct action. On August 28, 800 "orderly but noisy" civil rights demonstrators marched nearly four miles from the Lloyd Street School to MacArthur Square for a rally. As they approached the square, marchers were greeted by thirty picketers carrying signs asking, "Is this another Communist controlled demonstration?" In fact, more than fifty local civil rights, church, welfare, fraternal, and civic groups sponsored the "March Toward Freedom and Independence" to commemorate the second anniversary of the March on Washington and to highlight racial inequality in Milwaukee, particularly in jobs, housing, and education. MUSIC leaders hoped that this would reenergize the Milwaukee school desegregation movement at the beginning of the third year of planned protest. As Barbee explained, "The main thing is . . . we want our citizens to focus on local problems and local solutions rather than engaging in Afghanistanism—like problems and solutions in Alabama, Mississippi and Louisiana." The rally featured entertainers, floats, a motorcade, and speeches by Barbee, Dick Gregory, and Mississippi Freedom Democratic Party delegate Fannie Lou Hamer.[32]

As the boycott date approached, divisions deepened, rhetoric sharpened, and white community leaders outside of the school board frantically searched for a way to head off the protest. We-Milwaukeeans announced plans for a new study of racial imbalance in the Milwaukee public schools. MUSIC and MPS both agreed to the new study, but civil rights activists refused to call off the boycott; they had seen too many studies already. On October 13, Mayor Maier outlined his "War on Prejudice," an "intensive, year long experimental program to help change the distorted image that some people have of members of minority groups." He claimed that the efforts of civil rights advocates were "noisy" and "full of sound and fury" but "not meaningful." The mayor's proposal was long on rhetoric and short on concrete plans. It contained warmed-over calls for metrowide cooperation and increased acculturation programming, but the primary feature was a voluntary public relations campaign to create a new civic attitude on race. Although the plan did sketch out the view of civil rights from the perspective of an embattled inner city mayor dealing with the exodus of resources as individuals and businesses flocked to areas outside urban boundaries, many scoffed at the War on Prejudice as a political gimmick; it sounded good, promised much, but delivered little.[33]

On Monday, October 18, 1965, the second school boycott took place in Milwaukee. According to school records, an extra 7,300 students missed school that day. The figure dropped to 4,756 on Tuesday and hovered just above 4,000 on Wednesday, the last day of the protest. Vel Phillips, who headed up MUSIC's food distribution program, estimated that around 5,000 students attended one of the twenty-six freedom schools on the first day of the boycott. MUSIC also sponsored a direct action campaign to compliment the withdrawal. During the day, dozens picketed the school administration building. At night, Father Groppi, who was now serving as second vice president of MUSIC, led 265 young people on a thirty-eight-block march to school board President Foley's home, where they were joined by fifty others. Mayor Maier said that the demonstration, in front of a private home, exhibited a bigotry that "almost smacks of Ku Klux Klanism in reverse." Barbee called the mayor "bankrupt" on civil rights, stating that Maier's record "ranges from a mere whisper to a whining whimper." On Tuesday night, 313 young people, stretching for more than a block, snubbed their nose at the mayor by parading outside of his apartment. On Thursday, MUSIC leaders ended the demonstrations, citing fatigue among participants as well as a desire to preempt legal threats from the district attorney against boycotting students. A third, targeted boycott against North Division High School came off quietly in March of 1966; 500 students participated in the one-day walkout.[34]

Public support for MUSIC's direct action agenda waned in late 1965 as Barbee and Morheuser turned their attention increasingly toward the long march through the courts. In early December, MUSIC members conducted their last significant protest. It began with an all-night vigil at the construction site for the new MacDowell School. A MUSIC press release explained, "This construction is typical of northern style 'separate but equal' schools—schools well placed in neighborhoods which will obviously become racially imbalanced. Here the neighborhood school myth is unveiled for what it is meant to produce: Negro schools and white schools that operate outside the framework of democratic society." At 7:30 a.m., twenty-two demonstrators linked arms and blocked the entrance to the construction area. As workers began to arrive, five of them—two African American—shoved their way forcibly through the line of protesters. Soon after, a pickup truck, intent on entering the site, pressed into the human chain, pushing some of the protesters back three feet. Fearing an escalation of the conflict, the police asked demonstrators to move or be arrested. When protesters failed to budge, policemen began arresting activists. Several went limp and fell to the ground while officers carried them off to the patrol wagon. Others moved to the side and began singing freedom songs. Among those arrested were three clergymen and several members of the NAACP Youth Council (YC).[35]

Over the next two weeks, protests continued at the MacDowell site, resulting in twenty-one arrests, as activists continued to physically block construction. On December 8, three demonstrators temporarily blocked cement trucks from dropping their loads. The next day, twenty-year-old Robert Bundy chained himself to the construction gate for six hours in an attempt to impede work on the school. On December 10 and 14, protesters chained themselves to forklifts. There was an element of high jinks to these protests as activists attempted to create diversions to aid in the efforts of others. For instance, on December 10, several clergymen raced their cars up to one side of the site, brakes screeching, in an attempt to draw the attention of local authorities as four young protesters slipped through the gate on the opposite side to block construction equipment. Similarly, on December 14, one activist ran around the site as a decoy while another used the confusion created by the distraction to slip a chain around himself and a forklift. The

MacDowell protest ended on December 17, when 350 people took part in an "Equal Opportunity Day" march from the MacDowell site to the school administration building.[36]

The MacDowell protest illustrated the arc of change within the school desegregation movement from 1963 to 1965. Barbee and Morheuser, who had been so prominent early on, now spent most of their time and energy preparing the legal case. Whereas early demonstrations were overwhelmingly African American, toward the end white participation regularly ran as high as one-third to one-half of the total. And at the MacDowell protest, a smaller, tighter group of activists, centered on Father Groppi and the YC, had taken over MUSIC's direct action campaign, signaling the emergence of new civil rights leadership in Milwaukee. Soon, they would lead the local struggle in controversial new directions.

In the end, the school desegregation campaign revealed both the possibilities and limitations of civil rights insurgency. For the first time, MUSIC proved that it was possible to organize and sustain a mass protest campaign in Milwaukee. Although it did not desegregate the schools, it did result in some minor concessions by MPS, including an open enrollment policy, increased resources for compensatory education programs, and more black teachers placed throughout the system. More generally, the campaign pushed another important aspect of racial inequality into the public spotlight. In the process, it created awareness of segregation and educated the community, black and white, to its complex dynamics in the city. MUSIC provided thousands of ordinary inner core residents with opportunities to participate directly in the local black freedom movement. For a brief time, the school desegregation campaign gave voice to the voiceless, made what James Scott calls "the hidden transcript" of the poor and dispossessed audible.[37]

Nevertheless, it is equally clear that direct action alone was not enough to desegregate Milwaukee's public schools; it would take another decade of legal action to finally achieve that. Once again, a majority of white officials stood firm against racial change. The success of the Wallace campaign dramatically illustrated that the white reaction was not confined to official quarters but enjoyed broad support across the community.

Even so, the Milwaukee civil rights movement matured over the course of the school desegregation movement. MUSIC's organizing efforts did cultivate a pro–civil rights coalition as well as a new core of activists and leaders.

The campaign involved thousands of African Americans but also awakened young people, Catholics, and liberal whites to the cause of civil rights; each group would play a pivotal role in upcoming efforts. It became obvious that the status quo was deeply entrenched, and civil rights leaders increasingly understood what it was like to try to get social change moving in the city. They learned how to approach their struggle within the limitations of the local context and came to believe that the way to get action was to create tension and confrontation, to force the issue. Milwaukee civil rights activists, particularly Father Groppi and the YC, took this lesson to heart after the school desegregation movement. From that point forward, they increasingly relied on dramatic public confrontations, what Dr. King called "creative tension," to force change.

— 4 —

Father Groppi's
Civil Rights Awakening

In early March 1965, the combination of righteous cause, inspired leadership, courageous followers, and unjust brutality came together in Selma, Alabama. Selma had become the front line in the battle for national voting rights legislation. Responding to weeks of violence and unrest, which had culminated in the beating of several hundred peaceful protesters by Alabama state troopers on "Bloody Sunday," Martin Luther King Jr. issued a national ecumenical call for support. He asked people of conscience across the country to head south for a mass march from Selma to Montgomery. Northern white clergy and lay activists from all denominations, including hundreds of Catholic priests, nuns, and parishioners from more than fifty dioceses, responded to King's call. For the next few weeks, reporters and photographers from around the world trained their attention on the drama unfolding in Alabama as Christian witness combined with ecumenical protest in what NAACP chairman Roy Wilkins labeled the civil rights movement's "last great parade."[1]

On Friday, March 12, five days after the violence at the foot of the Edmund Pettus Bridge roiled the nation, four Catholic priests from Milwaukee— Fathers James Groppi, Patrick Flood, Matthew Gottschalk, and Austin Schlaefer—along with *Milwaukee Sentinel* reporter Bob Leipzig, set off for Selma by car. It was not the four clergymen's first trip south, but there was something different this time. News that James Reeb, a white Unitarian minister from Boston, had died the previous day from a beating at the hands of Alabama white supremacists had made its way to the group. As with the murders of James Cheney, Mickey Schwerner, and Andrew Goodman on the eve of the 1964 Mississippi Freedom Summer Project, the violence only stiffened the resolve of those going south. Religious people from across the country continued to stream into Alabama in a national display of conscience; the Milwaukee priests decided to press on as well. Frank Aukofer, who covered the story for the *Milwaukee Journal,* reported that "the atmosphere reeked of brotherhood and righteousness" and that the scene took on "aspects of a religious retreat." He also detected a prophetic sense among the visiting white congregants that "what they were doing was so right that they had to prevail, had to overcome."[2]

While in Selma, the Milwaukee priests lived with local people at the George Washington Carver Housing Project, where "a highly emotional sense of brotherhood and well-being pervaded." They worshiped each morning at St. Elizabeth's, a small Catholic mission church nearby, and attended meetings at Brown's Chapel, the spiritual home of the Selma voting rights campaign. The clergymen learned about the techniques of militant nonviolent direct action; debated civil disobedience; exchanged ideas with people of different faiths, classes, and races; marched in rallies; registered voters; challenged state troopers; conducted teach-ins with parents; knelt in interfaith prayer protests; and visited with local families.[3]

The dramatic high point of the trip came on Tuesday, March 16, when news arrived in Selma that Student Nonviolent Coordinating Committee (SNCC) volunteers in Montgomery had been attacked by club-wielding police officers on horseback. Alive to the moment, Father Groppi rallied his friends to the cause, certain that if there was work to be done, it was in the state capital. Other clergymen decided to join the Milwaukee contingent as they hastily packed their belongings and loaded the car. After a tense brush with an Alabama state patrolman on the highway, the caravan made it to Montgomery, where a gathering of local residents and civil rights workers directed them to a small house in which Martin Luther King Jr. and James Forman, then head of SNCC, discussed the campaign's next move. After more than four hours of waiting, a spokesperson for the civil rights leaders emerged to tell the clergymen that Dr. King and Forman would address a mass meeting at Beulah Baptist Church that evening.[4]

When the Milwaukee clergymen arrived at the church, ushers seated them in the second row. "[The old church] was so packed that some people were literally hanging from the rafters," recalled Frank Aukofer. An interracial throng of several hundred SNCC student volunteers, Southern Christian Leadership Conference (SCLC) operatives, visiting white clergymen, activists, and local black community members sat side by side in a scene one San Francisco reporter likened to a Beatles concert. The freedom songs sounded particularly fervent that night and the civil rights chants unusually raucous. According to Aukofer, when King stepped to the stage, the roar "almost lifted the roof off. It was like standing near the exhaust of a jet airliner." James Forman, still furious about the attack on SNCC volunteers earlier that afternoon, electrified the audience by angrily promising, "If we can't eat from the table of justice, we are going to kick the fucking legs out from under it." Forman's words caused a significant stir and signaled an ascending militancy within the Movement, particularly among younger activists. Ralph Abernathy quelled the disquiet by suggesting that the visiting religious community march to the state capitol to offer a prayer.[5]

Things were moving fast in Alabama, pervaded by a palpable sense that History—or was it the Holy Spirit?—had seized the moment. The Bloody Sunday attack and the death of James Reeb still hung heavily in the southern air. On Monday, hundreds of civil rights activists participated in an emotional memorial rally for the slain Boston minister. That evening, President Johnson, who had initially told Movement leaders to defer their quest for voting rights legislation, shocked the nation when he ended a historic address before a joint session of Congress in support of voting rights for African Americans, stating, "It's all of us who must overcome the crippling legacy of bigotry and injustice. *And—we—shall—overcome.*" The next morning, he delivered the Voting Rights Act to Congress. The day after that, Alabama troopers attacked student activists in Montgomery. With each new turn of events, every click of a camera, and fresh inch of newsprint, more and more supporters flooded into the state, and the sense of righteousness grew.

Following the mass meeting on Tuesday evening, the Milwaukee priests marched toward the front of a group of thirty-five clergymen and women to the state capitol. When they approached the stairs, a phalanx of troopers stepped forth to block the path of what some undoubtedly saw as a band of "outside agitators." Taking their cues from Father Daniel Mallette of Chicago, the demonstrators knelt in protest, refusing to budge before they offered a prayer on the statehouse stairs. After Father Mallette read from Saint Paul's epistle to the Hebrews, Father Groppi was the first to speak up. "God is the father of us all and we are all brothers in him," the Milwaukee priest reflected. "We have an obligation to help our brothers . . . If we go to Church on Sunday and preach the doctrine of Christ and then do nothing . . . we are hypocrites." The police ultimately relented, permitting three priests to mount the stairs and offer their prayer. As the demonstrators walked back to the church afterward, energized by the intoxicating sense of brotherhood and the dizzying pace of events, Father Groppi told his friends, "That's something I've always wanted to do—sit down in the heart of the segregationist South with a group of priests and ministers in an ecumenical protest." Father Gottshaulk smiled and retorted, "You just have a martyr complex is all."[6]

The next day, the Milwaukee priests again joined King, Forman, Abernathy, and John Lewis in a rainy march on the Dallas County Courthouse to protest the assault on SNCC workers the previous day. The group waited outside for nearly three hours as Dr. King negotiated with local officials inside. Ultimately, state troopers agreed to refrain from further violence against peaceful protesters, and a federal court lifted the injunction against a new Selma to Montgomery march. This soggy protest at the state capitol proved to be Groppi, Gottschalk, Flood, and Schlaefer's last in the state. That night, they slept in Montgomery's St. John the Baptist Church before heading back to Selma in the morning and then home to Wisconsin.

With the injunction lifted, the Selma voting rights campaign reached a quick conclusion. On March 21, an estimated 3,200 people set out again on the fifty-mile journey from Selma to Montgomery, under the trained eye of the national and international press, this time without incident. Three days later, more than 25,000 marchers entered Montgomery, where Harry Belafonte, Sammy Davis Jr., Tony Bennett, folk singers Peter, Paul and Mary, Nina Simone, and other celebrities performed at the Stars for Freedom rally. The next day, Dr. King delivered a speech at the foot of the capitol stairs. "They told us we wouldn't get here," he said. "And there were those who said that we would get here only over their dead bodies, but the world today knows that we are here and we are standing before the forces of power in the state of Alabama saying, 'We ain't goin' let nobody turn us around.'" President Johnson signed the Voting Rights Act into law on August 6, 1965. With that gesture, one important chapter in the national struggle for racial justice closed.[7]

The story of Father Groppi's journey to Selma underscores the crucial religious underpinning of his commitment to racial justice. For Groppi and many of the other white clergymen who had come south, the powerful resonance of Selma emanated from the fusion of politics and faith. To miss this dynamic is to fundamentally misapprehend Groppi's civil rights leadership. The animating spirit behind his dedication to the African American freedom struggle was his Catholic faith and his role as a priest. "He took it very seriously," recalled Margaret Rozga, a former NAACP Youth Council (YC) member who later married Groppi after he left the priesthood, "and I think that is something that gets overlooked a lot. He was really committed to the priestly life." This chapter attempts to explore the Catholic roots of Father Groppi's civil rights leadership and to situate his life within the broader context of what historian John McGreevy calls "the Catholic encounter with race" in the twentieth-century urban North. McGreevy singled out Milwaukee as the "site of the most sustained Catholic encounter with racial issues" in the postwar period. It is in this spiritual terrain that we might begin to understand how a white Catholic priest from Milwaukee's South Side became an important figure in the modern black freedom movement.[8]

The Catholic Church and Race Relations in Milwaukee

At the turn of the century, the unprecedented wave of southern and eastern European immigration to Milwaukee brought with it a sharp surge in the city's Catholic population, transforming what had been a strongly German church into a more diverse white, ethnic immigrant church. Roughly one-third to one-half of the city's population was Catholic throughout the mid-twentieth century, a demographic fact that ensured that the church would become a dominant local institution.

This urban immigrant Catholicism was firmly rooted in physical space. Church rules dictated that geography defined parish boundaries, guaranteeing a long-term commitment to a particular neighborhood. In turn, parishioners became church members by living within a prescribed area. As laborers and their families from Poland, Italy, Lithuania, Bohemia, Croatia, Ireland, and elsewhere flocked to Milwaukee for jobs in heavy industry, meatpacking, tanning, and other surging economic sectors, the urban landscape became transformed into a patchwork of immigrant neighborhoods. At the center of these ethnic enclaves often stood a Catholic church. As historian Gerald Gamm has written, "Catholics [could] be confident in their church's long-term commitment to its neighborhood, they [could] reasonably expect other Catholics to stay in the district, and those rational expectations [were] mutually reinforcing." This strong loyalty to territory was evidenced by the fact that many urban Catholics, when asked where they lived, responded with the name of their parish.[9]

White immigrant Catholics in Milwaukee by and large embraced a narrow and rigid traditional theology that emphasized hierarchy and tolerated little dissent. According to this view, church doctrines did not change, and obedience to religious authority was paramount. Most Catholics were taught doctrine from the *Baltimore Catechism,* a popular book used in Catholic schools throughout the country from the late nineteenth century through the 1960s. The approach advocated by the *Catechism* entailed memorizing a series of questions and answers and wholly embracing the theology it delineated. According to Father Eugene Bleidorn, a liberal pastor at St. Boniface Church, "Pray," "Pay," and "Obey" were its key words. The emphasis on order, discipline, authority, and uniformity ensured that "[Most Milwaukee Catholics] had no sense of social justice or that love your neighbor was just about as important as love God." In exchange for their obedience and devotion, the church defended members' interests and helped provide for their material needs. Parishioners turned first to their priest in times of celebration and stress, and clergymen often acted as a conduit between the laity and the broader community. Parishes established schools, insurance programs, acculturation classes, counseling services, burial and widow's benefits societies, free meal programs, and emergency shelters, and held numerous social activities. For many members, the church provided the only safety net when the world turned harsh or intimidating. Catholics who held prominent positions in business, unions, politics, and civic organizations were expected to serve as a further bulwark against perceived threats to their communities and the faith.[10]

In these ways, the church ordered Milwaukee Catholics' reality, literally and figuratively. For many, it was the single most important lens through which they viewed and understood the world. That perspective was insular and ill equipped to deal with the vast social changes sweeping urban America in the post–World War II period. Catholics were trained to interpret those changes through the lens of the church and its traditional teachings, and they turned to the church, rather than to the state or other secular institutions, for guidance and protection.

Because Milwaukee's black population remained relatively small until the mid-1950s, race played only a minor and occasional role in the Catholic world of Milwaukee. In general, church authorities opted for a hands-off approach to race relations, and when they did weigh in, it was usually to maintain the status quo. For most white Catholics, race, no doubt, went largely unexamined. When they did tune in, they often brought racist stereotypes to the issue or treated African Americans as another immigrant group, focusing on conversion and social programs more than on the struggle for racial justice.[11]

There was one notable exception to this general rule. In 1908, Lincoln and Julia Valle, a husband and wife team of black Catholic laypersons from Chicago, organized a small group of African American Catholics at a storefront on North Fourth Street in Milwaukee's inner core. In response, Archbishop Sebastian Messmer sanctioned the city's first African American mission the following year at St. Benedict the Moor chapel on North Fifth Street. A few years later, the largely white Capuchin community, which traced its history in the area back to the 1880s, assumed responsibility for this ministry. Over the next half century, Capuchin friars at St. Benedict ran a school, a day nursery, a summer camp for children, and a hospital.[12]

With the influx of poor African Americans and rural whites into northern cities and the concurrent flight of affluent whites to the suburbs, which transformed urban politics during the mid-twentieth century, the dynamics of the church were fundamentally altered. In Milwaukee, as in other urban centers, a new suburban Catholicism began to take root during the post–World War II era. Whites that moved outside the city limits from traditional urban neighborhoods became more affluent and better educated than previous generations, and they wanted more of the same for their children. Moreover, they were less tied to the ethnic character of their parents and grandparents' faith, and their lives and identities were no longer strictly defined by parish boundaries. Church authorities responded to these pressures by creating a ring of new suburban parishes and building a spate of new schools.

At the same time, growing unease spread throughout the increasingly working-class and poor white parish neighborhoods that these more affluent whites had left behind. As suburban Catholics and their neighbors made good on the promise of America, urban white ethnic Catholics and their neighbors worried about declining home values, crumbling urban infrastructure, rising crime rates, and the beginnings of a long economic slide toward deindustrialization. The rapid growth of the black community, with its rising demands for fair treatment in housing, work, and school, seemed like a threat to much of what many of these urban white Catholics valued. Consequently, they pressed clergymen and church authorities to defend their interests against both real and perceived threats.

Within the city's inner core parishes, urban demographic shifts played out differently. Because Catholic churches were rooted in geography, and not defined by the congregation, when populations shifted significantly, churches did not move with their flock (as Protestant churches and Jewish synagogues often did). Rather, they sought to continue their mission among the community's new residents. In Milwaukee during the 1950s, five parishes—St. Benedict the Moor, St. Boniface, St. Elizabeth, St. Francis, and St. Gall—felt the brunt of the city's racial transition. These churches lost much of their traditional white base as those residents fled the vanishing shelter of ethnic neighborhoods for the new security of suburban living. In their stead, African Americans, a group without a strong Catholic history, moved in. Widespread poverty among both the new and old residents, as well as urban blight, further challenged inner core churches during the 1950s and 1960s.[13]

If these parishes were to survive, they needed to stay connected to the communities around them. Priests and nuns in these churches developed new strategies to attract adherents. They reached out to those in the community, began to try to understand their condition and strivings, and sought to speak to those experiences. The same rootedness that had cost inner core parishes their old base now afforded white clergy a unique first-hand view of black life and community and, in turn, of urban inequality. Local African Americans tutored clergy on racial issues, and the result was a strong bond between inner core priests and nuns and the increasingly black communities around them. With more understanding, ultimately, came greater awareness of and participation in the local struggle for racial justice. Inner core Catholic churches became safe havens, providing refuge and resources for black Milwaukeeans in an urban world that was often indifferent, uncaring, or even hostile.

As a result of their efforts, the five inner core parishes attracted African American members. The promise of a better education for their children brought many black Milwaukeeans to the Catholic Church. St. Benedict the Moor,[14] St. Francis, and St. Boniface all ran parochial schools, with St. Francis and St. Boniface opening their doors to non-Catholics in a specific attempt to attract African American students. Similarly, St. Benedict's hospital was one of the few that tended to Milwaukee's black population without discrimination. The host of social programs sponsored by the churches—meals, shelters, acculturation programs, youth activities, and social events—also filled very real needs for community members and demonstrated Catholic compassion. By the early 1960s, St. Benedict had a 90 percent African American membership; St. Boniface's African American membership stood at 75 percent; St. Francis and St. Gall had African American majorities; and St. Michael, St. Leo, and St. Elizabeth each had substantial black minorities. Yet, even as the number of black Catholics increased, inner core parishes saw their overall membership drop precipitously during this period, as white residents continued to abandon the city for the suburbs.[15]

Nevertheless, until the civil rights movement and the Second Vatican Council, most local black Catholics, like most of their white counterparts, remained culturally and politically conservative. Few took leadership roles in the struggle for racial justice, choosing instead to work on institution building and traditional religious instruction and in schools. James Dorsey, who opposed the organizing efforts of the Milwaukee Negro American Labor Council, the Milwaukee Congress of Racial Equality, and the Milwaukee United School Integration Committee (MUSIC) and who headed up the Catholic Interracial Council of Milwaukee, was perhaps the most renowned and influential black Catholic in the city.

Similarly, church authorities continued to avoid controversial racial issues and to uphold the status quo. Inner core parishes emphasized conversion and social programming among African Americans but did not challenge racial discrimination in Milwaukee head-on. Demonstrating the continued hierarchical conservatism of the church, as late as 1963, one local priest wrote to the National Catholic Conference for Interracial Justice lamenting, "We would love to join you in the March On Washington but the Chancery office has said that it is very 'rash and imprudent' and has forbidden all priests [from] participating." Similarly, in the spring of 1965, conservative Catholics blocked an appearance by John Howard Griffith, author of *Black Like Me,* at a local Catholic youth convention. Liberal church members ultimately arranged an alternative appearance for Griffith. As the percentage of African Americans in the city steadily rose, the nation as a whole began to confront racial injustices. Church leaders inside and outside the inner core found it difficult to escape the divisive politics of race in urban America.[16]

By the late 1950s and early 1960s, the Catholic Church did not hold the same allure for younger African Americans that it had for their parents. This was, in part, because the Catholic Church in Milwaukee lacked significant and visible black leadership. In addition, the church's failure to work on grassroots issues, particularly racial justice, further distanced it from young people and the emerging civil rights movement. For the Catholic Church to appeal to a new generation of urban African Americans, it would have to transform itself once again, this time from a compassionate church to an activist church.

There was theological support for a more engaged and active approach to racial justice by inner core clergy and laypeople. Although the Catholic Church is often considered conservative for its emphasis on hierarchy and obedience and for its various attempts to control the human body, it has also established a more progressive tradition in its economic and social teachings. These lessons spring from a fundamental belief in the inherent dignity of human life. Basic dignity includes a right to work, health, and education. Each individual is to be respected and, in turn, to respect others. Moreover, the church teaches that humans are inherently social beings and that Catholics have a responsibility to help nurture social formations, starting with the family as the basic unit of society, and extending through communities, states, and even global society. Catholics are to seek out the ultimate unity, or solidarity, that ties all humans together, regardless of national, ethnic, racial, economic, or ideological differences. And according to the church, individuals have a special responsibility to take care of the environment. But perhaps most important, a concern for, and obligation to, the poor and disadvantaged is central to Catholic social teaching. Canon law states, "[Catholics] are . . . obligated to promote social justice and, mindful of the precept of the Lord, to assist the poor from their own resources." In public policy decisions, lawmakers and citizens are taught to maintain a "preferential option for the poor," a partiality for policies that ameliorate the conditions of the most vulnerable members of society. In this way, economic justice is intimately linked with the Catholic conception of social justice.[17]

The roots of this theology stretch back several hundred years, but it began to be systematized during the late nineteenth century. In 1891, Pope Leo XIII released *Rerum Novarum,* a powerful condemnation of unrestrained industrial capitalism. The encyclical addressed the vast economic inequalities and violent labor conflict that plagued numerous societies at the time and supported the rights of workers to join unions and collectively bargain for their interests. During the global depression of the 1930s, Pope Pius XI published a new encyclical, *Quadragesimo Anno,* which extended the idea that unrestricted economic forces alone do not produce a just society and which reiterated support for the poor and working class as well as for those who comfort them. During the 1960s, Pope John XXIII and Pope Paul VI released several writings that addressed the relationship between rich and poor nations, war and peace, and emphasized the church's solidarity with those who suffered and struggled for justice, including activists in the U.S. civil rights movement.[18]

Beginning in the 1920s and 1930s and gaining strength after World War II, the Vatican also encouraged greater involvement of laypeople in the mission of the church. "Catholic Action," as it was called, spurred a variety of localized movements.[19] In the United States, Catholic Action mainly took the form of small study groups; despite the name, reflection took precedence over action. It set off in new directions in 1938 when an Oklahoma priest named Donald Kanaly introduced the teachings of Father Joseph Cardijn to a clergy summer school for social action in Chicago. Cardijn, a Belgian friar, lived and wrote in response to the devastation of his country during World War I and with the hope of helping Catholic laypeople rebuild their lives and communities. According to Father Eugene Bleidorn, a strong Cardijn adherent in Milwaukee,

> "Observe, Judge and Act" was the humane way to exist [according to Cardijn]. You do an analysis of your life and of the lives of those around you, then you make an observation about how people are living, about their values. Observation is not my opinion but what in fact they are doing, what in fact they are saying. Having picked up what you think is an objective point of view, next, you make a judgment. Is that a good way for the human race to flourish? Or is it not? Would this be for the common good or would it not be for the common good? If the two are in harmony, then there is not much to do about it except live that way yourself. But if there is disharmony there, then there is an action choice . . . What action should we take to bring it in line?

This new technique, whereby people would systematically observe and judge a situation in light of the Gospel, and then act, was called the "inquiry method." Small groups of people met weekly, discussed important social issues, and ended each gathering with a concrete decision to act. The Cardijn Movement quickly spread from its nerve center in Chicago throughout the Midwest and across the nation. What distinguished the Cardijn Movement from other Catholic Action movements was its emphasis on action over education. "The action part was the most important part," explained Father Bleidorn. "It was easy to sit around and talk, but to decide based on the facts and judge what to do was the key." Father Patrick Flood agreed, stating "[the Cardijn Movement] taught us it is alright, it is correct, to be involved in politics." The crucial thing was to develop a sense of responsibility and action on the part of the laity. This further challenged another traditional conception of Catholic Action: the need for laypeople to act only under the strict control of the church hierarchy. The primary manifestations of the Cardijn movement in the United States were the Young Christian Workers, the Young Christian Students, and the Christian Family Movement.[20]

Due to Milwaukee's proximity to Chicago, the Cardijn reform impulse also beat strongly there. By the early 1940s, Father John Russell Beix helped establish several "cells" of the Young Christian Students and Young Christian Workers movements at local seminaries. According to historian of Catholicism Steven Avella, sympathetic young priests like Father Vernon Kuehn, Father Eugene Bleidorn, Father Francis Eschweiler, and Father John Michael Murphy "recruited a small, but tightly knit, corps of young adherents who were eager to bring Christ to [the community.]" One result of their work was the formation of several strong chapters of the Young Christian Family movement in the diocese. The success of these programs spurred Father Beix to establish a Cardijn Center on the upper floor of a deserted flophouse on North Water Street in February 1949. The center sponsored lectures and adult education programs, provided meeting space for Catholic Action groups, and included a bookstore as well as a supply of contemporary religious articles and artwork all aimed at spurring local Catholics to action. In Milwaukee, the Cardijn Center and Catholic Action formations were early strongholds of integration and social justice discussion and, later, of activism, particularly among the younger clergymen. Among the hundreds energized by these efforts were many of the leading African American members of MUSIC, including Carole Malone, Larry and Maxine Jeter, Lowell and Gloria Thomas, and Larry Harwell, as well as two young white seminarians, Patrick Flood and James Groppi.[21]

During the early 1960s, the reform movements moving through the church came together at the Second Vatican Council in Rome. Pope John XXIII convened the council in an attempt to reevaluate the church's role in the world. Delegates from all across the globe participated in these historic talks between 1962 and 1965. Out of their meetings came a series of statements and resolutions allowing for various alterations in church ritual: priests now faced the congregation; the vernacular replaced Latin; folk guitars and other contemporary music arrangements appeared on alters; churches were constructed in the round; many priests and nuns, particularly the young, shied away from "Father" and "Sister," opting instead to be addressed informally by their first name. Perhaps most important, Vatican II signaled a new conception of the relationship between church and community. The councils encouraged a move from a "hierarchical to a servant Church," from an authoritative structure to a common community of laypeople and clergy. Priest senates and parish councils were the primary outgrowth of this thrust of the councils. Vatican II also suggested that the church shift from an institution set apart from the world to one intimately concerned with modern life, and it reaffirmed Christian duty to the "lowliest" as well as the obligation of Catholics "to improve, not simply reject" the modern world. Finally, the councils urged the church to move from a Western to a more global and ecumenical vision.[22]

To reformers and liberals, like those in the Cardijn Movement or those in inner core parishes, the Second Vatican Council appeared to offer official sanction for their dissent. As Patrick Flood remembered, "All these currents within the Catholic Church said, 'Hurray to Vatican II! We've won. Everything we believe in has come to pass.'" What that meant on the ground in Milwaukee was that an increasing number of priests and nuns were sympathetic to the struggles of their parishioners and to issues of social justice generally, and they believed that they had the approval of church authority for their activities. To traditionalists, though, the changes in Vatican II were too much, too fast, and provoked reaction. A rift opened between American Catholics who supported or opposed the new reform efforts. This schism mirrored a similar cultural trend in the broader American society between old ways and new.[23]

The forces of change and reaction within the Catholic Church came to a head during the civil rights movement. At the same moment that church authorities in Rome were challenging members to reevaluate their roles in contemporary society, a national focus on race and urban poverty in the United States provided a way for liberal clergy and laypeople to put this new doctrine into action. For younger nuns and priests, the civil rights movement provided the hot moral center for their new religious identity in an era of applied Christianity. For those parishes located within inner core neighborhoods, the call to civil rights seemed even clearer. Vatican II appeared to sanction this activist spirit by speaking directly to the issue of race relations and civil rights in America. In April 1963, shortly before his death, Pope John XXIII condemned racial discrimination in *Pacem in Terris*. The following year, Pope Paul VI met with Martin Luther King Jr. in a show of support for the civil rights movement. The stage was thus set for greater Catholic involvement in local struggles for racial justice.

The "Conversion" of Father James Groppi

Father James Groppi emerged out of this Catholic cacophony of reform, renewal, and reaction. He was born in 1930 to Italian immigrant parents in Bay View, on the city's South Side. He credited his father as the initial inspiration for his commitment to racial justice. Giocondo Groppi, who had come to Milwaukee in 1913, "never allowed racial remarks or ethnic jokes or slurs . . . [if] someone used a term like 'Polack' or 'Nigger' he would voice his disapproval . . . 'That is like calling an Italian a "Dago," ' he would say."[24]

Groppi's commitment to civil rights was also rooted in his experience growing up on Milwaukee's South Side. The Groppi family lived and owned a grocery store in Bay View, a former mill town dominated by working-class Irish and Slavic immigrants. Groppi recalled feeling isolated and bullied as a youth, and he would often say that he knew what it was like to be an "outsider." He complained that "even the Church was guilty of discrimination" against Italian Americans in his South Side neighborhood. Italians were apparently so unwelcome at the local Irish Catholic Church that a group of Italians deviated from the geographic structures of the church and brought in their own priest each Sunday for an alternative mass in the back of a shoe store.[25]

But Groppi was quick to note that his experience as a white ethnic minority paled in comparison to the "terrifying discrimination" faced by African Americans. Referring to his parents' experience as immigrants, Groppi said, "The Italian was in pretty bad shape. But nothing as far as the black man is concerned. I don't like these comparisons between various ethnic groups and the black man because there are so many differences. Just the black man's color was enough."[26]

Groppi was pulled toward religion throughout adolescence and early adulthood. He told reporter Frank Aukofer, "To me, life, in order to have meaning, had to have religion. The brevity of life is one thing that always hit me—the shortness. You're here today and you're gone the next day. You've got to do something in this short expanse of time in order to make eternity meaningful." In 1950, at the age of twenty and with only tepid support from his parents, Groppi entered the Mt. Calvary Seminary in rural southeastern Wisconsin. In 1953, he transferred his religious studies to St. Francis Seminary, located a few miles from his boyhood home.[27]

The day-to-day racism and prejudice Groppi witnessed at St. Francis first stirred his interest in the African American community and race relations. "There were instances of prejudice that were terrible, really horrible," he remembered. "Nigger talk. Nigger jokes." He was particularly outraged when some of his classmates put on a minstrel show. In response, Groppi sought other outlets for his growing interest in racial justice. For instance, he and Pat Flood attended lectures and discussions at the Cardijn Center and participated in Catholic Action formations, where they discussed contemporary issues with other reform-minded Catholics.[28]

Father Matthew Gottschalk, a Capuchin friar at Blessed Martin, played a particularly important role mentoring Groppi and Flood during this period. "[Father Matthew was] a young priest who wore a beard down to his belly button and used to walk the streets all the time," Flood remembered. "He knew the inner city as a sociologist as well as a clergyman. He knew all the [black] families. Everybody knew him . . . he was really an authority on that population in Milwaukee." When asked about his long-standing interest in race relations, Father Matthew explained, "I was always a pseudo-scholar [of the civil rights movement]. I took several courses at Marquette [on race] . . . but I wanted to broaden my experience." So, Father Matthew began to walk the streets and, in the process, to get to know the local residents. On occasion, he brought along Groppi and Pat Flood. Gottschalk also enlisted the help of the young seminarians at a summer camp the Capuchins ran for African American children near the Hillside Housing Project in the heart of the inner core. For three successive summers, beginning in 1956, Groppi and Flood worked closely with local children at the camp. Dennis McDowell, a participant in the summer program and a future member of the YC and Commandos, fondly recalled, "[Father Groppi] was one of several white men who worked with [us]. He was like Mr. Droopy Pants because he always wore these big old baggy pants." Margaret Rozga claimed that Groppi's experience working with Father Matthew and the Capuchins "personalized a lot of the issues" of racism for him. Flood agreed, explaining,

> For the first time we came into contact with, and directly experienced, discrimination and racism. We took care of children in the mornings and then we called on families in the evenings . . . That whole experience brought about a conversion experience, you could say, or a change of will in all of us where we became . . . very committed to social justice around the issue of race.

From that point forward, Groppi's reaction to racism and discrimination was immediate, emotional, and personal, not abstract or intellectual. For him, the face of a young African American girl stung by a racial slur held "the pain of Jesus Christ as he hung on the cross. It was the pain of rejected love."[29]

James Groppi completed his work at the seminary in 1959 and was ordained as a Catholic priest. Although he requested an assignment in Milwaukee's inner core, the archdiocese sent him to St. Veronica, a primarily white, working-class parish located in a South Side neighborhood similar to the one where he grew up. Groppi's parish responsibilities at St. Veronica, which included the religious education of high school students, did not afford opportunities to address racial inequality directly, with one significant exception. During his tenure as an associate pastor, housing authorities announced that they were considering constructing low-income public housing units in the area. When a group of St. Veronica parishioners gathered to discuss the proposal and to consider a response, it became evident that their primary fear was an influx of African Americans. Groppi, outraged by the blatant displays of racism he witnessed, rebuked the group. For the next ten Sundays, the young priest preached against racism from the pulpit in what might best be described as a one-man protest. Groppi's actions strained relations with some adult members of the congregation but also gained the admiration of many students who later joined him and the YC in their many protests. Finally, in 1963, the chancery granted Groppi's wish and transferred him to St. Boniface Church in Milwaukee's inner core.[30]

St. Boniface proved to be a supportive place for Father Groppi's growing interest in racial justice. In addition to carrying out his duties as priest, the pastor, Father Eugene Bleidorn, was a sociologist and also worked as a high school social studies teacher. He had been greatly influenced by the Cardijn Movement and ran the Cardijn Center in Milwaukee for a stint during the 1950s. Like Gottschalk, Bleidorn understood the struggles of local African Americans and sought out ways to help. Throughout his tenure as pastor, Bleidorn supported Groppi's involvement in civil rights activism, from the pulpit to the press. The other young associate pastor at St. Boniface, Father Michael Neuberger, shared Groppi's commitment to young people through a series of youth activities at the church. These programs, along with the church's school and its close proximity to North Division High School, the city's largest African American high school, afforded Groppi the opportunity to continue cultivating close relationships with many black children in the neighborhood. Later, Pat Flood also joined the staff at St. Boniface. It is not surprising, then, that St. Boniface became the primary "movement center" in Milwaukee during the open housing campaign.

As important as these local factors were in the civil rights development of Father Groppi, a series of southern excursions between 1961 and 1965 had, perhaps, the most profound impact on him. On April 2, 1961, in the wake of the student sit-in movement and Freedom Rides, Father Matthew and Father Austin Schlaefer, both at St. Francis, gathered Groppi and another young priest, Father Robert Hoffman of St. Sebastian, and headed south. Over the next two weeks, the group visited thirty-one "Negro missions" in ten states, making thirteen stops in Mississippi alone. Schlaefer received official sanction for this "sociological tour" because he argued that it would help inner core clergymen to better understand the cultural roots of Milwaukee's black migrants. Spurred by the rational inquiry of the head, the trip struck the four clergymen in the heart. At Selma, they talked about "economic slavery" with sharecroppers, and in Montgomery they visited a segregated hospital. A New Orleans priest told them about a young African American football player who died from an injury after being denied care at two white hospitals, whereas in Yazoo, Mississippi, they learned that local white residents preferred to burn their old clothes rather than to donate them to poor African Americans. And everywhere the Milwaukee clergymen went, they saw Catholic priests and nuns enduring extreme isolation, alienation, and privation in pursuit of their mission. But the Milwaukee contingent was also inspired by the numerous everyday acts of survival, defiance, and resistance that they witnessed inside and outside the church. And the group even made its own contribution to the struggle when they unconsciously defied Jim Crow laws on a bus, on a cable car, and in a public restroom. In the end, as Father Schlaefer noted in his journal, "The beauty of the scenery was in sharp contrast to our feelings over the diabolic hate which was so evident in 'keeping the Colored in their place.' "[31]

The 1961 tour was the first of many southern excursions for the clergymen. Pat Flood, now Father Flood, joined Groppi, Gottschalk, and Schlaefer on a similar southern loop in 1963. "We went and visited areas where people were involved in [civil rights] and there was a Catholic church," Flood recalled. "And usually the Catholic Church was getting it on both sides. In the South, to be Catholic wasn't the greatest thing on earth anyway, and they [Catholics] were also working with the black community." That same year, despite a prohibition by church authorities, Father Groppi traveled to Washington, D.C., to attend the March on Washington.[32]

Just as Father Matthew had shared his experiences with a group of young seminarians, Groppi now shared his with a new generation of inner core students. During the summer of 1964, he drove to Jackson, Mississippi, with Nathan Harwell to work on voter registration with the Council of Federated Organizations. The pair took books, clothing, and food for the local people and, along the way, inadvertently "integrated" several restaurants.[33] In June 1965, Father Groppi drove five students from Alverno College to the SCLC headquarters in Atlanta, where they received training before joining a three-week summer voter registration project in Alabama; Groppi returned in August to visit the group. Later, in 1966, he and several YC members traveled to Mississippi to support the Meredith March against Fear, and in 1968 he drove the YC bus to an NAACP convention in Jackson, Mississippi.[34]

These southern excursions proved transformative for all involved. Margaret Rozga, an Alverno sophomore on the Alabama trip, called the experience "life changing." "I had grown up on Forty-Fourth and Oklahoma [Street in Milwaukee]," she explained. "I didn't know people who didn't have a bathroom. I didn't know that there were people that didn't have a set of dishes." Father Groppi argued that much of the change came from the personal collision with racial violence and fear each participant experienced in the South. Speaking about the 1964 trip with Nathan Harwell, he recalled,

> Going down to Jackson [Mississippi], we passed a plant where workers were letting out, white workers were letting out. They saw Nate and myself in the car. I was wearing a Roman, a clerical collar, at the time but it didn't matter. A Wisconsin license plate. Black and white in the front seat. They chased us down the highway. I am telling you, I was afraid. I took out my rosary and I prayed from Memphis to Jackson without stopping. We didn't stop. You couldn't go to the bathroom. You couldn't. You were afraid to stop to get something to eat. Nate and I were all alone. It was the beginning of our movement.

The directness of these encounters forced the young clergyman and his fellow travelers to clarify their commitment to racial justice. Summing up the impact of his various southern adventures, Groppi said, "what happened was that as you went along in the movement you got swallowed up in the cause. And the cause was the cause of righteousness. Pretty soon your fear was gone. Nothing mattered any more. The cause consumed you and the cause was more important than your life."[35]

Selma culminated in what Groppi and Flood referred to as their civil rights "conversion experience," which urged them toward a more militant and public role in the struggle at home. With hundreds of clergy in attendance, Selma appeared to fulfill the new spirit of the Second Vatican Council and to demonstrate the church's new conscience. It underscored the council's commitment to ecumenism, and it issued a profound challenge to northern clergy to work on these issues at home. A popular topic of discussion had been "Why Selma? And why Montgomery? Why not in your own back yard? What are we doing here when there are problems back home?"[36] The Milwaukee priests took this challenge to heart and returned transformed, imbued with a new sense of urgency and activism emboldened by faith. At a rally in St. Boniface shortly after their return, Groppi told a gathering of more than 200 people, "In the South there is a constant working to overcome [racial discrimination]. This is something we need to learn in the North . . . Bigotry is not confined to any one state. It is present here in Wisconsin." According to Father Flood, "[Selma] became an important consciousness raising event for us. [It] riveted us and made us totally committed to the cause. It was a great school of learning." And they were not alone. Hundreds of fervent northern white religious people from across the nation brought that same spirit of Selma home with them.[37]

The language of "transformation" and "conversion" that Groppi and Flood employed underscores both the spiritual and the very personal dynamic of their commitment to social justice. As a Catholic priest, Groppi was dedicated to a religious life. As a part of that life, he continuously grappled with the basic question of how to put faith into action. Margaret Rozga explained, "It wasn't a Protestant spirituality. It wasn't me and God and it wasn't the kind of thing where there was a point that you realized [that] you were finished with it, like I've been saved. It was an ongoing process in all aspects of life." For conservative Catholics, the answer to this fundamental question was obedience, but for Groppi, "the place of the priest is where the dignity of God is being trampled." In 1969, a reflective Groppi told a student reporter at the University of Cincinnati, "a priest has a prophetic role to play . . . and the prophetic role today is in the area of social justice and the eradication of racism." Catholic social teaching and the call to Catholic Action supported this view. Since the 1950s, Martin Luther King Jr. and the southern civil rights struggle had provided a powerful—and challenging—example of faith in action. Over time, through his years at the seminary, during his summers working with inner core kids, on his many travels South, and in his expanding relationship with the local African American community, Father Groppi's commitment to racial equality awakened and grew. In the end, he came to define himself and to build his entire religious (and day-to-day) life around the struggle for racial justice. Through this spiritual process—this "transformation" or "conversion"—he found a greater ability to take increasingly difficult stands and engage in more and more militant activism.[38]

Yet, there was another side to the Catholic awakening taking place in Selma and Milwaukee. Whereas liberals felt that the Catholic clergy were fulfilling their Christ-like duty to social justice by participating in civil rights demonstrations, traditionalists felt that priests should be praying and not protesting, obeying the law and not associating with "beatniks" and "communists." To them, Selma signified the culmination of all the factors that they perceived as a threat to their traditional way of life. As the commitment to civil rights deepened and broadened among reform-minded Catholics, so, too, did reaction and resistance grow among traditionalists. For inner core parishes, the call to social justice was clear: join the civil rights movement. The meaning of that call was less clear in working-class white parishes where discussions of racial equality paled beside fears of plummeting property values, the abandonment of traditional communities, and the beginning of broad-based economic problems. The influx of African Americans and the goals of the civil rights movement, in fact, seemed to fuel each of these threats. And now, representatives of the very institution that had fostered their sense of neighborhood and security seemed to sacrifice their interests on the altar of integration.

To these more conservative Catholics, Father Groppi embodied two threats simultaneously. On the one hand, he was a white ethnic from the South Side who increasingly represented the growing threat posed to white jobs, neighborhoods, unions, schools, and clubs by African American civil rights. In this way, Groppi was a race traitor. On the other hand, he personified the new church, with his challenge to authority, tradition, and obedience. Viewed this way, Groppi was also a religious traitor. Church reform and civil rights grew tangled, one leading to the other. Traditionalists saw in a priest like Father Groppi the distillation of what they feared and despised in the church, as well as in society, and they fought it.

By the mid-1960s, Catholic authorities across the urban North faced a serious dilemma. A growing number of priests and nuns were increasingly active in the civil rights movement out of conscience, but an even greater percentage of the church's core white constituency opposed civil rights as a threat to their most basic interests. The result was "two distinctly Catholic visions of church, community, and authority . . . clash[ing] in the streets, parishes and Catholic schools of the northern cities."[39]

Father James Groppi, Local Civil Rights Leader

Groppi brought back from Selma more than an invigorated spirit and expanded commitment to the cause. He also returned with a particular strategic approach to social change. According to Flood, "[Selma was] the basis for Jim [Groppi] when he came back, for the demonstrations [in Milwaukee], and for how to create a movement." The most basic principle in Groppi's approach was action. As Margaret Rozga explained,

> [What Groppi] saw as the main problem was that nobody was doing anything. So, he was going to do what was within his purview to do . . . There were lots of people who prided themselves on being great thinkers and great strategists but didn't do it. I think what [Groppi] saw was that people were so busy planning grand strategies that they never took step one.

This emphasis on action was consonant with the directive to "observe, judge and *act*" of the "inquiry method" that Groppi had learned from his mentors. Because action was central to his approach, specific issues—for example, housing, employment, education, and police brutality—were less important to Groppi. "It didn't matter what [issue you pursued]," Rozga explained, "because it was all this tangled ball of yarn and no matter which end you pulled on you ended up getting involved with the whole mess of racism." She continued, "A lot of the things that [Groppi] picked up on as issues were things that people brought either to St. Boniface or to the Youth Council and said, 'This is going on and nobody will help us except you.' And he would never say 'no' to somebody like that."[40]

Groppi was clear about the kind of action he wanted to see: nonviolent direct action. He pointed to a speech by Dr. King in Montgomery as a major inspiration:

> [Dr. King said] that hate was psychologically destructive and that the only way that you were going to survive, psychologically, in this movement, was through the adaptation of nonviolence, not only as a tactic . . . [but] as a philosophy of love. And he said that it is a state in life that none of us will ever attain to its greatest perfection, but it is a state that all of us must continually strive to attain.

Similarly, Groppi was deeply moved by the sight of a young black student in Alabama who, while being viscously clubbed by policemen, simply repeated again and again, "I love you." For the young priest this was "the ultimate in sacrifice and courage."[41]

But Groppi also understood that militant nonviolent direct action was rooted in confrontation. Here again, Groppi was deeply influenced by Martin Luther King Jr. Writing from a Birmingham jail cell in 1963, King revealed that the purpose of nonviolent direct action was "to create such a crisis and foster such a tension that a community which has constantly refused to negotiate is forced to confront the issue. It seeks to so dramatize the issue that it can no longer be ignored." With the help of the mass media making the world its witness, militant nonviolence promised the power to move recalcitrant public institutions and sway the public conscience to justice; the Milwaukee priests had experienced this firsthand in Selma. Groppi embraced this vision of a coercive nonviolence and would apply its lessons to a series of dramatic campaigns in Milwaukee over the next three years.[42]

There was a spiritual component to militant nonviolent direct action as well, for Father Groppi. It was through nonviolent activism, he thought, that individuals came face to face with racial inequality, met their fears, and were personally transformed. The direct standoff between good and evil clarified the issue of race relations and forced the individual to choose sides. In the emotional maelstrom that ensued, the individual often felt spiritually invigorated. With each new encounter, the commitment deepened. Groppi was confident that if he could get people active, they, like him, would be swallowed up by the cause. They, like him, would have their own civil rights conversion. On a large scale, this process might even "redeem the soul of the nation," as King liked to say. For Groppi, like King, nonviolence held out the possibility of individual, national, and even global redemption through change and reconciliation; it was a transformative force. Groppi concluded that nonviolence, like action, "is a tremendous Christian, spiritual doctrine."[43]

After Selma, Father Groppi plunged headlong into the ongoing school desegregation campaign. Within weeks, he was elected second vice president of MUSIC and was pushing the group to adopt a more militant strategy. MUSIC had been stymied after two years of work, inside and outside the system. Frustrated, Lloyd Barbee filed suit against the Milwaukee School Board in federal court. On May 17, MUSIC's executive board voted to organize a second school boycott in October, this time for three days, and approved a direct action program. A week later, MUSIC activists initiated a three-week "human chain-in" campaign outside several inner core schools.[44]

Father Groppi's first arrest occurred on June 4, 1965, while blocking a bus at Seifert Elementary School. It was the first time a Milwaukee priest had been arrested during the civil rights era and, as a result, caused quite a stir throughout the city's Catholic community. Church authorities and laypeople informally debated this curious young clergyman and the proper role of a priest. When traditionalists criticized Groppi for demonstrating in the streets and for breaking the law, he shot back that the role of the priest was to be involved in the community. When it came to "intact busing," Groppi believed that he had a spiritual responsibility to be out ahead of the flock (a flock that now embraced Catholics and non-Catholics alike), in front of the symbols of segregation, blocking buses. To him, faith, conscience, and priestly obligation dictated his response.

However important Groppi's individual leadership in Milwaukee, and regardless of the hot media glare he attracted, Groppi was not alone in his crusade. After Selma, Milwaukee Catholics in general played a larger and more visible role in local civil rights activism. Newspaper accounts of a MUSIC-sponsored Freedom March in August 1965, for example, noted that Catholics made up roughly one-half of the 500–600 total demonstrators. And, throughout that fall and winter, reporters curiously observed the increasing number of white collars and dark habits at civil rights demonstrations. On a more personal level, Pat Flood continued to be a primary ally and confidante of Groppi throughout the civil rights era. "What Jim and Pat said between each other," Margaret Rozga explained, "was that Jim was the person that shook the tree and Pat was the person that picked up the apples." Groppi was the public activist and outspoken voice of the movement; Flood worked largely behind the scenes by organizing meetings and negotiating. Activism also accelerated the associations among the five inner core parishes. According to Flood, "Priests and nuns in those five parishes came together into a very strong and committed community because of those boycotts and civil rights." That bond was formalized in the fall when the diocese established the Council on Urban Life (CUL), made up of members of the five inner core parishes. And the CUL was connected to a broader, interlocking network of individual nuns, priests, and laypeople; Catholic

Action formations; parish councils; and more formal bureaucracies, such as the Catholic Interracial Council and the Greater Milwaukee Conference on Religion and Race, which stood ready to act.[45]

Selma had also activated northern white clergy across denominational and theological lines. When Groppi and the others returned from Alabama, they met up with hundreds of other Milwaukeeans, Catholic and otherwise, who had been moved to action by news from Selma. Protestants and Jews had also heard Dr. King's call, and they responded in kind.[46] As was the case during the events in Birmingham, shocking television images from Alabama energized local liberal groups across the city and in every denomination. Nearly 3,000 black and white Milwaukee residents took to the streets in sympathy with those in Selma; it was the city's largest civil rights march to date. Church organizations and civic groups began discussing the issues and asking what they might do to help. Not all agreed on the causes of racial inequality or on the solutions or tactics necessary to overcome it, but there was a growing consensus that a problem existed and that it required action, if not always the confrontational direct action championed by Groppi. Overall, the public participation of white clergy in Milwaukee's civil rights activism heightened the ethical dimension of the local black freedom struggle and commanded attention from white residents who might otherwise have ignored it.[47]

These white activists joined the small but growing circle of local African Americans who had emerged as forceful advocates for racial justice in the city. Lloyd Barbee now represented the inner core in the state legislature, and Vel Phillips still served as the lone African American voice on the Common Council. Ministers, such as Reverend B. S. Gregg of St. Mathew CME, Reverend R. L. Lathan of New Hope Baptist Church, and Reverend Leo Champion of New Jerusalem Baptist Church, confronted racial injustices not only with words but also with deeds. Lathan had supported the Daniel Bell march back in 1958; Gregg and Champion participated in MUSIC demonstrations; and Champion, too, had traveled to Selma in 1965, as the official representative of the Milwaukee civil rights community. All of these leaders, in their own way, espoused an aggressive approach to racial change, and all, throughout the mid-1960s, worked in coalition with Father Groppi and the YC.

Even as Groppi found allies in other sectors of Milwaukee's spiritual community, his own denomination grew increasingly conflicted over the participation of their clergy and congregations in civil rights activities. Catholic divisions, which had been simmering for some time and which percolated after Groppi's arrest in June, boiled over completely during the lead-up to the second school boycott in mid-October. Throughout the summer, support mounted at inner core parishes for the upcoming protest. On September 28, twenty-four priests released a statement supporting the boycott. On October 10, the Sunday bulletin at St. Boniface announced that parishioners had voted 321–66 (or 83 percent to 17 percent) in favor of the boycott and had agreed to join four other inner core parishes—St. Benedict, St. Elizabeth, St. Francis, and St. Gall—by sponsoring a freedom school on church grounds. The archdiocesan school board initially voiced no objections to these plans.[48]

The clergy had reason to believe that there was recent precedent to support their participation in the boycott. For instance, there had been no public repercussions in 1964 when a group of priests and nuns protested George Wallace's appearance in Milwaukee. Nor had there been any church reaction to Father Groppi's growing leadership role within MUSIC or to his recent arrest. Moreover, the Greater Milwaukee Conference on Religion and Race, which included Archbishop Cousins, had reluctantly supported the one-day withdrawal in 1964. Given all this, inner core clergy were optimistic that church officials would continue to take a permissive stance toward their growing activism.

The inner core pastors' announcement went unchallenged for one week, but on October 14, Monsignor Edmund Goebel, the archdiocesan superintendent of schools, forbade the Catholic pastors and principals from participating in the boycott. The decree created more confusion than it cleared up: Did Monsignor Goebel have the authority to restrict individual clergy from participating in the boycott? Did it mean that church facilities could not be used for freedom schools?[49]

The following day, Bishop Roman Atkielski, acting head of the archdiocese while Archbishop Cousins attended the Vatican Council in Rome, deepened the confusion. In a letter to each of the inner core pastors, Atkielski referenced a letter from District Attorney Hugh O'Connell supporting his opinion that the boycott was illegal. He warned that parents and clergy risked "prosecution by civil authority" if they took part and concluded by stating that no parish facility was to be used for the boycott. When asked by reporters whether the clergy could participate individually in the boycott, the bishop reportedly stated that his order prohibited participation by any priest, nun, or brother. Because that specific command was not conveyed through official channels in writing but was reported only in the media, inner core clergy did not feel bound by it. As Father Eugene Bleidorn, pastor of St. Boniface, recalled, "We took our guidance from the official communication to us, and not from an unofficial interpretation in the daily press." Other pastors told reporters that "the order ran counter to the conscientious judgment of these priests most closely involved in the problem." Inner core clergy felt that Atkielski had sacrificed moral ground to legalism and vowed to continue their support of the boycott until a direct prohibition against individual participation came down. On October 16, the clergy joined several hundred people in a prayer vigil at the school administration building.[50]

Over the final few days before the scheduled boycott, a hail of conflicting and contradictory statements by church officials failed to settle the matter. The confusion had resulted from both the communication breakdown within the archdiocesan church structure in Cousins's absence and the strategic adherence to formal communications by inner core clergy. Father Mathew, acting as spokesman for the clergy, attempted to broker an agreement with Bishop Atkielski. The bishop refused to rescind his order, but he did allow the priests to release a statement to the press. The press release said that inner core parishes would run freedom schools if children showed up on Monday. Because they had committed facilities, personnel, and support to the boycott two weeks previously, they felt "that it [was] unreasonable to withdraw at this late hour." Of the conflict with the bishop, they argued,

> We respect him as holding an office from the hand of Christ. But it is with sorrow and regret that we declare that we do not think he understands the facts of the situation as they are.
>
> Accordingly, in our own consciences, we do not see his directions, based upon legal opinion, as morally binding with the force of Christ's words.

The statement made the front page in the Sunday morning newspapers, and some Milwaukee Catholics complained that the priests acted in direct disobedience to church authority. Many of the clergy involved in the conflict saw the bishop's lack of objection to the statement as a victory for freedom of conscience.[51]

The elation quickly gave way to disappointment. On Sunday morning, the chancellor of the archdiocese, Monsignor Leo Brust, called Father

Matthew and stated that the clergy's printed statement was in direct defiance of ecclesiastical authority. After another long meeting, the inner core pastors reluctantly withdrew their parishes from the boycott:

> since the prohibition has become a specific command of religious authority as such, and its violation interpreted as a direct defiance of ecclesiastical authority, we submit in obedience to the command of the Bishop . . . We also feel the obligation to protest the restriction put upon our freedom of action . . . Those working in the inner city should be allowed to make their own moral judgments and to act upon them.

The pastors also placed an ad in local papers explaining their view of the controversy to the community at large. The "Open Letter to Our People" stated, "With every protest short of direct disobedience and with the conviction that we are substantially betraying our people, but with the hope that we have not done so, we revert to the basic training we have been given and reluctantly close our parish facilities to the use of the Freedom Schools." It remained unclear whether individual participation by priests and nuns in freedom schools off church property was sanctioned. Having received no official ban, some priests and nuns, including Groppi, chose to participate as a matter of conscience.[52]

On Monday morning, the first day of the boycott, more than 500 students and parents showed up at St. Boniface expecting to attend a freedom school. In an effort to contain the situation and to stall until an alternative plan could be devised, Father Groppi led the children in singing and chanting before marching them to a site a few blocks away, where he taught them African American history for two hours. Later that night, Groppi walked thirty-eight blocks with 265 noisy African American students to the home of school board president John Foley, where they picketed and sang. The next day, Monsignor Brust ordered Father Groppi to withdraw from the boycott, and on Wednesday Father William Whelan received a similar order. Both priests reluctantly complied, but other Catholic clergy continued to teach and work in the freedom schools. The boycott ended that Thursday.[53]

The Catholic controversy during the school boycott generated significant national and local media attention. For the four days directly preceding the student withdrawal, Milwaukee newspapers carried headlines about the ongoing conflict. CBS and NBC sent television crews to cover the dispute, and Father Bleidorn received dozens of letters from across the country. Although the ecclesiastical jousting brought increased attention to the boycott and the freedom schools, it also shifted the emphasis, at a critical juncture, away from the details of de facto segregation in the Milwaukee public schools and toward a more general debate over the role of the clergy in nonviolent direct action and civil disobedience. "The story of the boycott," Rozga said, "became the story of Father Groppi leading 500 students away from St. Boniface Church."[54]

Like Selma, the "Catholic controversy" was a pivotal moment in Father Groppi's development. "That was a real moment of 'ah-ha' for him," explained Margaret Rozga. "When he went to St. Boniface he was supposed to make Catholics out of everyone in the neighborhood and here he was leading children away from the church because they couldn't have freedom school there. He thought something was wrong with that." Groppi realized that the struggle for racial equality was not only a contest to change local ordinances and alter the lives of African Americans. It was also a fight for the future of the institution to which he had devoted his life and which would alter the lives of thousands of Milwaukee Catholics. Both struggles fed back into each other. To overcome one would mean overcoming the other.

One important difference between the southern and northern civil rights movements was the central role of the Catholic clergy and laypeople as key supporters and opponents of racial justice in the North. In New York, Boston, Philadelphia, Chicago, Milwaukee, Baltimore, Cleveland, and elsewhere, Catholics numbered between one-third and one-half of the total urban population. Throughout the era, priests, nuns, and Catholic laypeople played a critical and growing role in local civil rights campaigns. At the same time, other Catholics in those same cities often served as a bulwark against change. In both instances, Catholics filtered the issue of race and reform through the lens of religion. It was left to church authorities to walk a careful line between the two camps, mediating competing, and in many ways contradictory, Catholic experiences.

Between 1965 and 1967, a dramatic new phase of the civil rights movement began in Milwaukee. As the school desegregation campaign moved into the courts, a more militant form of civil rights insurgency evolved behind the unlikely leadership of a white Roman Catholic priest and a band of passionate and dedicated inner core youth. Father Groppi and the YC confronted new issues with new tactics and a strategy that reflected the changing racial dynamics of the time. Their leadership would shape civil rights insurgency in Milwaukee for the remainder of the 1960s. Yet, even as Groppi received increasing media attention locally, nationally, and ultimately internationally for his work as a "civil rights leader," faith continued to be the source and the sustenance of his commitment to racial justice and a critical aspect of his leadership.

— 5 —

The Youth Council
and Commandos

On Sunday evening, August 28, 1966, Father Groppi and members of the NAACP Youth Council (YC) led a procession of 150 civil rights supporters on a six-mile trek from their inner core Freedom House, on poverty-stricken North Fifth Street, to the tree-lined comfort of suburban Wauwatosa. They had first come to this bucolic neighborhood ten nights earlier to make a statement against the membership of Judge Robert Cannon in the Fraternal Order of Eagles, a national organization with a strong local chapter. The Milwaukee Eagles Club (EC) had evolved into a key network for local politicians, judges, labor leaders, and businessmen, but, like several other major fraternal organizations, it restricted its membership to whites. Groppi and the YC hoped to convince the white jurist to resign his membership in the group, but Cannon defiantly resisted, telling the press, "I will remain in the Eagles as long as I live."

Initial pickets along the tree-lined sidewalk outside the judge's house were uneventful, but over the first weekend they quickly drew the attention of the media and thousands of raucous white onlookers. Although many whites were merely curious, others shouted obscenities, such as "Go back to the zoo, nigger" and "Nigger, go back to the jungle." Some held signs reading, "Groppi, Go Home"; "Nigger Lover!"; and "Keep Tosa White." A few spit or threw eggs, bricks, cherry bombs, rocks, and debris. On Sunday, August 21, the scene turned surreal when several robed Klansmen strutted in front of Cannon's home, their shiny regalia in strange relief against the well-manicured surroundings. As the protests continued through the week, tensions rose, and local police struggled to maintain order. By the following weekend, white anger had boiled over.[1]

Despite serious safety concerns, the demonstrators set out on August 28 in a festive mood, singing freedom songs and chanting anti-Eagles slogans. They walked behind a large U.S. flag, and several parents carried children on their backs and shoulders. One young man, stripped to the waist, had scrawled "Black Power" in charcoal across his shoulders, a sign of the shifting ideological terrain within the local struggle for racial justice. As demonstrators made their way past the EC headquarters near Marquette University, escorted by fifty Milwaukee police and fifty county sheriff's deputies, they clapped and chanted, "Eagles must go!" At North Fiftieth Street, the concrete slabs of the city gave way to the tree-lined streets and square-edged lawns of the suburbs. There, the marchers confronted a "carnival" of white reaction and racist hate dancing on the edge of chaos. Huge crowds of white onlookers, many visibly angry, lined block after block. Their obscene barrages and shouts of "Kill 'em, kill 'em! This is a white man's town. We don't want any cannibals here!" and "Kill the white nigger lovers!" ominously altered the tenor of the protest.

At the city limit, Milwaukee police handed over protection of the now 250 civil rights protesters—75 percent of them black and 25 percent of them white—to seventy Wauwatosa policemen clad in full riot gear and to hundreds more National Guardsmen standing shoulder to shoulder along both sides of Wisconsin Avenue. Four thousand hostile whites, sometimes five and ten deep, pressed menacingly against police barricades as Groppi and the YC walked the final ten blocks to Judge Cannon's home. The mobs shook their fists and heckled; they shouted "We don't want the niggers in Wauwatosa" and "Send them back to the Congo"; again they spit and threw stones, cherry bombs, and debris. Outside Cannon's house, a group of twenty counterdemonstrators calling themselves "The Boys from Tosa" waved a Confederate flag and held signs that read, "Groppi Is a White Uncle Tom," "Keep Tosa White," and "How Well Is Welfare?" Police reportedly confiscated several other signs that contained obscenities. A solid wall of steel-helmeted National Guardsmen from the Thirty-second division, carrying unloaded M-1 rifles and carbines with fixed bayonets, separated the two groups of demonstrators. It took a wedge of forty sheriff's deputies to lead Father Groppi and the YC back down Wisconsin Avenue after only a half hour of picketing. Police cars both trailed and preceded the embattled demonstrators, and guardsmen flanked the outer perimeter. As the group reached the Milwaukee line and police protection transferred back to city officers, "a wave of people swept across lawns and down the middle of the avenue to catch up." In that moment of transition and chaos, it appeared that a melee might ensue, as angry whites overtook the civil rights activists. During the noisy rush, a cherry bomb hit a fifty-two-year-old woman from Waterloo, Iowa, bloodying both of her legs. The police regrouped, separated the sides, and narrowly averted more serious violence; five whites were arrested in the process.

The EC campaign and the chaos outside Judge Cannon's home in Wauwatosa announced a dramatic new phase of civil rights activism in Milwaukee. Over the next three years, a potent alliance between a white Catholic priest and a group of inner core youths led thousands of people in a series of turbulent campaigns against police misconduct, segregated housing, employment discrimination, and welfare reform. These campaigns largely rejected liberal politics, instead mobilizing ordinary black citizens through direct action and civil disobedience. This chapter explores the origins of the collaboration between Father Groppi and the YC as well as their first major campaign against the EC and the creation of the Commandos.

Father Groppi and the NAACP Youth Council

Beginning in the early 1960s, a small nucleus of inner core students worked to move the Milwaukee YC from its traditional focus on membership recruitment and social activities to more active participation in local civil rights campaigns. In large part, this was a function of the new energy and militancy young people were injecting into the Movement through sit-ins, freedom rides, marches, and pickets. According to Alberta Harris, a key early YC leader, things began to change locally when she and another YC member attended the 1962 NAACP national convention in Chicago. Harris, who roomed with students from Jackson, Mississippi, called the experience "eye opening." "The number of times those kids had been in jail. The kinds of things that they had experienced. It was meeting them that really clued me in to what was going on and how much we were living in an isolated environment [in Milwaukee]," she explained. "I am talking to these people and the same problems that they are fighting, we have them, too, but ours are just more subtle, and we were sitting around doing nothing." Back at home, Harris began talking to her friends in the YC about turning the Milwaukee chapter into a more active one and vowed, "when the next convention comes, there's going to be more than two of us from Milwaukee and we're going to have done more than just sat around on afternoons and pat each other on the back for what good grades that we're getting." The following spring, several dozen YC members picketed three inner core Big Boy restaurants after a local black teenager claimed racial discrimination when he applied for a job. The brief protest, patterned on similar demonstrations by the Milwaukee Negro American Labor Council (MNALC), forced a quick settlement with the owner, Ben Marcus. Two months later, with the nightly news and daily headlines dominated by racial violence in Birmingham, Alabama, Milwaukee YC members participated in a nationwide sympathy protest against local Woolworth and Kress stores. After 1963, the Milwaukee United School Integration Committee's (MUSIC) endless meetings, lectures, fliers, dances, rallies, "Freedom Institutes," "Hootenannies," and "Freedom Camps" educated inner core youth about racial inequality in their city and told them that they had a crucial role to play in changing those conditions. Because the Milwaukee NAACP (MNAACP) was a member of MUSIC, YC members were free to join their actions. For many young people, participation in a MUSIC school boycott was their first taste of race rebellion.[2]

But institutional constraints within the NAACP continued to hold back the YC's nascent activist energies. "We weren't autonomous from the adult branch," Harris explained, "and we couldn't do anything without their permission." Following the Big Boy campaign, John Givens and Tom Jacobson resigned as YC advisors because a majority of the leadership in the adult branch opposed their direct action tactics. According to Givens, "The older people in the branch said, 'Oh, my God! We can't have this.' They wouldn't participate in the demonstrations. They didn't do anything." Rather than fight this "internecine war," the two men shifted their efforts to the recently formed Milwaukee chapter of the Congress of Racial Equality (MCORE). In response, Alberta Harris and other Milwaukee YC members joined a national push by high school and college students across the country inside the NAACP to separate youth councils from adult branches, a goal finally achieved at the 1965 convention in Denver.[3]

This bureaucratic change freed the Milwaukee YC to pursue a more aggressive strategy toward racial change. But first YC members needed an advisor who shared their belief in action. Again, Alberta Harris played a central role in this process. As she recalled years later,

> Father [Groppi] was transferred to our church [St. Boniface] and my mom invited him over for dinner and his conversation during dinner piqued my interest . . . He was talking about the urgency of race relations and the

problems we had in our city and he was saying things I needed to hear. He was talking about the problems of segregation, the problems with the schools, the police community that we were living in. He was on the money and you could tell he was really honest about what he was saying and how he felt about how black people were being treated in this community.

She continued,

I asked him if he would be interested in becoming the temporary advisor for the Milwaukee Youth Council. Initially, he said no. He didn't feel his duties at the church would allow him to do that. I kept after him and he finally agreed to take it on temporarily, so I took his name to the board and they authorized him to take over as a temporary advisor and the rest is history. He never left us.[4]

When asked why they chose Father Groppi, a white Catholic priest, over a member of the black community, Harris responded in a personal way, stating, "He was my priest. I didn't belong to a Baptist Church." She added, "[Groppi] was really just right on the money in terms of what the problems were in the community and wanting to do something. He was feeling like [we] were feeling, like what direction are we going to go? What are we going to *do?* How do we start this?" Velma Coggs, another early YC member, suggested that the group was also impressed by Groppi's commitment to the cause and his willingness to confront racial inequality head on, even if it meant personal sacrifice. Conversely, many established black leaders, including a number of prominent ministers, had consistently opposed direct action and criticized the leaders of MNALC, MCORE, and MUSIC for employing the tactic in their campaigns. To illustrate her point, Coggs referenced Groppi's June 4, 1965, arrest as a part of a "human chain." She claimed that several prominent black ministers were also slated to take part in the protest but balked. Paul Crawford suggested a more practical reason for selecting Groppi as the YC's new advisor. "Here you had youth," he said:

You had uneducated kids that tried to do something for the community. They needed guidance. They needed advice. They knew what they wanted to do, but even in terms of the press, [for instance,] can you imagine [one of us] standing in front of the press . . . there's no way. So, Groppi would do that. He was the vehicle. We had no one else, so we had to utilize him.

Margaret Rozga put it more simply, stating, "He was *doing* something. He had been in the school boycott. He was the second vice president of MUSIC . . . he gained an amount of visibility as someone who was going to take risks, be active, and do things. He'd been arrested in the spring and became advisor by the summer."[5]

For Father Groppi, the YC, like MUSIC, offered an institutional vehicle to formalize and focus his civil rights activism outside the direct institutional authority of the Catholic Church. With the school desegregation campaign moving into the courts, MUSIC's days as a direct action organization were likely numbered, and the old guard, which continued to dominate the adult branch of the NAACP, had made clear that they would not spearhead new direct action campaigns. The YC, with its recently achieved autonomy and wealth of untapped energy, provided an alternative. In addition, Groppi's special affinity for black children was well established by 1965, stretching back to his work at the Blessed Martin summer camp, through his travels south, and most recently in his work among inner core school children at St. Boniface. Groppi clearly possessed a unique ability to relate to young people's experiences and to speak their language. Journalist Frank Aukofer recalled this special connection in Selma:

> Father Groppi had little interest in publicity. He was much more interested in the black children who populated the shacks on the dirt streets of the Negro section of Selma . . . One minute he would be there, the next minute he would be gone—down a dusty side street, heedless of his own safety, to sit on a rickety porch or in the dust of a grassless yard to play with the little black children. Few shied away from him.

Groppi's various experiences working with poor African American kids, in both the North and the South, starkly highlighted for him the human impact of racial inequality, and the YC gave him a new opportunity to formalize his commitment. And Groppi believed that civil rights activism was a way to provide poor inner city black youth with a constructive outlet for their frustration and anger as well as to build their leadership skills and self-esteem.[6]

When Father Groppi agreed to serve as advisor for the YC in the late spring of 1965, the group was small and in need of direction and leadership. The young priest immediately set about drawing in schoolchildren at St. Boniface and other inner core parishes. One of these new recruits, Pamela Jo Sargent, recalled, "[Father Groppi] came into our classroom and asked us if we wanted to be a part of the civil rights movement." Though there was a nominal membership fee, it was not a barrier to involvement. "Walk in the door and you sign a card," according to Ed Thekan. "Even if you didn't have the $2, Father would say, 'Fine. You are a member. We will put in for you.' It wasn't a question of those who could afford it and those who couldn't afford it." Sargent was also quick to explain that Father Groppi's recruitment efforts were deeply infused with religious teachings. "We had mass before we had class," she said. "He would take the gospel of the Bible and relate it to what was actually happening in the world that we lived in. We heard these sermons every morning before we went to class." From Groppi's view, "[The civil rights movement] was our religious training. I did not teach a theology of the afterlife as much as I made the Gospel message relevant to the needs of the people in that community. I thought the best way to do that was to get [young people] involved in the civil rights struggle." "When you have a spiritual leader," Sargent said, "a man of the cloth, tell you Jesus . . . was an activist and you young people need to be a part of this world and get involved, we did." These daily sermons, blending the Gospel with the Movement, "put a fire" for civil rights activism into the hearts and minds of many St. Boniface students, particularly young women like Sargent, who played a central leadership role early on.[7]

This initial phase of the YC's partnership with Father Groppi was a time of excitement, growth, learning, and personal bonding. Alberta Harris explained, "St. Boniface was our base of operations. We were comfortable there . . . the rectory became our hang-out. We were almost always there. We could meet there. We could strategize there. We could be with Father there." While they hung out and forged the initial bonds of what for many would become lifelong friendships, YC members discussed Father Groppi's sermons, the problems facing black Milwaukeeans, and how they might become more active, as a group, and overcome them. "We started to learn from each other," Harris said. "We started to grow in the Movement from one another."[8]

The organizational structure of the YC was roughly democratic. A group of nine officers voted on all YC decisions, with Father Groppi offering advice but not voting. Despite this structure, early on most YC members followed Groppi's lead, mainly due to their lack of experience. The tactics and philosophy of the YC also reflected the views of their new advisor. The group embraced the confrontational nonviolent direct action that Groppi had learned from Martin Luther King Jr. in Selma. They sought out ways to foster "creative tension" within the community, flush out racial discrimination, and force people to choose sides and act. In addition, with the decline of the direct action phase of the school desegregation campaign, the YC under Groppi's advisement refused to work in formal coalition with other groups as MUSIC had done. Groppi explained,

> We had our own organizational attitude and that is why we did not form coalitions . . . we didn't have the patience for it . . . The decisions were made by [the YC]. They were an action group and the attitude was, look, we are going to do it. You want to come with us, fine. If you don't want to come with us, that's all right, too. But we didn't have any time to talk about what we should do and what we should not do. When it was a question of whether we should act or not act, we acted.

This emphasis on action and independence would lead to the most dramatic moments of Milwaukee's 1960s civil rights struggles.[9]

The obvious place for the YC to focus its energy, initially, was on the school desegregation campaign. As MUSIC's activism evolved in a more militant direction through 1965, the YC played an increasingly prominent role. Under the new leadership of Groppi and the Direct Action chairman, DeWayne Tolliver, YC members participated in boycotts, marches, pickets, and sit-ins; they disrupted school board meetings, attended planning sessions, made phone calls, went door to door, sang, chanted, and passed out flyers, all in the name of ending segregation in Milwaukee's public schools. In May, police arrested Tolliver, Nathan Harwell, and other YC members for their part in a MUSIC-sponsored demonstration. Again, on June 4, police arrested Harwell, along with five clergymen, including Father Groppi, for blocking a school bus with a human chain at Seifert Elementary School. Following the second school boycott in October, it was Tolliver and the YC who announced plans for continued demonstrations, including marches to the homes of Mayor Maier and the school board president, John Foley. And finally, in December, YC members and Father Groppi led MUSIC's last civil disobedience campaign at the MacDowell site, which resulted in dozens of arrests. By the end of 1965, Groppi and the YC had stepped to the forefront of the local Movement.

The Eagles Club Campaign

Following the MacDowell School protest in December 1965, the school desegregation campaign moved into the courts, and MUSIC's position as a vehicle for militant civil rights activism in the city diminished rapidly. This left Father Groppi and the YC casting about in search of new challenges. The continued inaction of local civic leaders fueled growing frustration and anger among many local people, particularly Groppi and the YC. The school board had remained steadfast in its unwillingness to correct racial imbalances in the public schools despite the mountainous evidence provided by MUSIC, the urging of several moderate and liberal community leaders, and a concerted campaign of direct action over a roughly two-year period. The Common Council similarly refused to act on housing and employment discrimination. Mayor Maier, for his part, continued to focus, rhetorically, on his "War on Prejudice" as the primary way to solve the city's problems but had failed to move any concrete proposals forward. By contrast, civil rights activists were growing impatient with traditional methods of redress. Petitions, meetings, hearings, negotiations, reports, articles, speeches, and peaceful demonstrations all seemed to have failed. More and more people searched for new avenues to change. As MUSIC activism declined, many felt that the broader civil rights struggle should be continued beyond the school issue and that the fight should be more aggressive.

As Father Groppi and the YC considered how to move forward, they worked to bolster their support and to cultivate leadership among inner core youth. During the spring of 1966, they established their first Freedom House in a dilapidated old slum house on Fifth Street in one of Milwaukee's most impoverished and overcrowded black neighborhoods. Groppi had learned about Freedom Houses during one of his trips to Mississippi, where they were used as safe houses and as voter registration centers, and thought it might work in Milwaukee as well. The YC explained in a fund-raising letter the reasons behind their decision to open the Freedom House: "Most of us have been raised in blight, and we know what it means to be Black and Poor. Our brothers need us badly there. Our purpose is to identify ourselves completely with the poor and to serve in every way that we know. Housing, education, employment, voter registration, etc., will be part of our activity." Richard Green, a future Commando, put it more simply: "It was a place we could all get together and talk about things." Alberta Harris, who was very active in the establishment of the Freedom House, agreed, stating, "That was where we met. We sat around and talked. We strategized. We had our local meetings there . . . and some state meetings. It became our formal base of operations."[10]

In part, the establishment of the Fifth Street Freedom House was a function of the need to create an independent space outside of St. Boniface. "We didn't always want to meet at the church," Dennis McDowell explained. "The church was a holy place. You did have a bunch of uneducated men who used a lot of vulgarity . . . [the Freedom House] was a separate space." Groppi concurred, saying,

> [I moved] out of the rectory because I always felt that the rectory was a kind of fortress that kept you away from your community and in order to reach the community, you had to get out of there . . . So, the 5th Street Freedom House, some of the Commandos and a few of the Youth Council members had to live there, and pretty soon some really good leadership developed.

McDowell added that the Freedom House was a place "that everybody could identify with . . . because you had Baptists that didn't want to go down to the Catholic church." Others claimed that the move was partly motivated by an underlying tension between Father Groppi and the pastor of St. Boniface over the presence of so many young people at the rectory.[11]

The primary function of the Freedom House was as an organizing tool. As Harris recalled, "Interest in Father Groppi was great in the community [at the time] and when we opened it, it was covered in the news media, so people just started to come." According to Dennis McDowell, "We had our information there and people came to sign up and join the NAACP YC. People also came there with their problems . . . The kids came [for a] place to hang out." Harris underscored the continuing spiritual aspect of the organizing work at the Freedom House, explaining, "[Father Groppi] would minister to these people in a variety of ways. He was a priest first and foremost . . . He was their spiritual advisor as well as their advocate for the problems [in their lives]."[12]

Fairly quickly, YC membership began to grow as a result of the group's work at the Freedom House, and the new recruits changed the class dynamic within the organization. Although all of the YC members lived in the inner core, the original nucleus of members, who were drawn primarily from St. Boniface, tended to come from more secure economic backgrounds with stronger family support networks and a greater emphasis on education than was found among the new recruits. According to Margaret Rozga, this "difference in orientation" led to minor tensions. "Every time a freedom house opened in a different neighborhood," she explained, "it brought in a whole different crowd and then there would be a period of adjustment." Alberta Harris described this dynamic as a "re-education" experience for everyone involved.[13]

Dennis McDowell's experience suggests that there was also a gendered aspect of the Freedom House organizing and the YC's early growth. McDowell's sister Vada and cousin Alberta Harris were two of the most active members of the YC in its earliest days. "My grandmother told me to join the organization in order to watch my sister [and cousin] because the gangs and stuff they were dealing with were a bunch of thugs," he recalled. "Dwight [Benning] and a few of the other boys got involved because we were the big boys, you know, to watch the girls and protect the priest." Alberta Harris agreed, explaining, "We ran into people that we would never have associated with [otherwise] . . . some of them were unsavory characters." She added, "The Freedom House could be a scary place at times. It was in a rough neighborhood and we were young girls . . . and it did help to have the guys there."[14]

Around the same time that the YC established the Fifth Street Freedom House, it decided to target the EC. With 5,400 members, the Milwaukee chapter of the Eagles was the second largest local branch in the country. Whites of all backgrounds belonged to the organization; blue-collar industrial workers, labor leaders, politicians, and business professionals all mingled at Eagles events. Consequently, it became an important network for the city's power brokers. In this way, membership was an imperative for ambitious local leaders. In 1966, EC membership included seventeen circuit and county judges, ten of twenty-four county supervisors, the district attorney, the county treasurer, the circuit court clerk, ten of nineteen aldermen, the city attorney, the city treasurer, the city comptroller, the city clerk, and the executive secretary of city elections. Congressman Clement Zablocki, who represented the city's South Side, and Mayor Maier also belonged, and Republican governor Warren Knowles held an honorary membership. Henry Reuss, who represented much of the city's black population, quickly quit the club after the YC brought the issue to public attention.[15]

As with most of the causes that Father Groppi and the YC took up, the initial impetus was a complaint brought to the group by a local person. "There was a [black] member of St. Boniface who swam on the swim team [but who couldn't practice with the team at the EC]," Margaret Rozga remembered. "It was just one person saying, 'They're making me feel like there is something wrong with me' and the YC saying, 'There is nothing wrong with you. There is something wrong with them.' That is how it started." Originally, then, the restrictive membership criteria alone was bothersome and wrong to the YC and was thus a legitimate source of protest.[16]

Over time, though, the YC refined and extended its critique of the organization. It questioned how public officials could be counted on to fulfill their duties impartially if they belonged to a group with a racist policy. The YC asked the community how African Americans could expect to get unbiased treatment from judges, politicians, labor leaders, and business executives if they maintained their membership in the EC. This was not an intellectual exercise for an organization whose members had been arrested numerous times during MUSIC-sponsored protests. In this sense, the YC argued, the EC was not a private association, and thus exempt from civil rights laws, but a quasi-public group under those laws' jurisdiction.

The YC was not the first to challenge the Eagles' "Caucasians only" clause. In July 1964, the Milwaukee Commission on Community Relations (MCCR) had asked the Wisconsin Advisory Committee to the United States Civil Rights Commission to look into the policy with an eye toward changing it, but the group was denied its request.[17] During that same summer, the local chapter of the Jewish antidefamation group B'nai B'rith cancelled a dinner at the EC ballroom because of its policy. The following January, an African American man urged the Milwaukee County Democratic Party to stop using the EC for its meetings and fund-raisers. After skirting the issue for several weeks, the Democrats did cancel an upcoming dinner at the club. MUSIC had also gotten into the act. On May 9, 1965, the school desegregation group picketed the EC to protest its membership policy. They targeted the club's manager, Milan Potter, who also served on the school board and had recently waged a divisive campaign to save the city's neighborhood school policy. In a letter to the executive secretary of the club, Lloyd Barbee wrote, "The Eagles Club . . . in addition to discriminating against Negroes in its Constitution, is now subsidizing a segregationist on the Milwaukee School Board of Directors." Last, in early January of 1966, James Stovall, an African American member of the local United Auto Workers Union, braved frigid temperatures to picket his union for meeting at the EC.[18]

In late February, YC members picketed outside the EC on Wisconsin Avenue. The protest continued through mid-March, but television and newspaper reporters largely ignored it. The demonstrations remained peaceful and without incident, except for one occasion. On March 16, an estimated 180 picketers marched along the sidewalk outside the EC as 1,000 people streamed passed to attend a St. Patrick's Day dinner sponsored by a local Catholic church. A scuffle broke out between plainclothes officers and a few protesters when police tried to break the picket line to enable a marching band to enter the hall. The incident resulted in the arrest of three YC members.[19]

The YC had a hard time making its case clearly to the public. Reactions to the YC's protest focused primarily on the EC membership policy and ignored the issue of local public officials' affiliation with the group. The EC consistently defended its freedom, as a private organization, to set the terms of its membership policy however it liked. It also threatened to seek a court order to halt the YC demonstrations, calling the NAACP a "left-wing extremist organization, part of a coalition of left-wing extremists seeking to create tension and conflict in this community." The EC attempted to hedge a bit by claiming that it had tried to get the policy changed at the national level but to no avail. Most of the public officials involved claimed that they deplored the white-only policy but would not quit, opting instead to "work from within" to change the discriminatory clause. In a show of support for the Eagles, Mayor Maier refused to terminate his membership and upheld the club's right to set its own policy. He did seek political cover, though, by announcing that he would not renew his membership in any private organization when each expired. Even some liberal civil rights advocates questioned the wisdom of challenging the Eagles' policy when more pressing issues, such as employment and housing, remained on the table. To them, however lamentable, the law seemed clear on this issue.[20]

The YC did register a couple of victories. WAWA radio, an R&B station out of West Allis, Wisconsin, which catered to Milwaukee's black community, announced that it would no longer sponsor dances at the EC. "The Eagles Club at that time was making a lot of money off of the black community because they would sponsor R&B groups," Alberta Harris explained. "They would let [black groups] perform there, so [African Americans] could go there and could pay [their] money to get in and see the Impressions or whoever, but you could not belong to the EC. If there wasn't a black group performing there, you couldn't go there." The Milwaukee County Labor Council also announced that it would not hold future meetings at the EC until the restrictive policy was changed, but almost immediately, in a display of the gulf between union leadership and some of the rank and file over civil rights, local 444 of the retail clerks union voted to continue meeting at the EC.[21]

It became evident to Groppi and the YC that they needed to alter their approach to the EC protest in order to clarify their position on public officials.

As they considered how to do that, a series of civil rights–related bomb blasts rocked the city. On July 1, a homemade explosive detonated in a South Side linoleum store owned by John Gilman. Gilman was a long-time leftist and outspoken supporter of racial equality as executive secretary of the Wisconsin Civil Rights Congress. A month later, on August 9, another homemade bomb tore apart the offices of the MNAACP. According to the *Milwaukee Journal*, "The explosion knocked down doors, blew out windows, knocked plaster off the walls and started a series of small fires which firemen extinguished with hand pumps." No injuries resulted from the blasts.[22]

At the end of September, Milwaukee police arrested two local men, Robert Schmidt and Roger Long, and charged them with the bombings. Both men belonged to the Wisconsin Ku Klux Klan (KKK) and had worked for the George Wallace campaign in Wisconsin in 1964. A report in the *Journal* referred to Long as the "former grand titan of the Wisconsin Klan." Schmidt served as secretary-treasurer of the Milwaukee Citizens Council, a group that opposed civil rights. The following day, police nabbed Turner Cheney, grand dragon of the Illinois KKK, in connection with the incident. Cheney and Long were convicted of the crimes, while Schmidt received partial immunity in exchange for his testimony against Cheney.[23]

There were signs of increased Klan activity in Wisconsin and Milwaukee in the months preceding the bombings. On June 18, 1965, a burning cross appeared on the lawn of an African American family who had recently moved into a white-majority neighborhood in Milwaukee. Then, in July 1965, the KKK announced that it planned to "open an office" in Wisconsin. In response, Mayor Maier denounced the Klan, saying, "The KKK has historically been anti-Catholic, anti-Jewish, anti-Negro, anti-Polish, anti-German, anti-decency. I'm sure the citizens of Milwaukee will reject this un-American organization." NAACP leaders also reported Klan activity in Lake Ivanho and Beloit. The Klan later appeared at open housing demonstrations in late 1967 and early 1968.[24]

The blasts significantly heightened racial tensions throughout the city. Civil rights leaders charged that the explosion was a deliberate attack on the NAACP and local efforts for racial equality. The head of the MNAACP urged local African Americans "not to retaliate," claiming that "rioting or going into the streets won't do any good." Lloyd Barbee was less restrained, calling the blast "a planned effort to destroy a symbol of established civil rights activity" and refusing to join NAACP leaders in seeking "community calm." "We've been calm long enough," he declared. "All the bigots and all the madmen are not in the South. We have an ample supply here in Milwaukee." Roy Wilkins, head of the national NAACP, telegrammed Maier to demand "vigorous action to apprehend persons responsible for bombing office of Milwaukee branch of NAACP and prosecution under Wisconsin statutes." Mayor Maier called the bombing "one of the most reprehensible acts which can be committed by any human being against another" and moved to "assure all responsible citizens that their person, their homes and their businesses will be protected." With a worried eye on possible retaliation, he concluded by stating, "I am not going to permit Milwaukee to become another Watts or another Chicago." The *Journal* called the bombing a "cowardly" and "deranged" act, and a host of local religious and political groups condemned the attack.[25]

On the morning after the bombing of the NAACP offices, Milwaukeeans awoke to news that several YC members, most in their late teens, had armed themselves with a loaded carbine and stood guard at the Freedom House. A picture on the front page of the *Journal* showed nineteen-year-old Dennis McDowell holding a gun. The article quoted Father Groppi as saying that the armed self- defense was his idea after the Freedom House and the St. Boniface rectory had received several telephone threats of further violence. "I will not remain non-violent in the face of some bigot coming at night and placing a bomb beneath the window," he said. "That is where my non-violence ends."[26]

The YC's protection of the Freedom House highlights the sometimes hidden history of armed self-defense within the civil rights movement. As historian Timothy B. Tyson has shown in his award-winning biography of North Carolina civil rights leader Robert F. Williams, nonviolence and armed self-defense often worked "in tension and in tandem" throughout the modern African American freedom struggle. Yet, this complexity has been submerged under the more popular and less controversial narrative of nonviolent direct action. In the aftermath of the bombings in Milwaukee, Father Groppi told YC members that they could use nonviolence as a tactic in civil rights demonstrations while not adhering to it as an absolute principle of their cause. "I've always believed in self-defense," Father Groppi said. "You know how cowardly the Klan is. They always strike at night. And this is Klan type activity . . . This sort of thing is so sneaky and so dirty that I believe in self-defense in a case like this."[27]

With Dennis McDowell sitting in the second-story window of the Freedom House, a gun in his hand, the YC began selling buttons with the slogan

"Burn Baby Burn" printed on them. The slogan had been chanted by Watts rioters and was increasingly popular among African Americans in cities across the country, but the Milwaukee YC was the only NAACP group known to use the slogan formally. According to Nate Harwell, the YC sold over 100 buttons. "Everybody loves 'em," he said. "They are going very well." Father Groppi told the press, "The buttons are a symbol of the struggle for freedom and a reminder of what happened in Watts." The head of the adult branch opposed the slogan and contacted Roy Wilkins in an effort to halt their sales. Henry Maier also pressured the national organization to rein in its Milwaukee youth chapter. In response, Roy Wilkins wrote to John C. Newcomb, Mayor Maier's chief administrator, "the sale of 'Burn Baby Burn' buttons is not indicative of a stand for law and order. We here in New York—off the record—were as astonished and dismayed as you must have been when we learned of this sale and of the sponsor." Wilkins ordered the YC to halt sales of the buttons.[28]

The YC's actions following the blasts shifted the attention of many white Milwaukeeans away from the bombings and to the civil rights group's reaction. The image of young, angry inner-city black men arming themselves against racist terror alarmed many white onlookers and seemed to confirm their worst fears about the intentions of Movement leaders. An editorial by WITI-TV captured this sentiment: "TV6 is well aware of the problems of our central city people . . . frustrating, sometimes desperate problems that must be solved. But, the answers will not be found by making threats . . . or spouting off with fiery thoughtless statements or by flaunting firearms." *Journal* opinion makers agreed: "It only furthers the destructive aim of the bomber to start brandishing firearms and parading inflammatory slogans on lapel buttons. The Watts slogan cannot be sugar coated as merely expressive of freedom aspirations in the Milwaukee context; it expresses nothing but more hate and violence like the bomber's." Conversely, Syd Finley, in town representing the national NAACP, asked a crowd of 150—two-thirds of whom were African American—at Mt. Calvary Church for restraint and calm but was quick to add that the NAACP had advocated self-defense since its founding in 1909. "Self defense is your right," Finley said. "I say to any white bigots: You want to step up and hit me, don't expect me to turn the other cheek." After meeting with Father Groppi, Archbishop Cousins told the press, "a man assigned to a specific work should be allowed to work in that field. I think that [Groppi's] action comes in the area of city ordinance. If he is violating any ordinance, then I think he is doing wrong." Shortly thereafter, the district attorney announced that the YC and Father Groppi had not violated any local law.[29]

In part, local anxiety over the YC's actions stemmed from a wave of racial violence that swept urban American during the summer of 1966. In mid-July, six nights of civil disorder erupted in Cleveland's predominantly black Hough neighborhood, claiming four lives and injuring more than thirty. Closer to Milwaukee, in the working-class Marquette Park neighborhood of Chicago, on August 6, Martin Luther King Jr. led hundreds of open housing advocates through a nasty gauntlet of thousands of screaming white residents. The level of hate was dazzling. Choruses of "I wish I were an Alabama trooper/This is what I would truly love to be/Because if I were an Alabama trooper/Then I could kill the niggers legally" filled the air. A rock the size of a fist struck King in the face, knocking him to the ground in a daze. A knife, hurled by another counterdemonstrator, missed the minister but lodged in the neck of a white marcher. Afterward, a clearly rattled King told the media, "I've been in many demonstrations all across the South, but I can say that I have never seen—even in Mississippi and Alabama—mobs as hostile and hate-filled as I've seen in Chicago. I think the people from Mississippi ought to come to Chicago to learn how to hate." At the same time, National Guardsmen in Dayton, Ohio, patrolled the city's predominantly black West Side in an attempt to quell racial violence. In Benton Harbor, Michigan, National Guardsmen stood by in the event that police in nearby Jackson needed help easing racial tension there. On September, 3, 1966, the governor of Illinois, Otto Kerner, called more than 2,250 National Guardsmen to another Chicago suburb, Cicero, to protect CORE activists. Four days later, 500 African Americans in Atlanta, Georgia, rioted after police shot a black suspect wanted for car theft. The disorder resulted in sixty-three arrests and fifteen injuries. Overall that summer, forty-three American cities were roiled by racial violence, an ominous foreshadowing of what was to come in Milwaukee.[30]

During the week of August 13, the YC sent letters to Circuit Judges Robert Cannon and Robert Hanson and to County Judges Christ Seraphim and John Krueger to ask that they resign from the EC. YC members hoped that by targeting these public officials, they would clarify their stance about the quasi-public nature of the EC. They were confident that one or more would resign in embarrassment, leading to other defections. In quick succession, though, Judges Seraphim, Hanson, and Cannon refused the demand, while Judge Krueger said he would not renew his membership but not because of the club's discriminatory policy.[31]

In response, the YC decided to take its campaign to Judge Cannon's home in suburban Wauwatosa. Some said the YC targeted Cannon, in part, because of his more liberal reputation as a jurist, but Alberta Harris suggested something different. He was symbolic of the way segregation worked at the time," she said. "On the surface he looked like one thing, but when you really started to look at what he was doing you could see he was a whole other kind of animal . . . the fact that racism existed but was hidden." Margaret Rozga suggested a religious angle. "It was a Catholic looking at a Catholic," she explained, "a Catholic priest looking at a devout Catholic layman and thinking he'll understand what I am talking about." But, she added, "Obviously, they had two very different ideas of faith."[32]

The conflict in Wauwatosa pitted differing conceptions of rights against one another. The YC asserted its right to peacefully protest, even in an affluent suburban neighborhood. Judge Cannon countered with his right to belong to any private club he chose, regardless of membership restrictions. And many white Milwaukeeans and public officials defended the judge and his neighbors' right to live in peace and tranquility. As a result, the YC protest was anything but clear-cut; considerable room for disagreement and conflict existed. YC members expected to confront Judge Cannon. What they did not bargain for was a confrontation with thousands of hostile whites.

For eleven straight nights, Father Groppi loaded up an old, beat-up bus and ferried civil rights demonstrators to the sidewalk in front of Judge Cannon's large brick colonial house in the suburbs. The YC led pickets, prayer vigils, and parades. Demonstrators chanted anti-EC slogans and sang freedom songs. Their numbers grew steadily from thirty to more than 250 over the course of the protest. But the YC underestimated Judge Cannon's resolve as well as the hostility their protest would elicit from local whites. "It was scary," Margaret Rozga remembered. "I spent ten weeks in Alabama [working for the Movement]. I never saw anybody in a Ku Klux Klan outfit, but I saw it in Wauwatosa." Frank Aukofer, who covered the protests for the *Journal*, recalled,

After about a week, it began to resemble a carnival. The Youth Council would arrive on the St. Boniface school bus, driven by Father Groppi. White spectators would either be waiting or would arrive shortly after. The crowd was always well salted with goons. Off to the side, a concessionaire sold popcorn, soft drinks, and candy bars from one of those neon lighted white trucks with windows in the sides.

After nine days of swelling crowds and increasing violence, Wauwatosa Mayor Ervin Meier asked Governor Knowles to dispatch the National Guard to protect the demonstrators. It marked the first time in Wisconsin's history that the National Guard was called out during a civil rights demonstration. Guardsmen patrolled the streets around Judge Cannon's home for three nights. The first night, over 400 soldiers were called to duty. The second night, over 500 were needed. By the third night, things had calmed down, and only 100 Guardsmen were called to the scene.[33]

The merits of the YC's argument were lost on many of the white Wauwatosans and their allies throughout the city. To those who already saw the general migration of African Americans to the city as a threatening "invasion," the Wauwatosa protests appeared to be the realization of their worst fears: a group of inner core African American children descending on their quiet, tree-lined neighborhood. As a result, many of the most reactionary white onlookers articulated in their shouts a kind of possessive, racialized defense of their neighborhood: "Keep Tosa White!" Others felt that a priest should not be leading young children in protests in the streets but should be in a church, praying. Such actions, they said, only encouraged lawlessness, disobedience, and violence. Still others opposed the YC's tactics. As in past campaigns, the demonstrations and the demonstrators themselves, rather than the underlying injustice of the EC's racially restrictive policy, became the primary issue for many whites. According to Aukofer, "The public, instead of focusing on the issue itself, focused on the dramatization of the issue." Father Groppi defended the YC's tactics, arguing, "Agitation is necessary. No one has ever been handed his rights on a platter . . . agitation is my motto."[34]

Local officials and opinion makers were also quick to react to the demonstrations in front of Judge Cannon's house. The *Journal* editorialists lamented, "There is shame in the fact that a state which enacted a forward looking law to open public accommodations to all races in 1895 now must summon its national guard to keep hundreds of whites from venting their intolerance on a group of peaceful Negro demonstrators." They suggested that the violent reaction of whites in Wauwatosa may have been inspired by similar events in Chicago around the same time. "The white mobs have been drawn to the scene purely for the sake of violence," the editors wrote, as "participants in some sort of insane fad that has developed as an outgrowth of the recent Chicago incidents." Mayor Maier attacked the civil rights activists for picketing private residences. In a public statement, Maier affirmed the general right to protest but also stated, "This community will never condone the organized harassment of a man and his family in their home, regardless of whether the family is white or Negro. In short, neither demonstrators nor counter-pickets belong in residential areas at night . . . The argument here is over tactics, not principle." In what was perhaps the YC's biggest coup, Probate Judge Michael Sullivan resigned from the EC in the wake of the Wauwatosa confrontation, stating that it was his opinion that membership in a segregated club was inconsistent with his oath of office. Circuit Judge Robert Hanson, on the other hand, stated that if he had to choose, he would rather be an Eagle than a judge. In words that prefigured Richard Nixon's 1969 "Silent Majority" speech, Hanson, who had served as national president of the Eagles, claimed that the "opinions of extremists dominate Milwaukee's civil rights debate while the views of the overwhelming majority are ignored."[35]

The issue split the NAACP. Both the MNAACP and the national organization opposed the EC policy and lent public support to the YC's demonstrations, but behind the scenes the adult branch of the MNAACP was less enthusiastic. At the regional NAACP Youth Council conference in April, the YC introduced a resolution asking all branches in the region to support a boycott of the EC in their home cities. In September, national officials announced that the protest would be carried to six other states: Ohio, Illinois, Indiana, Michigan, West Virginia, and Kentucky. They subsequently sent notices to 247 Youth Councils asking them to direct action against public officials who belonged to private clubs with racial restrictions.[36]

Not surprisingly, more than a dozen local liberal leaders and organizations rallied to the YC's defense with a flurry of resolutions and press releases. For example, the Council on Urban Life issued a news release that stated, "We agree with the NAACP Youth Council that it is unconscionable for a person holding an office of public trust to also hold membership in a racially restrictive organization. This is especially true of a judge who by his office represents the impartiality of justice." The group went on to defend the YC's tactics by drawing a parallel to the labor movement:

Picketing is within the constitutional and moral traditions of our nation. Perhaps many of those in the crowds which come to protest the peaceful picketing of the Youth Council have forgotten that much of their job security and their comfortable incomes were gained in large part as a result of the same kind of activity. We cannot deny the right to picket.

To liberals, the Wauwatosa campaign underscored the way racial discrimination was embedded in Milwaukee's political and economic power structures.[37]

Others were more conflicted. Many sympathized with the YC's position and opposed the white hostility in Wauwatosa but also bristled at the YC's confrontational tactics. Overall, there was a widespread feeling that no matter what the merits of the protest, initially, events in Wauwatosa had spiraled out of control. WTMJ-TV captured this sentiment in an on-air editorial:

> The demonstrations in front of Judge Robert Cannon's house may have had solid objectives, but they were reached long before this . . . The results since then are negative, dangerous and ugly.
>
> What we now have is a situation inviting physical danger—even if it does not come from any violent thoughts of the demonstrators. It has drawn to the Wauwatosa scene not only the morbidly curious who always get in the way, but the bigoted. Is this an objective desired by the pickets? . . .
>
> Can the NAACP's demonstrations really believe the Caucasian clause of the Eagles Club is worth the risk of violence and tragedy. Are there not greater racial injustices worth demonstrating against?

Given the recent bombings in Milwaukee, which were still unresolved, and the racial violence in Chicago, Cleveland, and elsewhere, the risk outweighed any potential benefit.[38]

The civil rights commotion in Milwaukee fed a noticeable upsurge in activity among far-right organizations in Wisconsin. Klan groups festered in Milwaukee, Lake Ivanho, and Beloit, cities with notable or historic African American populations. The *Journal* ran an article about the formation of Truth About Civic Turmoil, one of several John Birch Society front organizations dedicated to disseminating information about what it called the "civil rights fraud." The John Birch Society was headquartered in Appleton, Wisconsin, and enjoyed numerous links to Milwaukee. For instance, the Allen-Bradley Corporation, the city's largest employer during the 1960s, contributed significant funding to the group; cofounder Harry Bradley served as a leader in the far-right organization. In addition, local newspapers and radio and television stations all noted a significant increase in hate literature in Milwaukee in the months after the Wauwatosa protests. The MCCR issued a statement decrying the influx of racist propaganda.

Anti-Semitic and white supremacist pamphlets appeared in mailboxes and on windshields and back porches. At the University of Wisconsin–Milwaukee, students found copies of a superhero comic book called "Here comes White-man: Jews Commies Tremble . . . Nigger Criminals Quake in Fear . . . Liberals Head for the Hills . . ." Mayor Maier received copies of a fifteen-page red-baiting pamphlet written by far-right Christian evangelist Billy James Hargis, titled "Martin Luther King: Spokesmen for the Enemy." And in January 1967, six members of the American Nazi Party showed up at a speech by Father Groppi in Racine.[39]

Events in Milwaukee also garnered national and even international attention. Father Groppi received hundreds of letters during the protest. More than one-third came from outside of Wisconsin, including foreign countries, such as Canada, Pakistan, and Australia. The *New York Times* covered the Wauwatosa demonstrations and ran a favorable story on Father Groppi, titled "A Picketing Priest." The article quoted Groppi saying, "I will picket with the Negro. I will go South with him, and I will hang with him if need be." *Time* magazine took note of events in Milwaukee, too. Its piece, which included a small map of the inner core, described Groppi as "more of a Messiah than a leader" to the YC. The Associated Press put out similar stories over the wire. In a pattern that would persist, local and national media coverage, at first attracted by racial violence and the National Guardsmen, quickly trained in on the peculiar site of a white Catholic priest leading a militant civil rights campaign.[40]

The eruption in Wauwatosa prompted several attempts at a solution. A group of fifty local Catholic, Protestant, and Jewish clergymen met with YC members to offer their support on the issue but also to encourage the group to stop its demonstration. Archbishop Cousins, at the urging of Governor Knowles, called in Father Groppi for a talk. Although he personally opposed the continuation of the Wauwatosa demonstrations, he supported the priest's right to follow his conscience within the bounds of the law. Alder-man Vel Phillips and the city tax commissioner, Vincent Schmit, suggested that the EC's discriminatory policy might exclude it from the 66 percent tax exemption it enjoyed as a fraternal group. Joseph Fagan, chairman of the State Industrial Commission, held three days of "fact-finding" hearings on the question of discriminatory policies by private clubs. The city of Wauwatosa and Governor Knowles attempted to ban nighttime demonstrations in the suburb. When Wisconsin Attorney General Bronson LaFollette negotiated ground rules with Wauwatosa and Milwaukee city officials that sought to protect both the right of protest and domestic tranquility, the YC opposed these rules as an infringement on the constitutional right of free assembly. All of these efforts, though, went for naught.[41]

The YC sidestepped the Wauwatosa controversy, in part, by shifting its protest to the home of County Judge Christ Seraphim in Milwaukee and by threatening to lay siege to the home of Judge Robert Hansen. A few days later, the group picketed outside the home of South Side congressional representative Clement Zablocki. Both demonstrations were short-lived and uneventful.

The best opportunity for a settlement came in early September when University of Wisconsin–Milwaukee professor and experienced labor mediator Nathan Feinsinger offered to help smooth out the differences between the NAACP and the EC. Initially, the attempt looked promising. Father Groppi and the YC agreed to a temporary moratorium on demonstrations against prominent local officials while Feinsinger worked toward a negotiated settlement between national representatives of both organizations. In late September, Feinsinger announced a breakthrough: a meeting in New York on October 19, between Roy Wilkins, a small group of YC representatives, and D. D. Billings, the national president of the EC. Before that meeting came off, though, another controversy flared that would again change the dynamics of the civil rights insurgency in Milwaukee.[42]

The Formation of the Commandos and the Emergence of Black Power Politics in Milwaukee

At a news conference on October 4, 1966, Father Groppi announced that the YC had formed "a militant commando force" to aid in the group's civil rights activism. Groppi explained, "This is a direct action force that goes into very tense situations, that's very militant . . . They will be a police force. They will not be armed." The following day, local newspapers carried photographs of several young African American men clad in black berets, black ascots, green army fatigues, and black boots. Later, the uniform of the Commandos would be changed to lettered gray sweatshirts because most of the members could not afford the more elaborate clothing. In addition, the national NAACP preferred a uniform that clearly identified the Commandos as an NAACP group. The Commando uniforms were also an attempt to inject greater militancy into the movement as well as to project a bold, tough image to the public. But more than that, they also served a practical purpose.

Dwight Benning explained, "We felt that we could be distinguished from the crowd. If we had on the same thing that the crowd had on then they couldn't tell us from anybody else. By us having uniforms they could spot us in a minute and know who to go to. We even asked that the police come to us before they go into the line." Responding to charges that the Commandos were an example of "extremism" on the part of the YC, Groppi stated, "We are not extremists. We are militant. We are a vigorous direct action group. I don't think this is extremism."[43]

The creation of the Commandos emanated from several sources. In large measure, the group was a reaction to the bombing of the NAACP office in August and to the violence against YC members during the EC protests in Wauwatosa. In addition, the establishment of the Commandos reflected a lack of faith that local law enforcement would protect demonstrators in the face of violent white opposition. YC members regularly complained of aggressive behavior by white officers toward them. Prentice McKinney, a future Commando leader, recalled that during open housing demonstrations, Milwaukee police had a habit of "slipping with the teargas" and throwing it at civil rights protesters. Finally, the formation of the Commandos was a further attempt by Father Groppi to cultivate leadership and self-respect among poor, young African American men in the core and to channel their rage in constructive ways.[44]

Not everyone was enthusiastic about the formalization of the Commando group. Alberta Harris, who was the president of the YC at the time, "wasn't real big on the idea." She explained, "It felt like a private police force and . . . I didn't want them to go outside of the way we wanted to demonstrate or the way we wanted to present ourselves to the community. I didn't want them to turn into the Black Panthers. So, I was concerned about the paramilitary part of it." Father Groppi reassured her and other concerned YC members that the Commandos' primary role was to protect the Freedom House and to help marshal the lines.[45]

In fact, the Commandos fulfilled three primary roles in the Milwaukee Movement. In the most immediate sense, they formed a protective shield around civil rights demonstrators against hostile whites and rogue police officers. Dwight Benning, the first captain of the Commandos, explained,

> We decided we should take it upon ourselves to defend these people. You know, we asked them to march, now we had to protect their lives against people that we feared were biased toward us. We were youth, but we took

it upon ourselves to stand out and be noticed, like the militia, to protect our people from harassment from the various crowds.

Ed Thekan agreed:

We met with a lot of hostility. And the police did not necessarily separate us from the hostile crowds as quickly as they could have. There was a need there for a line of Commandos or a protective shield to keep their verbal abuses, their physical punches, and their rocks and bottles as far away from our marchers as we could.

In addition, the Commandos enforced order on the picket lines and in marches. Nonviolent direct action required strict discipline, and many young African Americans did not believe in it. It was easy for some to become angry and lash out in the face of flying epithets, obscenities, bricks, and cherry bombs. Robert Granderson recalled,

You know a lot of times different people got in the [demonstration] line just to raise hell, and a lot of times the people that were marching with them would raise hell to the outsiders; you know, say if he's walking along drinking a soda or something, they'd throw the can [out of the line]. This is what we'd try to stop.

Granderson also emphasized that Commandos imposed discipline on police officers, too: "A lot of times, the police would infiltrate the line. They would come into the line, they would put stuff in people's pockets. They would jump out of their cars and snatch people out of the line if they'd have a warrant or something. We got this understood with them that this wasn't going to happen." Later, during open housing protests in Milwaukee, Commandos also occasionally conducted their own demonstrations when a situation seemed dangerous.[46]

Although the vast majority of Commandos were African American, the Commandos adhered to a biracial philosophy and practiced what several members called "not-violence." According to Joe McClain, an early Commando leader, " 'Not-violence' meant we didn't carry weapons and we didn't start nothing, but we also didn't take nothing. If the police or the white crowds came after us or the marchers, we weren't afraid to mix it up. We fought back." Prentice McKinney agreed, stating,

We had a philosophy. [King's] was non-violence. [The Commandos'] was, "I am not-violent." There is a distinct difference, OK? I'm not violent, but if you hit me, I am going to take care of myself. See Dr. King at that point was teaching people non-violence, passive resistance. They dump sugar on your head, they kick you in the butt, they drag you, they beat you, submit to it. We had a little bit too much vinegar [for that].

This "not-violent" philosophy was also practical. "There was no way you could have adapted a violent philosophy on the South Side," Father Groppi explained. "You would have been hamburger. [So, not-violence] was a necessary survival method." He continued,

You see, it is very difficult to go out to the streets where [the Commandos] had been fighting with their fists and surviving in a violent sort of way their entire life, to say, look, we are going to be non-violent. I mean, it was just not the survival code. But [not-violence] was a method that we used . . . If we were going to save ourselves as human beings, if we did not want to become what our opposition was, we had to adapt [King's] philosophy. We struggled for it. And sometimes we were successful. Sometimes we failed.

Dennis McDowell credited not-violence with staving off greater violence against demonstrators:

It was self-defense that kept most of the people from really getting seriously hurt. If it wasn't for the brute strength and the out-going nature of the men in the Commandos at that time, the bulk of the people in those lines would have got hurt, somebody might have got killed, and I think the movement would have died, post haste, if it wasn't for the young men at that time.

Alberta Harris commented on this paradox by stating that despite the Commandos' embrace of not-violence and their willingness to mix it up with hostile whites or police, they were the "peacekeepers" of the Movement.[47]

Often lying just behind the public tactic of nonviolent direct action and unarmed not-violence was the presence of weapons. For instance, on the second day of the Wauwatosa protests, as white reaction and the potential for violence grew, Father Groppi and Tom Jacobson loaded up the old bus with YC members, many of whom would go on to become original Commandos. Nervous tension filled the air. The previous day, Groppi had called Jacobson to ask whether he would join the group and represent the YC in the event of arrests. He confided in the young civil rights attorney that he was fearful of white violence at Judge Cannon's home. Jacobson agreed to help. When the two men boarded the bus, they reminded the young demonstrators that they had agreed to practice nonviolence. Jacobson informed them that he could only represent them and defend their rights if they adhered to that philosophy. "If you have any weapons, you need to get rid of them now before we leave," he said. No one stirred. Again, he started, "I'm going to get off the bus and come back on." Jacobson exited the bus, and Father Groppi walked up and down the aisle. Clink. Clink. Clink. Brass knuckles, knives, and chains all appeared in a pile. Jacobson was shocked but relieved that the youths had relented. Ed Thekan explained, "You were dealing with street people who basically found a need in their own daily lives to protect themselves from whatever. You know, threats, assaults, et cetera, so they carried a bicycle chain, or . . . a switchblade or whatever was hot that day. But you could see where that wasn't required on the picket line." According to Alberta Harris, "people were showing up that just wanted to go out there and go to war, and [we] stopped that. We never had any violence from the people who were involved." Nonetheless, throughout the direct action era in Milwaukee, nonviolent direct action would coexist alongside a more shadowy version of armed self-defense.[48]

Public image was central to the thinking behind the formation of the Commandos. Alberta Harris recalled, "The media jumped all over them. This was something new. This small group of people was evolving into something bigger, and, of course, Father Groppi had taken on his own bigger-than-life image, and, then again, the Panthers were out there, people were familiar with what they were doing and they were afraid of them." Ed Thekan claimed, "The word 'Commando' itself was sort of a threatening word. I think it was chosen specifically for that . . . They weren't just rubber stamps. Or, they weren't just to pacify the crowds." Harris agreed, stating, "They were never armed and there wasn't one of them that would hurt anybody, but they scared the bejesus out of a lot of people, they really did, the establishment especially . . . that was the point." In this respect, the formation of the Commandos was a skillful tactical decision that was consonant with Father Groppi and the YC's philosophy of confrontation and agitation as the basis for change.[49]

Originally, the Commandos were a subgroup of the YC. Virtually all of the initial members also belonged to the YC. Nathan Harwell and DeWayne Tolliver, for instance, both early leaders of the YC, were founding members of the Commandos. They met at St. Boniface, looked to Father Groppi for guidance, and even traveled south with him. Similarly, Dennis McDowell had joined the YC to protect his sister and cousins working at the Freedom

House before becoming a Commando. In essence, the Commandos evolved out of the YC "line captains" that were established during the Wauwatosa protest. "When you go out [to a demonstration] with twenty individuals," McDowell explained, "you only need two people to captain. When you go out with 100 individuals, two will not do." Groppi agreed: "The Commandos, when it started, was a very small group . . . They were developed to become marshals of the [EC] demonstrations." As the job got bigger, the need for a more formalized unit evolved. Over time, the Commandos developed an increasingly distinct personality from the YC. But early on, there was considerable fluidity between the two groups.[50]

It is important to keep in mind the loose organizational structure and membership criteria that the YC and Commandos employed. In part out of secrecy and in part out of a lack of interest, neither group kept minutes of meetings, nor did they follow a concrete set of bylaws or articles of incorporation, though they were technically governed by NAACP regulations. "We came up with rules and guidelines on what it meant to be a Commando and how we were supposed to act as a Commando," explained Dennis McDowell. "Not being disrespectful, rude, crude, or lewd around the girls. You know, protect the womenfolk. Protect the old folks. [And protect the priest]." As the Movement evolved, the YC and Father Groppi developed the strategy and made decisions about when and where to march. The Commandos would then plan how best to "police" those demonstrations. There was a sense of mutuality between the YC, Commandos, and Father Groppi throughout the civil rights era and an acknowledgement that each subgroup and each member had an important role to play.[51]

The Commandos were not the only militant self-defense organization within the civil rights movement during the mid-1960s. In late 1964, a group of World War II and Korean War veterans in Louisiana formed the Deacons for Defense and Justice to protect local civil rights activists in the face of widespread Klan activity. The Deacons received considerable media attention in the Milwaukee newspapers. Similarly, the same month that Groppi announced the formation of the Commandos, Huey Newton and Bobby Seale established the Black Panther Party for Self-Defense in Oakland, California, to combat police brutality. Unlike the Commandos, both the Deacons and the Panthers carried weapons. And there were other examples of "commando" groups within the NAACP as well. Mark Rosenman, acting national youth director for the organization, told Milwaukee reporters that three other NAACP commando units existed at the time of the

Milwaukee group's founding, one in New England, one on Long Island, and one "working in four southern states." What tied all of these groups together was that they grew out of the specific needs of local circumstances, the appearance of anti–civil rights violence from whites and a general antipathy between local law enforcement and urban African Americans.[52]

The formation of the Commandos was just one aspect of the YC and Father Groppi's more general embrace of Black Power. In its broadest sense, the Black Power movement strove to express a new African American consciousness. It flowed out of earlier struggles for racial justice, but its meaning was vigorously debated. During the mid-1960s, Black Power became a slogan that meant different things to different people. To some, it represented race dignity and self-reliance. Others thought of Black Power in mainly economic terms. Black Power encouraged the improvement of conditions in African American communities and the cultivation of black institutions and indigenous leadership, rather than working for integration. Black Power also looked to black cultural heritage and history for the roots of African American identity. To cultural nationalists, Black Power related primarily to the arts and to cultural expression. Artists like Amiri Baraka tried to develop a new black aesthetic in poetry, drama, dance, music, writing, painting, and film that emphasized the centrality of self-representation and creative autonomy. Behind the afros and dashikis and other signs of race pride was the idea that beauty and self-esteem were critical to power relations as well as to self-image and self-expression. Furthermore, most Black Power advocates felt a necessity for black people to define the world for themselves, in their own terms, free from white control or domination. For some, this took the form of a political struggle against racism and imperialism and a more confrontational, demanding style. Many Black Power militants, like the Black Panther Party for Self-Defense, increasingly identified with pan-African struggles for liberation around the world. With this political evolution came an emphasis on urban ghetto poverty, a growing repudiation of nonviolent direct action, and an embrace of armed self-defense or even offensive violence as a "revolutionary tool."[53]

As Black Power grew, it caused heated debate and produced resistance from many whites and several prominent African American organizations, including the NAACP. Some criticized Black Power for what they perceived to be its "anti-white" message, arguing that it ran contrary to the integrationist ideal of American democracy. Others looked at Black Power as an invitation to lawlessness and racial violence and felt that it undermined established authority. Still others thought that Black Power did not offer a constructive solution to the increasingly desperate plight of African Americans, particularly in cities.

In Milwaukee, black and white newspapers printed dozens of stories about the new civil rights consciousness. They displayed pictures of leaders like Stokely Carmichael and H. Rap Brown, of the gun-toting Black Panthers in California, and of urban rioters in Chicago, Cleveland, Los Angeles, and elsewhere. Articles emphasized the incendiary rhetoric of national Black Power practitioners and stressed its menacing qualities over community organizing and race pride. Editorialists and letter writers argued over the merits of Black Power, while most conservative and far-right white leaders condemned the new ideology out of hand.

By the winter of 1966–1967, the YC and Father Groppi had clearly adopted the Black Power ideology. The sale of the "Burn Baby Burn" buttons, the armed defense of the Freedom House, and the formation of the Commandos as well as their uniforms, strategy, and style were all products of the new Black Power consciousness. At marches and rallies, civil rights activists regularly chanted Black Power slogans, held Black Power signs, and wore Black Power sweatshirts with "Soul Power," "Soul Sister," "Black and Beautiful," and other slogans printed on the back. At St. Boniface, priests placed banners in both Swahili and English around the church, they laced sermons with Black Power rhetoric, and Father Groppi refused to wear colorful priestly vestments during mass, preferring instead to wear black on the alter as a sign of racial solidarity.[54] Groppi also used mass and Christian theology to teach neighborhood children about the tenets of Black Power. For instance, an Associated Press report in May 1967 related the following exchange, in which Groppi asked a young African American girl why she thought the priest wore only black:

"Because it's a beautiful color," she responded.
"Because it's a beautiful color," Groppi repeated. "Wonderful. It is a beautiful color. All colors are beautiful—black, white, red, yellow—all colors. And why is that?"
"Because God made them," said a child.
"Because God made them," repeated the priest.

Groppi talked about black self-determination in religious terms as well: "The Lord ain't gonna help you and he ain't gonna help me unless we get out there and help ourselves. Jesus Christ was a civil rights worker. The greatest civil rights worker, greater than anyone here." Similarly, he preached:

> You must involve yourself as Christ did. The peace of Jesus Christ was the peace of inner conviction. He preached the peace of human dignity. He never meant that creative tension should be removed from earth. He didn't say that He came to bring peace to earth—that's part of the white lie—but rather to cast a sword upon the earth. You must be revolutionaries. Christ was a revolutionary. That's why he ended up on the cross.[55]

Father Groppi invited young people to gather around the altar, where they sang spirituals and discussed current civil rights issues. Journalist Frank Aukofer recalled one service, on October 13, 1967, which was attended by some Commandos and about a dozen YC members. They began by singing "Mary Had a Baby," "Nobody Knows the Trouble I've Seen," and "Swing Low Sweet Chariot." Groppi then proceeded with a "dialogue homily" about brotherhood and civil rights. After the mass, YC members began chanting "Black Power's coming, Black Power!" Groppi interrupted, and the following discussion ensued:

> *Groppi:* What do we mean by Black Power? Does it mean black people over white people?
> *Young people:* No, equal! It means opportunity.
> *G:* All right, do black people have much money?
> *YP:* No.
> *G:* Then what do we call it, what kind of power do we call it? . . . money power, economic power.
> *YP:* And in the political field and in the social . . .
> *G:* Political power. What do we mean by political power?
> *YP:* In the political field, we want some black people in office and not just white people.
> *G:* What do we mean by educational power?
> *YP:* We want to get a good education.
> *G:* What's one aspect of our education we don't get?
> *YP:* Negro history.
> *G:* Black history—all right, good.

Following this line of discussion, the young people, most in the sixth, seventh, and eighth grades, chanted again, "Move over whitey, Black Power!" but then ended by singing "We love everybody in our hearts." Groppi's attempt to make the liturgy relevant to the experiences of young black children was an important part of his mission.[56]

These and other unique features of Black Power in Milwaukee highlighted the way Groppi and the YC fit national Black Power ideology to their particular local circumstances. To many, the sight of a white Catholic priest leading chants of Black Power from the altar and the picket line no doubt seemed peculiar. And it was. The leading role of Father Groppi as a Black Power advocate and spokesman ran counter to the growing racial separatism of Black Power in some communities. In addition, the Commandos persistent embrace of interracial cooperation and not-violence as well as their refusal to brandish weapons, publicly, even as a symbolic act, set them apart from many other local Black Power organizations.

Official reaction to the formation of the Commandos was overwhelmingly critical. *Journal* editors called the announcement of the new unit "disturbing news" and compared them to the "Hitler Youth" and "the Red Guard of Communist China." The paper concluded, "The impasse [between the races] will only be made more bitter and more frustrating by the formation of this or any other commando force. Let's have an end to them in Wisconsin." The *Milwaukee Sentinel* concurred, stating,

> A band of vigilantes—and this is what the NAACP Commandos really are—might have a place in a community where the processes of law enforcement have broken down, where citizens must band together to protect themselves. Milwaukee is not such a place. Making the NAACP youth into a military cadre can only exacerbate the unfortunately and unnecessarily strained relations between the Negro community and our police department, which is all the uniformed force we need.

The *Milwaukee Star* covered the story but failed to comment editorially on it, while the city's other African American newspaper, the *Courier,* asked, "Will the Commandos' existence add to the 'domestic tranquility' or some egos? Will they excite, incite or possibly ignite? Or will their role fulfill their stated purpose? The Courier and many members of the community have very grave concerns about the wisdom of a Commando unit." The Milwaukee County Labor Council opposed the group by a vote of 225–1, and a state assemblyman, Republican Louis Cecil, called the Commandos "a Hitler-like group." Despite the broad opposition to the group, the national NAACP backed the formation of the Commandos, noting that other chapters had similar units. The local adult branch, though, privately opposed it. According to Prentice McKinney,

> It was the old plantation mentality . . . The older community—the NAACP, respectable leadership—had an investment in the system. They understood that there was discrimination, but they had learned to get along and live with it and not rock the boat. We were the young turks. We were having no part of it. We were standing up against it. We were defying it, which put their position in jeopardy because the system would look at them and say, "Why can't you control them?" And they tried.

In the end, though, the adult branch was powerless against the YC and maintained the united public front of the Movement.[57]

Most white Milwaukeeans reacted to the Commandos with a mix of surprise, fear, outrage, and opposition. For many whites, the Commandos conjured up images of marauding young black men undermining the rule of law and spreading racial violence. Taken together with the explosive string of recent events in Milwaukee and across the country, there was some basis to their fears. New concerns, like poverty, police brutality, urban education, housing, welfare, and employment, moved from the periphery to the center of the Movement's agenda. No longer were young civil rights activists asking nicely for basic civil rights and social equality. "We were about action," Prentice McKinney remembered. "I mean, we were teenagers and we said, 'This ain't right. Let's do something about it.'" More and more were making threatening demands behind the banner of Black Power. Racial violence was sweeping the nation's cities, and urban tensions remained high across the North. Many whites, and even some moderate and conservative African Americans, felt that the movement had moved away from dignified peaceful protest to confrontation. To them, urban violence seemed random, undirected, and, ultimately, counterproductive. Many whites did not understand or were ignorant of the experiences of black people in the inner core, particularly the antipathy many blacks had for local law enforcement. These whites looked on with growing fear of what might come to Milwaukee.[58]

Perhaps the most significant reaction to the creation of the Commandos, at least in the short-term, came from the EC leadership. D. D. Billings telegrammed Roy Wilkins that he would not meet with members of the YC or the Commandos, nor with national NAACP officials, if they did not repudiate the new Commandos unit. In response, Wilkins wrote,

You call upon me as national executive director of the NAACP to "disown" our Milwaukee youth unit . . . I cannot do this. Our Milwaukee youth unit is not violating any of the general programs set forth by the NAACP. Although its methods may strike some persons as being unorthodox, the situation to which it addresses itself in 1966, namely, a racial expulsion clause in the membership of, of all groups, a fraternal society, is also extraordinary for this day in this nation.

With that exchange, Professor Nathan Feinsinger's attempts to mediate a solution to the EC impasse fizzled, and the EC protest came to an effective end.[59]

Ultimately, little changed at the EC. The protest did net a few withdrawals of membership and even fewer cancelled meetings, but by and large the status quo remained. Father Groppi and the YC had successfully pointed to another instance of racial inequality in Milwaukee, but they achieved little that was concrete. As an organization, the YC continued to learn about racial inequality and the depths of white reaction in the city. According to Margaret Rozga, the EC campaign taught the YC a valuable lesson about the limits of negotiation. "People come and talk you to death so that nothing gets done," she explained. "[During the EC protest,] they said, 'we'll negotiate this for you,' and all it did was kill our momentum." As a result, the YC emerged from the EC campaign more skeptical of white officials and more committed to a confrontational form of nonviolent direct action.[60]

Their work also earned national recognition. At the NAACP convention in Boston in July 1967, the Milwaukee YC beat out more than 500 other youth councils across the country to win the Isabel Strickland Memorial award for "the most distinguished service in the fight for freedom." Similarly, Father Groppi received an award as "the most effective, outstanding advisor of any youth council in the country." The YC's activism and notoriety also paid off with increased membership. By the spring of 1967, as the group turned to new challenges, the YC counted 100 regular members, and the Commandos numbered more than thirty.[6]

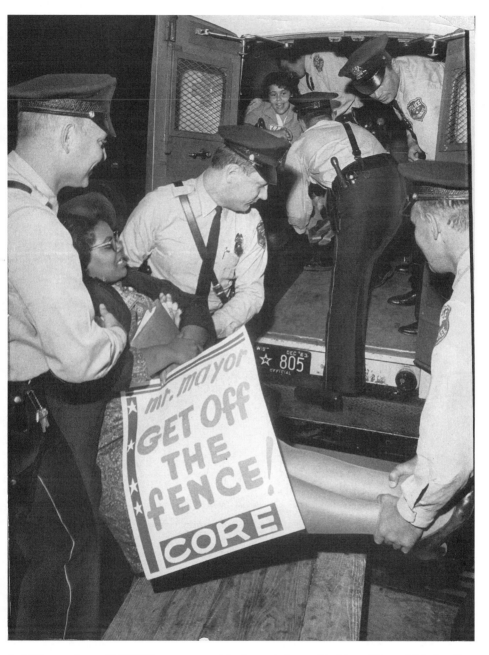

In 1963, members of MCORE were arrested during a sit-in outside Mayor Henry Maier's office. It was Milwaukee's first sit-in of the civil rights era. (*Milwaukee Journal Sentinel,* © 2007 Journal Sentinel Inc., reproduced with permission)

In 1965, members of MUSIC, led by Lloyd Barbee *(second from the right)*, formed "human chains" in front of buses to protest segregated public schools. (*Milwaukee Journal Sentinel,* © 2007 Journal Sentinel Inc., reproduced with permission)

Leading up to the second school boycott in October 1965, a controversy erupted over the role of clergy and church property in the protest. Father Groppi *(center)* led 500 young inner core students away from St. Boniface to a nearby church for a Freedom School after the auxiliary bishop forbade the use of the church in the boycott. (Wisconsin Historical Society, image no. WHi-40697)

Father Groppi *(right, wearing the hat)* and the YC protested the "Caucasian-only" membership clause of the Eagles Club in 1966. When they took their demonstration to suburban Wauwatosa, thousands of angry whites lined the streets, prompting the mayor to call out the National Guard. (Wisconsin Historical Society, image no. WHi-53595)

A few members of the Ku Klux Klan counterdemonstrated outside Judge Robert Cannon's home in suburban Wauwatosa during the Eagles Club protest. (*Milwaukee Journal Sentinel*, © 2007 Journal Sentinel Inc., reproduced with permission)

Members of the YC visited inner core schools to discuss the civil rights movement. Many young African American women played important leadership roles in the YC. (*Milwaukee Journal Sentinel,* © 2007 Journal Sentinel Inc., reproduced with permission)

In 1966, Father Groppi and the YC organized the Commandos, a defense group designed to cultivate black male inner core leadership and to protect civil rights marchers from hostile white onlookers and police. The Commandos practiced what they called "not-violence." (*Milwaukee Journal Sentinel,* © 2007 Journal Sentinel Inc., reproduced with permission)

In 1967–1968, Father Groppi, the YC, and the Commandos led 200 consecutive nights of marches in an attempt to compel the Milwaukee Common Council to adopt a strong citywide fair housing ordinance. Hundreds, and sometimes thousands, of marchers rallied in the courtyard at St. Boniface before each march to chant, hear speakers, and sing freedom songs. (*Milwaukee Journal Sentinel*, © 2007 Journal Sentinel Inc., reproduced with permission)

Open housing demonstrations became a powerful organizing tool in the inner core. Thousands of ordinary citizens joined Father Groppi *(center)*, the YC, and the Commandos and took to the streets for the first time to press for change. (Wisconsin Historical Society, image no. WHi-25167)

On the working-class South Side, thousands of white counterdemonstrators holding signs with White Power slogans lined block after block. The level of massive resistance to the open housing campaign in Milwaukee rivaled that of more well-known southern civil rights campaigns in Birmingham, Selma, and elsewhere. (*Milwaukee Journal Sentinel*, © 2007 Journal Sentinel Inc., reproduced with permission)

One of the most intriguing—and controversial—aspects of the Milwaukee open housing campaign was the image of a white Catholic priest (Father Groppi) leading a Black Power movement. In Milwaukee, Black Power was "not a color, but an attitude." (Wisconsin Historical Society, image no. WHi-1912; photograph by Howard M. Berliant)

On the second night of the open housing demonstrations, after 13,000 hostile whites attacked 200 peaceful open housing marchers on the south side of the Sixteenth Street Viaduct, Milwaukee police fired tear gas into the YC Freedom House, burning it down. The next afternoon, during a rally at the site, police arrested dozens of civil rights advocates. (Photograph courtesy of the Archdiocese of Milwaukee Archives)

Father Groppi's militant public leadership in Milwaukee's black freedom movement stirred significant debate within the local and national Catholic communities over the role of a parish priest and the relationship of the church to social change. (*Milwaukee Journal Sentinel*, © 2007 Journal Sentinel Inc., reproduced with permission)

At the height of the open housing campaign, the Commandos met privately with Father Groppi in the basement of St. Boniface to plot strategy for each march. The Commandos policed the lines and defended demonstrators from white mobs or hostile white police. They never started violence, but they were not afraid to fight back. (Wisconsin Historical Society, image no. WHi-53596)

Father Groppi, the YC, and the Commandos formed an alliance with Vel Phillips *(center)*, the only African American as well as the only female on the Common Council. Between 1961 and 1967, Phillips introduced a strong citywide open housing ordinance on four occasions, but each time, it was defeated by a vote of 18–1. (Wisconsin Historical Society, photo by *Milwaukee Journal Sentinel,* image no. MJS-48149)

Vel Phillips's participation in the open housing demonstrations represented an important alliance between the traditional African American leadership class and the new insurgent leadership of Father Groppi, the YC, and the Commandos. The Commandos even made her an honorary member of their group. (*Milwaukee Journal Sentinel,* © 2007 Journal Sentinel Inc., reproduced with permission)

Father Russel Whiton *(center)* emerged as an "anti-Groppi" during the open housing campaign. Whiton advised the Milwaukee Citizens' Civic Voice, a closed housing organization that espoused white supremacy. (*Milwaukee Journal Sentinel,* © 2007 Journal Sentinel Inc., reproduced with permission)

On April 8, 1968, 15,000–20,000 Milwaukeeans marched peacefully in honor of Dr. Martin Luther King Jr. It was one of the largest memorial marches in the country for the slain leader. (*Milwaukee Journal Sentinel,* © 2007 Journal Sentinel Inc., reproduced with permission)

In 1969, Father Groppi led the Welfare Mothers March from Milwaukee to Madison to protest cuts in the state social welfare budget. A multiracial coalition of social workers, civil rights activists, and welfare recipients, supported by thousands of students from the University of Wisconsin–Madison, took over the assembly chambers for eleven hours before being ejected by police. (Wisconsin Historical Society, image no. WHi-4934)

— 6 —

Police–Community Tensions
and the 1967 Riot

Rumors and fears of racial violence swirled about the inner core for months before it finally happened. The recent tumult in Wauwatosa during the NAACP Youth Council's (YC) Eagles Club (EC) protest stoked black militancy as well as white reaction, sharpening tensions throughout the city. The determined refusal of the school board, the city council, and the mayor's office to act on any of the mounting claims by black leaders and civil rights activists fueled popular frustration and anger. Deteriorating police–community relations, including a string of public disputes between YC members and the Milwaukee Police Department's "Tactical Squad" during the winter and spring of 1966–1967, fed the unease. Urban disorder in Newark, Detroit, and dozens of other cities the following summer combined with sensational media coverage of national Black Power leaders to buttress a growing belief that it was only a matter of time before Milwaukee joined the list. As inner core residents sought refuge from sweltering summer heat on porches, sidewalks, and in the streets, new rumors were born and passed along, old passions reignited.[1]

Third Street, where the violence began, had changed considerably since its heyday. At one time, the corner of Third and Walnut marked an active center for the black community, a concrete reminder that despite pervasive discrimination and inequality, local African Americans thrived. But by the summer of 1967, the nightclubs, restaurants, movie theater, offices, and retail stores that once flourished had deteriorated and given way to a desperate collection of bars, discount stores, small groceries, relief agencies, a Nation of Islam temple, and a growing association of vacancies. Blight had surrounded, and then devoured, the heart of Milwaukee's black community.

The initial confrontation started in front of a popular inner core night-club one late Saturday night, July 30, only a few days after the chaos in Detroit had ended. As two black women fought on the sidewalk, a group of 350 gathered to watch. When white officers arrived to break up the fight and disperse the crowd, several onlookers threw bottles, rocks, and garbage. The patrolmen radioed for reinforcements and proceeded to push the crowd down Third Street. The throng remained adamant, though; it took nearly fifteen blocks before it finally disbanded. The city got off relatively easy that first night; a few broken windows and a number of tossed garbage cans were the worst of it.[2]

In a pattern that repeated itself over the next few days, the daylight hours on Sunday remained calm, but stories continued to circulate and passions simmered. By sundown, Third Street came alive again with anger and anticipation. The specific trigger for Sunday's outburst is unclear. Some claimed it began when police roughed up a group of African American youths outside a dance. Squire Austin, a new Commando who lived near much of the action, was at a civil rights rally when the disturbance began. "The rumor we got," he recalled, "was that police had beaten up a kid pretty bad over on Third and Walnut . . . [when those rumors began circulating,] that's when the looting and firebombing started." Whatever the initial spark, by 10:00 p.m., a mob of nearly 300 people were moving along Third Street breaking windows, starting fires, and looting. Young people cruised the area, honking and yelling, while groups of two and three pitched rocks, bottles, chunks of concrete, cans, and garbage at passing vehicles driven by whites. Some spray painted the word "soul" on buildings. Police reported an overturned car, minor sniping, and even a Molotov cocktail. At one point, rock-throwing residents prevented firemen from tending to a series of fires in vacant inner core lots, while other local people raced around, urging calm and trying in vain to extinguish the flames. The vast majority of residents stayed indoors, away from the unrest, but inside the three-quarter-mile epicenter, events were out of hand; a mob psychology had seized hundreds of local people. More than 100 police and firemen struggled unsuccessfully to reassert order against what Squire Austin simply called "a mass of people destroying the neighborhood."[3]

Shortly before midnight, Chief of Police Harold Breier notified Mayor Henry Maier about the breakdown of civil order. Maier had been quietly planning for unrest since the EC disturbances in Wauwatosa more than a year earlier and quickly put his plan into action. Within a half hour, he called his staff together, asked Governor Reynolds to place the National Guard on standby, and notified presidential aid Joe Califano and Attorney General Ramsey Clark about the situation. Chief Breier set up a command post inside an inner core department store parking garage, where he monitored the situation and gave regular reports to the mayor. At the urging of Breier and against the advice of the fire chief, James Moher, Maier initially held back a formal request to activate National Guardsmen.[4]

As city officials struggled to coordinate a response, one of the worst incidents of the Milwaukee civil disturbance played out on Center Street. With his pregnant wife, John Tucker, a respected fifty-five-year-old janitor at Shorewood High School, spent the evening at home babysitting two of their great-grandchildren. At about 1:30 a.m., a white man in a station wagon reportedly passed by their house and shouted profanities, threats, and racial slurs at Tucker's grandson and some neighbors who stood in the driveway talking. One neighbor claimed that the man in the car shot at her. Tucker later testified that the incident prompted him to grab his shotgun, run outside, and return fire. Several minutes later, when five plainclothes white police officers pulled up in front of Tucker's house and barreled out of an unmarked car, the frightened homeowner again opened fire, this time from inside his house. In the darkness and confusion, one shot hit twenty-four-year-old patrolman Bryan Moschea in the chest and throat, killing him. Another bullet tore away part of Captain Kenneth Hagopian's face.[5] Police returned fire and lobbed tear gas into the home, which flames quickly swallowed, but Tucker kept shooting. Detective Leroy Jones received a blast to his right arm, patrolman David Kunde was hit on his left side, and a load of shot permanently blinded officer John Carter when it struck his face. Finally, Tucker surrendered. The next day, the bodies of Moschea and seventy-seven-year-old Anne Mosley were found in the ashes. The medical examiner later ruled that Mosley had been accidentally shot during the incident as she lay in bed.[6]

At 2:27 a.m., with two officers known wounded, one missing, and a number of small and large fires burning, Mayor Maier declared a state of emergency and formally requested help from the Wisconsin National Guard. The proclamation imposed a citywide twenty-four-hour curfew and closed all taverns, liquor stores, filling stations, and "petroleum supply points." Anyone who disobeyed the orders was threatened with immediate arrest and severe punishment. "Our chief concern is to restore law and order," Maier warned. "This must be the concern of *all* our citizens. We cannot permit irresponsible hoodlums to destroy property and endanger lives. We cannot allow lawless vandals to deprive others of their basic rights." Later that day, the Common Council ratified the mayor's actions and granted him sweeping emergency powers to "do whatever is necessary and expedient for the health, safety, welfare and good order of the city in such an emergency." Another resolution banned the sale of ammunition, guns, and other weapons for the duration of the crisis. Major General John Dunlop, commander of the Thirty-second division, notified the mayor that the 1,200 troops he was assembling would not be ready until 7:30 a.m. In the meantime, more than 1,000 Milwaukee police officers, with the help of a mild drizzle, began to reestablish calm in the inner core. At 4:30 a.m., a police inspector offered Mayor Maier his assessment of the night's casualties and damage: "six officers have been shot, which is verified; 3 citizens, 2 snipers, and 1 looter shot . . . these are not verified; much breaking of windows, looting, some fires. Fifth District Station was under sniper fire; all lights are out in station. Area of disturbance was roughly Holton to 20th, Capitol to Michigan." The police had made more than 180 arrests. At 4:50 a.m., Chief Brier finally reported, "Everything quiet."[7]

By Monday morning, the police and more than 500 National Guardsmen had blockaded the area around the disturbance. Another 1,000 stood ready at nearby staging areas.[8] Troops in combat gear and armored vehicles searched cars and patrolled inner core streets; most of the city remained desolate under the blanket curfew. Guardsmen ran special missions into the hardest hit areas to deliver milk and other basic provisions to cooped-up residents. That afternoon, police stopped Father Groppi and seven YC members as they traveled through the inner core to the Northcott Neighborhood House for a meeting with other African American community leaders. Joseph Fagan, head of the Wisconsin Department of Industry, Labor, and Human Relations, had issued Groppi and Fred Bronson, the president of the YC, unofficial "credential letters." The letters asserted that the bearer was one of several people working with the Industrial Commission to preserve order and prevent violence. Fagan later explained that the letters were "intended to assist [Groppi and the YC] in getting through police lines . . . on the theory that it might help him out because he has been of great help to the community and to us." Police and other city officials refused to accept the authority of the letters and promptly arrested the civil rights activists.[9]

The decision to take a hard line against Father Groppi and the YC threatened an already precarious calm. To Maier and many white onlookers, the incident was another example of Father Groppi and the YC's willingness to flaunt the law and instigate racial trouble. In their view, the civil rights leaders claimed special privileges not entitled to them. Civil rights activists and many inner core residents, on the other hand, viewed the arrests as an attempt to target Father Groppi and the YC for their past activism even though, in this instance, they worked for calm and order. According to this view, law enforcement officials were applying a dangerously stringent interpretation of the emergency measures. Fearing that the case might provide a rallying point for disgruntled inner core residents, Mayor Maier privately dispatched an aide to the courthouse to broker a speedy hearing and a quick release without bail for the activists. Though defused, the incident did not do much to build cooperation among the civil rights activists, the community, and public officials.[10]

For the next several nights, police officers, firemen, and hundreds of federal troops scrambled to keep a lid on a series of minor violent outbreaks, including occasional looting, sniping, a bomb scare, and arson. The most tragic turn came on Monday night when police shot and killed Clifford McKissick, an eighteen-year-old college student with no prior record, under murky circumstances. According to police reports, officers spotted McKissick and three other black youths throwing Molotov cocktails against a paint store wall across the street from the McKissick home. As the group fled, the police shot McKissick in the neck. Family and neighbors of the young man claimed that he had been sitting on the family's front porch when shooting broke out and everyone scrambled for cover. Moments later, Clifford appeared at the back door, choking from the bullet wound through his neck. The police surrounded the home, and all four young men surrendered. Clifford McKissick died on the way to the hospital. The county medical examiner ruled the death "justifiable"; many community members and civil rights activists felt differently. The following Saturday, 100 community members marched to the Safety Building behind Father Groppi and the YC to protest the incident. A few days later, more than 500 local people, including a full contingent of Commandos, turned out for Clifford McKissick's funeral.[11]

By the following Tuesday, the number and magnitude of these flare-ups had decreased, so the mayor loosened the emergency restrictions. In a major televised address, Maier announced, "[Tomorrow morning] the curfew will be over. The bans—the restrictions—will be gone." Yet, the physical and psychic damage had already been done. All told, the civil disturbance in

Milwaukee claimed five lives and caused 100 injuries (forty-four of them police), 1,740 arrests (the majority for curfew violations), and $570,000 in property damage. But, perhaps most significant, white Milwaukeeans could no longer comfort themselves with the myth that they were somehow exceptional or different from other large metropolitan areas, that they would somehow escape the worst of the spreading urban crisis. The burning rage had now come home.[12]

In the popular telling of the civil rights era, the southern Movement headed north after the historic legislative victories of 1964 and 1965, only to explode in a series of chaotic and violent urban riots, like the one that erupted in Milwaukee. Often, these conflagrations mark the first entrance of the urban North into the postwar civil rights narrative and are usually explained as part of a broader wrong turn for the Movement during the Black Power era, away from the nonviolent, interracial, and reform-minded activism of the first half of the 1960s and toward violence, racial exclusivity, and revolution in the late 1960s and early 1970s. In this light, urban disorders appear to be random, nihilistic, irrational, and tragic.

There are many problems with this standard trope. First, it obscures the rich history of struggle by African Americans and their allies in northern urban communities well before the urban violence of the mid- and late 1960s and implicates all community members in the violence of a few. In addition, it fails to situate these disturbances within their broader local histories of accelerating urban decline, deteriorating police–community relations, and growing popular frustration in black communities with the slow rate of change. Finally, it does not take into consideration the rational bases for violence in the face of chronic poverty, pervasive discrimination, and the determined inaction of white officials and civic institutions. In short, there is a more complicated story to be told around the civil disturbances of the 1960s.

The Deterioration of Police–Community Relations

The chain of events that began with the bombing of the NAACP office and extended through the Wauwatosa protests and the creation of the Commandos frayed relations between the YC and the Milwaukee police. Part of the problem was Harold Breier, the hard-line chief of police who ran the department with an iron fist and had little tolerance for civil rights activism. To many YC members and Commandos, Chief Breier was "an old fashioned, authoritarian, racist cop." Breier grew up in a working-class family on Milwaukee's South Side and joined the force in 1939 at the age of twenty-eight. The former head of detectives was bullheaded and liked things to be orderly; he set the tone for the entire department. A 1911 law that gave the chief of police lifetime tenure in office made Breier virtually untouchable politically and largely free from oversight. The same statute mandated that only "freeholders"—or those owning a home—could bring formal complaint against a police officer. This rule effectively prohibited complaints from the vast majority of Milwaukee's African American population. With overcrowding and rising crime rates in the inner core, Milwaukee police took an increasingly hard-line approach to law enforcement in black neighborhoods. A greater police presence meant more arrests and conflict. Because nearly 98 percent of the city's police force was white and working class and did not live in the areas they patrolled, few officers understood or respected the struggles of inner core residents. Local people, in turn, charged that police officers were overly aggressive, harsh or petty, and often failed to wear badges as required by law. Some black leaders pressed for the hiring of more African American patrolmen. Breier, in turn, scoffed at the idea of creating a police–community relations board.[13]

During the mid-1960s, Chief Brier turned the city's vice squad against civil rights activists. The squad had historically been used to monitor the activities of left-wing political organizations and radical immigrant groups and to regulate vice throughout the city. The Tactical Squad, as most called it, consisted of about six to eight detectives whose charge was to keep tabs on activities within the local civil rights movement. Officers wrote down license plate numbers at rallies, demonstrations, and church services. "We would hold rallies at St. Boniface," Prentice McKinney remembered, "and [the Tactical Squad] would go along and take everybody's license plate number. They would not hide. They'd get out of their car and just walk along . . . you'd come out of church and here's cops standing across the street blasting pictures. The harassment was not hidden." Police also took hundreds of photographs of marchers and YC members; tailed Father Groppi, the YC, and the Commandos day and night; and reportedly had a special room at the police station dedicated to their civil rights monitoring. Father Groppi later explained,

[Milwaukee police] followed us for something like six months. Everywhere we went! You got up in the morning, they were there. You went to visit your family, they were there. You went out to a restaurant, they were there. You took someone to a movie, they were there . . . At that time, we were preaching black, male leadership, and those young men got angry.

YC members and Commandos derisively referred to the officers who monitored them as the "Goon Squad."[14]

Throughout the civil rights era, police brutality was an increasingly potent civil rights issue across the urban North. Disturbances in Watts, Cleveland, New York, and many other places had either been directly precipitated or indirectly fueled by the clash between local law enforcement and black community members. A growing proportion of inner-city African Americans viewed the local police in adversarial terms, as "the enemy." Fuses ran short, and flare-ups occurred with regularity. Increasingly, social scientists and policy makers linked police brutality with urban violence. More and more, civil rights activists discussed the nexus between poverty, crime, and law enforcement and organized to "defend" their communities.

In Milwaukee, police–community relations had been tense in the core since the late 1950s, but they gained added heat during the summer and fall of 1966. After an incident in May, Reverend R. L. Lathan and Reverend Leo Champion, who had both been active in MUSIC-sponsored direct action campaigns, threatened trouble "like Watts" if city officials did not act to relieve inner core tensions over police conduct. A few days later, Assemblyman Lloyd Barbee, in Washington, D.C., for a White House conference on civil rights, called the pattern of harassment and intimidation by police in Milwaukee "as bad as it is in Mississippi." He claimed that Milwaukee authorities had tapped his telephone and followed him in unmarked cars because of his work against segregation in public schools. In July, Alderman Phillips publicly butted heads with Chief Brier when officers photographed civil rights activists who had come to support Phillips's open housing efforts at a Common Council meeting. She called the incident "intimidation and harassment of the highest order." Brier defended the policy as necessary and within the law. In August, a group of inner core pranksters painted "Burn Baby Burn" on the side of a local police station. In October, the YC's commando unit came to life and was viewed by many Milwaukee police officials, under these circumstances, as provocation.[15]

The feelings were mutual. Following the NAACP bombing, Milwaukee police placed the Freedom House under surveillance. Police officials claimed that they were acting to protect Father Groppi, the YC, and its headquarters after numerous threats. They cited public statements by YC leaders and the armed defense of the Freedom House as evidence of the need for police protection. YC members claimed that the police simply used safety and protection as a pretext to bully and intimidate them. "The danger is that it is constant intimidation and harassment . . . whenever [Chief Breier] puts a car out there to observe, observe, observe, observe what the Youth Council members are doing, he is intimidating them and they react to this. They don't want to be observed as common criminals and neither do I." According to Groppi, YC members, and Commandos, plainclothes officers in unmarked cars sat outside the Freedom House from sunup to late at night taking notes and photographs and hassling young people for petty offenses.[16]

As the YC's EC protest crested in early September of 1966, a series of seemingly minor confrontations with police set off a public storm. On Monday, September 5, the police arrested four YC members for shooting dice near the Freedom House. Officers confiscated just over $1 in the arrests. Father Groppi accused the Milwaukee Police Department of "harassment" and told reporters, "We don't know if we're being protected or attacked." He questioned the tactics employed by the officers, too: "The thing that disturbed us is that the thing could have been settled very easily if somebody would have just contacted us. I would have broken the game up. Now they took them downtown, finger-printed them, mugged [photographed] them, all for a $1.35 crap game." Groppi concluded, "We don't need this kind of protection." Breier responded, "If Father Groppi were really interested in protecting the place from bombing, he would not have revealed that it was being protected." The YC sent a formal letter asking the police to end their surveillance of the Freedom House. Breier replied, "In our opinion, you need protection and protection you're going to get, whether you like it or not. My advice to you is to not violate the laws and you won't have any problems." In court, Christ Seraphim, who had been targeted during the YC's EC protest, now sat in judgment over the four dice players. He called the Freedom House a "den of thieves" and suggested that Father Groppi "teach a respect for law instead of picketing." Groppi defended the YC and Commandos, saying,

> We didn't come here to alienate ourselves from the community, or the people in the community. This is why we came into the blight area. Several of our members have been in trouble with the police in the past. We don't

try to hide this fact. Many of our members have never been in trouble with the police whatsoever in the past. Some of them have had several years of college.

Seraphim ruled against the civil rights activists, levying a nominal fine on each defendant.[17]

Later that month, the police arrested a young woman outside the Freedom House and charged her with littering after she discarded a cigarette butt on the ground. Four YC members were also arrested for "interfering." Nathan Harwell, one of those involved in the incident, claimed that officers made critical remarks to the young people, including, "I hope you riot, then I can shoot off a few" and "I hope you have to go to Vietnam." Although the city attorney refused to prosecute the group, the police held them in jail over night. *Milwaukee Journal* editorialists called the police action "deliberate harassment" and "a shocking misapplication of the police power." Father Neuberger, one of Groppi's colleagues at St. Boniface, told a group of Catholic Worker members that Milwaukee police were often "unnecessarily harsh" when dealing with inner core teens. "It's the community which allows that situation to exist that will be responsible for the riots we will have," he stated. "The community has shown that the only time it will listen is when we do something wild enough."[18]

Following a failed meeting between police officials and YC representatives, YC members voted, in a satirical move, to provide Chief Breier with protection. Nathan Harwell explained, "We would like to thank Chief Breier for the fine protection he has given the Freedom House. We're going to protect Chief Breier's house very equally and without prejudice. We're going to take pictures and protect the chief . . . We think it's our responsibility and duty to protect him." YC members conducted two all-night "protective vigils" at Breier's house on September 30 and October 1. The following Friday, the newly formed Commandos, in full uniform, took over guard duty at the site. At the press conference announcing the Commando unit, Groppi quipped, "We want to make sure [the Chief's home] doesn't get bombed."[19]

The Freedom House was not the only site of police–community conflict in the core. Bars and other after-hours spots continued to attract discord as they had since the 1950s. For example, on September 10, a jeering crowd of more than 200 young African Americans threw rocks and bottles at two white policemen as they tussled with a black resident accused of stealing money from another bar patron. These kinds of incidents underscored the increasing willingness of young inner core residents to challenge police authority directly, at least when they were together in a large crowd.[20]

As tensions outside the movement continued to press upon Father Groppi, the YC, and Commandos, conflicts within the local Movement simmered. Moderate and conservative elements in the state conference and adult branch of the NAACP opposed the YC's confrontational tactics and militant strategy. The dispute took place mainly outside of the public eye, but many of the older generation of NAACP leadership criticized the armed defense of the Freedom House, the marches into Wauwatosa, the YC's embrace of Black Power, and the formation of the Commandos. Some complained that the Wauwatosa demonstrations marred a recent membership drive in Milwaukee. At the state conference in November, militant delegates rebuffed attempts by moderate and conservative members to rebuke the YC. Instead, the gathering passed a resolution praising the YC's activism and extending both financial and moral support to the group. The debate over tactics caused leadership friction within the adult branch, too. Reverend Walter Hoard, who represented the older and more moderate leadership group, narrowly held off an insurgent campaign by attorney Terrance Pitts for branch president. Pitts, who detailed a more activist approach to racial change, had the backing of the YC. Although the leadership remained in the older generation's hands, younger delegates served notice that a more militant spirit had infiltrated the NAACP. In 1967, the YC, not the adults, propelled civil rights activism in Milwaukee.[21]

There was some discordance within the YC and Commando ranks over Father Groppi's role in the YC. In early April 1967, "some officers of the local, state, and regional [NAACP] youth groups who are generally older members" publicly accused Groppi of being too militant and of controlling, not advising, the YC. To dispel any question about his role in the local Movement, Groppi asked the full YC membership for a vote of confidence at the next meeting. Nearly fifty members attended the meeting and unanimously voted in support of Groppi's leadership. A Commando spokesperson downplayed the challenge afterward, telling reporters, "There is dissention in every group, but dissention to what extent is the question . . . The vote was unanimous to retain Father Groppi as Advisor to the Youth Council . . . about 50 were present . . . the three individuals who were involved in this do exist, but I don't think they are as committed." He also stressed, "[Groppi's] function is as an advisor. We make our own decisions through deliberation and a process of parliamentary procedure." One week later, angry YC members threw stones and chunks of brick at the car of Thomas Leubenow, the *Journal* reporter who first reported the internal rift.[22]

Inherent in Groppi's leadership were questions of authenticity and legitimacy. To a certain extent, they were unavoidable; a white Catholic priest serving as a Black Power advisor to a militant civil rights group in 1967 and 1968 was necessarily controversial. Groppi himself expressed deep ambivalence about his role in the YC and often repeated his goal of cultivating young black leadership from within the community. On another level, though, periodic griping often had less to do with Groppi's leadership and more with the decidedly Groppi-centered media coverage. Journalists often assumed that Groppi made all decisions for the YC and that he was the leader of the Milwaukee Movement. Too often, they chose to focus on the heroic and passionate white religious figure and to ignore the many African American contributions pushed into the background. In fact, an eight-member executive committee made binding decisions for the YC after extensive deliberation. Groppi sat in on all meetings and regularly gave his advice, which the group often followed, but he did not have formal voting power. Similarly, Father Groppi attended most Commando meetings but acted only as an advisor. According to Shakespeare Lewis, who joined the Commandos in 1967, "The only time he'd [Groppi] say something in the [Commando] strategy meeting was if somebody asked him for his opinion. Otherwise, he'd sit and listen . . . But people on the outside say Father Groppi's leading them niggers down there. But people just didn't know." The relationship between YC members, the Commandos, and Father Groppi was organic and personal, with lines of authority purposefully vague. By the spring of 1967, though, Father Groppi had become a minor media celebrity, and no doubt some of the YC members and Commandos felt jealous.[23]

A more serious episode took place in May, when Dwight Benning, the original leader of the Commandos, Dennis McDowell, one of the group's other founders, and another young man told the district attorney that the YC and Father Groppi had planned a riot. They said that meetings had taken place and that riot plans had been drawn up, complete with maps of the inner core. They also claimed that Groppi had helped make homemade bombs and gasoline explosives. Groppi vociferously denied the charges. Nonetheless, the comments received substantial media coverage

and contributed both to the perception that Groppi was a rabble-rouser and
to the overall racial tension in the city. Those opposed to the civil rights
movement looked upon Groppi and the YC as a "lawless bunch," and the
riot charges, true or false, only confirmed their suspicions and fueled their
reaction. Upon closer scrutiny, the youths' story did not hold up, and they
admitted that they had fabricated the charges in anger because they wanted
to continue protesting the EC. Groppi felt that the situation in Wauwatosa
was too tense.[24]

Like most northern cities, Milwaukeeans approached the summer of
1967 with nervous anticipation. Each of the previous two summers had
produced significant urban racial violence, and many worried aloud: Will it
happen again? Will it happen here? Over a few short years, race relations
and civil rights insurgency in the city had been transformed. Activists had
moved from a faith in established institutions and the use of reason and negotiation as their primary weapons, through dignified and disciplined
protest, and finally to confrontation and civil disobedience. Similarly, many
Milwaukee whites had evolved from ignorance and indifference of racial issues, to concern and mild resistance, to open opposition and, in the most
extreme cases, violence. Divisions ran deep, and the atmosphere was
charged for conflict.

Much of the action, locally, continued to swirl around the issue of
police–community relations. In late April 1967, black youths pelted two
white police officers with stones as they fought with three African American
teenagers. That same month, police arrested Reverend Leo Champion and
Reverend Luscious Walker for interfering in the arrests of several inner core
residents.[25]

These flare-ups culminated when police clashed head-on with Father
Groppi. In early May, police arrested Groppi on charges of obstructing officers and resisting arrest when the priest intervened in a dispute between
youths and the police outside the Freedom House. Police officers claimed
that Groppi kicked, shouted profanities, and encouraged onlookers to "Start
the riot. Start the riot." Police also stated that a group of young African
Americans pelted them with bottles, bricks, and debris, resulting in minor
injuries to three officers. Father Groppi called the allegations a "dirty lie." A
few days later, the priest again clashed with police. "I was driving back [to
St. Boniface] and the police followed me. Right onto the property of St.
Boniface," Groppi remembered. "Now, I tell you, it wore me to such an extent that . . . I jammed the car into what I thought was reverse. And I

stepped on the gas. And by accident, I hit park . . . I jumped out of the car and told them to get off of Church property and the man turns to me and spits." The situation was tense, but Father Groppi was not defenseless. "It was a hot summer night," he explained:

> At that time on 12th Street there were all houses across the street from the parish. Black families were sitting on their [porches, asking] "You all right, Father? You need some help?" I said, "Yeah, come on over." So all these porches empty out, and the people came over. And as soon as those squad cars saw the fellows, they pulled out.

Nonetheless, police still ticketed Groppi for obstructing traffic.[26]

In the wake of these incidents, Chief Breier finally agreed to meet with Father Groppi and six members of the YC. The delegation told the chief that police were following and "harassing" them. Groppi warned Breier that the series of minor skirmishes and constant surveillance had escalated tensions nearly to the point of a riot. Breier responded, "It seems to me that you have caused that tension with your statements. In 27 years on the police department, we've always had friendly relations in that area until you came along . . . If you preach to your people that they are to do good things instead of bad, the tensions will disappear." Groppi retorted, "You just keep them off our back. If I have policemen on my back everywhere I go, I live in a Communist country . . . your presence is an intimidation." The meeting broke down amid fired-up passions. The next day, police captain George Sprague, in charge of a large portion of the inner core, told reporters that he remained unconvinced that "large tensions" existed in the area.[27]

Even though the mayor and Governor Knowles steadfastly supported Chief Breier and local officers, some local groups did try to head off the brewing conflict between the police and black residents in the core. A group of thirteen moderate African American ministers met with Chief Breier to demand the hiring of more black officers and to encourage police to "understand the problems of Milwaukee Negroes." Several prominent social scientists and clergymen wrote to Mayor Maier, stating that they were "strong in their convictions that the present stance of Mr. Breier and some of the policies of the Department constitute a major threat to peace in the core area." Lloyd Barbee introduced a measure to curb "police brutality" in the state assembly. Claiming that some young inner core African Americans threatened to bomb the homes of policemen and burn slum houses, the Milwaukee Commission on Community Relations and the Social Development Commission (SDC) announced that they would hold public hearings on police–community tensions. Similarly, the Greater Milwaukee Conference on Religion and Race and the Organization of Organizations set up "listening posts" throughout the inner core to collect claims of "police brutality." In lieu of official action, the *Milwaukee Star* suggested "citizen curbs" on Milwaukee's "conservative, almost all-white police department." The editors explained: "This could take the form . . . of responsible citizens, armed with radio-equipped cars, to answer police calls with tape recorders, photographic equipment and general legal knowledge to curb the enthusiasm of certain bigoted officers."[28]

The push for better police–community relations reached its public zenith on May 13, when the YC led thirteen organizations and 450 individuals on a march to the Public Safety Building to protest "police brutality" and "harassment." The YC president and vice president, Fred Bronson and Fortune Humphrey, posted a resolution on the door asking the mayor to "call off Chief Breier and to restore sanity to police operations." The notice further warned, "The black people of Milwaukee are controlled by a police force that is alien to them, that did not arise out of their community, that has little relation to the needs or desires of the community. This cannot continue."[29]

Storm clouds had gathered in Milwaukee. More and more local leaders began to issue riot warnings. Almost every Sunday, Fathers Groppi and Neuberger hammered away at racial inequality and police brutality in Milwaukee. "The black man in Milwaukee lives in a police state," Father Groppi claimed. "I have said the elements are all here and if they fall in the proper place on the proper night, there will be danger in Milwaukee this summer." When asked to explain the causes of urban disorder, he stated, "[It is] white apathy and white resistance and the white supremacist attitude that causes riots. Black frustration results when white apathy is that great." Father Neuberger attributed tensions to police harassment, stating, "Police are constantly hounding Father Groppi and the [Youth] Council, pushing them into a corner, baiting them, almost encouraging them to do something wrong . . . The seeds are planted. The fire is under the pot." Milwaukee, he added, was primed for "riot, bloodshed, suffering and mayhem." At a community meeting in May, Reverend Walker, Alderwoman Phillips, John Givens, representing the Milwaukee NAACP (MNAACP), Larry Harwell of the Organization of Organizations, and several university social scientists echoed the priests' sentiments, albeit in more restrained language.[30]

Pressures were compounded in late June when the YC and Commandos announced that they would next target housing discrimination and work for an open housing ordinance. "We're going to march," Father Groppi told a rally at St. Boniface. "We're coming off the reservation. We're going to move where we want. We're going to live where we want . . . Either we get what we want in this city, or we're going to turn this city upside down. If it takes the national guard out all summer, that's what the Youth Council's going to do." According to Groppi, open housing protests would not be confined to the inner core:

> We're going to go down and see some of these white aldermen on the South Side . . . We're going to see some of those realtors in Wauwatosa. They love us out there. The Commandos say to me, "Grops, When are we gonna go out to Tosa?" You know they say we can't picket out there. Well, we're going to Tosa, to Whitefish Bay, to Shorewood, and even out to Cudahy.

The YC began to hold regular open housing rallies at St. Boniface and to picket the homes of aldermen who opposed an ordinance. At one of the gatherings, Groppi again threatened to cross Milwaukee's "Mason-Dixon Line" to head to the working-class South Side to achieve an open housing ordinance. A few days later, the priest told the Common Council that without action on housing, Milwaukee could be turned into a "holocaust."[31]

Throughout this period, the YC and Commandos grew and changed as a new wave of recruits joined their cause. This influx was the result of a combination of factors. Many, aroused by media coverage, were inspired by the Movement and its promise of a more just society. Others joined because they no longer had faith in established institutions and leaders, while some got involved to help protect civil rights demonstrators from violent white reaction. A large proportion of the men were attracted by the image of Dennis McDowell sitting in the window of the Freedom House with a loaded shotgun and by photos of militant black Commandos making a defiant stand against police harassment.

The YC's community-organizing program at the Freedom House also began paying dividends. During the summer of 1967, the YC opened a new Freedom House on Eleventh Street after being evicted from the Fifth Street location. By July, the group boasted a membership approaching 100, and the Commandos numbered near fifty. For the Commandos, the addition of new recruits was particularly significant. Many of the second wave of men were "from the street," which meant that they were poor and tough, often without a strong family structure but in a gang; several had minor criminal records. According to Dennis McDowell, when the Commandos were not clashing with local police, they were sparring with inner core toughs. During this period, the group was primarily "involved with trying to get the kids to eliminate the gang [stuff] and the ignorance that was blatant throughout the inner-city . . . We were about getting the kids in tune with eliminating violence and preying upon each other" and redirecting their energy toward the Movement. The establishment of the Freedom House and the presence of the Commandos signaled a threat to turf controlled by local gangs with colorful names, like the Burleigh Boys and the Del Cronics. To make inroads, the Commandos had to be willing to stand up to the challenge of these local gangs when they came calling.

Prentice McKinney's experience provides an example of this dynamic. At seventeen, McKinney, who had a reputation as a smooth-talking hustler with a penchant for fighting, led an inner core gang called "Quickfists and the Retouchables." According to Dennis McDowell, some of the original Commandos had a weight-lifting club on Fifteenth Street, near McKinney's house; it was a part of their mystique and fed the aura of toughness surrounding the group. "Quite a few brothers from the neighborhood would challenge these big boys," McDowell remembered, "saying, 'You guys think you're something?' " When Groppi and the Commandos moved into the neighborhood, McKinney's crew paid them a visit. "I ended up in a fight with Dwight Benning," McKinney recalled, "and Groppi came out and said, 'No. No. You guys shouldn't be fighting.' " By standing strong, though, Commandos like Dwight Benning proved their street credibility, which earned them respect from local toughs like McKinney and opened up opportunities for dialogue and discussion about racial justice and the Movement. "That is how I got involved," McKinney explained. "That's how it started for me."[32]

But not all of the new Commandos followed this pattern. Joe McClain, for example, was in his twenties, older than the average Commando, worked at a local plant, and was married with kids. McClain, like many others, saw the demonstrations on television and decided to see what Groppi, the YC, and the Commandos were all about. McClain joined the Commandos and, because of his age and grounding, quickly became a mentor and leader within the group.[33]

As the YC and Commandos grew, they confronted new organizational challenges. "It was just like high school," McDowell explained. "You've got your seniors, who already have their program together, and they already went through the freshman, sophomore, and junior years . . . and all of a sudden the new freshmen come in and they think they can tell the juniors and seniors what to do. We had to set them straight." Over time, organizational growth led to the formalization of the internal structure and decision-making process in the YC and Commandos. It also meant that the tight personal connections that initially defined the YC loosened.[34]

With growing civil rights militancy and more combustible rhetoric came a quickening of white reaction. The mayor, Common Council, school board, and the bulk of the city's South Side legislators continued to form a bulwark against even modest racial change. The *Journal* reported on an inner core white man who had trained his dog to attack African American children and on an interracial family feud in a transitional inner core neighborhood, which resulted in the exchange of gunfire. Far-right organizations continued to crop up. In the spring of 1967, Klan members appeared at a rally for the recently burned-down Mt. Calvary Church, warning, "There'll be some bombings and some killings."[35]

Thanks to shared conditions and the amplifying power of the mass media, no city was an island. On July 12, 1967, the same day that a Milwaukee jury found Father Groppi guilty of obstructing police, an incident in Newark, New Jersey, between young black youths and police, escalated into four days of full-scale racial violence. New Jersey Governor Richard Hughes declared that the city was in "open rebellion, just like wartime." When the gunfire, burning, and looting subsided and the National Guardsmen had moved in, twenty-three African Americans lay dead, more than 1,500 were injured, and 1,300 had been arrested. Several blocks of Newark's urban black community stood charred and ruined, the result of more than 300 fires. The Newark riot was the largest urban unrest since Watts. Two weeks later, before anyone could catch their breath to understand what had happened in New Jersey, Detroit erupted. On the morning of July 23, Detroit police raided an illegal black after-hours bar, handcuffed its patrons, and forced them out. When an angry crowd of observers gathered at the scene, police retreated in fear, but the throng began burning and looting local businesses anyway. Again, hundreds of National Guardsmen were called out to quell the disturbance. In the end, the three days of unrest cost forty-three African American lives, 1,189 injuries, and 7,231 arrests.[36]

The nation looked on in horror at these and other urban conflagrations. Newark and Detroit worried everyone, particularly those living in cities.

Suddenly, the whole urban calculus dreadfully changed. A *Journal* headline declared, "Detroit Similar to Milwaukee." Rumors circulated that Milwaukee was next. The city sat waiting, awkwardly trying to reassure itself that it would not happen here, that Milwaukee was still uniquely exempt from the troubles that plagued other cities. Even the YC halted its open housing protests while newspapers and televisions covered the destruction in Detroit. Behind the scenes, though, city officials took no chances and began to prepare for the possibility of racial violence. Following the disturbances in Wauwatosa, police in seven Milwaukee suburbs united in an agreement to "enforce order" in the event of further civil unrest. It did not take long for them to get their chance.[37]

Making Sense of the 1967 Riot

Initial reaction to the civil disturbance in Milwaukee was swift and underscored the persistent local cleavages over race relations and civil rights. To be sure, most whites (and many black Milwaukeeans) condemned the violence. Mayor Maier called participants in the disorder "hoodlums" and chalked up the outburst to the city's urgent need for resources. Chief Breier and the county executive blamed the disturbance on "outside agitators," suggesting that the string of urban unrest across the country was the result of a "communist conspiracy." Many whites put the onus on civil rights leaders, particularly Father Groppi. "There will be no end to the riots," one letter to the mayor explained, "till the principal cause (Father Groppi) is removed." The major local media outlets and a number of prominent white civic leaders condemned the rioting, too, but also saw it as a strong indication that more vigorous official action was needed to address the problems of the inner core. Civil rights leaders and many African Americans viewed the outburst as the inevitable, if regrettable, result of building inner core frustrations and anger in the face of chronic inequality and half-hearted official action. Father Groppi, with his typical brio, likened the actions of rioters to those of Hungarian Freedom Fighters and stated that the disturbance "was not a riot at all, but young black people rebelling in frustration and anger because they had been relegated to second-class status in American society."[38]

In 1968, a study directed by Karl Flaming at the University of Wisconsin–Milwaukee painted a portrait of those who participated in the civil disturbance that challenged many of the official claims. Overall, researchers estimated that only 300 citizens took part in the violence and looting; well over 95 percent of all local African Americans did not partic-ipate in the disturbance. Overwhelmingly, rioters were young black men who lived in Milwaukee's inner core. Forty percent were migrants to the city, 35 percent were unemployed, and more than 20 percent could be clas-sified as poor. The study found no evidence of outside agitation, Commu-nist infiltration, or direct participation in the disorder by civil rights activists.[39]

That same year, the president's National Advisory Commission on Civil Disorders—commonly known as the Kerner Commission—issued its final report on the string of racial violence in the United States between 1965 and 1967 and came to similar conclusions. The report found no evidence of a conspiracy or of Communists or other outside agitators and instead argued that the unrest resulted from the "frustrated hopes" and "unfulfilled expec-tations" of inner-city residents living in deteriorating urban African Ameri-can communities. The Kerner Commission forcefully indicted white society as the primary cause of racial inequality, stating,

> Segregation and poverty have created in the racial ghetto a destructive en-vironment totally unknown to most white Americans. What white Ameri-cans have never fully understood—but what the Negro can never forget—is that white society is deeply implicated in the ghetto. White institutions created it, white institutions maintain it, and white society condones it.

The report also highlighted contentious police–community relations and widespread official inaction as significant contributing factors to urban vi-olence. It concluded with a stark warning—"Our nation is moving toward two societies, one black, one white—separate and unequal"—and called for massive governmental action, including "unprecedented levels of funding and performance," to reverse this trend. In 1968, though, it was unclear whether popular support at the local, state, or federal level existed for these prescriptions.[40]

The Kerner Commission's conclusions certainly resonated with the power of truth in Milwaukee. The city had undoubtedly been plagued by a long history of racial inequality and white complicity and was only recently waking up to that fact. Police–community relations had deteriorated to a dangerously adversarial position. The extent and duration of official inac-tion bordered on the absurd. And all the while, general conditions for black Milwaukeeans eroded to desperate levels. Hostility toward whites, distrust of political leaders, skepticism of established institutions, frustration, anger, and rage all blossomed in the inner core during the years leading up to 1967. The disorder made clear that at least a small segment of the community no longer had faith in even the militant activism of Father Groppi, the YC, or the Commandos; they turned instead to more violent and spasmodic means of expression and protest.

The big political winner coming out of the civil disturbance appeared to be Mayor Maier. For most residents outside the inner core, the story of the 1967 Milwaukee riot was a story of tragedy mainly averted, or at least contained, by the strong and decisive leadership of Henry Maier. For them, Maier dominated the experience. After all, it was the mayor's proclamation that placed the entire city under curfew, it was his request that brought troops in helmets and jeeps to patrol the streets, and it was his televised proclamation on August 8 that ended the formal state of emergency. Maier's efforts brought widespread plaudits. Hundreds of letters from Milwaukee residents and business owners poured into the mayor's office, praising his quick response to the crisis. "I am certain that if you had not acted as quickly and as decisively as you did this morning," wrote Douglas Pollack, a white resident of the city's affluent North Shore, "there would have been a great deal more chaos and suffering. By sealing off the troubled area and containing the lawless hoodlum element therein there will be far less property loss and fewer human tragedies."[41] Newspapers and television stations across the state similarly praised Maier's decisiveness, and journalists from NBC, ABC, United Press International, the Associated Press, the *New York Times*, the *Los Angeles Times*, the *Detroit News*, *U.S. News and World Report*, the *Chicago Daily News*, the *Chicago Tribune*, the *Chicago Sun-Times*, the *Chicago American*, the *Village Voice*, *Time*, and *Newsweek* wrote about him as a rising star on the national Democratic political scene.[42] Editorials, commentaries, and telegrams from civic leaders across the country, many of whom had rapped what they saw as indecisive leadership in Newark and Detroit, touted Maier's strategy as a model for other cities. *New York Times* editors wrote, "Like no other mayor of a northern city, Mr. Maier responded quickly with a tough, detailed plan for a curfew . . . It had the city transformed within hours." The *Chicago Sun Times* concurred, arguing, "Mayor Henry W. Maier views himself as a 'municipal scientist,' but behind his articulation of clinical solutions to his city's ills lies the muscle of a German general." The mayor of Charlotte, North Carolina, sent a telegram commending Maier's "foresight and judgment." Even the U.S. attorney called Mayor Maier to confer.[43]

The mayor's support was not unanimous or without question. Many inner core residents and most civil rights leaders believed that the mayor's emergency measures traded on white fear and were out of proportion to the actual threat.[44] These critics pointed out that although the state of emergency lasted for nearly ten days, the primary danger occurred during a five-hour period the first Sunday night. Moreover, they argued that the decision to impose citywide restrictions did not actually contain the impact of the disturbance but, in fact, amplified it and extended its reach into neighborhoods that would have otherwise been unaffected. This, in turn, fueled a mix of fear, guilt, and compassion among many of the city's whites.[45]

Maier used his enhanced political reputation to push forward his agenda on urban reform. "The central city of Milwaukee can no more finance the crucial problems of poverty, ignorance, disease and discrimination with the property taxes of relatively poor people," he argued, "than the city of Milwaukee can finance sending a man to the moon." The answer to chronic urban problems was not "a bigger and better billy-club," according to Maier, but greater urban–suburban cooperation and shared revenues at the federal, state, and local levels. To achieve this goal, he told a group of 100 local business leaders that he would wage a "Crusade for Resources." Over the next several weeks, Mayor Maier met with the Common Council, the county executive, Governor Warren Knowles, and sympathetic state legislators and even ran a full-page ad in the *New York Times,* paid for by Milwaukee religious leaders, pleading for increased support to central cities.[46] Although Maier's Crusade for Resources was met with a generally warm response from other civic leaders, not all were optimistic about its prospects. "So far in Madison," one WITI-TV editorial griped, "about all [that has] been promised [by Mayor Maier] are 'studies.' In most of the suburbs . . . he's received only hostility. Few outside of Milwaukee have shown any genuine interest or concern in the city's needs."[47]

The most forceful challenge to Mayor Maier's crusade came from Common View, an ad hoc group of approximately 100 black leaders representing a "broad cross-section of the Black community in Milwaukee," including Wesley Scott of the Urban League, Walter Hoard of the MNAACP, Fred Bronson of the YC, Father Groppi, Walter Jones of the *Star,* Melvin Hall of the SDC, Reverend Lucius Walker of the Northcott Neighborhood House, and Ray Alexander of the Northside Planning and Development Council. The group was "concerned about the long local history of smoldering racial conflicts, the immediate local crisis, and programmatic solutions to our problems." They issued a withering five-page indictment of city officials. "In the midst of the present confrontation," the statement read, "the white power structure continues to ignore the need for meaningful communication with the black community. The structure also refuses to recognize the long time deep-rooted circumstances and inherent consequences of not establishing plans and programs to resolve the situation." The report singled out Mayor Maier and his War on Prejudice as "superficial." It called the city administration "segregated" and "paternalistic" and claimed that white leaders had "circumvented the constant needs for equality of opportunity." The Common View statement also outlined the problems facing inner core residents in education, housing, and police–community relations. They termed Milwaukee's public schools "grossly inadequate" and complained that urban renewal really meant "black removal." The statement ended by laying blame for the recent disturbance squarely at the feet of city officials: "The paternalistic attitude of the white power structure, in 'knowing' all of the answers as to what is best for the black community has been the major contributing factor which led to the present confrontation . . . Black people want control of their community."[48]

The mayor countered by attacking "so-called civil rights leaders" for their militant rhetoric and direct action strategy, implying that they had contributed to, and perhaps even caused, the unrest. In a controversial move, Maier sought to blunt Common View's criticism by convening forty-seven local African Americans, including ministers, union stewards, bartenders, barbers, and businessmen, who supported his approach. Members of Common View complained that the move was an attempt to dictate African American leadership in Milwaukee. Reverend Lucious Walker told an audience in Pewaukee that the mayor's group was "not in touch" with the African American community and that Maier "wants to use them as a substitute for the real leaders." Others claimed that the mayor was making his choices based on stereotypical thinking in an effort to divide the black community. When asked about the makeup of the mayor's group, one civil rights leader derisively added, ". . . and porters, swampers and janitors." At the first meeting, Maier's group voted 44–3 to form a biracial council in conjunction with the Greater Milwaukee Conference on Religion and Race "to rise up in a time of crisis to meet the challenge." The commission, the mayor said, "will not be White Power. It will not be Black Power. It will be the power of the people." In response, a contemptuous Corneff Taylor remarked, "[Mayor Maier]'s up to his old tricks of appointing a new committee whenever he finds himself in a situation that needs immediate attention."[49]

The next day, Mayor Maier met with the Interdenominational Ministers Alliance, fifty-eight moderate-to-conservative African American clergymen with long-standing ties to the mayor's office. Former Commando Richard Green remembered,

> There weren't many ministers that we expected to get support from because they came from the old school. The mayor at that time had a group of black ministers who reported directly to [him] and he controlled that particular group and it was their responsibility to talk to their congregation and keep them in line. Then, after it [the open housing demonstrations] became a national thing and people were asking, "Where are your black leaders? Where are all of your black preachers?" Slowly but surely, they began to come in to give a little support.

Prentice McKinney concurred, stating, "[Most black ministers] were invested in the system just like the others [that is, the established African American leadership]." During the all-day conference, the mayor and clergymen hammered out a thirty-nine-point program of action against Milwaukee's racial problems. Whereas the Common View proposals focused on actions that the mayor could take, the "Statement of How (Milwaukee's Marshall Plan)" concentrated on measures that could be taken by other levels of government—the Common Council, the state of Wisconsin, and the federal government. As Frank Aukofer noted, "Most of the points led off with the words, 'That the mayor seek,' 'That the county furnish,' 'That there be a federal program,' 'That the state establish.'" Father Groppi agreed that action was necessary at all levels of government but complained that the mayor's plan emphasized what Maier could not do, instead of what he could do.[50]

In the end, what did the civil disturbance mean for race relations and civil rights insurgency in Milwaukee? Most immediately, it dramatically highlighted the problems of the inner core for local and national audiences; it exposed Milwaukee's racial inequality and forced it into the public discourse, a discourse that had, to date, largely ignored, minimized, dismissed, or explained away discrimination against black people in the city. In effect, the disturbance was a form of unorganized, semiconscious political expression. Even those who did not take part could understand the circumstances out of which those sentiments grew. The chaos carried many voices to those who would listen. It spoke in alternating tones of pain and disillusionment, frustration and disaffection, alienation and rage, mockery, catharsis, and even nihilistic delight. It raised a defiant protest against the dehumanizing stew of police harassment, persistent urban poverty, segregated schools, and physical confinement. It made clear that a growing number of inner core residents were unwilling to wait any longer for commissions and study groups, hearings and official protocols. It was at once a desperate plea for help and a boisterous rejection of business as usual.

The civil disorder also boosted Mayor Maier's national image and helped him consolidate local political power. Although the arrest of Father Groppi and members of the YC did nothing to cultivate a spirit of cooperation and trust between city officials and civil rights leaders, Maier had proven himself capable of handling large-scale urban unrest, a trait that appealed to a growing number of white residents fearful that the outbreak of racial violence was only a beginning, not an end. As an indication of the mayor's broad base of support, Milwaukeeans reelected him to a third term in 1968, in which he won over 80 percent of the total vote—the largest landslide in the city's storied political history. A significant portion of that unprecedented support came from white Milwaukeeans who perceived the mayor as a defender of their rights and interests against those of encroaching African Americans.

Undoubtedly, the civil disturbance contributed significantly to the ongoing awakening of Milwaukee whites, willing or not, to the concentrated problems of the inner core. The disorder served grim notice that in Milwaukee's center there resided volatile elements that were beyond white control and that demanded attention to stave off worse violence. In the process, the unrest gave lie to the fact that Milwaukee was somehow unique or different from other large American cities. Milwaukee had officially and undeniably taken its place alongside dozens of other deteriorating urban centers. The story of Milwaukee was increasingly the story of America. Some white residents responded to this challenge by calling for greater civic action through urban renewal, nondiscrimination, and social welfare policies. Others stressed the individual responsibility of those involved in the disorder and sought protection and containment from established civic leaders through increased policing and law enforcement. A small number moved to protect their families and property directly by arming themselves and organizing their neighbors. In the coming months, thousands would take to the streets to defend their neighborhoods, sometimes violently, from what they saw as a growing African American threat.

Father Groppi, the YC, and the Commandos viewed the disturbance as further evidence that dramatic, confrontational action—in this case, a civil disturbance—was the most effective, and perhaps only, means to compel white authorities to confront racial discrimination and to act in a meaningful way to overcome it. They realized that it was the present reality and future threat of social disorder and racial violence, the fear that "the problems of the inner core" were no longer geographically contained, which animated white residents and civic leaders. Recent history, though, had taught local civil rights activists that official promises and interracial commissions rarely brought concrete change. For that, they believed, the Movement would need to continue to pressure local officials and institutions. On August 24, 1967, just two weeks after Milwaukee's civil disorder, the YC announced that it intended to extend its open housing crusade by marching across the city, including into the primarily white working-class South Side.

Yet, even though the disturbance thrust inner core suffering into the public spotlight and created new opportunities for civil rights activism, it also came with costs and new challenges for the Movement. Unlike in the South, where images of racist whites attacking nonviolent civil rights activists stirred the conscience of the nation by exposing the depth and depravity of the Jim Crow system, thereby placing the Movement on high moral ground, in the urban North and West, the images were of poor inner-city residents burning and looting their own neighborhoods. These menacing, decontextualized pictures of black lawlessness, in turn, cast white police officers, firemen, National Guard troops, and city officials in the heroic role, battling to regain control and reestablish social order against nameless, rampaging black people. In this way, the disturbance reaffirmed popular notions about African American criminality and violence and fueled the white reaction against civil rights, generally. To the extent that the Movement was linked, correctly or incorrectly, directly or indirectly, with these more volatile elements of the inner core, the moral clarity of the northern Movement grew murky in white minds. Increasingly, civil rights activists had to contend with this intensifying popular white resistance. These trends culminated, dramatically, over the coming months when hundreds of open housing advocates marched headlong into a cauldron of white reaction on Milwaukee's South Side.

— 7 —

The Struggle for Open Housing

On August 13, 1967, just a few days after Mayor Maier lifted the citywide curfew in Milwaukee, a coalition of civil rights organizations and liberal clergymen held a tribute dinner for Father Groppi to honor the young priest's contribution to the local struggle for racial justice. Speaking to reporters after this conspicuous display of public solidarity, Monsignor John Egan called Groppi "a witness to the truth." Father Egan conceded that Groppi's voice could be, at times, "a little strident and shrill," but added, "the problems that are facing the poor and those who are dispossessed . . . is a strident voice, too, and it is being heard all over the world. Father Groppi is echoing that voice."[1]

Eleven days later, Father Groppi, the NAACP Youth Council (YC), and the Commandos made more noise when they announced that they would march into the overwhelmingly white, working-class South Side; demonstrators would walk from St. Boniface to Kosciuszko Park, located several blocks from the south end of the Sixteenth Street Viaduct. There, they planned to announce their "Declaration of Open Housing," unofficially claiming into law what the Common Council refused. YC representatives promised that the upcoming march would mark the start of a sustained direct action campaign.[2]

The day before the demonstration, the *Milwaukee Journal* printed a map detailing the march route. On Monday, August 28, about 100 civil rights activists gathered at St. Boniface for a rally. Demonstrators then set out across the Menomonee River Valley, "a natural boundary," according to the *Milwaukee Sentinel,* "that has unnaturally kept most minority groups out of South Side neighborhoods." A small group of South Side whites from Father Groppi's old church, St. Veronica, met demonstrators at the north end of the bridge with signs that read "Welcome." The half-mile walk across the viaduct was uneventful, but as the group approached the other side, they began to hear the sound of the more than 3,000 local whites who had come out to observe and oppose the open housing advocates. Many were simply curious but some held signs that read "Polish Power" and "A Good Groppi Is a Dead Groppi." Others yelled, "Niggers go home!"; "Go back to Africa!"; and "Sieg Heil." Soon, flying stones, bottles, garbage, and chunks of wood accompanied the chants and signs. At a number of intersections, Milwaukee police officers formed a wedge to get marchers through the throngs. An estimated 5,000 angry white locals awaited demonstrators in Kosciuszko Park, resulting in an outburst of scuffling. The violence injured twenty-two people, and the police arrested nine. As the civil rights activists left, Father Groppi promised that they would not only return the follow day but would continue to march until the Common Council enacted an open housing measure. The YC and its allies made good on their promise, marching for 200 consecutive nights in a campaign that became a national rallying point for fair housing advocates.[3]

The struggle for racial justice in Milwaukee had been gathering strength since its fitful start in 1958 and now entered a dramatic phase. The open housing campaign, which took on the most volatile issue in northern race relations, signaled the climax of civil rights insurgency in the city. It brought the Milwaukee Movement to nationwide attention and made Father Groppi a nationally recognized civil rights leader. The young activists of the YC and Commandos showed that a sustained, militant, direct action campaign could be carried out in the urban North without degenerating into anarchic violence or racial separatism. But it was a long struggle.

Housing the American Dream

Throughout American history, private property and homeownership have been at the core of an evolving conception of the American Dream. The nation's founding documents enshrined private property and individual liberty as key pillars of American democratic republicanism. Until the end of the nineteenth century, a variation of Thomas Jefferson's "agrarian ideal"— which envisioned a democratic nation of independent and autonomous small landowners—dominated the American view of the good life. The opening of the West to homesteaders by the federal government deepened this commitment to private property and independent homeownership.

With urbanization, homeownership and a strong sense of neighborhood—usually organized around ethnicity and religion—came to replace the agrarian ideal at the center of the American Dream. Suburbanization, in large part, was fueled by the desire of middle-class and affluent Americans to achieve this conception of the good life. Historian Stephen Grant Meyer has pointed out that pervasive phrases like "Home sweet home," "There's no place like home," "A man's home is his castle," "Good fences make good neighbors," and "not in my backyard" underscore the tremendous significance of homeownership in American culture.[4]

New Deal programs and political idealism further solidified housing as a central feature of the reformulated postwar American Dream. To middle- and working-class citizens, these policies held forth the promise of economic security through private homeownership. President Franklin Roosevelt frequently spoke of the ideal of a nation of free homeowners in his speeches, and he included the right to a decent home in his 1944 "Second Bill of Rights." This idealism resonated with urban white ethnics who had long struggled to buy homes in the city without the benefit of federally backed mortgages and loans. The Home Owners Loan Corporation, the Federal Housing Administration, and the G.I. Bill put homeownership within the grasp of thousands of middle-class and working-class Americans, often for the first time. For many, a home became the only significant asset that they owned; it represented real property and thus economic stability. Most viewed these new federal benefits as entitlements earned through hard work and good citizenship. According to Thomas Sugrue, "Homeowners' rights were . . . a reward for sacrifice and duty." Indeed, throughout the postwar era, many U.S. policy makers saw private homeownership as a key ingredient to American national security as well as to personal self-sufficiency. In Roosevelt's formulation, "A nation of homeowners is unconquerable."[5]

Most white Americans believed that homeownership was grounded in an implicit set of property rights: the right of free association, to live where and among whom you choose; the right of choice, to be free to dispose of property in any way the owner sees fit; and the right of peace and tranquility, to avoid criminal behavior, urban decay, noise, traffic, and other hazards of urban living. Federal loan and mortgage policies reflected these assumptions by promoting racially homogenous neighborhoods and suburbanization at the expense of urban redevelopment and integration.

Although many black people no doubt also subscribed to this postwar conception of the American Dream, homeownership and open access to housing bore a special historical resonance for African Americans. During slavery, black people, themselves defined as "chattel," were denied property rights. The unfulfilled promise of "forty acres and a mule" during Reconstruction condemned tens of thousands of African Americans (as well as an increasing number of poor, rural white people) to landless poverty well into the twentieth century. In urban America, black people faced not only residential segregation but also significant barriers to homeownership. For example, in 1960, only 3 percent of Milwaukee African Americans owned their own homes.

Many white residents supported African American homeowning rights as long as blacks remained a significant urban minority limited to their own distinct neighborhood. As the black population in Milwaukee surged during the 1950s, many white residents came to view the expanding African American inner core as a threat. Some did not believe that black people had earned the new entitlements in the same way whites had. Others associated African Americans with declining property values.[6] Still more thought black rights came at the expense of white rights and that public policy seemed increasingly at odds with white working-class interests.

As the northern struggles for racial justice accelerated during the mid-1960s, open housing emerged as the most divisive and often violent civil rights issue in the urban North. A 1961 report by the National Commission on Race and Housing summarized the problem: "There are probably not fewer than twenty-seven million Americans, or nearly one-sixth of the national population, whose opportunities to live in neighborhoods of their choice are in some degree restricted because of their race, color or ethnic attachments."[7] The upsurge in popular agitation pushed housing onto the national civil rights agenda. By 1965, President Johnson became convinced that the problem of racial discrimination in housing was so invidious and pervasive that legislation was required to root it out. He sought to capitalize on his hard-won successes in the 1964 Civil Rights Act and the 1965 Voting Rights Act, as well as the growing urban unrest, to push for a federal open housing law as the centerpiece to the 1966 Civil Rights Act, but legislators, backed by powerful housing and real estate lobbies, defeated the measure. A disappointed Martin Luther King Jr. suggested that the demise of the legislation "surely heralded darker days for this social era of discontent."[8]

The failure of federal legislators to come up with a strong open housing bill spurred a series of local open housing campaigns in the urban North between 1966 and 1968. A number of these efforts resulted in significant racial conflict. In addition, the failure of federal legislation and the devolution of the issue to states and localities pit city against suburb, local government against state government. A federal measure would have had the virtue of setting a national standard to which all states and localities had to adhere, thus eliminating the fractured conflicts that erupted between the different layers of government.

From the first, housing discrimination was a significant issue for Milwaukee African Americans. Whereas some argued that black Milwaukeeans were steadily making economic progress on the back of the industrial economy, housing segregation appeared intractable. The inequality was self-evident in the local landscape, and it literally shaped most black people's experience. Restrictive covenants, biased loan and mortgage policies, discriminatory real estate practices, social custom, and choice ensured the creation and perpetuation of the inner core. Overcrowding and dilapidation followed its slow north and westward expansion throughout the late 1950s and 1960s. Yet, according to Stephen Meyer, official policies did "play a role in maintaining the dual housing market . . . [but] the weight of the evidence demonstrates that they reflected a popular unwillingness on the part of whites to have African Americans living in their midst."[9] As Milwaukee's black population shot up, pressing at the boundaries of the core, and the urban crisis deepened, housing inequality became more acute, and residential segregation became nearly total. A national report in 1965 revealed that Milwaukee suffered from the lowest "Suburban Negro Ratio" in the United States; 98 percent of all local African Americans lived in the central city—the largest concentration in the nation.[10]

Although social custom and various institutional mechanisms usually maintained residential segregation without conflict, occasionally incidents did occur. In 1949, a group of more than 100 angry white residents at the Greenfield trailer camp, on the city's West Side, mobilized to oppose the presence of Albert J. Sanders, an African American navy veteran, and his family. According to Wisconsin state historian William Thompson,

> many of them signed a petition declaring that "the Negro should not be permitted in a white camp." The crowd then moved to the Sanders' trailer, threatening: "If you stay here, we'll break up your car. We'll hurt you and your wife and your children, too." Although sheriff's deputies made it clear they would protect him and his family, and other residents encouraged him to stay, Sanders left the camp with his family for the night.

In a more recent incident, in 1963, Matthew Anthony, a black arc welder, and his family returned from church to their new home in a predominantly white West Side neighborhood to find a flaming cross on their front lawn. A seventeen-year-old white adolescent confessed that he and four other neighborhood youths had committed the act after overhearing a group of white adults express indignation over the presence of an African American family in the neighborhood. White anxiety and reaction over the perceived "threat" posed by African Americans grew along with the black population during the 1950s and 1960s.[11]

By the early 1960s, Milwaukee civil rights advocates had begun to push housing onto the public agenda. In 1960, the Wisconsin NAACP drafted model open housing legislation aimed at the state legislature. That same year, Lloyd Barbee and Tom Jacobson led a fourteen-day sit-in at the state capitol in Madison to force a "human rights" bill, including a strong fair housing provision, out of committee. Liberal and civil rights organizations publicized housing discrimination and circulated "Good Neighbor Pledges" to Milwaukee homeowners. The Milwaukee Urban League and the Milwaukee NAACP (MNAACP) worked to field housing complaints and to place African Americans in available housing on a case-by-case basis. State legislative activity on open housing spurred opposition from a string of new property owners associations dedicated to defending "property owners' rights" against "forced housing." Hundreds of citizens filled out "stop forced housing legislation" cards and returned them to their representatives. John Carroll, president of "The Citizen," an organization dedicated to "better government," took to the television airwaves to oppose "any open occupancy bill that seeks to destroy my personal freedom and abolish private property under the guise of 'civil rights.'" "Under the 'forced' occupancy bill," Carroll claimed, "the state controls to whom you may rent your home; the state controls to whom you can sell your home; and, in effect, controls who may play in your yard with your children." In 1963, the Milwaukee Board of Realtors endorsed the National Association of Real Estate Board's "Property Owners' Bill of Rights" and distributed it widely in the city, including as a full-page ad in local newspapers. "The erosion of these freedoms," the realtors warned, "will destroy the free enterprising, individual American." In the 1963 and 1964 legislative sessions, state representatives rejected various legislative measures that banned discrimination in the sale, rental, or financing of private housing.[12]

Undaunted, Assemblyman Barbee and other civil rights advocates reintroduced a strong open housing bill in 1965. The real estate industry and

South Side representatives again led strong opposition to the measure. In April, the Milwaukee Board of Realtors paid for a full-page advertisement in the *Journal* opposing all "forced housing legislation." In response, civil rights advocates placed more than 450 personal ads in the newspaper demonstrating popular support for the open housing law and urging passage of the bill. In Madison, 300 people attended a march and rally at the state capitol to support open housing.[13]

On December 3, the Wisconsin legislature finally enacted a bipartisan compromise measure supported by Governor Warren Knowles. The new statewide open housing law was limited to buildings with five or more units—30 percent of the total housing units in the state—and exempted the vast majority of inner core housing. In addition, legislators granted enforcement powers for the law to the State Industrial Commission, which had faced past criticism from civil rights advocates. Even so, WTMJ-TV editorialists called the bill "a fair, middle of the road approach in attempting to solve a nagging problem of the state's bigger cities, mainly Milwaukee." Despite the law's shortcomings, many open housing activists viewed the bill as a beginning. Because state officials would not go further, however, Milwaukee open housing advocates moved their fight to the local level.[14]

Vel Phillips's Lonely Fight for Open Housing

In Milwaukee, Alderwoman Vel Phillips led the legislative charge to enact a comprehensive, citywide open housing ordinance. Born in 1924, Velvalea Rodgers grew up in relatively secure surroundings on North Eighth Street. Rodgers's mother taught her and her two sisters middle-class propriety rooted in the church, and her father, a small business owner, taught her the virtue of self-help and race pride. In high school, the hard-working Rodgers won a college scholarship during a speech contest and attended Howard University. Howard introduced Rodgers to a much broader spectrum of African American life. While in Washington, D.C., she learned from esteemed black scholars, including E. Franklin Frazier, Alaine Locke, and Howard Thurman, but also confronted Jim Crow directly for the first time. In 1951, Rodgers became the first African American woman to earn a law degree from the University of Wisconsin–Madison, where she met her husband, Dale Phillips, a fellow law student. After law school, the couple moved to Milwaukee, where they both played a prominent role in the MNAACP.[15]

During the mid-1950s, Vel Phillips worked for the League of Women Voters, registering black voters throughout the inner core. These door-to-door visits brought the young lawyer into stark contact with the poverty and depravation that many Milwaukee African Americans endured; dilapidated housing conditions left a particularly deep impression on her. Phillips credited her work with the League of Women Voters for influencing her decision to run for a seat on the Common Council and place housing at the center of her legislative agenda.

Personal experience also fueled her concern for the issue. When Dale and Vel Phillips attempted to move from their inner core home on Walnut Street, they had a difficult time finding a white property owner willing to sell to them. Phillips explained, "People then could just say, 'We don't rent to you people. We don't sell to you people.'" Even sports icon Henry Aaron, a friend of the Phillipses, encountered difficulty buying a house beyond the boundaries of the core. "He suffered terribly," Phillips recalled.[16]

In 1956, a long overdue redistricting plan created new political possibilities for African Americans in Milwaukee. The plan carved out a new ward—the Second Ward—that was situated primarily within the inner core. Although the new district contained a significant concentration of black voters, it was still necessary for candidates to garner a portion of the white vote to earn a majority. With the quiet support of traditional black leaders, including her peers at the MNAACP, Phillips decided to seek the open Second Ward Common Council seat.

As a measure of the importance of race and gender politics at the time, Phillips felt compelled to shape her campaign to obscure her identity. She did not print photos on any of her campaign materials and legally changed her name to Vel—from the more feminine Velvalea—so that it could appear on the ballot. Phillips also made few public appearances, relying instead on the power of a good campaign organization, and hid the news that she was pregnant until after election day. As the lone woman and the only African American on the council, many saw Vel Phillips as the representative of all minorities in Milwaukee.

Alderwoman Phillips initially worked to establish more public housing projects in Milwaukee, but these efforts stalled in the face of white opposition, prompting her to turn her attention to the statewide struggle for open housing legislation. Phillips introduced a strong citywide open housing ordinance in the Common Council four separate times between 1962 and 1967.

The measure, which covered the sale, lease, and rental of most property in the city, went down in defeat each time by a vote of 18–1, with Phillips casting the lone supportive vote. "It was embarrassing," Phillips remembered years later. "I'd come home and practically cry myself asleep. I never got any support."[17]

The unanimous opposition to Phillips's ordinance suggested the significant obstacles facing open housing advocates in Milwaukee. Some public officials argued that residential segregation was not the result of racial discrimination but of the inability of African Americans to afford higher rents and mortgages. To be sure, economic inequalities prohibited most African Americans from more affluent neighborhoods, and there were even some civil rights advocates who believed that employment and economic issues should be the leading issue of the movement. Yet, as early as 1952, a report from the mayor's Commission on Human Rights concluded that segregation in Milwaukee was "widely and openly practiced." That report, and another in 1966, found evidence of "block-busting" among Milwaukee realtors.[18] Block-busting refers to a practice whereby realtors sell homes to one or two pioneering African American families in white neighborhoods located on the fringes of segregated black neighborhoods at an inflated price. The realtors would then turn around and encourage the white homeowners to sell their homes at a loss because, they suggested, the presence of African Americans would bring down property values. These newly available "white properties" were then sold to more African American families over the market value. In addition to lining the pockets of real estate agents, the practice deepened racial animosities, fueled white flight, and fostered segregation. Mortgage and lending practices as well as widespread popular opposition to integration in many white neighborhoods compounded the difficulty. Moreover, it was simply not politically sensible for white council members or the mayor to support open housing when popular opposition among white Milwaukeeans ran so high. Opponents of open housing were given cover by City Attorney John Fleming's opinion that a local ordinance intruded on the jurisdiction of the state and by Mayor Maier's continued insistence on a countywide law.[19]

There were more indirect obstacles to open housing advocates' efforts, too. Between 1963 and late 1965, the main action on open housing in Wisconsin remained at the capitol building in Madison; no local political will existed because politicians and city leaders continually deferred to state action. Closer to home, the Fred Lins controversy, the school desegregation campaign, the EC protest, and police–community relations successively held center stage in the struggle for civil rights. Events in Birmingham, at the March on Washington, and in Selma further diverted local civil rights energies to pressing national affairs. In this broader context, Phillips's open housing crusade, though supported by most liberal and civil rights organizations, remained one issue among many.

By 1967, open housing had built momentum nationally and locally. The failure of the federal Civil Rights Act of 1966 brought out simmering racial divisions within the Democratic Party. The widespread urban violence of 1967, much of which had grown out of the general squalor of segregated black communities, put the open housing issue in a different context, prompting legislators and activists to again push for a law. "One of the burning frustrations Negro residents carry with them in city ghettos," the NAACP's Roy Wilkins proclaimed, is "the knowledge that even if they want to and have the means to do so, very often they cannot get out."[20] The Kerner Commission, which released its report on civil disturbances in March 1968, indicted housing discrimination as a major reason behind African American frustration, racial strife, and urban violence.

Open housing activists in dozens of northern cities took to the streets during the mid-1960s to pressure state legislatures and city councils to pass open housing laws. The most visible and violent campaign took place in Chicago, a short hour-and-a-half drive from Milwaukee down the shores of Lake Michigan. There, in 1965 and 1966, a contentious and fragmented coalition of local civil rights organizations and Martin Luther King Jr.'s Southern Christian Leadership Conference (SCLC)—"the Chicago Freedom Movement"—led a series of open housing marches through several white working-class neighborhoods. To many, the demonstrations symbolized King's attempt to prove that his brand of confrontational nonviolent direct action could work in the urban North. The campaign attracted national media attention when thousands of angry white counterdemonstrators pelted nonviolent demonstrators with a hail of bottles, rocks, cherry bombs, and racist epithets. The Chicago Freedom Movement degenerated into internal bickering among local and national civil rights leaders, resulting in a hasty retreat from the city by King and the SCLC after they negotiated a severely compromised agreement with city officials. Some saw the failure of the Chicago open housing campaign as a repudiation of King and the SCLC's nonviolent strategy in the North. In fact, it was farther up the shores of Lake Michigan, in Milwaukee, where many said that the interracial, nonviolent, and church-based Movement made its "last stand."[21]

Crossing Milwaukee's "Mason-Dixon Line"

In Milwaukee, as the school desegregation and EC campaigns subsided and police–community relations simmered, Father Groppi and the YC, like their allies in cities across the North, shifted their attention to open housing. As early as October 14, 1966, Father Groppi announced that the YC would next target open housing. "We think we have exhausted the demonstrations against the school board and the Eagles Club," he told a group of clergymen in Appleton. "Next we are going to protest in the area of Negro housing."[22]

Ronald Britton, a recent Vietnam veteran and inner core resident, first drew the YC's attention to the issue. Shortly before Christmas, Britton, his wife, and child were told by a white property owner along the fringe of the inner core that she would not rent to them. "What would the neighbors think?" she asked. The ex-Marine brought the case to Father Groppi, who saw it as "Jesus, Mary and Joseph being told there was no room at the inn." Groppi referred the issue to the YC, which decided to get involved. In keeping with the season, their first move was to serenade the racist landlord with Christmas carols outside her duplex.[23]

Father Groppi also telephoned Vel Phillips and invited the alderwoman to St. Boniface to discuss the YC's plans. "He asked me if I would mind having some help," Phillips remembered, "and I said of course not." For the YC, the move represented an attempt to coordinate its direct action campaign with the legislative process. "She was our mouthpiece," Squire Austin recalled, "She was a real asset. She was in the right position to make things work." An alliance with Phillips also lent a degree of official sanction to the YC's protest. For the alderwoman, it was clear that she had reached an impasse within the council; the previous five years had brought only frustration. In order for her fellow council members to act, the political dynamics needed to be altered. Nonviolent direct action held out that possibility. By exerting external popular pressure on aldermen who had opposed the open housing measure, the legislative process might respond.[24]

The embrace of direct action by Alderwoman Phillips was significant. Vel and Dale Phillips were important members of the traditional African American leadership in Milwaukee. As a lawyer, legislator, and prominent member of the MNAACP brought up in a family culture that emphasized middle-class propriety, Vel Phillips preferred a more "dignified" and deliberate approach to social change through established institutions. She had spent her professional career working through the courts and the Common Council to achieve racial equality. She had registered voters, attended fundraisers, worked on campaigns, brought suit, circulated petitions, and run for office. In the past, she and other members of the MNAACP leadership had been skittish about direct action. But once Phillips publicly supported the marches, she then felt compelled to participate. "They were fighting for my bill," she remembered. "I felt like I had to go."[25]

In March 1967, YC members picketed Mayor Maier's home to protest a rent increase at the Parklawn housing project. In a new twist, as fifteen people marched, sang, and chanted outside, six demonstrators entered the mayor's apartment complex in an attempt to talk to him directly. Maier said that the tactic was evidence of the YC's "lust for headlines." After the Common Council again voted down an open housing ordinance in June, Father Groppi promised more demonstrations during the upcoming summer and warned, "Either we get what we want or we turn this city upside down."[26]

From late June through late July, the YC and Commandos targeted six North Side aldermen who had opposed the open housing ordinance despite the fact that they represented portions of the inner core. On June 19, an interracial group of sixty to eighty-five young people rallied at St. Boniface Church and then marched to Alderman Martin Schreiber's home on West Auer Avenue, chanting "We want Black Power" and singing freedom songs. Signs read, "Down with Slum Landlords" and "We Want a 'Home Sweet Home' Too." As the group marched in front of the home, four YC and Commando representatives—YC President Fred Bronson, Prentice McKinney, James Pierce, and Lawrence Friend—rang Schreiber's bell. The alderman invited the delegation inside to discuss the issue. During the half-hour meeting, Schreiber told the open housing advocates that he opposed the city ordinance because the state of Wisconsin already had a law covering the issue. A frustrated Bronson said afterward, "We're going to march all over the city to get that bill passed. If it takes all summer, all right!" Aldermen Francis Dineen, Eugene Woeher, James Maslowski, Robert Ertl, and Robert Dwyer, as well as City Attorney Fleming, faced similar protests, but each maintained his opposition.[27]

Reaction to the initial phase of the open housing campaign was mild. The two daily newspapers buried coverage of the story far from the front page while editors at the *Milwaukee Star* wrote that the aldermen's "unacceptable excuses for continued fair housing opposition show them to be merely phony liberals, unqualified to representing Negro citizens" and commended the YC "for helping our Aldermen display their true feelings." Vel Phillips and Assemblyman Lloyd Barbee encouraged civil rights activists at pre-march rallies; Father Groppi and the YC vowed to press on. Alderman Maslowski, on the other hand, called the YC protests "harassment," while his colleague, Robert Dwyer, argued that housing segregation in Milwaukee could be solved only through "voluntary cooperation between people of goodwill." In a more ominous sign of things to come, on July 11, an irritated crowd of more than 100 white residents gathered across the street from Maslowski's home to taunt, jeer, and threaten civil rights demonstrators.[28]

The following weekend, civil order broke down in the heart of the inner core's commercial district. The 1967 Milwaukee riot dramatically changed the local political and social context for open housing advocates. Suddenly, the inner core had forced its way into the public consciousness. As Mayor Maier sought support from civic leaders for his "39 Points" and his "Crusade for Resources," Father Groppi, the YC, and the Commandos plotted a dramatic new course for their open housing campaign. Targeting North Side aldermen had not provoked significant media attention or elicited white reaction as the civil rights activists had wanted. They moved to seize the postriot moment and keep pressure on city officials by expanding their direct action campaign into the South Side.

But why head into the South Side? In part, the decision was symbolic. The Menominee River Valley, often referred to as the city's "Mason-Dixon line," powerfully signified Milwaukee's racial divide. Crossing that threshold poked through an important physical and psychological boundary. Few black Milwaukeeans were anxious to actually move to the white working class neighborhoods of the South Side, but most did not want to be told they could not solely because of their race. In effect, the decision to march across the Sixteenth Street viaduct was a direct challenge to the physical confinement of African Americans in the city and to the policy of racial containment. Father Groppi acknowledged this dynamic when he told reporters, "We are coming off the reservation."[29]

There were also practical reasons for crossing the Sixteenth Street Viaduct and heading toward Kosciuszko Park. The South Side was a working-class area of the city and thus affordable to many African Americans. The more affluent North Shore suburbs and many West or far South Side neighborhoods remained out of the economic range of most local black residents, an illustration of the interconnections between economic inequality and racial segregation.

The choice to march into white working-class neighborhoods was also an act of defiance. In the weeks leading up to the announcement, the YC office received a string of threatening phone calls from "Polish bigots" suggesting that African Americans should be confined to the inner core. A sarcastic Prentice McKinney explained to reporters,

> We got a couple of threatening telephone calls saying that if we march on the South Side we're going to march in blood. And I thought it was an open city. Everybody says Milwaukee's an open city and you can walk any place you please, but it seems like that 16th Street Viaduct is the "Mason Dixon Line" so now we're going to march across that and walk around on the South Side a little bit and go out to [Kosciusko Park] and have a little Black Power picnic out there and see what the people out there think about it, especially that Mayor Maier.

When asked if the march was planned as retaliation for the calls, McKinney shot back with a cocked grin, "No, we always planned on marching on the South Side and seeing what real grass looks like and nice houses and stuff, so we're going to march out there and look at it."[30]

For many local African Americans, the issue was less about integration than it was about self-determination. As far back as 1963 Janis Carter had articulated a common sentiment among many black inner core residents:

> Living next door to white neighbors is probably the furthest thing from our minds. We wish only to live where we choose in an environment conducive with our economics. This is what whites are fighting. They are fighting to keep us huddled together in the vilest ghettos possible.
>
> Won't someone please inform them we don't give a tinker's damn about living next door to them? All we want is our constitutional right to live wherever our money affords us!

Framed in this way, Carter cast open housing as a Black Power issue, with the emphasis on freedom, autonomy, and empowerment. The argument cut to the heart of the containment policy that had historically bound African Americans to the overcrowded inner core and made clear that black residents were not seeking approval from whites for their rights.[31]

Perhaps most significantly, strategic reasons lay at the heart of the decision to head south. Even the civil disorder had not altered the political balance on the Common Council regarding housing; each time Vel Phillips introduced her ordinance, it went down to defeat, 18–1. It was obvious that only a dramatic change in the political landscape would break the impasse. Strong evidence suggested that a foray into the South Side provided the best opportunity to foster the kind of "creative tension" necessary to compel such a transformation. "The whole point of direct action was to open up negotiations where there had been no negotiations," explained Margaret Rozga. "Where there was a refusal to negotiate, direct action was a way to force people to the table." In order to compel civic leaders to the negotiating table, it was imperative to provoke a response from hostile whites. "What determined a lot of targets for us was reaction," said Prentice McKinney, "whether or not there would be a reaction . . . When we marched to the aldermen's houses, the neighbors stayed indoors. They didn't like us out there in white people's neighborhood, but there was no uproar of real hostility." By contrast, popular resistance to racial change among white working-class South Side residents was strong and could more likely be counted on to react against demonstrations. YC and Commando leaders hoped to exploit that reactionary energy within the community to flush housing discrimination into the public spotlight. According to Jesse Wade, "We knew when we went that we were walking into danger . . . and we announced that we were coming and let them [white residents] get real prepared." "We needed the exposure and the media to draw attention to why we were there," said McKinney. "We didn't march to the South Side because we wanted to buy a home . . . We needed the media to air it out to the people." Local newspapers obligingly played their role in the plan by devoting front-page coverage to the announced demonstration.[32]

Crossing over the Sixteenth Street Viaduct into the heart of working-class white Milwaukee indeed proved explosive and transformed the local campaign into a national crusade for fair housing. The massive white resistance on the South Side and the burning of the Freedom House during the first two nights of protest convulsed the city and drew the attention of media outlets across the country and around the globe. Although the YC and its allies expected stiff resistance, few anticipated the massive outpouring of racist venom displayed by thousands of local white residents. The *Journal* said that the violence was the result of "shameful bigotry," while WITI-TV editorialists labeled the incident "the ugliest display of mass hatred that has ever been witnessed in our city." The *Catholic Herald* editorial staff, who termed the chaos on the South Side of the bridge a "hate-in," also offered one of the more colorful and poetic condemnations of the white violence. They wrote, "It was as if a sharp lance had finally pierced a nasty carbuncle on the Body, Mystical and political. Suddenly, out spewed a fetid mass of hate. An estimated 13,000 white human beings behaved as if they had fled their humanity—as if they had never heard of Jesus Christ and His commandment to love. Presumably and sadly, many were Catholics. If so, they became human and Christian dropouts."[33]

The initial marches were particularly shocking for many YC members and Commandos. Squire Austin remembered those harrowing early forays across the viaduct:

> First thing, I was scared. Really scared. I went through those neighborhoods going to work . . . I didn't have any problems. But when they knew a protest march of black people was coming in formation, they were scared. I didn't know what they would do. Crossing the bridge seemed like it took forever. As we got closer and closer to National [Street], you could hear them. You could hear the echo. You could hear the chants of White Power and it was really frightening and we knew that the police weren't going to protect us. So, we cupped arm-in-arm, everybody was really snug that first time we went over, sort of like a snake winding and the closer we got the more scared I got. The initial contact we had, the first time, was a lot of glass being thrown, beer bottles . . . [The police] actually had to clear the way, get people off the streets. We couldn't march on the sidewalks anymore and had to go into the street. That's when most people got hurt.

According to Dennis McDowell, "That was like walking from the gates of heaven into the bowels of hell." Jesse Wade called the experience "frightening, really frightening," and Pamela Jo Sargent stated that she "had never seen hatred like that in my life . . . To this day I wear a scar on my forehead where I was hit by a brick."[34]

Father Groppi denounced the response from local residents as a "white riot" and criticized Mayor Maier for not calling in the National Guard. At a press conference on Wednesday, an impassioned Groppi complained,

> When we had a so-called riot here in the [inner core] . . . Mayor Maier called in the National Guard and put the entire city under a curfew. Now last night you had a riot on the South Side and the Mayor had not called in the National Guard. We nearly got killed there last night . . . What we are

asking is that the Mayor give us the same protection that he gave the white businessman here in the core when we had a disturbance a number of weeks ago.

When reporters asked whether it was wise to return to the South Side after such a violent outpouring, Groppi responded,

We're going to exercise our constitutional right to picket and protest. We have tried every means possible to bring fair housing legislation to Milwaukee, and we're going to continue to march. It is up to the government of this city and this state to see to it that we can exercise our constitutional right of freedom of speech, and we're going to exercise that regardless of the danger. We'll die for that right.[35]

Vel Phillips did not participate in the first march across the Sixteenth Street Viaduct, but after seeing the massive resistance that Father Groppi, the YC, and Commandos encountered, she decided to join the protest. Both her mother and husband opposed her participation as too dangerous, and, in fact, she regularly received hate mail and threats for her work in the Common Council. During the coming direct action campaign, a bullet shattered one of the Phillips's apartment windows and lodged in the face of their steel kitchen range, prompting the alderwoman to send her two sons to stay with relatives. Phillips herself confessed that she initially hesitated to march out of concern for the safety of her two young children but ultimately felt morally obligated to support the hundreds of young people, citizens, and clergymen who were turning out to support her legislative effort. "I can't fight the good fight as an alderman and be on hand for every demonstration," she explained, "but there are times—if you believe in the right of protest and demonstration and open occupancy—that you have to show this." The fact that the local movement remained interracial, nonviolent, and rooted in the church no doubt also facilitated Phillips's embrace of the direct action campaign. Moreover, her endorsement of the contentious campaign ensured the public support of traditional black leaders.[36]

Authorities differed on who was responsible for the racial violence on the South Side. The *Journal* wrote, "If the civil rights demonstrators led by Father James Groppi were trying to show that our community is poisoned by hate, the point has been made . . . The shameful bigotry shown by whites . . . was a rejection of everything Americans and Christians should stand for. The sight of children with their parents joining in chants of hate was enough to sicken decent people." The *Sentinel* agreed: "There's no min-imizing the shame that Milwaukee should feel at the events of two recent nights. The city has been disgraced by the show of naked hatred, which must shock those who believe in the innate tolerance of all men." The arch-bishop and Priests' Senate issued statements supporting Groppi and urging white Milwaukeeans not to confuse the young priest with the real problems, which, as they saw it, were a lack of justice and compassion for the inner core residents. Most liberal churches and organizations concurred, and a major-ity of the citizens polled by the *Journal* condemned the white violence.[37]

Most official voices also believed that the demonstrators had made their point and should not continue. Archbishop Cousins, for example, said that although the marches had "brought some reactions that are hard to con-done," further demonstrations "served little or no purpose." That same day, Mayor Maier summoned to city hall a group of thirty Milwaukee-area clergymen—including a few black ministers and several from the city's South Side—to help during the civil rights unrest. The clergymen endorsed the mayor's countywide open housing ordinance and agreed to convene the Greater Milwaukee Conference on Religion and Race to rally support for the "39 Points." Governor Knowles tried to find a group of Milwaukee busi-ness or civic leaders—perhaps We-Milwaukeeans—to mediate the dispute, but nothing came of it.[38]

Maier felt that the South Side marches squelched the chance for legisla-tive action in the wake of the riot. "There was a chance," he believed, "for a united effort to gain resources and meet the problems of the central city. However, the Groppi marches, ostensibly over a symbolic issue—central-city-only open housing—created a degree of violence and civic tension that destroyed the possibility." Maier believed that the marches hardened lines between people and races, which actually made it more difficult to solve the city's problems. Even as the mayor urged white residents to stay away from the demonstrations, he deflected the primary responsibility onto "provoca-tive marchers." He attempted to set Father Groppi apart from the issues by calling him a "man of violence." Mayor Maier also exploited the widespread misperception among white Milwaukeeans that the Commandos were vio-lent by repeatedly referring to them as "hoodlums" and "street criminals."[39]

The mayor also continued to deflect criticism toward the suburbs. "Shouldn't they have open housing where there are no Negroes?" he asked. "Wouldn't it be logical to have open housing in the suburbs to absorb some of the poor?" Another time, he explained, "I would be delighted to have central city open housing if [the suburbs] would build 50,000 low income units to help break this up and help these people." What would really help Milwaukee African Americans, the mayor claimed, was more state and federal money to stem economic decay and to rebuild urban communities across the country. Father Groppi countered, saying,

> We agree with Mayor Maier that there should be a housing ordinance on a county-wide basis. In fact, the YC may very soon be marching in some of the suburban communities that do not have fair housing legislation, but we think that the Mayor is also passing the buck. We need fair housing legislation here in the city of Milwaukee and he's always talking about the federal government, the state government and the county and he never talks about Mayor Maier and his city of Milwaukee.

Prentice McKinney added, "You gotta remember . . . Maier has to represent the city that elects him." The liberal Milwaukee Citizens for Equal Opportunity was not as gracious:

> The city should assume leadership, not avoid it. As to Mayor Maier's claim that a city ordinance would result in an "apartheid society," all of our research into the effect of city fair housing ordinances in Wisconsin and elsewhere proves this statement to be false . . . Our society is segregated now and what we need are practical solutions, not continued attempts to shift the burden of responsibility to others.[40]

Following the South Side chaos on August 28 and 29, Maier imposed a voluntary curfew and a thirty-day citywide ban on marching between 4:00 p.m. and 9:00 a.m. "Our target is not people who want to meet peacefully," he explained. "We must try to keep the extremists, who seem to want a civil war, from tearing at each other. We are trying to do all this without abridging entirely the rights to speak, to march and to parade and to demonstrate." A clearly frustrated Father Groppi told reporters, "For heaven's sake we have a white riot on the South Side for the last two nights and what did [Mayor Maier] call for, a voluntary curfew. He didn't have any voluntary curfew when a few blacks tore up part of 3rd street. That is a double standard of justice." As ACLU and MNAACP lawyers challenged the ban in court, the YC and Commandos challenged it in the street. On August 30, the group led dozens of people through city hall, then on to Mayor Maier's home, and finally to a large rally on the property of the burned-out Freedom House.[41]

The YC and Commandos viewed the fire at the Freedom House the previous night as an attack by local police. Prentice McKinney told reporters, "The fire . . . was premeditated, deliberately set by the police force. The firemen were held out deliberately by the police force . . . They don't like us down there and I guess they figured this is one way to get us out, but one house don't stop no show." Father Groppi, holding up a burned-out teargas canister and several shotgun shells, concluded, "[Police] filled the house with teargas and that's what started the fire. The police are what burned the place down." Police and fire officials consistently denied any involvement with the blaze.[42]

Milwaukee police, equipped with riot sticks, helmets, and orders to arrest any infraction of the mayor's proclamation, stood watch over the restless crowd of more than 300 that gathered outside the burned husk of the Freedom House. According to Groppi, the YC did not intend to lead a march that evening. "We merely wanted to get together to discuss our mutual problems, discuss the events of the past few days and perhaps discuss the future," he explained. When Prentice McKinney introduced Alderwoman Phillips from the steps of the Freedom House, club-wielding police moved in to disperse the crowd, which had spilled onto the sidewalk and the street, a technical violation of the mayor's proclamation. In response, open housing advocates hurled a barrage of rocks, debris, and shouts of "Nazis!" and "Gestapo!" at police. The normally composed Phillips stood on the charred Freedom House porch, events spiraling out of control, shouting, "What the hell is going on here?" Father Groppi, who had not attended the first part of the rally, walked up as police continued to break up small groups of people. After conferring with YC and Commando leaders, Groppi shouted to police, "Why didn't you tell the people here to get on the [Freedom House] property instead of beating those ladies with clubs?" He complained that Maier and Chief Breier were more willing to use force against nonviolent African Americans than against violent white counterdemonstrators on the South Side. As the priest and law enforcement officers traded barbs, the crowd again swelled to 150. Civil rights advocates attempted to reclaim their space from police through sound, alternating songs like "We Shall Not Be Moved" and "Ain't Gonna Let Nobody Turn Us Around" with chants of "We hate coppers," "We hate Maier," and "Get off the North Side, cops." Meanwhile, police darted back and forth across the street to arrest the slightest infraction; Justice Department officials stood by, watched, and took notes. After forty minutes, officers, now armed with shotguns, again descended on the crowd, this time with orders to arrest the whole group. According to one member of the Milwaukee Congress of Racial Equality (MCORE), "[the police] were not making many arrests but rather swinging those long night sticks hitting people in the head and back. It seemed as if they were more interested in punishing people, than maintaining law and order." Father Groppi and a few Commandos slipped out the back door of the Freedom House and made their way to St. Boniface, where they picked up the bus and returned to aid fleeing civil rights demonstrators. In the end, police arrested fifty-eight people around the Freedom House property that night. At a press conference the following day, Father Groppi concluded, "When people in a community cannot discuss, peacefully, the problems of that community without having the police department come up with clubs and bust open our heads, it is time for citizens that are interested in justice and rights and the American System, to stand and protest." With each passing day, the crisis in Milwaukee deepened.[43]

Marching on the Selma of the North

Despite the massive resistance by thousands of local whites and the continued confrontations with local police, Father Groppi, the YC, and the Commandos promised to press on with the campaign. "We're going to get fair housing not only for the city of Milwaukee," Groppi promised, "but we're going to get it on the national scene and it's going be this consistent type of courageous protest that's going to bring [it]." Referencing abolitionist freedom fighter Fredrick Douglass, the priest concluded, "You've got to fight for [your freedom]. You've got to struggle for it and that's what we are doing by protesting, and we're going to keep at it, and we'll keep protesting until we get what is ours."[44]

The Thursday night rally began as a fund-raising event to collect bail and fine money for demonstrators arrested at the Freedom House. As Father Groppi spoke, he became increasingly enraged by the mayor's proclamation. "We're getting tired," he said. "Every time something happens, the Mayor issues another proclamation." Groppi argued that the latest decree was aimed at the YC for "exercising our American constitutional right of free assembly." He concluded by telling the crowd of over 430 nuns, clergy, and black and white youth and adults, "Unless we are ready to die we have no business in the civil rights movement." Just then, Vel Phillips arrived and was swept onto the shoulders of several Commandos to a roaring cheer.

Father Groppi then asked the crowd if they were ready to march, and they shouted, "Yeah!"[45]

During the ensuing march through the North Side, club-swinging police again waded into the raucous demonstration, setting off another melee. Protesters smashed the window of a squad car and then tossed burning papers on the front seat. All told, Milwaukee police arrested 137 open housing advocates for violations of the mayor's ban, including Father Groppi, Alderwoman Phillips, and twenty workers from the Inter-City Development Project, the majority of them under age eighteen. Later, hundreds of angry African Americans pelted firemen as they tried to extinguish two suspicious inner core fires.[46]

On Friday, September 1, the beginning of the Labor Day holiday weekend, the Milwaukee open housing campaign began to attract national support. NAACP Field Secretary Syd Finley and regional Youth Director Bill Hardy traveled to the city to take part in another attempted rally and march. The next day, Mark Rossman, National NAACP Youth Director, arrived. More than 400 open housing supporters sang, chanted, listened, and rallied for nearly four hours while a team of attorneys drove to Madison in pursuit of a restraining order against the ban. Shortly after 10:00 p.m., a judge in the capital city denied the YC's request. Father Groppi and the YC and Commando leadership conferred and then decided to march anyway. When they did, police once more moved in to stop them. After officers slugged one Commando to the ground, several demonstrators threw bottles and stones at the police. Multiple scuffles broke out as officers attempted to arrest the throwers. The fracas resulted in nineteen injuries and fifteen arrests, including Groppi—for the second night in a row—Syd Finley, and Bill Hardy. The remaining 400 marchers staged a brief sit-in at North Division High School before riot-clad police dispersed them with their sticks. Demonstrators retreated to the supposed sanctuary of the St. Boniface parking lot, but officers pursued them onto the grounds and shot several canisters of tear gas that landed in front of the rectory and convent. Over the next several hours, nuns and parish staff administered wet towels to the stinging eyes of protesters. Some angry YC members and Commandos called for retaliation, while others condemned demonstrators who threw bottles and rocks. One demonstrator, a retired army captain, died of a heart attack.[47]

Over the long Labor Day weekend, the open housing demonstrations grew. The national NAACP put out a call to its branches to join the Milwaukee open housing demonstrations. Nationally renowned comedian and civil rights activist Dick Gregory, who had supported the school desegregation campaign two years earlier, joined the protest. Sympathizers poured into the city from across the country, particularly on weekends, and many began to call Milwaukee "the Selma of the North" because of the violence on the South Side of the Sixteenth Street Viaduct. On Saturday and Sunday, demonstrators staged at least a half-dozen long marches through Milwaukee and into two suburbs in an all-out effort to make the city a national focal point for open housing. On Saturday, Mayor Maier lifted the ban on evening marches. That afternoon, Maier toured the inner core with local and national media to trumpet the progress being made to combat urban ills while more than 1,000 integrated protestors, led by Father Groppi, the Commandos, and Dick Gregory, set off on a sixteen-mile march to city hall and then through the South Side. Although thousands of white onlookers again lined the streets south of the Sixteenth Street Viaduct, no serious incidents occurred. After the demonstration, Father Groppi told remaining open housing supporters, "When we see that fair housing bill passed and on our desk, we might consider going home for a rest." Later that night, more than 800 people marched around the North Side.[48]

On Sunday afternoon, more than 1,000 open housing supporters walked through downtown and around the North Side. That night, nearly 800 mostly black demonstrators again marched for two hours through North Side neighborhoods. On Labor Day, a diverse group of 650 open housing advocates paraded past Judge Christ Seraphim's home and around his neighborhood in suburban Shorewood, while a dozen YC members staged a sit-in at Alderman Dineen's office. At night, more than 1,300 demonstrators, in two groups—one led by Father Groppi, the other by YC President Fred Bronson and Dick Gregory—marched through the North and West sides of town, including Wauwatosa.[49]

The momentum gained over the holiday weekend carried into the work week. On Tuesday night, Dick Gregory, Father Groppi, the YC, and the Commandos led more than 500 civil rights supporters and several cars on a noisy three-hour North Side march. On Wednesday, nineteen-year-old YC leader Jean Matthews led fifty YC members in an afternoon protest through downtown. That evening, 1,000 people packed St. Boniface to hear a parade of speakers blast the mayor and Common Council for their inaction on open housing. Dick Gregory encouraged supporters to boycott Milwaukee's Schlitz brewery. Afterward, 450 demonstrators walked six miles in five hours of protest. Police arrested eleven marchers for using profanity, resisting arrest, assaulting an officer, obstructing an officer, and carrying a concealed weapon.[50]

A controversial incident took place at the mayor's office on Thursday afternoon. Twenty-five YC members, led by a cocky Prentice McKinney, staged a "sit- and lie-in" inside city hall, demanding to meet with the mayor. Before leaving the office for another inner core press tour, Maier told the protesters, most of who were middle and high school age, to stay as long as they would like. In a telegram to National NAACP Director Roy Wilkins, Maier wrote, "I have issued orders that they [protesters] are to be protected, stay as long as they like. Purpose is to show the nation their bad manners and put lie to contention of police brutality and lack of police protection." Police stood by but said that they would not act unless Maier formally complained. By 3:00 p.m., the crowd of demonstrators had swelled to seventy-five, the media had arrived, and the tenor of the protest became rowdy. Each new batch of participants drew loud applause and cheers of "Soul Brother!" and "Soul Sister!" Prentice McKinney, playing to the young protesters as well as to reporters, called the mayor a "nigger," later explaining, "a nigger is a lowdown shiftless person."[51] He blew in the faces of plastic helmeted officers, taunting one, "You look like a monkey with a banana," and calling another "an orangutan."[52] "We might bring Stokely Carmichael here and Rap Brown," one Commando warned reporters. "If Mayor Maier says something about it we're going to burn the town down." A scuffle broke out when demonstrators tried to block the entrance of several police into the room, resulting in the arrest of McKinney and four others. According to *Journal* reporter Mildred Freese, chaos ensued:

> While they watched [the police arrest McKinney and others] the teenagers sang, clapped and beat on the walls. They took coat hangers off a coat rack and used them to rip chairs, and put a hole through a window. They went through a receptionist's desk and threw the contents on the floor, ripped up paper and a dictionary and used lipstick to write on a $400 aerial photograph of the city mounted on the wall. They grabbed memos, made paper airplanes and sailed them through the office.[53]

Another reporter wrote, "They slashed and ripped expensive leather chairs, seized the office switchboard, shattered a window and plastered the walls with city promotional stickers proclaiming, 'Milwaukee—Great for Business, Great for Living' and with 'Black Power' labels. Wastebaskets were emptied and tossed about the room. Cigarette butts littered the carpets." The mayor's office estimated damage in excess of $3,000.[54]

Newspaper editors at the *Journal* called the incident "a wild outbreak of destruction," the result of "hoodlum outrage." The Journal Company's television news division, WTMJ, said that the incident was an attempt to "deliberately taunt police into action. And then again charge police brutality." The *Sentinel* called on Archbishop Cousins "to prevent a Catholic church from being used as a center for inciting civil disorder and a priest from fanning the flames of hate and violence in a horrible perversion of Christ's teachings." WITI-TV told viewers, "This is proof . . . unequivocal proof . . . of the hoodlum element that exists in Milwaukee's so-called civil rights movement." And a *New York Times* editorial claimed that the outburst "undid all the good they had previously accomplished." James Newcomb, the mayor's chief administrative officer, shifted the blame to Father Groppi. "This is not civil rights. It never was," he said.

> I wish that every clergyman and nun who has clucked sympathy for Father Groppi's poor little youngsters had been here to watch the exhibition . . . It was a display I hope everyone in urban America will see on their TV screens tonight and tomorrow. It will give them an idea of the tactics being employed by a Roman collar in Milwaukee.

Mayor Maier argued that the civil rights organization did not respect "law and order" and courted arrest because their movement was losing steam. He concluded with an appeal to liberals and to what he called the "Militant Middle." "It is about time," he said, "that the Militant Middle of our society becomes organized in such a fashion that the cries of the extremists to both the right and the left can be rejected and that the community as a whole, whites and non-whites working together, can once again proceed on the path of progress."[55]

Despite the bad press that came with the destruction at the mayor's office, momentum continued to build within the open housing campaign. Over the first few weeks of contentious protesting, open housing advocates picked up a broad range of new support. Local, state, and national liberal and civil rights organizations, as well as dozens of churches from all denominations, voiced their sympathy for the marchers and endorsed a citywide open housing ordinance in Milwaukee. Newspapers and televisions news programs across the country covered unfolding events in Milwaukee, and Father Groppi became an increasingly identifiable national civil rights leader. Some speculated that Martin Luther King Jr. and H. Rap Brown would come to town to join the protests. Although the high-profile visits never materialized, King did telegram Groppi, praising his ability to "be militant and powerful without destroying life or property." Like King in Selma, Father Groppi sent out an ecumenical call through the National Council of Churches and the National Catholic Conference for Interracial Justice for religious men and women to come to Milwaukee to bear witness to racial injustice through participation in the open housing demonstrations. Dr. David Hunter, of the National Council of Churches, argued that city officials had shown a greater unwillingness to act than in any other northern city. Bill Hardy sent out an alert to all youth and adult units to support this "historic moment" in Milwaukee. The Chicago and Minneapolis-area Catholic Inter-racial Councils put out similar calls. Much of the organizing was aimed at the coming weekend.[56]

More than 1,000 people attended a rally at St. Boniface the night of the incident at Mayor Maier's office. Jeanette Strong of Gary, Indiana, and chairperson of the regional NAACP told the crowd that she had sent a telegram to all units to join a "gigantic mass rally" at St. Boniface Church the following Sunday afternoon. Charles Evers, brother of slain Mississippi civil rights leader Medgar Evers, criticized Milwaukee's black clergy, saying, "It's a disgrace to Milwaukee that we don't have more Negro preachers out there [marching]." Several speakers exhorted open housing supporters to expand the boycott of Milwaukee breweries to include Schlitz, Pabst, Miller, and Blatz. Syd Finley, who said that NAACP branches in seven states had already passed proposals supporting the beer boycott, defended the policy: "They [that is, the brewers] represent the economic power structure of your city and they are tied in with the administration." After the rally, a diverse group of over 400 marched through the city's East Side, then again to Judge Seraphim's suburban home. At 7:30 the next morning, civil rights demonstrators in five cars clogged the exit ramps of the North-South freeway near North Avenue for a half hour, blocking hundreds of cars during rush hour traffic, in what might best be described as a "stall-in."[57]

The hard work of the YC and its allies across the country paid off. The following weekend, hundreds of civil rights supporters poured into Milwaukee to participate in open housing demonstrations. On Saturday, the thirteenth day of protests, an estimated 750 demonstrators—200 from the Chicago Catholic Inter-racial Council—marched through jeers and taunts on Milwaukee's South Side. The march covered nearly twenty miles over seven hours, through Kosciuszko and Humboldt Parks, then home on Lincoln Avenue. On Sunday, more than 5,000 marchers—the largest of the entire Milwaukee open housing campaign—crossed the Sixteenth Street Viaduct once again. Participants represented more than a dozen states and included Dick Gregory and the head of the Chicago NAACP. Demonstrators faced hundreds of white opponents along their trek, some carrying signs that read, "Kill the Black Devils," "Communists," and "Who Needs Niggers?" Chants of "nigger" and "Wallace for president" competed in the air with choruses of "We hate Polacks" and "Move over whitey, blackey's coming in." Police made five arrests, including one Commando for blocking a police van and fighting with officers, but no serious incidents occurred.[58]

The outpouring of national support for Milwaukee's open housing campaign fanned reaction among many local whites. Over the next few days, as civil rights activists continued to march peacefully through other sections of the city, thousands of white South Side residents and their allies organized increasingly large counterdemonstrations. Both sides of the housing controversy engaged in a dangerous dance of march–countermarch on the streets of Milwaukee. Several times, the two groups narrowly avoided direct confrontation by a few city blocks or a thin line of riot-clad police. The situation seemed dire in Milwaukee. "I think a major confrontation is inevitable," one anonymous "leading citizen" told *U.S. News and World Report*. "The prejudice in Milwaukee is such that almost anything could set it off. I see two speeding freight trains bound on a collision course. Neither is trying to apply the brakes."[59]

Saturday, September 16, marked the twentieth consecutive night of demonstrations. Dick Gregory led more than 650 marchers back to the South Side under heavy police protection. On Sunday, Father Groppi appeared on CBS-TV's news program, *Face the Nation*. He told the audience, "The white man won't do anything for the black man until he is disturbed. He needs disruptive tension." In addition, he said that the church ought to be the "most radical civil rights leader in the country" because "nothing attacks the teachings of Christ more than racism and self-righteousness." Responding to criticism of his role in the demonstrations, Father Groppi told the moderator he would leave his leadership position if it would help the open housing movement. The national NAACP board of directors telegrammed their support to Groppi, the YC, and the Commandos and condemned Mayor Maier and the Common Council for their lack of action. That night, more than 1,000 open housing advocates from across the country marched over the Sixteenth Street Viaduct while chanting, "We're Gonna Be Your Neighbors!" As they proceeded down Sixteenth Street, crowds of white people gathered and began catcalling and taunting the demonstrators; one teenager threw a bottle but was promptly arrested. Signs in windows read, "Niggers and Clergy! Pray for forgiveness for destroying property" and "Niggers Don't Waste Your Time Marching—Fix up Your Homes and Yards!" Again, no violence resulted, but Gregory warned afterward, "Don't think those South Side crackers aren't mean or that they're backing down. They knew the police meant business today."[60]

The open housing marches sponsored by the YC and Commandos continued every day into the fall of 1967 and beyond. The number of supporters fluctuated from several dozen to several hundred, cresting on weekends and ebbing on weekdays, but Father Groppi, the YC, the Commandos, and their allies continued forward. "We will not stop our marches," Groppi and the YC promised. "We will not stop our direct action until we get a law."[61]

Making History in Milwaukee

As marches and counterdemonstrations continued and the national media debated the meaning of what was happening in the streets of Milwaukee, city officials scrambled to address the crisis. In early September, Mayor Maier spoke before the Common Council and urged support for his nighttime ban on marches. A few days later, Maier announced that he would support a citywide open housing bill in the Common Council after fourteen of twenty-six suburban communities passed their own law. He also sent a proposal to Madison for stronger statewide measures and more money for urban development, but legislators rejected extra funds and did not act on housing. At the county level, the legislative committee of the County Board of Supervisors refused to discuss countywide open housing, saying it was a state matter.

The Common Council held its first fall meeting—also the first since the outbreak of South Side violence—on September 12. Father Groppi and seventy-five other open housing supporters marched to city hall to watch the proceedings. Alderwoman Phillips offered a new version of a citywide open housing ordinance. By a now familiar 18–1 vote, the council voted to support the mayor's emergency ban on marching and by the same tally refused to let Phillips reintroduce her measure before the legally specified ninety days had elapsed since the last attempt. Two weeks later, with civil rights activists singing "We Shall Not Be Moved," Vel Phillips reintroduced the citywide open housing ordinance. The council immediately referred the measure to the Judiciary Committee for study. On October 16, 625 people jammed the Common Council meeting room for public hearings. The Judiciary Committee endorsed a proposal by Ben Barkin, the city's most prominent public relations executive, to establish a subcommittee of interested parties to hammer out a compromise ordinance. Such a plan, he argued, could boost the city's image as well as solve the crisis. Vel Phillips called the plan "a ray of hope."[62]

Meanwhile, grassroots opponents of open housing announced that they were gathering signatures on a petition calling for a citywide referendum on the issue. The vote would trump legislative action with a more direct measure of public opinion. Sponsors—and civil rights leaders—felt confident that open housing would go down in an overwhelming defeat in a popular vote. The plan aimed at cloaking continued housing discrimination in a veneer of democratic legitimacy and underscored the contradictory visions of democracy held by many black and white Milwaukeeans. Vel Phillips called the proposed referendum "another great dodge."[63]

With each new violent episode in the streets and each new national news story, pressure mounted on the Common Council to act. The Open Housing subcommittee sequestered itself in the Governor's Suite at the Pfister Hotel from October 21 to October 23. The subcommittee consisted of five aldermen, including Vel Phillips, the president of the Milwaukee County Labor Council, the director of the League of Women Voters, the president of the Milwaukee Board of Realtors, and one representative each from the YC, the Greater Milwaukee Committee on Equal Opportunity (MCEO), and the Greater Milwaukee Conference on Religion and Race. During the three-day parlay, the real estate industry, which normally provided the backbone to formal opposition to open housing, remained quiet and debated the issue internally. In the end, the industry opposed any new measures, stating that the existing state law was sufficient. After a final nineteen-hour marathon session, the subcommittee had still failed to reach a compromise. Instead, they presented three alternatives to the full Judiciary Committee: (1) enact a law that mirrored the current state law; (2) enact a law that was stronger than the current state law; (3) enact a law that exempted all rental property. Father Groppi griped, "We want that bill, not proposals." The Judiciary Committee refused to recommend any ordinance to the full Common Council and instead remanded the issue to committee for further study. The Judiciary

Committee then delayed action on the issue completely until it could certify the 27,000 signatures that the Milwaukee Citizens' Civic Voice submitted to demand a citywide open housing referendum. The bureaucratic buck passing only confirmed the lessons civil rights activists had learned in previous campaigns.[64]

The impasse between marchers, counterdemonstrators, the mayor, and the Common Council continued for six more weeks. On November 25, a meeting between Father Groppi, Commando leaders, and Maier failed when activists walked out after the mayor appeared to skirt the open housing issue. Three days later, the Common Council approved an April referendum on the issue authorizing a two-year ban on any statute. Then, on December 12, the council passed an open housing ordinance that mirrored the state law by a vote of 13–6; both sides agreed it would have little impact on local housing or the ongoing demonstrations. The *Journal* editorialized, "It is as if some evil force were compelling the aldermanic majority to sink the open housing question deeper into the mud every time they have to face it."[65]

Reaction to this flurry of activity from the civil rights community was swift. Vel Phillips, who opposed the ordinance, called the move a "face-saving device, a way out" for her colleagues and complained, "Thanks for nothing. You are very much too late and very much too little." The MCEO newsletter lamented that "Milwaukee is proving to continue in the path that led a local black citizen as far back as 1941 to say, 'Milwaukee is a southern town that lost its way 100 miles north of Chicago.'" Father Groppi, who described the gesture as "tokenism and crumbs," stated, "It reminds me of Mississippi. They're fooling around here, insulting black people by insulting their God given constitutional rights." The YC promised to march for five years if necessary. Walter Hoard, president of the MNAACP, summarized open housing advocates' feelings when he said, "It has destroyed the hope many people had. It's not just fair housing: it's tied to everything in the struggle for equality."[66]

Despite continued frustration on the Common Council, broader community support for an open housing ordinance continued to grow through the fall and early winter. By early December, six suburbs had passed open housing laws. The Japanese-American Citizens Organization, Manpower Incorporated, the Wisconsin Council of Churches, the Wisconsin Council of Rabbis, and the Milwaukee Jewish Council all offered more high-profile official support to the campaign. The spiritual heads of Milwaukee's Catholic, Episcopalian, Lutheran, Methodist, Presbyterian, Baptist, and

Jewish communities issued a joint appeal to their members and city leaders for citywide open housing. Two hundred delegates of the state AFL-CIO voted to condemn the inaction of Mayor Maier and the Common Council, and 350 South Side residents and clergy ran a supportive ad in a local newspaper. Business leaders, feeling the effects of decreased tourism and downtown shopping, increasingly pressured city officials—often behind the scenes—to end the racial conflict.

As local support grew, so too did national, and even international, attention. Daily newspapers and evening news telecasts across the country covered racial strife in Milwaukee. The three major television networks all had crews in town. In addition, *Time, Newsweek, U.S. News and World Report,* and *Esquire* ran pieces on the open housing campaign while Voice of America broadcast reports across the globe. An editorial in the *New York Times* labeled Milwaukee "the most segregated [city] in the U.S." *U.S. News and World Report* asked, "Will Milwaukee Become Another Detroit or Newark?" One Milwaukeean even wrote home to say that the Nigerian press was covering events in Milwaukee. Father Groppi travelled the country to tell his stories and solicit support.[67] Maier and Father Groppi testified before the National Commission on Civil Disorders in Washington, D.C. Groppi warned the panel, "more riots are possible." The NAACP National Youth and College Association published and distributed "March on Milwaukee," an eighteen-page booklet with numerous photos. Many Americans came to see Milwaukee as the center of the national open housing struggle.[68]

Much of the national attention continued to focus on Father Groppi and Mayor Maier. An exasperated Roy Wilkins compared Maier to Pontius Pilate, passing responsibility for open housing to other levels of government. *Newsweek* magazine referred to Father Groppi as "a priest gripped by that elemental Christian belief which ordains that all men must love each other." As Groppi's stature as a national civil rights leader rose, so too did interest in Mayor Maier's longer-term urban political strategy. Catholic parishioners in many American cities debated the role of the young Italian priest in Milwaukee's civil rights movement while policy makers studied the merits of metropolitan politics, shared revenues, and the need for an "urban Marshall Plan." In December and January, Father Groppi received a series of accolades. The national NAACP announced it would honor the priest in New York City in January for "the living demonstration he provides of the continuing need for interracial cooperation in the fight for freedom." *Esquire* magazine named Groppi a "notable person" for 1967, and the Associated Press voted the priest "the newsmaker of the year" in religion.[69]

As with the local scene, perhaps the best measures of growing national support for the Milwaukee open housing campaign were the throngs who aided the movement. Thousands of individuals from around the city and across the nation flocked to Milwaukee's inner core to participate in demonstrations. Seventy-five-year-old Ignatius O'Connor from Boston came to Milwaukee in September and stayed for three months. O'Connor, a lifelong Catholic activist, had also attended the 1963 March on Washington and the 1965 Selma to Montgomery March, and in 1967 he felt he needed to be in Milwaukee. Rallies and marches averaged several hundred supporters, dipped as low as seventy-five, and peaked at 5,000. As many as 40 percent of the marchers at any given event were white. Weekend rallies tended to draw larger numbers, more out-of-towners, and higher numbers of white participants. Membership in both the YC and Commandos also soared during the campaign, and Father Groppi continued to be deluged by hundreds of letters of support, encouragement, and thanks. As in Selma, northern white clergymen and women religious heeded Father Groppi's ecumenical call and traveled to Milwaukee to bear witness. "They come in the habits of nuns, wear the roman collars of priests or answer to the Protestant title of 'Reverend' or 'Doctor,'" wrote *Catholic Herald* reporter Thomas Smith. "They came to join the battle for open housing."[70]

The Milwaukee open housing campaign, which ultimately stretched on for 200 consecutive nights of marching, represented an impressive organizing effort by hundreds of people. It was this structure, this conscious effort, which sustained a movement day in and day out despite considerable adversity. The home of this organizing effort was St. Boniface Church. St. Boniface, which the *Journal* called the "Marchers' Mecca," became a unique Movement center, perhaps unlike any other Catholic Church in the United States. It was an organic parish, democratic, experimental, and committed to social justice through social action. In many ways, St. Boniface personified the promise of reform laid out during the Second Vatican Council. As Squire Austin explained, "St. Boniface was a live church."[71]

At the height of the open housing campaign, St. Boniface throbbed with activity. Commandos guarded the church around the clock and made sure that no drinking, profanity, violence, or gambling took place on the premises. The thousands of people who flocked to Milwaukee to participate in civil rights demonstrations came to St. Boniface. It was an educational laboratory where people from all over the country learned and took their insights back to their hometowns. According to the *Journal*, St. Boniface served as "a refuge, rally hall, medical station, housing and transportation bureau and cafeteria. Its function is similar to Brown's Chapel . . . in Selma, Alabama, which was home to civil rights demonstrators during protests there more than two years ago." In a one-week period, a small army of volunteers at the church treated more than 125 minor injuries, collected $5,000 in donations, served 1,500 meals twice daily, recruited more than 300 hosts for out-of-town visitors, and ran a "pick-up service" to shuttle demonstrators back and forth. Most YC members and Commandos did not recall regular nonviolence training at St. Boniface, but Squire Austin stated, "We had a guy come in teaching us martial arts and he taught us self-defense. We had classes on how to protect yourself if you are attacked with billy-clubs and what parts of the body to protect so you don't get hit on the head or in certain areas of the body that are vulnerable." Daily and weekly masses were packed as the line between church and Movement dissolved; the Gospel infused the Movement, and the Movement infused the Gospel. Behind the scenes, Ben Barkin led a quiet, successful campaign to raise financial support from Milwaukee corporations and business leaders. A team of lawyers worked to free the endless stream of arrested demonstrators and thwart the various challenges to their right of assembly and peaceful protest. Outside St. Boniface, cameramen and reporters from all the major television stations, along with press, TV, and radio personnel from Milwaukee, milled around searching for a new angle. Down nearby side streets, police vans sat waiting for orders to join another march through the city. Tactical Squad members continued to keep tabs on civil rights activities. All of this required resources, coordination, and effort.[72]

At the center of what had become a national crusade for open housing were Father Groppi, the YC, and the Commandos. Despite the media's overemphasis on Groppi's leadership, there was a definite structure and protocol between the groups. Father Groppi and YC and Commando leaders would meet daily—sometimes with their legal team—to decide the goals and overall strategy for the upcoming night. The Commandos would then privately plan the route of the march and how to protect marchers. Fred Reed recalled Commandos and Groppi using matchbooks, cigarettes, and other everyday items to map out strategy on the floor of their meeting room. Demonstration participants were not notified of the final plans until the pre-march rally. Although Father Groppi served as a trusted aide and often offered his suggestions, he did not have a vote in either group. Yet, because of the deep personal intimacy between the young civil rights activists and their advisor, by and large there was consensus.[73]

The organizing effort, tactics, and leadership of the movement were not static. The open housing campaign was in motion and changed over time in response to developing circumstances. From the beginning, there was an improvisational—some said disorganized—quality to the campaign. Margaret Rozga called it "a constant process of rethinking." Father Groppi and the YC acted from the heart. They saw what they believed was an injustice and moved to change it. As a result, the open housing campaign was often short on long-term planning. Leadership in the Commandos was particularly fluid as influence often flowed toward those with personal charisma, regardless of their official rank. "The Commandos was an evolution," according to Prentice McKinney, "as was leadership within the movement itself."[74]

Over the first few months of the open housing protests, the leadership dynamic within and between the YC, Commandos, and Father Groppi changed subtly. The civil rights leadership core became smaller and more secretive as relations with Milwaukee police deteriorated; this was to keep law enforcement off guard about the details of their plans. In addition, as Groppi became a national figure, he traveled more and left an increasing amount of local responsibility to YC and Commando leaders. The young priest's time and energy, while still primarily focused on events in Milwaukee, was pulled in more directions, a burden that took a physical and emotional toll. Similarly, the media's focus on Father Groppi's charismatic leadership created jealousy, tension, and even periodic rifts between young civil rights activists and their advisor. "There was resentment against Groppi at times," admitted Prentice McKinney, "but there was also resentment against me. Anybody that got to a leadership position, you have people sitting over there that are not in the limelight but who are desirous of the limelight. So, there was this undercutting going on, always." Most Commandos were quick to explain that the emphasis on Groppi was not his own doing but a function of the media's need to create leaders and to privilege a white Catholic priest over black youths.[75]

National media attention also brought hundreds of outside supporters into the open housing campaign, which posed a new set of challenges and opportunities. Whereas early marches attracted 100–200 mainly local people, later demonstrations brought in thousands of outsiders, sometimes with little nonviolent training or experience. It was the task of YC and Commando leaders to organize and guide this mass of protesters so that the philosophy and tactics of the open housing campaign could be maintained. It became more difficult to keep demonstrators in line, literally and figuratively, as more people participated; not everyone bought into nonviolent direct action, particularly in the face of South Side violence and police brutality. Similarly, swelling membership in the YC and Commandos altered the character of both groups. Many of the new Commando recruits were physically tougher, more volatile, and less disciplined than the original members. This created some internal divisions. In addition, because many had served in the military, the organization formed ranks and a chain of command to cope with their numbers.

By December of 1967, the Commandos eclipsed the YC as the primary organizational focus of the demonstrations. They moved from an auxiliary security force to central leadership within the Movement and then ultimately to an independent life apart from the YC and Father Groppi. In part, this was the realization of Father Groppi and the YC's original desire to cultivate young, black, male inner core leadership through the group. It also sprang from the intense media attention the Commandos received. In addition, Groppi's diminished time in Milwaukee as well as the practical reality of a widespread violent reaction to the open housing demonstrations and the need to protect and organize a large following contributed to this shift. Last, as school restarted, regular student involvement dropped, forcing the Commandos to play a larger role in organizing the open housing demonstrations.

As fall began to turn to winter, Milwaukee open housing advocates intensified the economic dynamic of their protest. The racial violence that began with the July civil disorder and continued through the first month and a half of the open housing campaign had leveled a serious blow against tourism revenues. In September, Dick Gregory issued a formal boycott against several local breweries.[76] The boycott was intended to put economic pressure on local businesses to gain their support for open housing. By October, it was not unusual to hear marchers chanting "No more Schlitz" as they walked by inner core taverns. Sales declined out of solidarity with the boycott and because many tavern owners feared reprisals if they continued to sell targeted beers. NAACP chapters in seven states and CORE affiliates in thirteen states adopted resolutions supporting the Milwaukee boycott. On October 3, 200 demonstrators marched to the Schlitz and Blatz brewery to accentuate their protest. The mayor's economic development advisor said that the protest was "bad for the city's image." One inner core Schlitz distributor told the *Wall Street Journal* that his orders had sunk from ninety cases to one case per week.[77]

In November, the YC urged Milwaukee African Americans and their allies to boycott Christmas shopping and traditional holiday decorations. The aim of "Black Christmas" was to accent the spiritual side of the holiday and to focus more pressure on business leaders to get involved with the open housing issue. "No housing bill, no dollar bill," Father Groppi explained. "That is the only language the man downtown understands." Most business leaders and civic officials opposed the campaign out of economic self-interest. The *Milwaukee Courier* called the protest "unrealistic," and African American business owners in the inner core complained when the YC refused to exempt them from the boycott. John Givens, the former chairman of MCORE, opposed the boycott, explaining, "In a community like Milwaukee's inner city, you've got a lot of Christmases where people have done the very best that they can do and got whatever little bit they could get, so now we are going to propose a Christmas that is going to be black, in which they don't get anything. I see enormous psychological damage in that, and I won't participate."[78]

As a part of the Black Christmas campaign, civil rights marchers paraded through the downtown shopping district and into some of the major department stores. They sang "I'm Dreaming of a Black Christmas" and "Freedom Bells" and chanted "Black Christmas" and other Black Power slogans.

In one of the more bizarre turn of events, a white supremacist group, the Milwaukee Citizens' Civic Voice, joined a black separatist group to establish "Yule Patrols" to "protect" downtown shoppers from open housing protesters, a move that seemed to heighten fears, rather than allay them. It was somewhat ironic for the two separatist groups to work together to achieve their goals. On December 18, twenty members of the Yule Patrol, wearing white armbands with the words "Merry Christmas" on them, confronted roughly 200 Black Christmas demonstrators in the major downtown shopping area. YC members shouted "Uncle Tom" at the black separatists, to which the Yule Patrol replied, "Go follow your white slave master." Beyond the contesting chants, though, no incident occurred.[79]

Many reports indicated that business was significantly diminished in the downtown shopping area during the holiday shopping season. The *Wall Street Journal* wrote that the Black Christmas campaign promised to "leave a coal in the stocking of many a downtown merchant." Its analysis suggested that retail, restaurant, and theater patronage were all down an average of 20–30 percent over the previous year. Hotels and motels reported a 20 percent drop in business since the July civil disturbance, restaurants a 25 percent dip, and convention inquiries a 40 percent decline. The *Milwaukee Journal* reported that daytime sales in the inner core remained steady but that nighttime sales were off by 25 percent. It was unclear to what extent that the impact was the result of the Black Christmas campaign. Undoubtedly, months of racial violence had put fear in the minds of many white shoppers who then declined to come downtown because they deemed it unsafe.[80]

The Black Christmas campaign definitely had an effect on the inner core, over all. Frank Aukofer wrote that the protest was "highly successful in that it kept the inner core area bleak for the holidays." Few residents strung holiday lights or made Christmas displays, though some put out images of a black Jesus instead. Frank Aukofer suggested that "a lot of the celebrating of Christmas was done covertly." It is unclear to what extent the lack of holiday decorations was the result of community support for the Black Christmas campaign and to what extent it emanated from a fear of retaliation. Rumors of threats, violence, and intimidation by the Commandos against those who did not go along with the protest were common. The Commandos denied the allegations.[81]

The Black Christmas campaign culminated at midnight mass on Christmas morning. Father Groppi, wearing only his black vestments, asked the integrated standing-room-only crowd, "I wonder how many of the 27,000 people on the South Side who signed that [referendum] petition realize they are playing the part of the innkeeper in turning out Christ? I wonder what the members of the Common Council think tonight when they hear the words, 'No room in the inn,' and when they vote against open housing?" The mass ended with a series of Christmas carols "with a little bit of soul added." Afterward, 425 supporters took to the streets for a two-hour march through the North Side, the 120th consecutive day of open housing protest in Milwaukee.[82]

The YC and Commandos continued to lead daily marches into March, but the Milwaukee open housing campaign began to lose steam after the holiday season. The number of supporters at rallies and demonstrations fluctuated between several hundred and a few dozen while the proportion of white participants grew to 40–70 percent. With the Wisconsin winter freeze setting in, school in session, and open conflict in the streets diminished, national media attention strayed to other pressing issues, particularly the war in Vietnam and the upcoming presidential election. To be sure, the December compromise on the Common Council tempered some passions in the city over the issue.

Even within civil rights circles, the open housing campaign began to wane. Father Groppi, still traveling extensively, began to drift into other issues. Martin Luther King Jr. asked the priest and the Commandos to lead the Midwest contingent in the upcoming Poor People's Campaign. The death of another inner core black man at the hands of Milwaukee police stirred new enmity in the community. In February and March, the Commandos supported a series of protests at inner core schools over the absence of black history textbooks and the lack of "soul food" in cafeterias. Urban League Chairman Wesley Scott suggested that the Commandos might be hired as guards at schools and in the core. Internal divisions also emerged within the Commandos that ultimately led to a split between those who advocated direct action and those wanting to move into a social service role. Mayor Maier continued his "Crusade for Resources," now focusing on securing federal monies through the Model Cities Program, a massive federal effort to fund local projects aimed at combating slums and revitalizing urban neighborhoods. In March, Father Groppi resigned as direct action advisor for the MNAACP, which was followed quickly by the resignation of Walter Hoard as president of the MNAACP. Those moves signaled a return of the local NAACP branch to a more cautious approach to racial change.

Even as the YC's direct action campaign in Milwaukee slowed down, the tide began to turn in support of open housing. At the national level, spurred mainly by the wave of racial violence the previous summer, Congress again debated new civil rights legislation. In February, liberal Democratic Senators Walter Mondale and Edward Brooke implored their colleagues to pass open housing legislation. On the floor of the Senate, Mondale raised up Milwaukee and the courageous, but to date futile, struggle of Father Groppi and the YC as examples of the dire need for change. Afterward, in a letter to the Milwaukee priest, Mondale wrote, "Your contribution to this effort, whether we are defeated or are successful, has been most significant, and I do appreciate it." Despite the renewed focus on housing in Washington, D.C., congressional liberals struggled to line up the requisite votes to enact legislation.

In Milwaukee, attention had turned to the upcoming referendum. Civil rights supporters, acknowledging that victory was probably impossible, feared that the vote might spur a new round of conflict between extremists on both sides, further damaging the city's national reputation. Salvation came on March 4, when an ACLU lawsuit challenging the constitutionality of the referendum finally made its way to Federal Judge Robert Tehan. Judge Tehan ruled, "in an historic decision with implications for cities all over the country," that the city could not hold a referendum that would prohibit passage of an open housing measure. In turning away the plebiscite, Judge Tehan called it "patently unconstitutional if enacted into law" and said that it would "do great irreparable injury not only to the plaintiff and his class [that is, African Americans] but to the city as a whole" by encouraging "further racial unrest" and "a longer, hotter summer in 1968." The decision placed open housing back squarely in the lap of the Common Council.[83]

Following the ruling, the YC and Commandos decided to suspend their open housing campaign on March 14, the 200th consecutive night of protests. Alderwoman Phillips and Father Groppi led 325 supporters, one final time, through North Side neighborhoods. "Open housing isn't the only civil rights struggle," Richard Green said. "In order to obtain all our equal rights, we're going to have to work on all our problems, such as employment, education and what have you." Margaret Rozga called it "a period of questioning." With that, Milwaukee's dramatic open housing demonstrations came to a decidedly anticlimactic end.[84]

The assassination of Martin Luther King Jr. on April 4 provided a tragic final chapter to the Milwaukee open housing movement. In the wake of King's death, a spasm of racial violence ripped through dozens of American cities, but not Milwaukee. At a requiem mass at St. Boniface, Father Groppi told the gathering,

I know tensions are going to rise in our community. It's not really a question at this time of what we would want to do. It's a question of what Dr. Martin Luther King would want us to do. Dr. King was a nonviolent man. Many of us disagreed with him . . . [But] at this time we must do what he would want us to do—he being of the nonviolent philosophy, I think this is the honor we owe to him.[85]

YC members and Commandos patrolled the inner core to urge calm and visited local taverns to encourage them to close their doors out of respect to King.

On the following Sunday, 7,000 local residents attended a formal memorial service sponsored by the Interdenominational Ministers Alliance. Because Mayor Maier was a featured speaker, the YC and Commandos boycotted and held their own service in Garfield Park. Father Groppi continued to urge the younger, more militant crowd to remain nonviolent. On Monday, April 8, an estimated 15,000–20,000 people participated in a memorial march through the inner core and downtown Milwaukee. Although a few young people broke some windows along the route, the march remained overwhelmingly orderly, especially compared with incidents in other cities. The demonstration was also one of the largest held for the slain civil rights leader anywhere in the nation. Frank Aukofer credited the Commandos with maintaining order. "[They] did the yeoman duty in policing the march," he said. "They kept the ranks dressed, chased youngsters who threw rocks, guarded stores where windows had been broken, and generally maintained order while city police stayed inconspicuously in the background."[86]

Shocked that the nation's leading advocate of nonviolence had been brutally slain, and reeling from the massive wave of urban violence that followed, Congress quickly moved to pass the 1968 Civil Rights Act, which featured a strong open housing measure. President Johnson signed the bill into law three days after the Milwaukee memorial march. Many years later, Ben Barkin, who became a friend of the president, recalled that Johnson thanked him for the important contribution made on the streets of Milwaukee to the federal open housing law.[87]

Seizing the political moment, Mayor Maier reversed course and endorsed a local ordinance that mirrored the new federal bill. According to Vel Phillips, "[The Mayor's switch] smacks of what white America has done to black America for centuries. It's gutless and heartless at the same time." Then, on April 30, the Common Council, which had seven new members after elections on April 2, surprised most people by passing a citywide ordinance that surpassed the federal law and covered an estimated 90 percent of all Milwaukee dwellings; the vote was 15–4. Father Groppi called the council's vote "a significant victory" and said, "We're not forgetting we had to pay for the victory at a great price. A lot of people went to jail. A lot of people got sore feet." Vel Phillips was cautiously optimistic: "The council has given me hope. Maybe the white power structure recognizes the frustrations of the black community." Years later, she reflected, a bit more sardonically, "Even Milwaukee had to concede it was part of the United States."[88]

— 8 —

Black Power Politics

In late September of 1967, Father Groppi, five members of the Commandos, and two other local white clergymen set off from Milwaukee to Washington, D.C., to lobby liberal politicians for a national "fair housing" law and to attend the Conference on the Churches and Urban Tension. The conference, organized by the Methodist Church with the support of several other liberal denominations, sought to bring greater national attention to the explosive open housing drama unfolding on the streets of Milwaukee. For nearly a month, hundreds of civil rights advocates had clashed with thousands of white working-class residents on the city's South Side. Milwaukee was only the latest in a string of housing clashes that rocked urban America during the mid-1960s, marking the issue as a key civil rights battleground in the North. Conference organizers in the nation's capital hoped to dramatize the need for congressional action on this pressing issue by spotlighting the Milwaukee campaign.[1]

On the first day, at a session featuring Father Groppi and the Commandos, leaders of Pride Inc., a local black nationalist organization founded by Marion Barry, opposed Father Groppi's close relationship with the Commandos and his role as primary spokesperson for the Milwaukee open housing campaign. A line of critics rose to castigate the white priest and his young black companions with a list of derogatory names and Black Power barbs. "Father Groppi has one thing wrong with him," one member of Pride Inc. declared, "his color. It's the same old case of whites using Negroes." During this verbal onslaught, Groppi said nothing, instead retreating to a corner of the room. The five Commandos stepped forward to defend the young priest and to explain that, in fact, they were the leaders of the Milwaukee campaign and that Groppi was their advisor. They went on to reaffirm their conviction in Black Power but also their commitment to a "not-violent," interracial, church-based movement in Milwaukee.

A series of testy exchanges between the contending sides followed. One Washington Black Power leader bristled at the Commandos' defense and shouted, "You men had better get guns and use them." One Commando responded with a question of his own, "Do you have guns?" The man replied, "Yes, we have guns." "Where are you from?" "Los Angeles." The Commando then reportedly said, "We haven't heard anything from you in Los Angeles. Don't you have the guts to use them?" Another Black Power challenger demanded, "You had better get with us!" Commandos then began chanting, "You're too late, Baby! You're too late, Baby!" Charles Harper denounced the whole Washington lot as "big mouths . . . who aren't doing nothing." The meeting quickly degenerated into chaos, necessitating a wedge of Commandos to get Father Groppi out.[2]

Over the next two days, the local militants continued their efforts to undermine the conference. As Groppi and the Commandos met with legislators, members of Pride Inc. told reporters that the Commandos were not authentic Black Power leaders because they allowed a white man to advise them. The group also tried to block the Milwaukee activists from participating in a scheduled march and prayer vigil at the Washington Monument. Their challenge divided the conference into black and white caucuses, and few African Americans participated in the public actions. In the end, the conference broke upon the rocky shoals of competing visions of Black Power. The organizers' attempt to bring the Milwaukee campaign to a broader national audience fizzled as the media focused more on the internal strife than on the issue of housing.[3]

Yet, the confrontation solidified the alliance between Father Groppi and the Commandos and reaffirmed their commitment to their own brand of Black Power politics. "Father Groppi and ourselves are together," one Commando told reporters after the conference ended. "We would die together, even if it meant going to hell. This movement is black and white. It contains people of all colors. We do not turn anyone away who is seeking justice for the blacks and who is willing to work and sacrifice to bring it into existence." Another wrote as he left the capital city, "I advocate Black Power, but not to the point that it stops any people or any man from identifying himself with a Black Power movement, even if he be white, yellow or green." When the Milwaukee delegation returned home, a multiracial throng of several hundred met them at the airport, mingling Black Power slogans with chants of "We love Father Groppi!" and "Freedom!" Later, at St. Boniface Church, the delegation received a standing ovation as they reaffirmed the principles of their campaign. Vel Phillips called the interracial open housing campaign "beautiful" and warned that Milwaukee might prove to be "a last ditch stand for non-violence, a last ditch stand for the church and a last ditch stand for an integrated movement." According to the *Catholic Herald Citizen,* "[The hundreds of activists who come to Milwaukee] see in the events here a revival of the civil rights movement on an interracial front. Active in their own cities in this area, they feel obliged to lend their moral, financial and physical support to a cause which they conceive of as a crusade for decency and justice." Comedian Dick Gregory argued that Black Power advocates nationwide were becoming less antiwhite because of the Milwaukee demonstrations. "What we are doing here in Milwaukee," he said, "is convincing a lot of cats that black nationalism is not a color, it's an attitude." When Groppi rose to speak, several Commandos swept him onto their shoulders as the crowd roared, a powerful affirmation of the priest's role in the local movement.[4]

Father Groppi and the Commandos had weathered a serious storm in the nation's capital. In response to the challenge posed by Washington Black Power advocates, the Commando leadership had not only stepped forth to defend Father Groppi as a person, but also went further to articulate an alternative vision of Black Power that emanated from unique local circumstances and remained nonviolent (or at least, not-violent), interracial, and church-based. The episode illustrated both the challenge the Milwaukee Movement posed to the dominant formulation of Black Power at the time and the difficulties of rebuilding the old civil rights coalition.

The Milwaukee open housing campaign forces us to reconsider the story of Black Power. This history suggests the need to look beyond simple slogans and orthodoxies to find out just what Black Power meant on the ground; to find out how local activists combined direct action and nonviolence with self defense, civil rights with Black Power, demands for housing and school integration with expressions of social and cultural autonomy. It challenges us to consider how local civil rights activists fashioned their own versions of Black Power politics that made sense in the context of their community. In short, it underscores the contested nature of Black Power. When we look at Black Power in new ways, we are able to see new things. This chapter steps back from the narrative approach to mine some of these deeper meanings. In the process, it affords the chance to explore other important dynamics of this story. In particular, closely linked to Black Power politics are issues of gender and massive resistance to racial change by whites.

The Evolution of Black Power Politics in Milwaukee

Many of the traditional trappings of Black Power were apparent in Milwaukee during the open housing campaign. It was evident at rallies and mass at St. Boniface. It could be heard in the fiery rhetoric and rebellious tones of march leaders and in the songs and chants of demonstrators. Black Power was proclaimed on signs and emblazoned across the chests and backs of Youth Council (YC) sweatshirts, which read "Freedom Fighter," "Soul Brother," "Soul Sister," "Black Is Beautiful," "Sock It to Me Black Power," "Remember McKissick," and "Stop Police Brutality." Commandos often wore dark sunglasses and fatigues and carried themselves with an aggressive toughness and assertive masculinity typical of the Black Power era. They had a bit of a swagger. They were strident and combative, uncompromising, defiant. Black Power was present in the organized, collective economic power of the Black Christmas campaign and in the increasing links Movement leaders drew between their struggle and the war in Vietnam.

Yet, Father Groppi, the YC, and the Commandos tried to cut their own path between extremes by fashioning a form of Black Power that made sense within the local context. According to Squire Austin, "We intermingled with the Panthers. We sat down [with Stokely Carmichael] and listened to him talk. We did that to broaden our minds as to what we were doing. But a lot of stuff they were doing we didn't agree with."

It is clear from existing evidence that Black Power in Milwaukee meant different things to different individuals, adding another level of complexity to the concept. For most, it was simply a source of unity, strength, and pride. "Black Power meant confidence" to Squire Austin. "It was strong. Unity. Together. If I was out there [marching] by myself I would be weak and afraid. When you say Black Power, I got all of these people with me and I don't fear nothing." Prentice McKinney said that Black Power "countered the [stereotypes] that 'Black is ugly' and that 'Black is powerlessness.' It was a new way of seeing yourself. It was empowering . . . [It meant] we ain't taking that shit anymore." Margaret Rozga, who is white, stressed that in Milwaukee "you could be all for Black Power and not be black." To Rozga, Black Power meant "acknowledging or asserting the rights of black people. It meant the push to get black people full equality, but it wasn't separatist. It was simply a more forceful articulation of what we'd been struggling for all along." YC President Fred Bronson agreed: "We're not anti-white; we're just pro-black. We defined Black Power for ourselves some time ago. To us, it means a struggle for political and economic unity and self-determination for the black man." But Bronson was also quick to add, "Blacks cannot reach full economic strength alone. Whites control the money and the economic strength, and it's going to take white help to bring the black man to equality." Moreover, alongside Black Power slogans, YC members sweatshirts also read "Black and White Together," "We Love Father Groppi," and "We Love Everybody." Father Groppi taught in his dialogue homilies that Black Power meant "equal" and "opportunity" for African Americans, but "in our hearts we love everybody." Vada Harris defined Black Power in terms of race pride and an expanding self-awareness that, according to historian Jack Dougherty, "bolstered her political commitment to integration rather than conflicted with it." Dougherty also noted that during the open housing campaign, demands for Black Power were often uttered in the same breath as calls for "fair housing," a more integrationist objective. A banner hanging in the basement of St. Boniface stood as a reminder of this relationship. It read, "Black Power + White Power = Community Power," and along the left and right were two phrases, "United we stand" and "Divided we fall." Yet, although many YC members and Commandos shared the belief that integration and race pride were complementary, not competing, Dennis McDowell acknowledged that for some Commandos Black Power was, in fact, "a black thing."[5]

Black Power was present in Milwaukee in many ways that were less obvious, too. For example, the educative aspects of the open housing marches might reasonably be understood as a form of Black Power. Dennis McDowell explained,

> Back in the day most people [in the inner core] were really only concerned with what was happening in their neighborhood or on their porch. But when they saw us walk past, when we were passing out flyers, or ran up to their house, or people would run down to us wanting to know what was going on and we told them what we were doing would make a difference, then pretty soon that line went from twenty to forty to a hundred to 200 people.

He concluded, "We motivated a lot of people. There were many people who were ready to get up out of their seats, but they needed a leader." In this way, the open housing campaign raised the collective voice of the migrant, working-class community and organized black political power.[6]

The Commandos' philosophy of "not-violence" continued to distinguish Black Power in Milwaukee as well. Throughout the first two months of the open housing campaign, spiraling antagonisms between marchers, white onlookers, and police resulted in a number of violent clashes. "It was a matter of survival," explained Prentice McKinney. "When the tear gas came in and you had to run off and there's thousands of white people throwing shit at you and cops swinging at you, I mean, Big D [Dwight Benning] and I used to go back to back. He'd get my back and I'd get his and we'd just start wailing." Circumstances on the ground increasingly propelled the self-defense aspect of not-violence to the fore. And although Commandos did not employ weapons, they made good on their promise of "armed" self-defense with their fists.[7]

Throughout the open housing campaign, the Commandos staved off a number of challenges to their authority from activists and community members who advocated violence. For instance, at a September 11, 1967, rally, a group of sixty to eighty young black "toughs"—armed with sharpened sticks and rocks—tried to join a YC march. The Commandos ejected them from the protest. A few days later, several young Milwaukee African Americans wearing sweatshirts that read "Deacons for Defense" arrived at a St. Boniface rally to challenge the Commandos leadership. The Milwaukee Deacons, which was not formally affiliated with the more well-known Deacons for Defense and Justice in Louisiana, advocated a separatist black nationalist stance and armed self-defense. During a brief private conference, the Commandos told the Deacons that they wanted no part of their group but welcomed individual members to participate in open housing demonstrations as long as they adhered to the established rules. The Deacons refused and instead joined with the white supremacist Milwaukee Citizens' Civic Voice to oppose the open housing campaign. In response, members of the Louisiana Deacons for Defense came to Milwaukee in December to repudiate the local group and to support the Milwaukee Movement.[8] A week after the initial Deacons challenge, twenty-five "anti-white Negroes" from Chicago gathered at St. Boniface after a march to organize violent activity in Milwaukee. The group passed out images of Malcolm X and Stokely Carmichael and told local activists that they should burn the city down, not march. Again, the Commandos invited the Chicagoans to participate in demonstrations but only if they agreed to remain "not-violent." Despite these and other challenges, in the end, the Commandos maintained control of the open housing campaign and "not-violence" carried the day in Milwaukee.[9]

As the opening story in this chapter illustrates, Father Groppi's public leadership in the local movement complicated Black Power politics, locally and nationally. In addition to his skin color, Groppi's continued fusion of faith with his vision of Black Power also set racial politics in Milwaukee apart. Throughout the demonstrations, Groppi's vision of Jesus became increasingly black and increasingly radical. He spoke of Jesus as a revolutionary activist, an advocate for the oppressed engaged in a struggle for justice. He endowed Black Power—race pride, community development, and black political and economic development—with a spiritual legitimacy and force. Over time, as Groppi reached deeper levels of commitment to the cause, the line between himself and the black community receded. Groppi moved from ministering to the African American community to struggling with them. By 1967, Father Groppi spoke of "us" and "we" when discussing the injustices facing black Milwaukeeans.

Moreover, as the open housing demonstrations stretched on without significant progress, Father Groppi's rhetoric became increasingly militant. More and more, Groppi drew distinctions between the philosophy of "not-violence" and Kingian nonviolence. At the end of September, he told the president's National Advisory Commission on Civil Disorders that African Americans turned to violence because other means had not gotten results. "When Rap Brown says that violence in the American system is as common as cherry pie," he explained, "I don't know who in the world can give him an argument because it is true." He called violence "a constructive way of social protest" and said that in the face of persistent white apathy it was "morally and objectively justified," although he also thought that "not-violent" civil rights activism might channel that anger "into a constructive pattern of social action."[10]

Over the following six months, Father Groppi moved in an ever more radical direction, repeating and extending his ideas to audiences across the country. Calling himself a "radical" rather than a liberal because "a liberal leaves the room when the action begins," Groppi questioned whether nonviolent direct action would be enough to "move white people to conscience" in Milwaukee. He told a Chicago audience, " 'We Shall Overcome,' and 'Black and White Together' are still being sung in Milwaukee, but maybe we should sing 'We Shall Overthrow.' " At a college in St. Paul, Father Groppi said that the YC's motto was "Total liberation or death." He praised Rap Brown and Stokely Carmichael as "great men and great heroes" in the black community. In St. Louis, Groppi caused a minor stir in the national media when he used the word "fuck" on live television while describing the harassment he and other civil rights activists faced in Milwaukee. In January, he explained the morality of African American violence by way of a comparison to Joan of Arc: "She led armies. She swung a sword. She killed people. She's one of the greatest saints we have. You can talk to me about the evil consequences of violence and blood in the streets. You can talk and you can argue with me about violence as a technique . . . but if you talk about it morally, that is sheer hypocrisy." He criticized the U.S. government for spending billions of dollars each month "killing innocent people in Vietnam" and then rebuking African Americans for using "the same technique." That same month, in Dubuque, Father Groppi stated that riots were "a necessary aspect of the black revolution." Two months later, the priest told a group of civil rights advocates in Providence that most "socially acceptable means for gaining freedom had failed for black Americans." Moreover, Groppi said that conditions had not "degenerated to riots" but were "escalating into revolutionary acts."[11]

As the most recognized public spokesman for the YC and Commandos, Father Groppi walked a fine line between understanding, explaining, and advocating racial violence. For example, the priest told the National Advisory Commission on Civil Disorders that he was studying the usefulness of violence as a tactic. "The Milwaukee NAACP Youth Council Commandos are giving non-violence its last chance," he warned. "If it doesn't work, I'm not saying what our future action will be . . . We've just about had it." Many in his audience undoubtedly failed to draw the same fine distinctions as the young priest and saw the words as justification for more radical actions. Some viewed Groppi as a provocateur and others as a prophet of doom. He believed he was simply delivering a warning based on the circumstances as he saw and experienced them. The FBI, who as recently as the summer of 1967 debated whether Groppi even belonged in the "Rabble-Rouser Index," now labeled him an "agitator" and expressed concern about what they saw as the priest's growing "propensity for violence." They tracked and recorded his movements, speeches, and activism via the media, field agents, and community informants. Yet, despite his numerous explanations and warnings, Father Groppi consistently adhered to the nonviolent ethos in his own life and activism. He came to see Black Power, particularly political and economic power, as the only way to stave off racial violence and full-scale "guerilla warfare" in the United States. "Communication is useless," he said, "unless both sides have power. If you don't have it, you have no voice."[12]

In addition to massive white resistance, conflicts with Milwaukee police continued to propel much of the violence during the open housing demonstrations. Admittedly, the relationship between law enforcement officers and civil rights marchers was complicated throughout the open housing campaign. No doubt, the river of animosity separating the two sides was deep, and the recent history was contentious. However, although Milwaukee police clashed openly and often with civil rights activists during the mayor's ban on marching, on other occasions, police officers incurred serious harm to protect demonstrators and their rights. Commando Richard Green recalled,

> I was arrested many times and sometimes [police] would say, "Hey. I support what you're doing and I'm only doing my job." And I could respect that . . . But we are talking about white officers who had worked the inner city for X number of years saying, "What you are doing is right" . . . but then you had those other kind who lived on the South Side and who were probably many of those folks who were throwing rocks and calling names and they looked for an excuse to rough us up. You never knew what to expect.

Nonetheless, Prentice McKinney felt that when push came to shove, "This was Harold Breier's town. Just like Bull Connor down South . . . He kicked ass and took names. Either you went along and you were a good Negro or you had to deal with Breier, and Breier was no lightweight. He was the law and whatever happened to you it was going to be 'justifiable.'" Squire Austin agreed, "It was like they [Milwaukee police] were siding with the people, the hecklers, the racism, the racist people that didn't want us on the South Side."[13]

Tensions with police culminated in October of 1967. During the first part of the open housing campaign, mutual distrust evolved into open conflict as strict enforcement of the mayor's ban on evening marches resulted in dozens of arrests and skirmishes between Commandos and the police. The Commandos felt that the police too often interfered with their attempts to maintain order in the marches. They believed that many officers intimidated demonstrators in an attempt to interrupt the open housing campaign. Others said that the police taunted and threatened Commando leaders with the hope of goading them into fighting. Many recalled law enforcement officers using the word "nigger." And demonstrators continually complained that many Milwaukee policemen did not wear badges during demonstrations or that they wore black tape across their name and badge number, making it hard to identify officers who brutalized marchers. In this context, the Commandos felt increasingly challenged by the police to establish their own authority and power through some sort of direct conflict.

The straw that broke the camel's back came on Sunday afternoon, October 8, when more than 400 people participated in a "jovial" march led by Father Groppi and Dick Gregory. Later, a smaller group of YC members and Commandos went out looking for white counterdemonstrators. Police tried in vain to steer the two groups away from each other. When they finally met across a North Side intersection, choruses of "The Battle Hymn of the Republic" competed with chants of "Black Power."[14] An estimated sixty-five police officers armed with nightsticks and helmets stepped in front of civil rights demonstrators and shoved them backward when the marchers began to cross the street toward their adversaries. As those in the rear pressed forward, marchers in the front had trouble retreating. Police then began swinging their clubs to disperse the crowd. The South Side protesters quickly left the scene, but a number of Commandos lined up opposite police while the remaining open housing advocates chanted, "Eight fingers two thumbs, send those cops to Vietnam." Civil rights supporters ultimately re-formed their ranks and pressed on. A few minutes later, Groppi and Gregory arrived, and the march paused while leaders met. Meanwhile, demonstrators chanted, sang, and taunted the police. During the break, police officers left the scene, and the march continued. After 10:00 p.m., the police returned and demanded that the marchers get out of the street. When they refused, police again waded into the crowd with swinging clubs. Many marchers fought back. The *Milwaukee Journal* reported, "One Negro youth fell to the street as a policeman was taking him to a patrol wagon. The policeman slugged him several times, yelling at him to get up. He continued to hit the youth with his riot stick on his head and body as the youth cried: 'I'm getting up, man, I'm getting up!' " Police arrested thirteen, including Dick Gregory, and at least seventy-five protesters were treated at the hospital for injuries.[15]

The Sunday night incident enraged many YC members and Commando leaders. The next evening, the Commandos planned an organized confrontation with the police by using the "box-in trap." According to Shakespeare

Lewis, who was in charge of creating a subgroup of Commandos to carry out the plan, "The strategy was that when we tie up the traffic [at the intersection] we knew that the police was going to rush in. And when they rush in, we opened up [the marching line] and let them into the square [the center of the intersection] where we had blocked off traffic."[16] Once surrounded, Commandos would converge on the trapped officers and fight it out.

At the pre-march rally, the Commandos did not tell other demonstrators that they planned a confrontation with the police. "We knew this was coming but we didn't want the marchers going out there looking for this because it could have gone the other way," explained Lewis. He went on,

> The police could have changed their plans and maybe not charged that night. Some of the marchers on some of the marches, we Commandos have taken weapons from the marchers—big knives, pistols. If they would have known there was going to be a confrontation they might have come prepared for anything; see, then there might have been people dying, because that way the police would have a reason to shoot them down.[17]

Father Groppi introduced eight Commandos who had been injured by police at the previous night's demonstration. He told the audience, "Police, like most of white society, are infected with the disease of prejudice. When they go home at night, they talk about 'niggers.' They've marched for 42 days and they're getting mad. All they want to do is use that club on a black person." The priest promised that the Commandos and YC leaders would no longer tolerate police brutality and would resist. "Call it what you want," he said, "but I call it Christian self-defense."[18]

Father Groppi, the Commandos, and YC leaders set off through the North Side from St. Boniface with 275 open housing supporters. They sang freedom songs and again chanted, "Send the cops to Vietnam" and "Burn, baby, burn!" When the group reached the busy intersection at North Avenue and Twentieth Street, they began to march slowly across each intersection, blocking traffic. With the "box" established, cars began to back up for blocks in all directions. Eight policemen, in full riot protection, decided to break up the roadblock by rushing toward the demonstrators. As they did, Commando leaders yelled for marchers to open up and let police into the middle of the intersection. As the box closed back in around the officers, several Commandos rushed toward them. "The police started swinging fists and clubs when they saw they were trapped. The Commandos responded and the fighting was hard and bad. While the police had helmets, we didn't and many [Commando] heads were knocked. Both sides had casualties who had to go to the hospital." Civil rights marchers scattered as Commandos battled the police. Several threw bottles, umbrellas, and even a garbage can lid into the intersection. As more officers joined the fray, they collared and clubbed demonstrators indiscriminately, and many marchers fought back with fists, rocks, and even, reportedly, a lead pipe. When the fighting subsided, civil rights demonstrators made their way back to St. Boniface. Police arrested eleven during the conflict, and twenty-seven people received treatment at area hospitals, including six officers. Paradoxically, Commando leaders claimed that the violent altercation marked the end of police intimidation and aggression in the open housing campaign.[19]

Outside the bounds of organized demonstrations and planned confrontation, other dangerous embers burned in Milwaukee and racial conflict often spun of its own accord. The same night that tear gas canisters pursued open housing advocates into St. Boniface, twenty-six suspicious fires were set throughout the inner core. Over the full Labor Day weekend, firemen reported more than 100 fires, the majority set by Molotov cocktails. Firehouses fielded dozens of other false alarms. Hostile crowds hindered inner core firefighting efforts, injuring two and prompting police protection for fire squads. Several white-owned businesses boarded up their windows. One anonymous caller threatened, "We're going to burn this town down." By the end of September, more than 200 inner core fires, sometimes as many as fifteen per day, had broken out since the civil disturbance two months earlier.[20]

Racial unity, one of the central tenets of Black Power, was hard to come by in Milwaukee. Although the majority of inner core organizations, leaders, and residents publicly supported the open housing campaign, some, particularly older residents and traditional leadership, privately questioned the YC and Commandos' confrontational tactics. Prentice McKinney believed that the rift was primarily generational. "You had African Americans who were young, who were born in the North with a totally different set of values than their parents who were born in the South," he explained. "Who are less afraid of whites and more cognizant of the injustice, of the difference in treatment [in the North]. Who this country is placing demand upon to go in the service and to fight for this country. Who have virtually no employment opportunities—and there is real frustration there—and virtually all of them have police records."[21] The *Journal* noted a similar class gap among local African Americans. And old tensions continued to simmer within the leadership ranks of the Milwaukee NAACP (MNAACP) as well as between the YC and the national office. "They did not [always] support our tactics," Richard Green explained:

> They threatened to take our charter [at one point] . . . but it wasn't going to stop us from doing what we were doing. We felt there was a need for it, whether the NAACP supported us or not, or any other black organization. This was something that we felt we had to do for Milwaukee . . . so we had very heated talks with the national NAACP.[22]

But some did criticize Father Groppi and the YC publicly. Reverend Louis Beauchamp, speaking for the Interdenominational Ministers Alliance, identified the direct action campaign and militant Black Power posturing of the Commandos as the primary reason that the Common Council had not passed an open housing ordinance. In response, seventy-five demonstrators marched to Reverend Beauchamp's home on Capitol Drive to chant, "What side are you on, Reverend Beauchamp? What side are you on?" Throughout the open housing campaign, Beauchamp reported to the mayor's office on inner core activities, including meetings he attended with other ministers and civil rights leaders.[23]

There were very real limits on Black Power possibilities in Milwaukee. Because the African American community remained comparatively small and black people did not possess significant political power or strong community institutions with deep historical roots, it was important for the Movement to form coalitions with supportive whites. The leaders of the open housing campaign advocated a Black Power that emphasized race pride over racial exclusivity and encouraged the use of economic, political, and educational power to gain equal rights. The same numerical disadvantage dictated that protesters embrace "not-violence." Father Groppi's role and the special place of St. Boniface further ensured that the Milwaukee campaign stayed rooted in Christianity.

In the end, the Black Power that emerged in Milwaukee was ground out of local circumstances, more than national slogans, and emphasized racial consciousness over skin color. Despite criticism like that from the leaders of Pride Inc., Groppi and the Commandos felt that they were Black Power advocates. Born out of official intransigence and violent white opposition, their version of Black Power emanated from the ethnic, racial, and class relations in Milwaukee. Cultivating indigenous African American leadership, particularly among young black men and projecting a masculine verbosity and toughness of style, it included building African American institutions and encompassed race pride, self-determination, and not-violence. But it also meant a pragmatic, interracial approach to coalition politics in a city where angry white working-class residents far outnumbered African Americans and their allies. It allowed space for sympathetic whites and religious people to participate in their movement and acknowledged that a more public display of armed self-defense might court slaughter. Practical experience had taught Milwaukee's civil rights leaders that their best chance for success lay in this mix of approaches. As a result, many civil rights activists across the country saw the Milwaukee open housing campaign as an alternative to other national trends, and as a unique formulation of "Black Power."

A Gendered Movement?

Historian Steve Estes has written, "The civil rights movement was first and foremost a struggle for racial equality, but questions of gender lay deeply embedded within this overtly racial conflict." In Milwaukee, the open housing campaign highlighted these gendered dynamics in the black freedom movement. Notions of manliness were central to the creation and development of the Commandos and their conception of Black Power. Many years later, Groppi reflected on this dynamic: "The Commandos . . . were a very chauvinistic group. There were no women that were in the Commando group. It was looked at as a very macho thing." Ed Thekan extended this idea, stating, "There was a perceived need, I think, to identify with the black male who had in many instances been emasculated . . . downgraded by the white society . . . Here [was] a case to exemplify the black man as being the leader in the sense of protector." According to Dennis McDowell, "[The Commandos] made us aware of who we were. There was a lot of self-involvement with all the men that became Commandos because of what Father Groppi instilled in us. Pride came about that was hidden, and I mean really hidden . . . We didn't know we had the right to stand tall as men." Margaret Rozga stressed that the focus on black men and masculinity within the Commandos was not a source of tension within the local Movement. "I think the rationale for the Commandos was more or less accepted by most people," she recalled, "and it was pretty well understood that that was not what women were doing and nobody made much ado about it and in fact supported it."[24]

According to Estes, manhood entailed an economic, social, and political status ideally achievable by all men, but which has been out of reach for most African American males throughout U.S. history. For example, men were to be heads of household, with the ability to economically provide for their families and to offer protection when needed. Men were also to have a political voice in the decisions affecting the community, state, and nation. And finally, men were to have access to all women who were not married. On each count, African American men were restricted from achieving their full manhood. In this light, the Commandos' assertion of black masculinity might be viewed as a claim on gendered rights that they had been historically denied. Just like the slogan "I Am a Man!" in Memphis during the garbage workers' strike in 1968, the very creation and presence of the Commandos was both "a demand for recognition and respect of black manhood as well as black humanity."[25]

This emphasis on developing black male leadership—what Estes calls "masculinist uplift"—aided African American men but also reinforced a set of ideas that bolstered a sense of dominance over women. Often, Commandos acted to prove their manhood, rather than to transform the community. They were to be tough and strident. They were willing to fight to protect women, children, and clergy during marches. Their entire persona, from the clothes they wore to the rhetoric they employed and the attitude they projected, was designed to suggest a strong black masculinity and a threat to whiteness. The danger was that this masculine posture could become an end in itself, rather than an avenue to more transformative change in the community. The flamboyant, assertive leadership style of the Commandos ensured that men became the public leaders in Milwaukee, despite the fact that women were heavily involved in all aspects of the Movement. The manly aggression and violence countenanced by the Commandos' philosophy of not-violence might also lead to physical violence outside the tightly controlled bounds of marches and demonstrations, as the vandalism at Mayor Maier's office proved. It could just as easily slip into nihilistic violence or domestic abuse. The sexual energy underlying this definition of manliness might also put young women in the YC at risk. As more and more men flooded into the Movement largely because of media images of the Commandos, rather than a serious consideration of philosophy, tactics, and strategy, these risks increased.

Outside the black community, an aggressive black manhood might also be dangerous. In the white mind, which was already primed with frightening stereotypes of black manhood linked to criminality, hypersexuality, and pathological violence, an assertive black masculinity might actually reinforce preexisting negative ideas about African Americans and justify white reaction. Given the media's emphasis on the most extreme aspects of Black Power, it was likely that whatever positive attributes might be associated with an assertive black manhood would be minimized, distorted, or ignored altogether.

Nevertheless, there were clearly positive dimensions to masculinist uplift, at least for those directly involved in the Commandos. The idea that manliness was tied to a protective role in the Movement led the group to corral the most troubling aspects of this aggressive manhood. According to Dennis McDowell, Commandos were not to be "disrespectful, rude, crude, or lewd around the girls." The point, he said, was "protect the women folk. Protect the old folks. And protect the priest." Moreover, McDowell suggested that this union of men "meant being a part of a family. My family was all busted up. It meant belonging to something, and we had a purpose."

Just as Father Groppi's skin color confounded ideas about Black Power, so too did his leadership convey competing messages about gender. As a priest, Groppi embodied a kind of soft masculinity but also a legitimacy because of his spiritual designation. Yet, as a militant civil rights leader, he projected a hard masculinity, an assertive manliness found in his rhetoric, his tone, his crusading energy, his uncompromising stance in the face of injustice, and his willingness to directly confront white supremacy, regardless of the potential risks. Black Power masculinity in Milwaukee, then, was complicated and even contradictory.[26]

The emphasis on black manhood in the Commandos, in the public leadership of Father Groppi, and in the powerful images of Black Power pervading the media often obscured the contributions of women to the Milwaukee civil rights movement. Yet, interestingly, few complained about this imbalance. According to Betty Martin, "Everybody had their own place. We all had our own spot. We knew our territory . . . I knew that the men's job was to get out there and protect that line. I knew I couldn't step over there into their line. Everybody had a defined role . . . There was no conflict." Margaret Rozga put it another way: "When your friend is getting arrested for dropping a cigarette on the sidewalk, you aren't going to say to other members, 'Why are more men in leadership positions?'" Alberta Harris, on the other hand, conceded, "We had some power struggles within the organization itself over the fact that we had males that had too much power." Yet, as

Martin explained, these discussions took place behind the scenes rather than in public. "If we have dissension among ourselves, then we project that to the public and we can't project that to the public," she said. "So we ironed out all of our grievances behind closed doors and when we got outside that door you didn't know we had grievances."[27]

Despite the powerful image of black masculinity projected by the Commandos, Father Groppi, and the media, women played key roles in the open housing campaign. "There were a lot of devoted women behind the scenes," recalled Martin. "A lot of people don't know that . . . Women were out there and put their lives on the line every day along with the men." The primary vehicle for women's participation and leadership in Milwaukee was the YC. Vada Harris, Alberta Harris, Velma Coggs, Pamela Jo Sargent, Margaret Rozga, Betty Martin, Shirley Butler and many others performed critical roles within the group. Women participated in every level of decision making. They marched, were arrested and jailed, and usually led freedom songs at rallies and on the line.[28]

An older group of women, known as "the mothers of the civil rights movement," played a special role in the YC. Collectively, these "mothers" served as an informal council that gave advice and protected the young women in the group. "They were the women who groomed us," Martin explained, "who taught us confidence and what was at stake . . . [They] communicated with our real mothers to let them know the children were alright and being watched over." Martin suggested that the "mothers" also policed a kind of middle-class respectability among the young women that might be seen in a similar light as Father Groppi's cultivation of black manhood in the Commandos. "They made sure that we stayed in line," she said, "because the media was there and they could say here's Groppi and a bunch of young girls who are loose. The mothers saw to it that none of that took place." They also put the brakes on any advances by members of the Commandos.

Martin also explained that outside of their collective role, individual "mothers" took on unique duties. Mother Butler "made sure we stayed where we were supposed to be . . . If you weren't on that line, she'd find out where you were at. She was in charge of the tracking system." Mother Campbell "had her own PhD. She was a physician of home development." According to Martin, "[Campbell] was the one who told us that we were out among men and there are ways that women should act." Mother Miller was "the overseer." If any women "got out of line," Mother Miller called a "hen party, where all the mothers would get together and when they were finished with us after the hen party, whatever was wrong was corrected."[29]

A small group of St. Boniface parish women played a particularly important role in the organizing effort at the church. "Mrs. Campbell and Mrs. Yarborough were the people who did most of the cooking, and I think everyone just took them for granted," said Margaret Rozga. "But they were good at it, and people loved it." Years later, Dick Gregory concluded that one of the things that gave the Milwaukee open housing campaign a unique cohesion was the nightly meals that women like Mrs. Campbell and Mrs. Yarborough worked hours to prepare and serve after every march. "That's why it was one of the greatest demonstrations of the civil rights era," Gregory explained, "because everyone got fed. If you marched, you got fed. They even had a system to make sure you actually marched and didn't just get the food." Local restaurants, grocery stores, and individual community members donated most of the food, but it was women like Mrs. Campbell and Mrs. Yarborough who prepared and served it.[30]

In these and other ways, civil rights insurgency in Milwaukee during the open housing campaign was gendered and contradictory. Although the struggle was primarily about breaking down racial inequality, Father Groppi, the YC, and the Commandos employed gendered strategies to achieve their goals.

Massive Resistance

In some ways, the flip side of Black Power was the outpouring of massive resistance by white Milwaukeeans to racial change and their assertion of a collective racial identity. Just as symbols of Black Power were evident throughout the open housing campaign, so too were expressions of White Power. The breathtaking number of white residents participating in resistance—totaling as high as 13,000 at the peak of conflict—was itself a powerful indication of the depth of white hostility to racial change in Milwaukee. Counterdemonstrators waved confederate flags and wore George Wallace campaign stickers. In a direct challenge to Black Power, they held signs proclaiming, "White Power," "Polish Power Fights Back," "Niggers wake up! Marching won't make you white," and "Keep Our Neighborhood White." During one counterprotest, a group of young white men tied a stuffed gorilla with a noose around its neck to the top of their car.

The inability or unwillingness of most white Milwaukeeans to understand the experience of local African Americans and to empathize with their plight testified to what George Lipsitz has called "the possessive in-vestment in whiteness." Similarly, the near total dominance of local institu-tions by whites, and their steadfast refusal to make even minor concessions to the demands of African Americans, might rightly be viewed as a form of White Power as well.[31]

Stories of massive resistance during the open housing marches are par-ticularly shocking and challenge the idea that white racial violence was pri-marily a southern phenomenon. Following the first two nights of conflict on the south side of the Sixteenth Street Viaduct, the high point of massive resistance came in mid-September. On Sunday, September 10, hundreds of white South Siders grew violent and openly battled with police, who needed six hours, several canisters of tear gas, and twenty arrests to disperse them. Roving groups of counterdemonstrators called police "nigger lovers," threw firecrackers, and made known their intention to fight civil rights marchers. The final altercation of the night came just after midnight, when police turned back a group of whites headed north over the Sixteenth Street Viaduct.[32]

Monday, more than 200 white opponents of open housing attended a rally at Humboldt Park, where Gerald Janka, a machinist from Racine and a self-proclaimed representative of the National Association for the Advance-ment of White People, told the crowd, "We're setting up the platform for a White Power march . . . to the jungle where Groppi operates . . . We're go-ing to end the black scourge." That evening, a mob of more than 1,000 hos-tile counterdemonstrators again met 650 open housing proponents south of the Sixteenth Street Viaduct. Many held signs reading, "Polish Power," "White Power," "Black Slaves Forever," "Open Housing in Africa," and "Block Them off, Nobody Goes South." Others chanted "E-i-e-i-e-i-o, Fa-ther Groppi's Got to Go!" and "We Want Slaves." Some white people wore swastika stickers; several threw bottles, bricks, rocks, and debris at demon-strators; and a number of civil rights marchers tossed them back. The two sides clashed openly for fifteen minutes before police moved in to break it up, sending open housing supporters scurrying back to St. Boniface. When white counterdemonstrators attempted to pursue the marchers back over the viaduct, police again blocked them. One man yelled, "we'll get them yet!" In the end, police made thirty-two arrests, and at least three people were hurt. Mayor Maier said the city "verged on civil war" but refused to call out National Guard troops to maintain order. The *Milwaukee Courier* complained that the failure of city officials to act had "brought the city to the precipice of an open war." *The Catholic Herald Citizen* called Milwaukee "a city teetering on the brink of complete madness." Father Groppi matter-of-factly told reporters, "If we had gone any further, they would have slaughtered us."[33]

This outpouring of massive resistance was increasingly organized. Some angry South Side whites called themselves "White Power Rangers," while the John Birch Society and National States Rights Party, both with ties to the Wallace campaign, organized formal opposition groups, such as the Milwaukee Organization for Closed Housing and Milwaukee Citizens' Civic Voice.[34]

The Catholic Church became a vehicle for white reaction as well. In another strange symmetrical twist to the open housing unrest in Milwaukee, one of the most visible leaders of the organized opposition was a young white Catholic priest, Father Russell Witon, of Port Washington. Witon grew up in the same neighborhood as Father Groppi, and the two men had attended the same grade school and high school, although they apparently did not know each other. Witon opposed "forced housing" and the "means and methods" employed by the YC. Yet, even though he and his followers attempted to project a moderate stance, Father Witon's comments often suggested a darker motivation. For instance, after a night of marching, including a near confrontation with civil rights protesters on the streets, Witon told a crowd, "We are not going to let those savages—those black beasts—take our rights away." He also challenged his followers to confront the church's role in civil rights. "It is the very devil that is behind these people," he said, "and we have to pray for their souls." Father Witon served, at least in the media, as the "anti-Groppi."

On Tuesday evening, September 12, 650 opponents of open housing intended to march to St. Boniface. When Milwaukee police officers blocked them from crossing Wisconsin Avenue, the group headed to Archbishop Cousins's residence. Carrying a casket that read "God is White" and "Father Groppi Rest in Hell," the counterdemonstrators demanded that the archbishop censure the young priest. The group chanted White Power slogans from the sidewalk as a half-dozen representatives spoke with Cousins inside. The archbishop told the leaders he would take their demands under consideration. As the protesters headed home, marchers taunted police and clashed with them in several minor disturbances.[35]

On Wednesday night, several hundred civil rights demonstrators followed Father Groppi and YC leaders in a march to Alderman Martin

Schrieber's home to call for an emergency Common Council session to deal with the open housing crisis. At the same time, an estimated 2,000 white people joined counterdemonstrations on the South Side to oppose open housing legislation. The counterprotest began when 200 people rallied at Kosciuszko Park and then headed for the Sixteenth Street Viaduct under the protection of twenty-seven white teenagers wearing armbands that said "White Power Rangers." Along the way, the crowd—now 450—met two members of the Chicago Nazi Party, who passed out signs decorated with swastikas and the words "Symbol of White Power." The group crossed the viaduct and headed for Archbishop Cousins's residence at the chancery. Again they confronted the archbishop, and again he addressed the crowd. Speaking through a bullhorn, he said, "We're making a mistake if we make this—one side or the other—a hate campaign. It's not a question of one man. It's a two-way street. We ask your cooperation." The crowd applauded and began to leave. By the time the group reached the south side of the Sixteenth Street Viaduct, though, their mood had changed, and they began chanting "Father Groppi's Got to Go!" As they proceeded up National Avenue yelling White Power slogans, more than 1,500 cheering white onlookers lined Sixteenth Street. When the mob encountered a car being driven by an African American, they surged at the vehicle chanting, "Let's get the nigger." The driver sped away as Milwaukee police launched tear gas and smoke bombs into the throng. The white teens then turned on police officers, throwing bottles and rocks and smashing store windows. "The cursing mobs turned [several streets] into a battleground," one reporter wrote. "Grey teargas . . . fogged the six block area, which was virtually sealed off by police. Streets were littered with rocks, bottles, beer cans and shattered glass as rioters pelted police cars and passing Negro motorists." It took several more volleys of tear gas, smoke bombs, and shotgun blasts to quell the disturbance.[36]

Later that week, Archbishop Cousins wrote directly to the laity of the Milwaukee archdiocese through the editorial and opinion page of the *Catholic Herald Citizen*. In the letter, Cousins stated that although he did not agree with Father Groppi's every act or statement,

> If Father Groppi were out of the picture, the NAACP Youth Council would not go out of existence. Its Direct Action committee would continue to determine tactics. Its large legal staff would still advise. The parent-organization would maintain its present position and lend its support. More to the

point, the underlying causes of unrest pointed up the Youth Council would go on plaguing us. They existed long before Father Groppi's advent.

In a reference to recent violence in the streets, the archbishop wrote, "We are being diverted by emotion and mob psychology into fighting a straw figure while the real enemy goes unscathed."[37]

Signs of counterorganizing continued throughout September and early October. Two Nazi Party members announced plans to rally political opposition to open housing in Milwaukee on September 22. The next day, Nazis participated in a South Side rally led by Father Whiton, who called the YC advisor "unchristian" and "unpriestly." In October, the Ku Klux Klan announced its own organizing drive. Hate literature circulated widely.[38]

As the open housing campaign garnered national attention and support, civil rights advocates continued to confront this deep well of massive resistance. Despite the often-repeated claim that white hostility was limited to working-class white neighborhoods, in fact, it came from every section of the city and virtually every state, from all economic classes, from each of the major religious denominations, and from both major political parties.[39]

The thousands of letters that Father Groppi received offer a unique window into the breadth of white opposition to open housing in Milwaukee.[40] The largest segment of letters could be rightly termed hate mail, including death threats and charges of "nigger lover" and "traitor." Of those that more accurately fell under the heading "constructive criticism," perhaps a majority held firm to the acculturation model, which stated that black migrants from the South did not possess the necessary skills to succeed in the urban North. A significant portion made accusations of Communist infiltration and outside agitation in the local movement, reflecting the pervasive Cold War politics of the time. Others were critical of Black Power, racial exclusion, and black nationalism. A large number of white ethnics believed in an immigrant mythology. They asked, "Why should African Americans be given 'special treatment' when my parents, who were immigrants to this country, never received any help from anyone? They had to make it on their own—why can't black people?" These people often forgot or ignored the special measures that had helped many of them and their parents go to school, start a business, buy a home, or get a job. Still others complained that open housing laws infringed on the property rights of white homeowners. Catholics continued to ask hard questions about the role of priests and nuns in political action and the future of the faith. The conflict between progressive Catholics and traditionalists revealed a deeply divided church. For many religious and nonreligious alike, Father Groppi became the primary issue. Others expressed support for the overall goal but opposition to direct action tactics. A significant proportion of the letters appealed to racist or stereotyped thinking that cast African Americans as inherently lazy, immoral, stupid, dependent, criminal, and violent.[41]

Intriguingly, much of the correspondence articulated a sense of white solidarity that was in sharp relief to the long history of white ethnic rivalry and conflict in Milwaukee. Before the rapid influx of African Americans to the city, ethnicity, religion, and language severely divided white ethnic groups. During the postwar period, rivalries among whites subsided. In part, this was a function of suburbanization and the breakdown of traditional neighborhoods. In addition, the letters to Father Groppi and other public officials during the civil rights era suggest that the perceived threat that black people posed to white interests in the form of increased competition for jobs, schools, housing, and public resources also fueled the decline of white ethnic identity and the embrace of a more general "white" self-identification. This shift in racial solidarity appears to undergird the emergence of white backlash politics in the 1960s and 1970s, but more work is needed in this area before any firm conclusions can be drawn.

Although letters of opposition to racial change came from every corner of the city and crossed ethnic and class boundaries, anecdotal evidence does suggest that working-class white Milwaukeeans formed the bulk of massive resistance in the streets. In part, this was no doubt a function of the fact that Father Groppi, the YC, and the Commandos chose to target working-class neighborhoods in their initial marches. Even though civil rights advocates occasionally marched to the suburbs during the open housing campaign, white residents of those communities remained relatively secure from the "black threat" compared with their working-class white neighbors left behind in traditional neighborhoods. In addition, as labor historian Steve Meyer has explained, many working-class industrial workers asserted a "rough manhood" that could be explosive and violent in defense of their interests. In addition, because many working-class white residents associated African Americans with urban decay and social disintegration, when civil rights activists clamored for equal access to historically white schools, jobs, labor unions, churches, fraternal organizations, and housing, whites reacted to defend their perceived interests.[42]

This willingness to defend what white residents viewed as theirs also contained a gendered dynamic rooted in physical space. Racial superiority was tied up with ideas of "whiteness," which were, in turn, largely rooted in the containment of "blackness" within separate racialized space. The physical division of the races was one of the most powerful and visible indications that African Americans were subordinate to whites. Thus, civil rights activists' challenge to segregation undermined the concept of whiteness, which was the foundation for racial superiority. If African Americans lived in the same neighborhoods, attended the same schools, worshiped in the same churches, participated in the same clubs, and worked alongside whites in unions and industry, what then was the basis for racial superiority? Just as African American men stepped forth to protect Movement activists out of a sense of manly duty, so too did white men move to defend their racial advantage by defending their families, neighborhoods, and homes from the "threat" of an encroaching "blackness." Moreover, these racial challenges took place at a time when the world that had anchored white male identity was being challenged on a number of fronts. Traditional religious practices, gender roles, sexuality, nationalism, and industrial labor, all important components of male identity, were in decline, fueling a sense among many white working-class men that their very existence was imperiled. But just as the focus on black manhood obscured the contributions of women to the struggle for racial justice, so too does this analysis of white working-class men cloak the role of white women in massive resistance. It is clear from photos and television news footage that women participated in all of the major street conflicts during this period. Further research is needed to probe the depth and extent of their role in white racial opposition to civil rights.

There was also a psychological dynamic to the physical separation of the races that reinforced negative ideas about African Americans and blocked integration. In large measure, Father Groppi—a white man from the South Side—learned to love and trust African Americans out of direct experience with black people in the inner core. Similarly, African Americans at St. Boniface, in the YC, and in the Commandos had come to love and trust this white priest through their own direct experience with him. Exposure was the key to undermining racist ideas of whiteness and blackness. For most white Milwaukeeans, though, the geography of race and the fear of integration blocked that same kind of exposure to the new, fast-growing black community. As such, most white and black Milwaukeeans knew each other not as human beings but as symbols of blackness and whiteness, with all the stereotypes that those symbols conjured, more often negative than positive.

Again, these initial observations about massive resistance require more work before firm conclusions can be drawn. One of the difficult aspects of probing white opposition to the civil rights insurgency, particularly in the North, is the relative lack of sources. Unlike Movement activists, white residents who participated in counterdemonstrations, shouted racist slogans, threw rocks, bricks, and cherry bombs, or attacked peaceful protesters with their fists are often unwilling to speak about it today. Moreover, closed housing organizations rarely kept minutes or donated their papers to archives. What insights we might glean come through scattered newspaper accounts, television footage, and photos. This is why the trove of letters contained in the papers of Father Groppi, Mayor Maier, Congressman Zablocki, and others are so unique and valuable. Despite these challenges, it is important to find creative new ways to explore white resistance to racial change.

The alliance between Father Groppi, the YC, and the Commandos and their embrace of Black Power politics defy easy characterization and challenge a number of fast assumptions about the civil rights movement. The very fact of a white Catholic priest leading a Black Power movement was confounding. In the face of massive white resistance, Father Groppi modeled a very different kind of white identity that pointed toward new racial possibilities. His articulation of a Black Power politic rooted in the Catholic Church suggested a more complex relationship between religion and racial militancy. The Commandos' philosophy of not-violence called into question the false dichotomy between nonviolence and armed self-defense. Their adoption of "masculinist uplift" was simultaneously elevating and limiting. The YC's ability to reconcile race pride and community empowerment with integrationist goals, such as open housing, indicated a much more fluid connection between concepts like "integration" and "Black Power." And as in other struggles for racial justice across the country, women played a crucial but hidden role in the open housing campaign.

In response to the civil rights insurgency in Milwaukee, thousands of hostile white residents took to the streets to defend what they perceived as their interests. This vigorous white reaction was shocking in its scope and appalling in the depth of racial hatred it articulated. Just as Father Groppi's role in the Movement challenges pat notions of Black Power, so too does the massive resistance by whites in Milwaukee's streets demand a reconsideration of the concept in the urban North.

As controversial as Groppi's public leadership in the Milwaukee Movement was, his presence also drew the attention of many. Unlike the militants in Washington, D.C., it was the fact that this white Catholic priest was working with young inner core black militants in a not-violent, interracial, church-based movement that held out hope for many of an alternative way forward. Martin Luther King Jr., who in 1967 was searching for his own new direction against the challenges of urban poverty, racial exclusivity, and rising violence, understood the important meaning of what was happening in Milwaukee when he telegrammed Groppi and the YC at the height of the open housing campaign. "What you and your courageous associates are doing in Milwaukee will certainly serve as a kind of massive nonviolence that we need in this turbulent period," he wrote. "You are demonstrating that it is possible to be militant and powerful without destroying life or property. Please know that you have my support and prayers."[43]

— 9 —

The Decline of Direct Action

On Sunday, September 21, 1969, Father Groppi led a coalition of welfare mothers, social workers, college students, poor African Americans, and Latinos on a weeklong march from Milwaukee to Madison to protest proposed cuts in the state's welfare budget. Republican Governor Warren Knowles had called a special session of the legislature the following week to consider his own proposal to provide more aid to urban antipoverty programs. As the "Welfare Mothers March" made its way toward the state capitol, local people brought homemade casseroles, breads, and fruit to sustain the poverty advocates. Farmers and churches opened their doors each night to the weary protesters. John Dequardo, Waukesha County Deputy Sheriff, joined the marchers as they moved through his territory. Demonstrators gave him buttons with slogans like, "I support a guaranteed adequate income for all Americans" and "Welfare Rights Now!" When the protesters left Waukesha County, Dequardo told Father Groppi, "Give 'em hell Father," while his white partner raised his fist in salute. Others were not so gracious or supportive. A man standing outside an Oconomowoc tavern shouted, "Fight poverty, get a job!" Many local businesses locked their doors and set out "Closed" signs as marchers strode by. One tavern owner closed up instead of allowing marchers to seek shelter from sub-50° temperatures and a driving rain. In Hubbleton, Wisconsin, the entire business district shut down for the day, and Waterloo residents directed "considerable hostility" toward the demonstrators.[1]

The ranks of the Welfare Mothers, which had averaged thirty-five during the week, swelled to over 100 as the state capitol came into view. On Sunday, September 28, the group made its way to Library Mall, on the campus of the University of Wisconsin–Madison, for a rally. Madison was in the midst of its own revolution during the late 1960s, fueled by New Left radicalism and a strong countercultural presence. More than 1,000 people—including dozens of welfare recipients from across the state and many University of Wisconsin–Madison students—turned out to greet the weary protesters and hear mothers on welfare demand that the legislature restore funds to programs aiding the poor. Diane Neitzel, president of the Washington County Welfare League, told the crowd, "We are the people, all of the people . . . These cuts are aimed at the children and we fight for them." A Mexican American welfare mother from Milwaukee spoke in broken English and fought back tears as she questioned the priorities of a state budget that allocated millions of dollars for airline and transportation services but only 16 cents per meal for adult welfare recipients. An impassioned Groppi told the crowd, "There's something wrong with a country that places so much emphasis on the military and cannot feed its own children." He further promised, "We did not march 90 miles for nothing. We will be as nice as we can be and as mean as we have to, to see that something is done for the children of the mothers on the march . . . We're tired of getting crumbs off [the legislature's] table of abundance. We're going to knock that table right out from under them."[2]

A similar rally on Monday drew a crowd of more than 3,000, many of them students and antiwar activists. Afterward, the group stretched nearly three blocks as people walked up State Street to make their case to the legislature. The demonstrators, following the lead of Father Groppi, several Commandos, and a group of Latino "Brown Berets," circled the capitol building, blocked traffic, and chanted "Power to the People." Local police officers watched as the protesters mounted the capitol stairs and entered the building. Father Groppi told the throng, "We have taken over the Capitol building. We have captured the building. We need people to bring in food. We don't intend to leave." The crowd responded with cheers, peace signs, and more choruses of "Power to the People." Assemblyman Lloyd Barbee was the only legislator to meet the group inside the capitol. He welcomed them and said, "Don't worry about accusations of stopping the legislature's work. The legislature has not done any significant work all year." He went on, "I am happy to see you recognize the need for change and that you are using your own rules to bring about change, rather than the system's rules." Groppi and Jesus Salas, director of the United Migrant Opportunity Services, then led demonstrators to the doors of the assembly chamber as several hundred others filled the upstairs gallery. Finding the heavy leather doors locked, Father Groppi and Salas summoned a group of Commandos and Brown Berets to knock them down with a few well-placed shoulder charges. The doors broke from their hinges and slammed to the floor, allowing nearly 1,000 to stream inside.[3]

The protest quickly took on a carnivalesque atmosphere. According to reports in the *Milwaukee Journal,*

> Where the clerks normally sit and record the day's events, angry welfare marchers strode on the desk top, leading songs, chanting slogans and making speeches amidst loaves of bread, jars of peanut butter and mayonnaise and packages of baloney.
>
> The thronelike chair where the assembly speaker should sit was occupied, at various times, by mothers, squirming children and orators who were using it and the speaker's podium for something to stand on. The last occupant was a bushy haired young man, leaning back with his feet folded comfortably on the rostrum, making a call on the speaker's telephone.

Speaker after speaker rose to talk about the plight of poor people in Wisconsin. As they spoke, paper airplanes made from legislative documents sailed through the air, college students strummed guitars, and welfare mothers chased after their children. Following a brief attempt by legislators to enter the room, the speaker of the assembly moved to adjourn the session, and most lawmakers fled the building. The welfare protestors occupied the capitol building for a total of eleven hours before law enforcement officials ejected them around midnight. The takeover was an unprecedented chapter in the history of the Wisconsin legislature.[4]

The next day, welfare marchers again circled the capitol. Hundreds of National Guardsmen with fixed bayonets kept order while angry legislative leaders, most of them conservative Republicans, vowed to kill the governor's emergency poverty measures and make Father Groppi pay. Turning to a long-ignored 1848 law, Assemblyman James Sensenbrenner Jr. introduced a bill declaring Groppi in contempt of the legislature and ordering him to jail for six months or until the legislative session ended. Father Groppi's supporters argued that legislators had circumvented due process, and Lloyd Barbee complained that to "sock it to a priest is as low as you can go." Legislators claimed that the move was necessary to preserve order and stave off anarchy. In the end, the assembly voted 72–24 in favor of the contempt citation, but local police had already arrested Father Groppi at a nearby Catholic church for disorderly conduct. As officers led him away, he said, solemnly, "Pray for me."[5]

Ten days after the assembly's vote, a federal judge overturned the citation and freed Groppi. An appeals court disagreed, but in 1972 the U.S. Supreme Court unanimously ruled that the assembly had violated the priest's rights. Father Groppi ultimately served more than a month in jail, and the experience rattled him. According to Father Dismas Becker, it "killed his spirit."[6]

The Welfare Mothers March was the last major direct action campaign of the civil rights era in Milwaukee. Following the open housing demonstrations, Father Groppi, the NAACP Youth Council (YC), and the Commandos headed off in new, and often different, directions. Civil rights insurgency, overall, waned as local, state, and national circumstances changed during the late 1960s and early 1970s. This chapter looks at the decline of direct action in Milwaukee during the late 1960s

Dr. King's Last Crusade

The open housing campaign in Milwaukee caught the attention of civil rights leaders across the country, particularly advocates of nonviolence and interracialism who were searching for a way forward in the face of Black Power racial exclusivity and urban rage. Early in 1968, Martin Luther King Jr. invited Father Groppi, the YC, and the Commandos to join him on a new crusade against poverty. King had become distressed as the spiraling cost of war in Vietnam forced steep cuts in Great Society and War on Poverty funding. In response, he envisioned a "Poor People's Campaign," in which thousands of impoverished Americans of every racial and ethnic background descended on Washington, D.C., in an attempt to compel lawmakers to pass an "economic bill of rights," patterned on the G.I. Bill, for the poor. King asked the Milwaukee activists to help organize and lead the Midwestern contingent of this interracial movement of the poor; they agreed. After King's assassination in April, the Southern Christian Leadership Conference decided to press on with its fallen leader's "last crusade," despite evidence that a majority of white Americans opposed it for fear of racial violence.[7]

From February through May of 1968, as the open housing campaign dragged on, Father Groppi, several YC members, and the Commandos helped recruit participants to the Poor People's Campaign in Wisconsin, Indiana, Michigan, Georgia, Pennsylvania, Ohio, and Mississippi. In May, Father Groppi flew to Atlanta to greet 500 marchers as they arrived there. Appearing with Coretta Scott King, Ralph Abernathy, Stevie Wonder, and Diana Ross and the Supremes, Father Groppi told the crowd of 10,000,

"We're going up to Washington and march around the capitol the same way Joshua marched around Jericho, and before we give up, the White House is going to come crumbling down."[8] Later that month, Groppi and several Commandos flew to Detroit, where they joined the Midwestern caravan to the Poor People's Campaign, officially led by Dr. King's younger brother, Reverend A. D. King. Because A. D. King was largely a symbolic leader, the Commandos took on the primary responsibility of managing the group and maintaining order.

Following a preliminary rally, demonstrators in Detroit returned to Cobo Hall to find police officers readying to tow away the marchers' stalled communications car. Several Commandos quickly encircled the vehicle and blocked police action, explaining that a new battery was on its way. The standoff escalated as the two sides exchanged harsh words and a series of threats. After a battalion of mounted police arrived and civil rights activists still refused to budge, a fifteen-minute melee broke out, with mounted police clubbing marchers and reporters indiscriminately. The "Detroit Incident," which resulted in sixteen injuries, was the only serious violent confrontation involving Poor People's Campaign demonstrators during the entire protest.[9]

In Washington, D.C., Father Groppi told U.S. Attorney General Ramsey Clark that if legislators did not act, poverty advocates would tie up traffic and create a dramatic confrontation with government institutions. Yet, despite these and other threats, the Poor People's Campaign fizzled under persistent rain, police repression, a reactionary political climate, and a general lack of organization. At "Resurrection City," the makeshift encampment of poverty protesters near the capitol, internal unrest mushroomed. According to historian Gerald McKnight, "Turf battles, drunken brawls, protection rackets, and petty theft became common occurrences." FBI informants inside the city identified Milwaukee Commandos as one of the four groups taking advantage of the deteriorating circumstances and claimed that they were armed with "knives, guns or clubs." When police finally moved in to disband the site, Groppi and the Commandos peacefully returned home.[10]

Back in Milwaukee, the tight coalition of YC members and Commandos that had sustained the open housing campaign disintegrated. At the same time as Father Groppi and one contingent of Commandos organized for the Poor People's Campaign, another group moved away from direct action. During the summer of 1967, Julius Modlinski, a social worker at Marquette University, helped a group of Commandos establish a youth employment and recreation program and encouraged the group toward a social service approach to civil rights. In September 1968, three Commando leaders— Hank Walters, James Pierce, and Johnnie Davis—approached Modlinski for help finding jobs. Modlinski, Wesley Scott of the Urban League, and Joe Fagan of the state Industrial Commission worked with ten Commandos to craft a plan of action. According to Jesse Wade,

> There were like six or seven of us moving around the universities trying to figure out how we could get some programs started for those guys that the [police] started picking up and putting in jail because a lot of those people who had been marching went to jail who had warrants out for them, but still came out and marched knowing that if they got caught they were going to jail. So we noticed that there were a lot of parolees and probationers out there . . . So, we began to mobilize in that area.

On November 8, the group met with several inner-city school principles to discuss the possibility of developing youth programs. In January, the Commandos submitted a proposal to the state for a $160,176 grant to start "Commandos, Inc." Shortly thereafter, they received $47,000 for a six-month trial program to counsel African American parolees. The group dubbed the effort Commandos Project I (CPI). As Wade recalled, "[We] had to prove to the fathers of the city that we weren't just a storm-trooping group." Increasingly, this nucleus of Commandos turned their attention away from open housing and toward youth development and the ex-offender program. CPI continued its community service programs into the mid-1970s.[11]

Many civil rights activists, including a number of YC members and Commandos, claimed that Commandos, Inc., represented the co-opting of the Movement by "the system." Prentice McKinney called it a "buyout."[12] Dismas Becker, another white priest active in the civil rights movement, agreed. "A lot of the people who were a part of [the civil rights insurgency] got institutionalized," he explained. "Basically, it was the government's best weapon. They got those people that were causing the trouble and gave them an institution to run . . . The Commandos Project I. A lot of them went into community service, and the fire went down. The civil rights doors closed."[13] Many Commandos, particularly those loyal to Father Groppi, preferred that the group stay independent from the "system" and continue to focus on direct action. For those involved with CPI, the program offered a chance to do long-term community work on issues they cared about while also getting paid. According to Paul Crawford, "The original idea was to hire all the Commandos, really, because there were so many guys out of work."[14] Regardless of these internal dynamics, the establishment of Commandos, Inc., signaled not only a split and a move away from direct action but also the decline of the Commandos.

With his base fragmenting, Father Groppi resigned as advisor to the YC in November of 1968. The reasons for this break were myriad. Many of the original members of the YC and Commandos had already moved on to college, marriage, or full-time jobs. The tight personal bonds that had brought Groppi into partnership with young people in the first place were no longer present, at least not within the formal framework of the YC or Commandos. In addition, Groppi continued to face criticism from some for his leading role in the local black freedom movement. Even though Milwaukee had stood against the dominant national tide of racial separatism and Black Power during the open housing campaign, those trends eventually overwhelmed the local scene. Both Milwaukee black newspapers embraced cultural nationalism and welcomed the priest's ouster. Others groused that Groppi was "profiting" off of the Movement when he traveled the country for speaking engagements. Father Groppi publicly denied claims that he had been forced out of the YC, instead telling reporters that he resigned to organize his parish "along the lines of militant social action involvement." He also justified the move by explaining that his job as advisor had always been "self-liquidating." Now that the YC was self-sufficient, he argued, he was no longer needed.

In addition, Father Groppi's vision of social justice expanded as he gained national prominence, taking him in new directions. Slowly, Groppi became more involved with antiwar activism. On September 24, 1968, fourteen men, including five priests and a minister, removed more than 10,000 draft cards from Milwaukee's draft board office and burned them in a nearby public square dedicated to fallen soldiers in U.S. wars. Faced with harsh penalties and stiff jail terms, Father Groppi agreed to co-chair the Milwaukee 14 Defense Committee, which publicized the case and organized demonstrations outside the courthouse. The Milwaukee 14 gained national notoriety alongside other similar trials from that time period, including those of the Chicago 7 and Catonsville 9.[15]

Father Groppi's role in the Milwaukee 14 campaign, coupled with the national media exposure he received during the open housing demonstrations, opened up new worlds of activism, particularly among antiwar

activists, New Left radicals, and counterculturalists. In June 1971, police arrested Groppi during a strike by university workers at Yale. In October of
that year, he supported the Nixon Eviction campaign in Washington, D.C.
There, he participated in a "people's panel," a "grand jury investigation of
citizen grievances and American power"; spoke on the telephone to North
Vietnamese representatives about their recent peace proposal; and marched
on the White House, where he and hundreds of others hoped to serve an
"eviction notice" to the president. Instead, police arrested more than 300
activists, including Groppi and radical pacifist Dave Dellinger. On December 10, Father Groppi took part in the Free John Sinclair concert in Ann
Arbor, Michigan, where he shared the stage with John Lennon, Yoko Ono,
Stevie Wonder, Archie Shepp, Commander Cody, Phil Ochs, Jerry Rubin,
Bobby Seale, Allen Ginsberg, and Jonnie Lee Tillmon. Sinclair, a colorful
radical poet and political activist best known as the manager of the left-
wing proto-punk band MC5 and founder of the White Panther Party, had
been sentenced to nine years' imprisonment on a minor marijuana charge
and was widely viewed in New Left circles as a political prisoner.[16]

Following Father Groppi's resignation as advisor, the YC virtually disappeared from public notice. The group continued to meet at St. Boniface and
consulted Groppi when necessary. Members staged brief demonstrations
for increased job opportunities at inner core laundries, supported Groppi-
led protests against the Allen-Bradley Company and for welfare rights, and
later worked with the short-lived Milwaukee Black Panther Party to protest
racial discrimination at a local movie theater, but the YC quickly became a
marginal player in local racial politics.

The Allen-Bradley Protest

Even as the direct action coalition that had sustained the open housing
campaign disintegrated, specific issues still had the potential to mobilize
short bursts of civil rights insurgency. In between the open housing protests
and the Welfare Mothers March, employment discrimination at the Allen-
Bradley Company spurred a targeted direct action campaign. Employment
discrimination had continued to plague the inner core community ever
since the initial organizing efforts of the Milwaukee Negro American Labor
Council (MNCALC) almost a decade before.

The controversy began at a Washington, D.C., gathering of black newspaper editors when Ken Coulter, the brash, young publisher of the *Milwaukee*

Star, confronted President Johnson about employment discrimination at Milwaukee's largest employer. Allen-Bradley, which received in excess of $30 million in federal contracts, employed a paltry twenty-five black workers out of a total labor force of 7,500. In addition, the company refused to make any efforts toward recruiting or retaining African American, Jewish American, or Latino workers, despite a series of presidential executive orders stretching back to 1941 that outlawed employment discrimination in companies that received federal contracts. For many decades, the company and local 111 of the United Electrical, Radio and Machine Workers of America (UE) maintained a preferential hiring procedure whereby friends or family members received priority in employment decisions with a recommendation from a current employee. Because white workers had historically dominated the labor pool, this "friends and family" policy effectively reinforced the color line at Allen-Bradley, even though the plant was located in the heart of the city's burgeoning Latino community.[17]

Caught off guard by Coulter's caustic rebuke, Johnson looked searchingly around the room, stretched out his finger toward one of his assistant counselors, and said simply, "Do something." Shortly thereafter, the solicitor of labor summoned James Jones, a young African American lawyer in the Labor Department, and commanded him to issue a complaint against Allen-Bradley. With a small staff of three lawyers, Jones boarded an airplane to Milwaukee and began to pull together a case. According to Jones, the Allen-Bradley suit was the first attempt by federal officials to enforce the long string of nondiscrimination executive orders dating back to Franklin Roosevelt's historic Executive Order 8802.[18]

In April, Jones formally accused the company of failing to fulfill its fair employment obligations as a federal contractor based on the terms of President Johnson's Executive Order 11246. Although the notice made no claim of overt discrimination in hiring, it did highlight the general lack of minority employees at the company and the failure of Allen-Bradley to take "affirmative action" to remedy this discriminatory pattern as mandated by the order.[19]

Despite its complicity in the friends and family policy, UE leadership at local 1111 quickly moved to a public stance in support of federal action. On May 26, the UE issued a statement to the press demanding that Allen-Bradley agree to a nondiscrimination clause in their labor agreement. The union's support emanated from practical considerations over moral or ethical concerns; they feared the potential loss of 1,500 jobs for their members if government contracts were revoked. The union leadership's public support for an antidiscrimination clause sent a rush of rumors throughout the plant. White workers worried that any changes might result in loss of jobs, reduced pay, or a change to the seniority system. Many attacked the new policy as a "quota" and "reverse discrimination." The declining industrial economy and growing white reaction against civil rights, in general, fueled these fears.[20]

As federal officials and union leaders grappled with Allen-Bradley's team of sixty lawyers, a small group of African American and Latino activists initiated a direct action campaign against the company. In July 1968, Father Groppi and several members of the YC and Commandos joined the brewing controversy. Fresh from their open housing victory, Father Groppi told local and national media that picketing would begin outside the company gates unless Allen-Bradley promised to hire more minority workers. "Allen-Bradley neither said they had a program nor had any desire to hire black people," he explained. "That is why we feel we are justified in taking direct action." Echoing past arguments by Calvin Sherard and the Milwaukee Negro American Labor Council (MNALC), Groppi also suggested that the company should "have a number [of black workers] comparable to the percentage of Negroes in Milwaukee, about 12 percent." In a new twist on Milwaukee civil rights activism, a group of Latinos, primarily Mexican American, also formed a direct action organization and joined forces with the YC, creating a strong coalition dedicated to ending discrimination at the South Side manufacturer. Under the leadership of Armando Orellana, the Milwaukee Latin-American Union for Civil Rights also demanded that Allen-Bradley hire Latinos based on their proportion in the community, about 5 percent.[21]

On August 17, 275 African American, Latino, and white demonstrators gathered at St. Boniface for a rally. The group heard speeches by Groppi; YC President Lawrence Friend; Commando direct action chairman Joe Mc-Clain; and Bill Robinson, vice president of the UAW local 1486 at the International Harvester plant. Following the rally, the protest supporters set out for the South Side. The demonstration grew to more than 400 as activists picketed outside the company's front gates. The scene was repeated over the next few days without serious incident.[22]

The impact of the direct action campaign was significant. With pickets, demonstrations, and a few disorderly conduct arrests came a new wave of local and national media attention. Milwaukee's two mainstream newspapers failed to give more than cursory coverage to the case between March and July but published nineteen articles on the Allen-Bradley controversy in August, focusing primarily on the actions and statements of the coalition. The *New York Times* also ran a lengthy article on the picketing at Allen-Bradley. With heightened media attention came increased local awareness and outrage, which placed further pressure on Allen-Bradley executives to act. As James Jones recalled, "[The civil rights coalition] generated important community pressure by demonstrating. The newspapers and media covered it. Their direct action supplied the media story that only the black press had carried previously. So, they drummed up the political firestorm necessary to get Allen-Bradley moving."[23]

On April 24, 1969, after an exhausting series of meeting, hearings, and considerable wrangling and under renewed threats of debarment, federal officials and Allen-Bradley lawyers hammered out an agreement. Father Groppi, speaking on behalf of the YC, called the agreement "too weak" and "just a lot of words. We're not interested in words." He further stated, "We want information. We want to know how many blacks and Latins the company employs and where they are working." Disappointed, Father Groppi and more than a dozen YC members and Commandos briefly picketed the company again in August of 1969. Dr. Benjamin Spock, the noted pediatrician and ardent antiwar activist, joined the protest. The brief spate of protest turned ugly when a group of white workers attacked several demonstrators as they blocked the entrance to the plant. During the melee, police arrested Father Groppi and three other activists on charges of disorderly conduct.[24]

Latino community leaders maintained a more upbeat outlook. Armando Orellana stated, "We consider the ruling . . . a victory for the Latin American people. We are encouraged. More Latin Americans are working for Allen-Bradley." Orellana also suggested that because of the decision against Allen-Bradley, other Milwaukee businesses had become more concerned about their executive order obligations. In retrospect, James Jones concluded, "Without the pressure of local people, I don't think this would have happened."[25]

The Welfare Mothers March

Fast on the heels of the Allen-Bradley demonstrations, a diverse group of Milwaukee welfare mothers and social workers approached Father Groppi through the Council on Urban Life to lead a protest against proposed cuts in the state budget. The welfare reform movement in Wisconsin mirrored a national political trend during the late 1960s and early 1970s. A renewed acknowledgment of persistent poverty collided with a growing national fiscal crisis and the "new conservatism" to make for contentious politics. President Richard Nixon, federal lawmakers, and welfare rights advocates tussled over the direction and content of reform. In Wisconsin, conservative state legislators spearheaded an effort to trim benefits to the poor. The move outraged civil rights leaders, poverty advocates, and liberal politicians throughout the state but particularly in Milwaukee, where a disproportionate number of poor people and people of color lived. The link between racial discrimination and poverty was clear to many activists. "Most people saw the connection between welfare reform and racism," Father Dismas Becker explained. "While the majority of people on welfare were not black, proportionally there were more black people on welfare than white people. So, people made the connection that poverty and minority-ism were [linked]. The result of racism was a lack of jobs and poverty."[26]

As the march from Milwaukee to Madison proceeded, the campaign appeared to pick up steam with growing popular support. In large measure, this was due to Father Groppi and the Commandos' participation. Their national reputation and proven activist record drew significant public attention to the cause. According to Becker, one of the main organizers of the march, that attention took a problematic turn in Madison: "The thing exploded [when Groppi] went to campus and gave a talk there encouraging students to join them and 3,000 students joined them. That just magnified and terrified everyone when they saw 3,000 people walking up State Street." With the takeover of the assembly chamber, the Welfare Mothers March lost the head of steam it had built over the previous two weeks of planning, organizing, and peaceful marching. Immediately, the media and public opinion turned harshly against the demonstrators. Again, Father Becker explained:

[The impact of the takeover was] negative, very negative. We were working to put together a good coalition of people to pressure [the legislature]. The governor was on our side, and it basically tied the hands of the governor because it became so political, and people were so upset by this rowdy crowd that he wasn't able to do anything . . . Groppi had essentially taken over the seat of government, and the legislature met across the street, in essence a government in exile if you want to put it that way. I said to

[Groppi,] "What are you doing here? This is no longer a protest, this is a revolution." And he just shrugged it off. We lost everything there.[27]

The seizure of the capitol highlighted the lack of long-term planning in Father Groppi's civil rights leadership. Moved by injustice, he acted, sometimes without considering the full impact of those actions. During the open housing campaign, this willingness to confront racial justice head on had, on balance, worked to the advantage of the Movement. A year later, the political context had changed enough that now the militancy of poverty rights advocates was cast in a negative public light.

While the Welfare Mothers March linked to the protest politics of the previous decade, it also underscored the changed dynamics of the late 1960s. Despite Father Groppi's leadership and the presence of a number of loyal YC members and Commandos, the priest no longer operated from a formal institutional base outside the church. In addition, the significant participation of Latinos in both the Allen-Bradley demonstrations and the Welfare Mothers March suggested that the urban demographics of race and ethnicity were rapidly changing. No longer would city politics play out along simple lines of black and white. A growing influx of Mexican Americans, Puerto Ricans, and other Latin American populations would complicate coalition politics in most large northern cities, including Milwaukee. In addition, the welfare issue pushed poor black, brown, and white women to the forefront of the Movement, giving a public voice to those who were often invisible. Moreover, the massive infusion of student participation in the takeover of the assembly chambers indicated the degree to which Vietnam and the antiwar effort had eclipsed civil rights as the galvanizing activist issue of the day. Welfare activists also confronted the new politics of white backlash as conservative political leaders moved to curtail the liberal gains of the previous decade, and a fatigued public increasingly opposed confrontational direct action tactics and the growing radical spirit. The liberal moment had passed, and a new era of conservatism and "law and order" dawned. Reform possibilities diminished in proportion to these altered political trends. According to Father Dismas Becker,

[The Kennedy and Johnson administrations] were liberal, and liberalism stimulates protest. Nixon came in and was much more [conservative] . . . and people didn't see the opportunity there. Federal money was thrown into communities and was basically used as a divider between the different political forces. Then that money dried up . . . It was a trough. Good people, but needy people got money. Then, not so good people got a lot of money [and civil rights activism declined.][28]

Civil rights activism in Milwaukee, of course, did not simply revolve around the YC, the Commandos, or Father James Groppi; there were many others struggling for racial justice in various ways during the late 1960s. Vel Phillips and Orville Pitts, the second African American Common Council member, continued to work on a variety of issues through traditional political channels.[29] Similarly, Lloyd Barbee kept raising his voice for racial justice and human rights in the state legislature. Moderate local civil rights groups attempted to register black voters to increase African American political power. For his part, Mayor Henry Maier still pushed his metropolitan-wide political agenda as well as his "Crusade for Resources." In addition, the Organization of Organizations, a confederation of social welfare and inner core groups, fought to secure federal and state monies earmarked for urban renewal and civil rights and to make local institutions live up to the promise of "maximum feasible participation of the poor" in the use and distribution of that funding. There were innumerable formal and informal expressions of race pride, cultural nationalism, community organizing, and economic independence within Milwaukee's African American community. And in personal relationships across the city, residents of all races attempted to navigate the new politics of race and ethnicity in the emerging "post–civil rights era."

Perhaps the most significant new organization to arise out of the changed circumstances of the late 1960s and early 1970s was the short-lived Milwaukee chapter of the Black Panther Party (MBPP). The group, which embraced racial separatism and armed self-defense, was established in 1969, only to be dissolved by the central committee of the national organization that same year due to "counter-revolutionary leadership" and then reincorporated for a brief time in 1971. Although the MBPP never became a significant force in the city, it did institute a number of social service programs for inner core residents, including free busing to prison for convicts' family members, a free health center, a free daycare center, an egg cooperative, a community blood bank, and a free breakfast program for poor children. The MBPP also published a newsletter, monitored local police activities, and performed other practical services for inner core black residents, including filling in potholes, finding temporary housing for African American evictees, and pressuring local businesses to hire more minority workers. Most of these efforts were small in scale and short-lived.[30]

In many ways, by the early 1970s the era of direct action in Milwaukee had ended. Activists had effectively seized the moment, identified a set of problems facing local African Americans, organized around them in a series of discreet campaigns, achieved some gains and suffered some defeats, and, in doing so, transformed the political landscape. The local and national contexts changed dramatically after 1968, and the civil rights movement needed to reassess its goals, strategies, and tactics by responding to the altered circumstances. This new phase of political activism was no less important than the era of direct action, but it was distinct. By 1970, the era of sustained militant direct action had ended in Milwaukee, and an era of community organizing and cultural and electoral politics had begun.

Even so, most of the leading civil rights figures in Milwaukee continued to work for racial justice even after the direct action era faded. Calvin Sherard, who led MNALC's economic boycotts during the early 1960s, left Milwaukee for Detroit, where he worked with the United Auto Workers union and the A. Philip Randolph Institute. John Givens, the former head of the Milwaukee Congress of Racial Equality, became a labor negotiator at General Motors Corporation and was ultimately the first African American appointed as an advisor to the mayor of Milwaukee. Lloyd Barbee kept pressing the school desegregation lawsuit to victory in 1977 and pushed a wide array of human rights issues in the assembly until the end of his tenure in 1976. Vel Phillips worked on a variety of inner core issues in the Common Council until 1971. She went on to become the first female black judge in Wisconsin, the first person of color elected to statewide office in 1978—as secretary of state—and an active leader in several Milwaukee civil rights organizations. Father Groppi became an important antiwar activist and worked on numerous other progressive issues, locally and nationally. During the mid-1970s, he appeared with Marlon Brando in northern Wisconsin to support the rights of indigenous people, attended international peace conferences in Montreal and Paris, and traveled to Ireland at the request of a Catholic bishop to support the growing drive for independence. After leaving the priesthood in 1972—a move common among activist clergy from the 1960s—Groppi married a former YC member, Margaret Rozga, in 1976; became a Milwaukee city bus driver; and organized a statewide union before succumbing to brain cancer in 1985. Mayor Henry Maier worked for shared revenues and a metropolitan-wide politics until his tenure in office ended in 1986. Many of the YC members and Commandos moved on to college or full-time employment, often in social services, teaching, or government. Dozens of priests, nuns, and ministers returned to their churches, where they promised to continue to work for change. And a large segment of the ordinary people that supported the civil rights insurgency in Milwaukee by participating in marches, demonstrations, and rallies were profoundly affected by their experiences and remembered that time as the most exhilarating and meaningful of their lives.

Conclusion:
"We Are Destined . . ."

On February 28, 1990, Milwaukee alderman Michael McGee announced the formation of the Black Panther Militia. The group's manifesto, like that of the original group in 1966, turned the promise of America's founding document on its head. "We are destined," it said, "for incarceration, death and complete and absolute sadness, instead of life, liberty and the pursuit of happiness promised by the Declaration of Independence." In March, McGee threatened all-out guerrilla warfare in Milwaukee—including sniper attacks, severed electrical wires, and burning tires on freeways—if government officials did not direct millions of dollars toward economic development, health care, and emergency employment programs in the inner core by the end of 1995. "The kind of fight I'm talking about bringing to Milwaukee," he said, "is the kind that once it starts here, it's gonna spread throughout the country. It's the white establishment's worst nightmare. You can't cope with an internal enemy, underground, tied up into the fabric of society. So that means that any black anywhere could be a sympathizer or a member—and I've got white members."[1]

But Michael McGee did not appear to be a typical radical situated along the fringes of society. Happily married for twenty years and the father of nine children, he had much to lose. McGee earned a bronze star for his service in Vietnam and worked with a variety of established institutions on community development before being elected to the Common Council in 1984, where he represented the inner core. During the ensuing years, McGee became frustrated with the inaction of local government in the face of an ever-deepening urban crisis in Milwaukee. Large-scale economic and demographic changes had continued to ravage communities of color. By

1990, he decided that more confrontational tactics were needed to prod the city's power structure to action.

Michael McGee's incendiary comments and apocalyptic vision brought the urban crisis in Milwaukee renewed national attention. Some people dismissed his threat as the misplaced rantings of a lunatic. Others were enraged and recoiled at the suggestion of violence as a means to change. Many took McGee's promise seriously. Regardless of what people thought about Michael McGee, the Black Panther Militia, or their warning, it was impossible to deny that the urban crisis that had animated thousands of local people during the 1960s continued to rage unabated in Milwaukee's central city more than twenty years later.[2]

The story of race relations and the civil rights insurgency in Milwaukee during the 1960s forcefully illustrates that the urban North was, in fact, the site of dramatic and important struggles for racial justice. Between 1958 and 1970, a series of indigenous leaders, local organizations, and coalitions coalesced around a string of issues—employment, public education, the membership of public officials in private clubs, police–community relations, housing, and welfare rights—to challenge racial inequality. Early on, groups such as the Milwaukee Negro American Labor Council and the Milwaukee Congress of Racial Equality experimented with protest politics with varying degrees of success. Over time, a new generation of community leaders, more in tune with young people and the migrant working class, began to voice a challenge to traditional community leadership and its cautious approach to change. As the national climate on race and civil rights shifted during the early and mid-1960s, local activists seized new opportunities to act. The Fred Lins controversy sparked the first sit-ins and galvanized inner core leaders, at least momentarily, by tapping into popular support. The school desegregation campaign mobilized thousands of inner core residents and educated a whole new generation of young people about civil rights and social action. Lloyd Barbee's unique mix of legalism, intellectualism, and activism was effective in the context of this fight against segregated public education. Even so, throughout, white civic leaders remained unmoved, prompting Barbee to go into the courts and others to head into the streets.

The Eagles Club (EC) protest marked the dramatic entrance of Father Groppi and the YC onto the local scene and ushered in a more confrontational phase of civil rights insurgency in Milwaukee. The scale of massive white resistance in suburban Wauwatosa as well as growing tensions between law enforcement officers and activists prompted the formation of the Commandos, a unique self-defense group that practiced "not-violence." Though the EC campaign was both controversial and unsuccessful, civil rights activists learned valuable lessons that they applied in subsequent demonstrations.

The open housing campaign took place at a critical transitional moment in the national struggle for racial justice. As a growing number of activists nationwide embraced a vision of Black Power that included violence, racial separatism, and political radicalism, Milwaukee civil rights activists stood against the tide by fashioning their own version of Black Power rooted in local circumstances. The Milwaukee Movement seemed to reject the idea that race pride, self-determination, and integration were antithetical. Instead, activists offered a vision of civil rights insurgency that emphasized consciousness as well as color. Like Birmingham and Selma, the local movement in Milwaukee carried national significance. At its height, the open housing campaign seemed to many the last stand of a nonviolent, interracial, church-based movement. Even Martin Luther King Jr. was deeply inspired by what was happening in Milwaukee, suggesting that Father Groppi, the YC, and the Commandos had found a "middle ground between riots and sentimental and timid supplications for justice." Unlike Dr. King's failed effort in Chicago in 1966, the Milwaukee open housing campaign provided evidence that nonviolent direct action could be an effective tactic in the urban North.[3]

Father Groppi's faith and his role as a priest were central to his commitment to racial justice as well as to his particular brand of leadership. "Marching is not only a protest," he said, "it is a prayer." Conversely, many whites who resisted racial change also viewed the world through a Catholic lens, only a far more traditional one.[4] We are just beginning to appreciate the complex, and often contradictory, roles Catholics played in the urban North during the civil rights era, an important dynamic considering the large proportion of Catholics in the region.

The principal tactic in these campaigns was nonviolent direct action, though it evolved into "not-violence" and riots did occur. Milwaukee civil rights activists hoped to use an increasingly confrontational direct action strategy to pressure entrenched institutions and unwilling city fathers to respond to the problems facing inner core residents. Beyond a few basic tenets, Father Groppi, the YC, and the Commandos did not adhere to any uniform ideology or doctrine. Their approach was pragmatic and experimental, rooted in the real-life needs of inner core residents. As circumstances shifted and new issues emerged, the YC and Commandos learned and grew, refining their tactics and strategies. Along the way, they provoked massive resistance and street violence from thousands of white Milwaukeeans that rivaled any of the more famous episodes of white reaction in the South.

This history supports the growing body of scholarship that underscores the limits of postwar racial liberalism. Official white intransigence, perhaps more than any other factor, fueled civil rights insurgency in Milwaukee. "In the whole Movement," Margaret Rozga explained, "in any of those actions, if [white civic leaders] would have responded reasonably in the first place, it would have never happened . . . people got frozen into their position as soon as you pointed out something that could be changed." In truth, despite strong progressive, labor, socialist, and liberal traditions in Milwaukee, white supremacy pervaded local politics.[5]

Even with the national attention "the Selma of the North" generated between 1965 and 1968, the story of civil rights insurgency in Milwaukee has largely fallen from public memory. Unlike the 1965 campaign for voting rights in Selma, the YC and Commandos' campaigns offered no clear moral divisions, nor did they hold forth a tidy redemptive narrative of American institutions overcoming an obvious injustice. Competing ideas of private property, free association, individual rights, and the American Dream collided with an insurgent racial militancy, resulting in a series of explosive clashes. Race relations, civil rights insurgency, and Black Power were, in many ways, considerably more murky in the urban North than in the Jim Crow South. And because most of these issues persist, the story of the civil rights movement in places like Milwaukee requires a reckoning with contemporary racial issues that historians and the public have been reluctant to entertain. To be sure, we are still early in the process of excavating important Movement stories outside of the South. Perhaps with time this imbalance will change, and northern struggles for racial justice will take their places alongside the more well-known stories of the South.

It is difficult to assess the successes and failures of the civil rights insurgency in Milwaukee during the 1960s. For instance, although activists ultimately succeeded in forcing the Common Council to pass a relatively strong citywide open housing ordinance, a temporary exemption of two-unit apartments barred African Americans from access to a significant portion of the city's housing. Even with full coverage after 1974, housing discrimination persisted, in part because of the informal aspects of real estate practices that make the industry hard to regulate, as well as continuing racial bias in loan and mortgage decisions. And the issue of fair housing has always been interconnected with other persistent inequalities that have yet to be fully addressed or overcome.

Similarly, the protracted legal battle against segregated public schools was not tried until 1973–1974, more than eight years after Lloyd Barbee brought suit in 1965. It took two more years for the judge to rule that segregation did exist. After the school board appealed the decision, the U.S. Supreme Court remanded the case to district court to decide whether the segregation in Milwaukee's schools had been intentional and, if so, to determine its present effects. In 1978, the federal district court ruled that public school officials had intentionally acted to perpetuate the racial imbalance in the Milwaukee schools since 1950 and that the effects of these policies were currently citywide. Even after a 1979 settlement, the results were unclear. Of the 8,500 students reassigned to new schools to combat segregation, 80 percent were African American. At the same time, white parents increasingly fled the public system or moved to lily-white suburban school districts outside the grasp of the Milwaukee city school system.

Large, macrolevel trends continued to foster racial inequality in Milwaukee despite the real gains of the civil rights era. The boundaries of the inner core steadily pushed northward and westward as suburbanization and deindustrialization continued to fuel the decline of urban neighborhoods from the 1970s through the 1990s. The national economic malaise of the 1970s, the shift away from social welfare and toward a punitive public policy, and the Reagan-era policy of urban neglect perpetuated widespread African American poverty and social decay at the root of the urban crisis. As a result, author Jonathan Coleman wrote in 1997 that Milwaukee had "one of the nation's highest rates of black-to-white unemployment, one of the highest rates of black teen pregnancy, one of the highest turndown rates for minority loan applications, one of the lowest percentages of black owner-occupied housing, and one of the highest percentages of blacks living below the poverty line." These circumstances provided the seedbed for a new black radicalism in the city. Yet, unlike in the 1960s, Alderman McGee and other black radicals did not inspire grassroots support, an indication that there were critical differences between the two historical periods.[6]

Perhaps Milwaukee civil rights activists succeeded in something other than tangible gains. What unified the struggle for racial justice during the 1960s was an underlying effort to convince white Milwaukeeans and the existing power structure that the problems of the inner core were legitimate, that they emanated chiefly from racial discrimination and systemic inequality, and that they required significant and sustained action by the entire community. White people had long viewed the growing African American community as a cancer on an otherwise idyllic city. They often pushed responsibility for complicated urban problems onto this embattled minority population. As historian William Thompson has suggested, the Milwaukee civil rights movement "insisted upon . . . the acceptance of the idea that black people were an integral and essential part of the city."[7]

At the beginning of the twenty-first century, race continues to be, perhaps, the most salient and pressing issue facing community leaders in Milwaukee. According to the 2000 census, minorities make up 55 percent of the total Milwaukee population, with Latinos accounting for 12 percent and Asian Americans numbering 3 percent. The Latino community is concentrated in the neighborhoods just south of the Menominee River valley, forming a human buffer between the still largely white working-class South Side and the African American North Side. The Asian American community is scattered throughout the city.

Although there have been certain gains, pervasive racial inequality continues. Approaching 2010, black people make up roughly 40 percent of the total population of Milwaukee and can be found in all segments and at all levels of local society, but their representation is still not proportional. During the 1990s, the Common Council selected its first African American president, and in 2004 Marvin Pratt was sworn in as the city's first black mayor after a scandal forced John Norquist to resign. But overall, African American political participation remains low. The Eagles Club Ballroom was converted into a music venue—"The Rave"—where young people and musicians of every race gather to listen, play, and dance. At the same time, the downtown area has experienced a housing, business, and entertainment resurgence that is no doubt good for all residents in some ways, even as it diverts needed resources away from inner core programs.[8]

However, the overriding reality of race and the African American experience in Milwaukee continues to be dominated by poverty and inequality. Census data reveal that Milwaukee is one of the most segregated cities in the country. In 2007, the black male unemployment rate was 43 percent, the second highest in the nation. Most African American residents still live in or near the inner core; the South Side remains overwhelmingly white, as does the North Shore and the western suburbs. Even at the height of the mid-1990s economic boom, unemployment rates hovered as high as 30 or 40 percent in the most depressed inner core neighborhoods. Chronic poverty led to crime, drugs, and violence and bred hopelessness and despair. African American incarceration rates jumped, far outpacing whites. Also in the 1990s, Milwaukee's public schools began to resegregate, graduation rates in inner core high schools plummeted, and truancy rose. Henry Maier's vision of revenue sharing and metropolitan-wide political cooperation remains unfulfilled, and police–community relations are still tense.[9]

The Sixteenth Street Viaduct is now officially called the Groppi Unity Viaduct, but fewer and fewer people are aware of the meaning behind that designation. St. Boniface was razed in the mid-1970s to make way for an expansion of North Division High School and the old Commandos Project I sign no longer hangs outside its inner core headquarters. Civil rights veterans are getting older, and some have since passed away. During the 1960s, the civil rights insurgency emerged out of the dire circumstances facing most inner core black residents and the repeated inaction and indifference of both established black leaders and the broad white power structure. As the racial crisis in Milwaukee persists, the question remains today as it was back then: Are community leaders and Milwaukee residents of all races and ethnicities moving vigorously enough to address these mounting problems?

In late September 2007, a diverse group of several hundred Milwaukee residents, including a few dozen former YC members and Commandos, gathered with scholars from across the country at the University of Wisconsin–Milwaukee for the "March on Milwaukee" conference to commemorate the fortieth anniversary of the 1967–1968 open housing campaign and to probe the contemporary dynamics of the urban crisis. On a beautiful Sunday afternoon, people gathered again after all those years at the north end of the Sixteenth Street Viaduct. Vel Phillips, now eighty-two, linked arms with Margaret Rozga, Mayor Tom Barrett, who is white, and Willie L. Hines Jr., the African American president of the Common Council, to once again head south across "the longest bridge in the world." Joe McClain, Betty Martin, Dennis McDowell, Pamela Jo Sargent, and other civil rights veterans peppered the crowd, and several of the women led freedom songs.

Many who were there wore navy blue t-shirts that read "Milwaukee NAACP Youth Council 1967" in big white block letters, and a few had on black uniforms trimmed in gold that said "Commandos Phase II." Local reporters and their camera crews buzzed about looking for a good angle or a usable quote. At the center of the bridge, more than 100 members of the Latino community that now inhabits the blocks just south of the viaduct joined the commemoration in a display of solidarity. Many held signs that read "No Racism," "Fight for Justice," and "Si Se Puede/Yes We Can." A band of African drummers and two dancers pounded out a driving rhythm as people milled about and found seats in front of the stage. After a series of remarks by prominent officials and former movement leaders promising a renewed effort against intractable inequalities, Dick Gregory regaled the crowd with his old routine.

It was clear that weekend that the Milwaukee Movement mattered. It mattered in very personal and transformative ways for those individuals who had heard the call forty years ago and participated in the various marches and demonstrations. And it mattered to the city, which passed laws and broke down barriers. But the Movement mattered in another way. The speeches and stories and memories of the past served as a powerful reminder that there was still work left to be done, still chasms yet to be bridged.

Notes

Introduction

1. The following narrative is culled from various news accounts and personal interviews with participants. See *Milwaukee Journal,* August 30, 1967, p. 1; *Milwaukee Sentinel,* August 30, 1967, p. 1; *Milwaukee Star,* September 2, 1967, p. 1; and *Milwaukee Courier,* September 2, 1967, p. 1; Betty Martin, interview with Arlene Zakhar, January 20, 1984; Vel Phillips, interview with Patrick Jones, December 3, 1999, and April 20, 1999; Joe McClaine, interview with Patrick Jones, December 3, 1999, and March 29, 1999; Prentice McKinney, interview with Patrick Jones, January 11, 1999, and March 27, 1999; Margaret Rozga, interview with Patrick Jones, July 9, 2005, and July 26, 2005; Dennis McDowell, interview with Patrick Jones, August 11, 2005.

2. Throughout this text, I use the word "Movement." People who participated in the struggle for racial justice often called it "The Movement." They understood that their particular local work was a part of something bigger—The Movement—that was happening across the country. This language also underscores the social movement dynamic of what I am writing about.

3. A booklet published by the national NAACP Youth and College Division on the open housing campaign in Milwaukee states, "Early Wednesday, August 30th, some YC members returned to the Freedom House and found a tear gas canister and shotgun shell in the gutted cottage. Police claim no tear gas was thrown into the civil rights headquarters." Then, on August 30, Fire Chief Edward Canavan told reporters that his department's investigation concluded that a firebomb, not a tear gas shell, ignited the fire at the Freedom House. Canavan argued that it would have taken a tear gas canister several hours rather than several minutes to start the fire. The YC believed that this was an official whitewashing of the event. See "March in Milwaukee," NAACP Youth and College

261

Division, 1967, MNAACP Papers, State Historical Society of Wisconsin; *Milwaukee Journal,* August 31, 1967, p. 9.

4. See Jacquelyn Dowd Hall, "The Long Civil Rights Movement and the Political Uses of the Past," *Journal of American History* 91 (2005): 1233–1263; Charles Eagles, "Toward New Histories of the Civil Rights Era," *Journal of Southern History* 66, no. 4 (November 2000): 815–848.

5. Aldon Morris, *The Origins of the Civil Rights Movement: Black Communities Organizing for Change* (New York: Free Press, 1984); John Egerton, *Speak Now against the Day: The Generation before the Civil Rights Movement* (Chapel Hill: University of North Carolina Press, 1994); Patricia Sullivan, *Days of Hope: Race and Democracy in the New Deal Era* (Chapel Hill: University of North Carolina Press, 1996); Glenda Gilmore, *Defying Dixie: The Radical Roots of Civil Rights, 1919–1950* (New York: W. W. Norton, 2008).

6. John Dittmer, *Local People: The Struggle for Civil Rights in Mississippi* (Urbana: University of Illinois Press, 1994); Charles Payne, *I've Got the Light of Freedom: The Organizing Tradition and the Mississippi Freedom Struggle* (Berkeley: University of California Press, 1995). Other excellent recent local studies include Glenda Alice Rabby, *The Pain and the Promise: The Struggle for Civil Rights in Tallahassee, Florida* (Athens: University of Georgia Press, 1999); Kim Lacey Rogers, *Righteous Lives: Narratives of the New Orleans Civil Rights Movement* (New York: New York University Press, 1993); Adam Fairclough, *Race and Democracy: The Civil Rights Struggle in Louisiana, 1915–1972* (Athens: University of Georgia Press, 1995); David Cecelski, *Along Freedom Road: Hyde County, North Carolina and the Fate of Black Schools in the South* (Chapel Hill: University of North Carolina Press, 1994); Emilye Crosby, *A Little Taste of Freedom: The Black Freedom Struggle in Claiborne County, Mississippi* (Chapel Hill: University of North Carolina Press, 2005).

7. Joanne Grant, *Ella Baker: Freedom Bound* (New York: John Wiley & Sons, 1998); Chana Kai Lee, *For Freedom's Sake: The Life of Fannie Lou Hamer* (Urbana: University of Illinois Press, 1999); Vicki Crawford, Jacqueline Anne Rouse, and Barbara Woods, *Women in the Civil Rights Movement: Trailblazers and Torchbearers, 1941–1965* (Bloomington: University of Indiana Press, 1993); Bettye Collier-Thomas and V. P. Franklin, eds., *Sisters in the Struggle: African American Women in the Civil Rights–Black Power Movement* (New York: New York University Press, 2001); Constance Curry, ed., *Deep in Our Hearts: Nine White Women in the Freedom Movement* (Augusta: University of Georgia Press, 2000); Lynne Olson, *Freedom's Daughters: The Unsung Heroines of the Civil Rights Movement from 1830 to 1970* (New York: Scribner, 2001); Barbara Ransby, *Ella Baker and the Black Freedom Movement: A Radical Democratic Vision* (Chapel Hill: University of North Carolina Press, 2002); Premilla Nadesen, *Welfare Warriors: The Welfare Rights Movement in the United States* (New York:

Routledge, 2004); Rhonda Williams, *The Politics of Public Housing: Black Women's Struggle against Urban Inequality* (New York: Oxford University Press, 2005); Kimberly Springer, *Living for the Revolution: Black Feminist Organizations, 1968–1980* (Durham, NC: Duke University Press, 2005): Annelise Orleck, *Storming Caesars Palace: How Black Mothers Fought Their Own War on Poverty* (Boston: Beacon Press, 2006); Felicia Kornbluh, *The Battle for Welfare Rights: Politics and Poverty in Modern America* (Philadelphia: University of Pennsylvania Press, 2007).

8. Glen Eskew, *But for Birmingham: The Local and National Movements in the Civil Rights Struggle* (Chapel Hill: University of North Carolina Press, 1997). See also Steven Lawson and Charles Payne, *Debating the Civil Rights Movement, 1945–1968* (Lanham, MD: Rowman & Littlefield, 1999); J. Mills Thornton, *Dividing Lines: Municipal Politics and the Struggle for Civil Rights in Montgomery, Birmingham, and Selma* (Tuscaloosa: University of Alabama Press, 2002); Mary Dudziak, *Cold War Civil Rights: Race and the Image of American Democracy* (Princeton: Princeton University Press, 2000); Thomas Borstelmann, *The Cold War and the Color Line: American Race Relations in the Global Arena* (Cambridge, MA: Harvard University Press, 2001); Brenda Gayle Plummer, *Rising Wind: Black Americans and U.S. Foreign Affairs, 1935–1960* (Chapel Hill: University of North Carolina Press, 1996); Penny Von Eschen, *Race against Empire: Black Americans and Anti-Colonialism, 1937–1957* (Ithaca, NY: Cornell University Press, 1997); Michael Krenn, *Black Diplomacy: African Americans and the State Department, 1945–1969* (Armonk, NY: M. E. Sharpe, 1999).

9. Timothy Tyson, *Radio Free Dixie: Robert F. Williams and the Roots of Black Power* (Chapel Hill: University of North Carolina Press, 1999); William Van DeBerg, *New Day in Babylon: The Black Power Movement and American Culture* (Chicago: University of Chicago Press, 1992); Komozi Woodard, *A Nation within a Nation: Amiri Baraka and Black Power Politics* (Chapel Hill: University of North Carolina Press, 1999); Peniel Joseph, ed., "Black Power Studies I," *The Black Scholar* 31 (2001): 2–56; Peniel Joseph, ed., "Black Power Studies II," *The Black Scholar* 32 (2002): 2–66; Jeffrey O. G. Ogbar, *Black Power: Radical Politics and African American Identity* (Baltimore: Johns Hopkins University Press, 2004); Peniel Joseph, ed., *The Black Power Movement: Rethinking the Civil Rights–Black Power Era* (New York: Routledge, 2006); Judson L. Jeffries, *Black Power in the Belly of the Beast* (Urbana: University of Illinois Press, 2006); Peniel Joseph, *Waiting 'Til the Midnight Hour: A Narrative History of Black Power in America* (New York: Henry Holt, 2006); Cynthia Williams, *Soul Power: Culture, Radicalism, and the Making of a U.S. Third World Left* (Durham, NC: Duke University Press, 2006); Peniel Joseph, ed., "The New Black Power History," *Souls: A Critical Journal of Black Politics, Culture, and Society* 9 (2007): 277–374; Akinyele O. Umoja, "The Ballot and the Bullet: A Comparative Analysis of

Armed Resistance in the Civil Rights Movement," *Journal of Black Studies* 29 (1999): 558–578; Akinyele O. Umoja, " 'We Will Shoot Back': The Natchez Model and Paramilitary Organization in the Mississippi Freedom Movement," *Journal of Black Studies* 32 (2002): 271–294; Simon Wendt, " 'Urge People Not to Carry Guns': Armed Self-Defense in the Louisiana Civil Rights Movement and the Radicalization of the Congress of Racial Equality," *Louisiana History* 45 (2004): 261–286; Christopher Strain, *Pure Fire: Self-Defense as Activism in the Civil Rights Era* (Athens: University of Georgia Press, 2005); Simon Wendt, *The Spirit and the Shotgun: Armed Resistance and the Struggle for Civil Rights* (Gainesville: University Press of Florida, 2007); Yohuru R. Williams, *Black Politics/White Power: Civil Rights, Black Power, and Black Panthers* (St. James, NY: Brandywine Press, 2000); Jama Lezerow and Yohuru Williams, eds., *In Search of the Black Panther Party: New Perspectives on a Revolutionary Movement* (Durham, NC: Duke University Press, 2006); Curtis Austin, *Up against the Wall: Violence in the Making and Unmaking of the Black Panther Party* (Little Rock: University of Arkansas Press, 2006).

10. Among the numerous excellent memoirs and biographies, see Ben Green, *Before His Time: The Untold Story of Harry T. Moore, America's First Civil Rights Martyr* (New York: Free Press, 1999); Daniel Levine, *Bayard Rustin and the Civil Rights Movement* (New Brunswick, NJ: Rutgers University Press, 2000); Cynthia Griggs Fleming, *Soon We Will Not Cry: The Liberation of Ruby Doris Smith Robinson* (Lanham, MD: Rowman & Littlefield, 1998); John Lewis, *Walking with the Wind: A Memoir of the Movement* (New York: Simon & Schuster, 1998); Andrew Manis, *A Fire You Can't Put Out: The Civil Rights Life of Birmingham's Reverend Fred Shuttlesworth* (Tuscaloosa: University of Alabama Press, 1999); Juan Williams, *Thurgood Marshall: American Revolutionary* (New York: Times Press, 2000); Stokely Carmichael and Michael Thelwell, *Ready for Revolution: The Life and Struggle of Stokely Carmichael (Kwame Ture)* (New York: Scribner, 2003).

11. Jeanne Theoharis and Komozi Woodard, eds., *Freedom North: Black Freedom Struggles outside of the South, 1940–1980* (New York: Palgrave, 2003); Jeanne Theoharis and Komozi Woodard, eds., *Groundwork: Local Black Freedom Movements in America* (New York: New York University Press, 2005).

12. Robert Self, *American Babylon: Race and the Struggle for Postwar Oakland* (Princeton: Princeton University Press, 2003); Peter Levy, *Civil War on Race Street: The Civil Rights Movement in Cambridge, Maryland* (Gainesville: University Press of Florida, 2003); Martha Biondi, *To Stand and Fight: The Struggle for Civil Rights in Postwar New York City* (Cambridge, MA: Harvard University Press, 2003); Matthew Countryman, *Up South: Civil Rights and Black Power in Philadelphia* (Philadelphia: University of Pennsylvania Press, 2006). See also James Ralph Jr., *Northern Protest: Martin Luther King, Jr., Chicago and the Civil*

Rights Movement (Cambridge, MA: Harvard University Press, 1993); Gerald Horne, *Fire This Time: The Watts Uprising and the 1960s* (Charlottesville: University Press of Virginia, 1995); John McGreevy, *Parish Boundaries: The Catholic Encounter with Race in the Twentieth-Century Urban North* (Chicago: University of Chicago Press, 1996); Kenneth Jolly, *Black Liberation in the Midwest: The Struggle in St. Louis, Missouri, 1964–1970* (New York: Routledge, 2006); Rusty Monhollon, *This Is America? The Sixties in Lawrence, Kansas* (New York: Palgrave, 2002).

13. Locally, very little research has been done on race relations and civil rights activism in Milwaukee. The only major historical works on the African American community in Milwaukee are Joe Trotter, *Black Milwaukee: The Making of an Industrial Proletariat* (Urbana: University of Illinois Press, 1985); and Jack Dougherty, *More Than One Struggle: The Evolution of Black School Reform in Milwaukee* (Chapel Hill: University of North Carolina Press, 2003). Frank Aukofer, an urban beat reporter for the *Milwaukee Journal* during the civil rights era, wrote a useful account of civil rights activism in Milwaukee in 1968, but the work is incomplete and fails to place the local Movement within a broader historical context. See Aukofer, *City with a Chance* (Milwaukee: Bruce Publishing Company, 1968). In addition, a smattering of doctoral dissertations and master's theses deal with particular aspects of Milwaukee's racial history. On education, see Jack Dougherty, "More Than One Struggle: African-American School Reform Movements in Milwaukee, 1930–1980" (PhD diss., University of Wisconsin–Madison, 1997); and William Dahlk, "The Black Educational Reform Movement in Milwaukee, 1963–1975" (master's thesis, University of Wisconsin–Milwaukee, 1990). On the 1967 riot, see Karl Flaming, "The 1967 Milwaukee Riot: A Historical and Comparative Analysis" (PhD diss., Syracuse University, 1970). On the history of the city's Social Development Commission and the development of community action programs in the city, see Mark Braun, "Social Change and the Empowerment of the Poor: Poverty Representation in Milwaukee's Community Action Programs, 1964–1972" (PhD diss., University of Wisconsin–Milwaukee, 1999). On the intersection of race, religion, and Cold War politics in Milwaukee during the 1950s, see Kevin Smith, " 'In God We Trust': Religion, the Cold War, and Civil Rights in Milwaukee, 1947–1963" (PhD diss., University of Wisconsin–Madison, 1999). On African American migrations to Milwaukee from the South, see Paul Edward Geib, "The Late Great Migration: A Case Study of Southern Black Migration to Milwaukee, 1940–1970" (master's thesis, University of Wisconsin–Milwaukee, 1993). On the short-lived chapter of the Black Panther Party in Milwaukee, see Andrew Richard Witt, "Self-Help and Self-Defense: A Reevaluation of the Black Panther Party with Emphasis on the Milwaukee Chapter" (master's thesis, University of Wisconsin–Milwaukee, 1999). For a history of the Milwaukee Urban

League, see Michael Ross Grover, "'All Things to Black Folks': A History of the Milwaukee Urban League, 1919 to 1980" (master's thesis, University of Wisconsin–Milwaukee, 1994). On highway construction and racial dislocation, see Patricia House, "Families Displaced by Expressway Development: A Geographical Study of Relocation in Milwaukee" (master's thesis, University of Wisconsin, 1968).

14. Peter Ling and Sharon Monteith, *Gender and the Civil Rights Movement* (New Brunswick, NJ: Rutgers University Press, 1999); Steve Estes, *I Am a Man! Race, Manhood, and the Civil Rights Movement* (Chapel Hill: University of North Carolina Press, 2005); Douglas Massey and Nancy Denton, *American Apartheid: Segregation and the Making of the Underclass* (Cambridge, MA: Harvard University Press, 1993); Stephen Grant Meyer, *As Long as They Don't Move Next Door: Segregation and Racial Conflict in American Neighborhoods* (Lanham, MD: Rowman & Littlefield, 2000); Ronald Formisano, *Boston against Busing: Race, Class, and Ethnicity in the 1960s and 1970s* (Chapel Hill: University of North Carolina Press, 1991); J. Anthony Lukas, *Common Ground: A Turbulent Decade in the Lives of Three American Families* (New York: Random House, 1985); Michael Novack, *The Rise of the Unmeltable Ethnics: Politics and Culture in the Seventies* (New York: Macmillan, 1971); Andrew Greeley, *Why Can't They Be Like Us? America's White Ethnic Groups* (New York: E. P. Dutton, 1971); Thomas Sugrue, *The Origins of the Urban Crisis: Race and Inequality in Postwar Detroit* (Princeton: Princeton University Press, 1996); Becky Nicolaides, *My Blue Heaven: Life and Politics in the Working-Class Suburbs of Los Angeles, 1920–1965* (Chicago: University of Chicago Press, 2002); Lisa McGirr, *Suburban Warriors: The Origins of the New American Right* (Princeton: Princeton University Press, 2002); Kevin Kruse, *White Flight: Atlanta and the Making of Modern Conservatism* (Princeton: Princeton University Press, 2005); Matthew Lassiter, *The Silent Majority: Suburban Politics in the Sunbelt South* (Princeton: Princeton University Press, 2005); Jason Sokol, *There Goes My Everything: White Southerners in the Age of Civil Rights, 1945–1975* (New York: Vintage, 2007); Joseph Crespino, *In Search of Another Country: Mississippi and the Conservative Counterrevolution* (Princeton: Princeton University Press, 2007).

15. For a more contemporary look at race relations in Milwaukee, see Jonathan Coleman, *Long Way to Go: Black and White in America* (New York: Atlantic Monthly Press, 1997).

1. Ethnic Milwaukee and the Black Community

1. The subsequent narrative of the attack at New Butler is culled from several news reports. See *Milwaukee Leader*, July 28, 1922, p. 1; *Milwaukee Journal*, July 28, 1922, p. 1; *Milwaukee Sentinel*, July, 28, 1922, p. 1; *Wisconsin Daily News*,

July 28, 1922, p. 1; *Milwaukee Leader,* July 29, 1922, p. 1; *Milwaukee Journal,* July 29, 1922, p. 1; *Milwaukee Leader,* August 1, 1922, p. 1.

2. Daniel Hoan also supported separate black unions in Milwaukee and federal antilynching legislation and opposed the expansion of the Ku Klux Klan into Milwaukee later in 1922. See Elmer Beck, *The Sewer Socialists: A History of the Socialist Party of Wisconsin, 1897–1940* (Fennimore, WI: Westburg Associates Publishers, 1982).

3. John Gurda, *The Making of Milwaukee* (Milwaukee: Milwaukee County Historical Society, 1999), pp. 1–58. See also Beck, *The Sewer Socialists.*

4. According to historian Ruth Kohler, Henry Anderson came to Milwaukee in 1830 but moved to Green Bay, where he married Georgiana, before returning to Milwaukee around 1841. The patriarch of Henry's family, Sully Watson, had purchased his freedom years earlier, whereas Georgiana's family had never known slavery. See Ruth Miriam De Young Kohler, *The Story of Wisconsin Women* (Koehler, WI: Committee on Wisconsin Women for the 1948 Wisconsin Centennial, 1948), p. 14. On the Andersons and their extended family, the Watsons, see John B. Lundstrom and Albert A. Muchka, "The Legacy of Sully Watson: From Slave to Citizen of Milwaukee," *Wisconsin Academy Review* 40 (1994): 4–8.

5. William T. Green, "Negroes in Milwaukee," *Milwaukee Sentinel,* October 16, 1895, reprinted in *Milwaukee History Magazine* 51 (1968): 10–11; Kohler, *The Story of Wisconsin Women;* William J. Vollmar, "Negro in a Midwest Frontier City, Milwaukee, 1835–1870" (master's thesis, Marquette University, 1968).

6. Henry E. Legler, *Leading Events of Wisconsin History* (Milwaukee: Sentinel, 1898), pp. 226–229.

7. John G. Gregory, "Negro Suffrage in Wisconsin," *Transactions of the Wisconsin Academy of Sciences, Art and Letters* 11 (1898): 94–101; Joseph A. Ranney, *Trusting Nothing to Providence: History of Wisconsin's Legal System* (Madison: University of Wisconsin Law School, Continuing Education and Outreach, 2000); Leslie H. Fishel Jr., "Wisconsin and Negro Suffrage," *Wisconsin Magazine of History* 46 (1963): 180–196; Zachary Cooper, *Black Settlers in Rural Wisconsin* (Madison: State Historical Society of Wisconsin, 1977).

8. Vollmar, "Negro in a Midwest Frontier City, Milwaukee, 1835–1870," pp. 25–27, 39–44, 51, 65–72, 84–87; Jack Dougherty, "African Americans, Civil Rights and Race-Making in Milwaukee," Conference Paper, Symposium on Milwaukee History, University of Wisconsin–Milwaukee, September 27, 2004, pp. 3–4.

9. Dougherty, "African Americans, Civil Rights and Race-Making in Milwaukee," p. 14.

10. Leslie H. Fishel Jr., "The Genesis of the First Wisconsin Civil Rights Act," *Wisconsin Magazine of History* 49 (1966): 324–333; Harry H. Anderson, "Landmark

Civil Rights Decision in Wisconsin," *Milwaukee History Magazine* 51 (1968): 22–29.

11. Gurda, *The Making of Milwaukee,* pp. 170–182.

12. Ibid.

13. Ibid., p. 175. See also Harry Anderson and Frederick Olson, *Milwaukee: At the Gathering of Waters* (Tulsa: Continental Heritage Publishing, 1981); Bayard Still, *Milwaukee: The History of a City* (Madison: Wisconsin State Historical Society, 1965); Joe William Trotter, *Black Milwaukee: The Making of an Industrial Proletariat, 1915–1945* (Urbana: University of Illinois Press, 1988).

14. Jim Arndorfer, "Cream City Confidential: The Black-Baiting of Milwaukee's Last Pink Mayor," *The Baffler* 13 (1999): 72.

15. Beck, *The Sewer Socialists;* Gurda, *The Making of Milwaukee;* Anderson and Olson, *Milwaukee: At the Gathering of Waters;* Still, *Milwaukee: The History of a City.*

16. William Thompson, *The History of Wisconsin,* vol. 6: *Continuity and Change, 1940–1965* (Madison: State Historical Society of Wisconsin, 1988), p. 336.

17. Paul Geib, "From Mississippi to Milwaukee: A Case Study of the Southern Black Migration to Milwaukee, 1940–1970," *Journal of Negro History* 83 (1998): 229–248; Charles O'Reilly, *The Inner Core North: A Study of Milwaukee Negro Community* (Milwaukee: University of Wisconsin–Milwaukee, 1963), p. 2.

18. Gilbert Osofsky, *Harlem: The Making of a Ghetto, Negro New York, 1890–1930* (New York: Harper & Row, 1966); Thomas R. Buchanan, "Black Milwaukee, 1890–1915" (master's thesis, University of Wisconsin–Milwaukee, 1974), pp. 1–10, 54, 78.

19. H. Lewis Suggs, ed., *The Black Press in the Middle West, 1865–1985* (Westport, CT: Greenwood Press, 1996), pp. 325–348; O'Reilly, *The Inner Core North,* pp. 43–64; Thomas Imse, "The Negro Community in Milwaukee" (master's thesis, Marquette University, 1942), pp. 10–16, 46–47; Thompson, *The History of Wisconsin,* vol. 6, pp. 309–314.

20. Trotter, *Black Milwaukee,* pp. 116–119. For more on Walnut Street, see Paul Geenen, *Milwaukee's Bronzeville, 1900–1950* (Chicago: Arcadia Publishing, 2006).

21. Trotter, *Black Milwaukee,* pp. 39–79; Charles O'Reilly, Willard Downing, and Steven Pflanczer, *The People of the Inner Core-North* (New York: LePlay Research, 1965), pp. 65–80; Thompson, *The History of Wisconsin,* vol. 6, pp. 315–319.

22. "Policy" is a street lottery played in many poor urban neighborhoods.

23. Trotter, *Black Milwaukee,* pp. 80–114; Thompson, *The History of Wisconsin,* vol. 6, p. 367.

24. See MNAACP Papers and Milwaukee Urban League Papers, State Historical Society of Wisconsin, Madison; Thompson, *The History of Wisconsin*, vol. 6, p. 321; Trotter, *Black Milwaukee*, pp. 80–114.

25. Allan H. Spear. *Black Chicago: The Making of a Negro Ghetto, 1890–1920* (Chicago: University of Chicago Press, 1967); Trotter, *Black Milwaukee*.

26. Gurda, *The Making of Milwaukee*, p. 359.

27. Trotter, *Black Milwaukee*, pp. 147–195; Jack Dougherty, *More Than One Struggle: The Evolution of Black School Reform in Milwaukee* (Chapel Hill: University of North Carolina Press, 2004), p. 24

28. O'Reilly, *The Inner Core North*, p. 2. It is also important to note that this increase, as dramatic as it was, was probably even greater in magnitude than official census data reveals. As William Thompson has pointed out, census enumerators were often hesitant to approach African American homes or apartments and instead relied on estimates from nearby business owners. At the same time, blacks were sometimes unwilling to report the actual number of residents in overcrowded dwellings because it violated city building codes. The Milwaukee Urban League estimated that the true number of African American residents in Milwaukee during the 1940s and 1950s may have been underreported by 2,000–6,000. See Thompson, *The History of Wisconsin*, vol. 6, pp. 309–310. See also Geib, "From Mississippi to Milwaukee."

29. See O'Reilly, *The Inner Core North*, pp. 70–79; Mark Braun, "Social Change and the Empowerment of the Poor: Poverty Representation in Milwaukee's Community Action Programs, 1964–1972" (PhD diss., University of Wisconsin–Milwaukee, 1999), pp. 31–33.

30. Patricia House, "Families Displaced by Expressway Development: A Geographical Study of Relocation in Milwaukee" (master's thesis, University of Wisconsin, 1968), p. 76; Anderson and Olson, *Milwaukee: At the Gathering of Waters*, pp. 66–76.

31. The median household income of all families in Milwaukee during the 1960s was nearly $7,000. By contrast, the median African American household income during the same time period was roughly $4,000. See Braun, "Social Change and the Empowerment of the Poor," p. 24.

32. Thompson, *The History of Wisconsin*, vol. 6, p. 331.

33. In Chicago, for instance, there was a black "submachine" that received patronage from the Daley administration in return for political support. In Cleveland, a coalition of whites and blacks helped bring about the election of Carl Stokes, the first African American mayor of a major American city, in 1968. See Estelle Zannes, *Checkmate in Cleveland: The Rhetoric of Confrontation During the Stokes Years* (Cleveland: The Press of Case Western Reserve University, 1972); Carl Stokes, *Promises of Power: A Political Autobiography* (New York: Simon & Schuster, 1973).

34. Vel Phillips, interview with Patrick Jones, January 31, 2000; Gurda, *The Making of Milwaukee*, pp. 360–361; Thompson, *The History of Wisconsin*, vol. 6, pp. 322–323. The lack of political power in Milwaukee stood in sharp contrast to the situation in other northern cities that had experienced a larger and earlier migration of African Americans. For instance, in Chicago, even though Mayor Richard Daley sought to maintain racial separation within the city throughout his career, the presence of a large black population forced the Democratic machine to make certain concessions to this constituency. In fact, there existed a black "submachine" that wielded moderate power. See William Grimshaw, *Bitter Fruit: Black Politics and the Chicago Machine, 1931–1991* (Chicago: University of Chicago Press, 1995); Adam Cohen and Elizabeth Taylor, *American Pharaoh: Mayor Richard J. Daley: His Battle for Chicago and the Nation* (New York: Little, Brown, 2000).

35. O'Reilly, *The Inner Core North*, pp. 70–79; Braun, "Social Change and the Empowerment of the Poor," pp. 31–33.

36. Gurda, *The Making of Milwaukee*, pp. 157–319; Anderson and Olson, *Milwaukee: At the Gathering of Waters*, 151.

37. Arndorfer, "Cream City Confidential," pp. 73–77; "The Shame of the Nation," *Time*, April 2, 1956, http://www.time.com/time/magazine/article/0,9171,862056,00.html?promoid=googlep (accessed June 2006); Gurda, *The Making of Milwaukee*, p. 363.

2. Early Protest Politics

1. The following narrative is culled from the "Facts of the Case" section of a 1983 appeal of a civil suit brought against the city of Milwaukee by Daniel Bell's father, Patrick Bell Sr. Until 1978, the events surrounding Bell's death remained murky and disputed. According to court records, "In 1978 [Officer] Krause went to successor District Attorney E. Michael McCann and revealed that he and Grady had lied about what occurred during the Bell shooting in 1958." Krause's testimony formed the foundation of a renewed inquiry into the case and the criminal prosecution of Officer Grady. On August 29, 1979, Thomas Grady pled guilty to homicide by reckless conduct and perjury in connection with the Daniel Bell inquest. Grady received a sentence of seven years' imprisonment and was paroled after serving three years. See United States Court of Appeals, Seventh Circuit, *Patrick Bell, Sr. v. City of Milwaukee*, September 4, 1984, pp. 10–20. For another overview of the Bell case, see Sylvia Bell White and Joanne LePage, *Her Brother's Keeper: A Sister's Quest for Justice*, an unpublished manuscript in the possession of the author, ca. 2003, pp. 161–176.

2. This quotation is based on the testimony of Officer Krause in 1978. Grady denied making the statement, but his employment records show that his superiors

had criticized him for having too few arrests. A report from his probation officer in 1980 claimed that Grady had admitted making racial slurs during the 1950s. See *Patrick Bell, Sr. v. City of Milwaukee*, p. 11; White and LePage, *Her Brother's Keeper*, p. 169.

3. Again, this statement is based on court testimony by Krause and disputed by Grady. See *Patrick Bell, Sr. v. City of Milwaukee*, p. 11.

4. Ibid., p. 12.

5. White and LePage, *Her Brother's Keeper*, p. 170. According to court documents, Krause contrived the somewhat bizarre, self-incriminating declaration. See *Patrick Bell, Sr. v. City of Milwaukee*.

6. Sylvia Bell White, interview with Patrick Jones, July 23, 2007; see also *Patrick Bell, Sr. v. City of Milwaukee*, p. 13.

7. *Milwaukee Journal*, February 5, 1958, pp. 1, 3; *Milwaukee Sentinel*, February 6, 1958, pt. 2, p. 1. See also *Patrick Bell, Sr. v. City of Milwaukee*.

8. *Milwaukee Sentinel*, January 30, 1955; *Milwaukee Sentinel*, November 3, 1956. See also "Report on a Survey of Social Characteristics of the Lower Northside Community," by John Teter and students, in the appendix of the Milwaukee Commission on Human Rights, *Annual Report*, 1956, Milwaukee Human Rights Commission Vertical File, University of Wisconsin–Milwaukee Archives, Milwaukee.

9. "Memorandum on Conference with Chief of Police—Howard O. Johnson," undated, Milwaukee NAACP Papers, box 2, folder 16, State Historical Society of Wisconsin, Madison; *Milwaukee Journal*, February 16, 1958, p. 5; *Milwaukee Journal*, February 21, 1958, p. 20; *Milwaukee Journal*, February 15, 1958, p. 8; *Milwaukee Defender*, March 1, 1958, p. 1; *Milwaukee Journal*, February 26, 1958, p. 8.

10. *Milwaukee Journal*, March 1, 1958, p. 7.

11. *Milwaukee Journal*, March 17, 1958, pt. 2, p. 1; *Milwaukee Journal*, March 18, 1958, pt. 2, p. 1; *Milwaukee Defender*, March 1, 1958.

12. *Milwaukee Journal*, February 16, 1958, p. 5; *Milwaukee Journal*, February 21, 1958, p. 20; *Milwaukee Journal*, March 11, 18, and 21, 1958; *Milwaukee Sentinel*, February 21, 1958; *Milwaukee Defender*, March 1, 1958; *Milwaukee Journal*, March 21, 1958, pt. 2, p. 1; *Milwaukee Journal*, March 24, 1958, p. 10; Calvin Sherard, interview with Patrick Jones, February 17, 2001; White interview. See also White and LePage, *Her Brother's Keeper*, pp. 177–178.

13. "Statement of Frank P. Zeidler, Mayor, at Meeting on 'Social Problems of the Core of the City,' Thursday, 9/3/59," in Mayor's Study Committee of Social Problems in the Inner Core Area of the City, *Final Report to the Honorable Frank P. Zeidler, Mayor* (hereafter referred to as the Zeidler Report) (Milwaukee: Mayor's Study Committee, 1960), pp. 1–32.

14. Zeidler Report, pp. 1–32; William Thompson, *The History of Wisconsin*, vol. 6: *Continuity and Change, 1960–1965* (Madison: State Historical Society of

Wisconsin, 1988), p. 371; Oscar Handlin, *The Newcomers—Negroes and Puerto Ricans in a Changing Metropolis* (Cambridge, MA: Harvard University Press, 1959); Jack Dougherty, *More Than One Struggle: The Evolution of Black School Reform in Milwaukee* (Chapel Hill: University of North Carolina Press, 2003), p. 60.

15. Zeidler Report, pp. 1–32.

16. Henry Maier would go on to preside as mayor of Milwaukee for the longest term in city history, an astonishing twenty-eight years. See Henry Maier, *Challenge to the Cities: An Approach to a Theory of Urban Leadership* (New York: Random House, 1966), pp. 44–45; Henry Maier, *The Mayor Who Made Milwaukee Famous: An Autobiography* (Lanham, MD: Madison Books, 1993), pp. 38–40.

17. *Milwaukee Journal*, June 13, 1960, p. 1; *Milwaukee Journal*, June 14, 1960, p. 1; see also *Wisconsin Blue Book, 1960*, p. 21; Ralph Whitehead Jr., "Milwaukee's Mercurial Henry Maier," *City* 6 (1972): 10–20; Frank Aukofer, *City with a Chance* (Milwaukee: Bruce Publishing, 1968), pp. 9–10; Sarah Ettenheim, *How Milwaukee Voted, 1848–1968* (Milwaukee: UW Extension, Institute of Governmental Affairs, Milwaukee Office, 1970), pp. 24, 128.

18. Sherard interview.

19. Tom Jacobson, interview with Patrick Jones, November 1, 1999.

20. Sherard interview; *Milwaukee Journal*, May 29, 1960, p. 8.

21. Sherard interview; Dougherty, *More Than One Struggle*, p. 78.

22. *Milwaukee Journal*, October 29, 1960, p. 1; Flier, titled "Mass Rally Defends Negro Youth against Police Brutality," John Gilman Papers, box 1, State Historical Society of Wisconsin, Madison.

23. Interestingly, Calvin Sherard was not from New York and had never lived there.

24. *Milwaukee Journal*, December 6, 1960, pt. 2, p. 2; *Milwaukee Sentinel*, December 6, 1960, pt. 2, p. 1; *Milwaukee Sentinel*, December 7, 1960, pt. 2, p. 9; Reuben Harpole, interview by Patrick Jones, November 17, 1999; Dougherty, *More Than One Struggle*, pp. 77–79.

25. Eddie Walker to Gloster Current, December 7, 1960, part 3, section C, box 166, "Milwaukee, 1959–1960" folder, National NAACP Papers; see also Dougherty, *More Than One Struggle*, p. 79.

26. *Milwaukee Journal*, May 27, 1960, p. 14; *Milwaukee Journal*, May 29, 1960, p. 5; *Milwaukee Journal*, May 30, 1960. On the NALC, see Paula Pfeffer, *A. Philip Randolph, Pioneer of the Civil Rights Movement* (Baton Rouge: Louisiana State University Press, 1990), pp. 214–239; Jervis Anderson, *A. Philip Randolph: A Biographical Portrait* (New York: Harcourt Brace Jovanovich, 1972), pp. 305–306, 309–310; Sherard interview.

27. *Milwaukee Journal*, August 4, 1962, p. 9; *Milwaukee Star*, August 25, 1962, p. 1; *Milwaukee Star*, September 1, 1962, p. 2; *Milwaukee Star*, September 8, 1962, p. 1; *Milwaukee Star*, September 22, 1962, p. 1; Sherard interview.

28. *Milwaukee Star,* May 4, 1963, p. 2; *Milwaukee Star,* May 18, 1963, p. 4; *Milwaukee Star,* June 1, 1963, p. 3; *Milwaukee Star,* August 3, 1963, p. 5; Sherard interview.

29. *Milwaukee Star,* June 1, 1963; Sherard interview.

30. *Milwaukee Journal,* October 30, 1962, pt. 2, p. 1; *Milwaukee Star,* November 3, 1962, p. 1; *Milwaukee Star,* November 5, 1962, pt. 2, p. 1; *Milwaukee Sentinel,* December 10, 1962, p. 1; Sherard interview.

31. Jacobson interview.

32. Martin Luther King Jr., *Why We Can't Wait* (New York: Harper and Row, 1964), pp. 3–4.

33. "The Negro in Milwaukee: Progress and Portent, 1863–1963," Milwaukee Commission on Human Relations, January 1, 1963, State Historical Society of Wisconsin Pamphlet Collection; Nathan Glazer and Daniel Patrick Moynihan, *Beyond the Melting Pot: The Negroes, Puerto Ricans, Jews, Italians, and Irish of New York City* (Cambridge, MA: MIT Press, 1968); Thompson, *The History of Wisconsin,* vol. 6, p. 377.

34. *Milwaukee Journal,* January 19, 1963, p. 1; *Milwaukee Star,* January 19, 1963, p. 1; Maier, *Challenge to the Cities,* pp. 47–48; Maier, *The Mayor Who Made Milwaukee Famous,* pp. 39–41.

35. *Milwaukee Journal,* June 12, 1963, p. 24; *Milwaukee Sentinel,* June 13, 1963, p. 10; *Milwaukee Star,* June 15, 1963, p. 1.

36. *Milwaukee Star,* April 27, 1963, p. 1; *Milwaukee Star,* May 18, 1963, p. 1; *Milwaukee Sentinel,* June 15, 1963, p. 5; Milwaukee Journal, June 15, 1963, p. 3; *Milwaukee Sentinel,* June 15, 1963, p. 5; *Milwaukee Journal,* June 16, 1963, pt. 2, p. 8.

37. *Milwaukee Journal,* June 13, 1963, pt. 2, p. 1; *Milwaukee Sentinel,* June 13, 1963, pt. 2, p. 1.

38. *Milwaukee Journal,* June 13, 1963, pt. 2, p. 1; *Milwaukee Sentinel,* June 13, 1963, pt. 2, p. 1; *Milwaukee Journal,* June 14, 1963, p. 16; *Milwaukee Star,* June 29, 1963, p. 4; *Milwaukee Star,* July 13, 1963, p. 5; *Milwaukee Star,* July 30, 1963, p. 3; *Milwaukee Journal,* June 17, 1963, pt. 2, p. 10; *Milwaukee Sentinel,* June 17, 1963, pt. 2, p. 1; *Milwaukee Sentinel,* June 20, 1963, p. 1; *Milwaukee Star,* June 22, 1963, p. 1; *Milwaukee Sentinel,* June 19, 1963, p. 4; "Statement of Concern," *Milwaukee Star,* July 27, 1963, p. 1. The ad also appeared in the *Journal* and *Sentinel* on July 25, 1963.

39. Milwaukee Congress of Racial Equality Papers, State Historical Society of Wisconsin, Madison; August Meier and Eliot Rudwick, *CORE: A Study in the Civil Rights Movement* (Urbana: University of Illinois Press, 1975); John Givens, interview with Patrick Jones, November 17, 1999.

40. Jacobson interview; Givens interview; *Milwaukee Journal,* August 29, 1963, p. 4; *Milwaukee Journal,* August 30, 1963, pt. 2, p. 6; *Milwaukee Journal,* September 8, 1963, pt. 2, p. 1.

41. For an overview of the Social Development Commission, see Maier, *Challenge to the Cities*, pp. 43–58; Maier, *The Mayor Who Made Milwaukee Famous*, pp. 37–50; Mark Braun, *Social Change and Empowerment of the Poor* (Lanham, MD: Lexington Books, 2001).

42. *Milwaukee Journal*, July 26, 1963, p. 1.

43. *Milwaukee Sentinel*, July 29, 1963, pt. 2, p. 7; *Milwaukee Journal*, July 30, 1963, pt. 2, p. 1; *Milwaukee Sentinel*, July 30, 1963, pt. 2, p. 1; *Milwaukee Journal*, August 27, 1963, pt. 2, p. 1; "CORE Press Release," August 28, 1963, Thomas Jacobson Papers, State Historical Society of Wisconsin, Madison; Givens interview.

44. *Milwaukee Journal*, August 28, 1963, p. 1; *Milwaukee Star*, September 7, 1963, p. 1; *Milwaukee Journal*, August 29, 1963, p. 1

45. *Milwaukee Journal*, September 3, 1963, p. 1; *Milwaukee Star*, September 7, 1963, p. 5; *Milwaukee Journal*, September 17, 1963, p. 1; *Milwaukee Journal*, September 18, 1963, p. 1; *Milwaukee Journal*, September 19, 1963, pt. 2, p. 1.

46. *Milwaukee Journal*, September 1, 1963, p. 1; *Milwaukee Star*, September 7, 1963, p. 5; Givens interview; Jacobson interview.

47. *Milwaukee Star*, September 7, 1963, p. 4; WITI-TV Editorial, September 6, 1963, Tom Jacobson Papers, Milwaukee County Historical Society; *Milwaukee Journal*, September 9, 1963, p. 7; Givens interview.

48. *Milwaukee Journal*, September 22, 1963, p. 1; *Milwaukee Star*, September 28, 1963, p. 3.

3. The Campaign to End School Segregation

1. *Milwaukee Courier*, May 29, 1965, p. 1; *Milwaukee Journal*, May 24, 1965, p. 1; MUSIC Press Release, May 24, 1965, Barbee Papers, box 13, folder 11, State Historical Society of Wisconsin, Madison; *Countdown* Newsletter, vol. 1, no. 3 (May 1965), MUSIC Papers, box 1, folder 1, State Historical Society of Wisconsin, Madison.

2. The MUSIC Papers and Barbee Papers contain miscellaneous press releases, fliers, and statements from this period.

3. Frank A. Aukofer, *City with a Chance* (Milwaukee: Bruce Publishing Company, 1968), p. 61; *Milwaukee Journal*, June 16, 1965, pt. 2, p. 1; *Milwaukee Star*, June 19, 1965, p. 1; Lloyd Barbee to NBC, May 25, 1965, Barbee Papers, box 12, folder 6.

4. Lloyd Barbee, interview with Patrick Jones, January 30, 1999; "Lloyd Barbee: I Remember Milwaukee," WMVS/WMVT, April 19, 1995; Biographical Sketch, Barbee Papers; Jack Dougherty, *More Than One Struggle: The Evolution of Black School Reform in Milwaukee* (Chapel Hill: University of North Carolina Press, 2004), pp. 74–75.

5. Ibid.

6. Ibid.

7. Thomas Jacobson, interview with Patrick Jones, November 1, 1999; Barbee interview; Maxine Aldridge White and Joseph Ranney, "Lloyd Barbee: Fighting Segregation 'Root and Branch,'" *Wisconsin Lawyer* 77 (2004), http://www.wisbar .org/AM/Template.cfm?Section=Wisconsin_Lawyer&TEMPLATE=/CM/Con tentDisplay.cfm&CONTENTID=47649.

8. On school desegregation, see Gary Orfield, *Must We Bus?* (Washington, DC: Brookings Institute, 1989); J. Harvie Wilkinson, *From Bakke to Brown: The Supreme Court and School Integration, 1954–1978* (New York: Oxford University Press, 1981); Barbee interview; Dougherty, *More Than One Struggle,* pp. 71–80.

9. Barbee interview.

10. Minutes of the Special Committee on Equality of Educational Opportunity, December 10, 1963, Radtke Papers, State Historical Society of Wisconsin, Madison; Barbee interview.

11. *Milwaukee Journal,* January 27, 1964, pt. 2, p. 1; *Milwaukee Journal,* January 28, 1964, pt. 2, p. 1; *Milwaukee Star,* January 25, 1964, p. 1.

12. Barbee interview; John Dahlk, "The Black Educational Reform Movement in Milwaukee, 1963–1975" (master's thesis, University of Wisconsin–Milwaukee, 1990), p. 42.

13. Barbee interview; Dougherty, *More Than One Struggle,* p. 94; Aukofer, *City with a Chance,* p. 54.

14. For a full overview of Wallace's career as well as the 1964 presidential primary campaign, see Dan Carter, *The Politics of Rage: George Wallace, the Origins of the New Conservatism, and the Transformation of American Politics* (New York: Simon & Schuster, 1995), esp. pp. 202–215 (on the 1964 primaries). The *Journal, Sentinel,* and *Star* all covered the Wallace campaign extensively from late February to early April.

15. *Milwaukee Journal,* March 23, 1964, p. 1; *Milwaukee Journal,* March 26, 1964, p. 16; *Milwaukee Journal,* March 31, 1964, p. 1; *Milwaukee Journal,* April 2, 1964, p. 1.

16. *Milwaukee Journal,* April 2, 1964, p. 1; *Milwaukee Sentinel,* April 2, 1964, p. 1; Carter, *The Politics of Rage,* p. 206.

17. *Milwaukee Journal,* March 10, 1964, p. 1.

18. Barbee interview; Aldon Morris, *The Origins of the Civil Rights Movement: Black Communities Organizing for Change* (New York: Free Press, 1984), pp. 40–76.

19. Jacobson interview; Barbee interview; Reverend B. S. Gregg, interview with Patrick Jones, November 10, 1999.

20. Dougherty, *More Than One Struggle,* pp. 104–130.

21. For a basic characterization of Morheuser, see interviews with Barbee, Gregg, Jacobson, and John Givens (interview with Patrick Jones, November 17, 1999. See also Dahlk, "The Black Educational Reform Movement in Milwaukee, 1963–1975," p. 48; *Milwaukee Journal,* April 19, 1964; *Milwaukee Journal,* May 17, 1964; *Milwaukee Star,* February 26, 1966, p. 1.

22. *Milwaukee Journal,* March 2, 1964, p. 1; *Milwaukee Sentinel,* September 20, 1963, p. 1; *Milwaukee Journal,* April 29, 1964, p. 12; *Milwaukee Courier,* May 24, 1966, p. 1; *Milwaukee Journal,* August 20, 1966, pt. 2, p. 1; *Milwaukee Star,* May 14, 1966, p. 1. See also Dahlk, "The Black Educational Reform Movement in Milwaukee, 1963–1975," pp. 49–50; *Milwaukee Sentinel,* May 18, 1964, p. 1.

23. *Milwaukee Journal,* March 25, 1964, p. 1; *Milwaukee Sentinel,* March 25, 1964, p. 1.

24. *Milwaukee Journal,* May 19, 1964, p. 1. The MUSIC Papers, MNAACP Papers, and Barbee Papers all contain lesson plans, curriculum, assignments, and other documentation of the freedom schools. See also Aukofer, *City with a Chance,* pp. 57–58.

25. *Milwaukee Courier,* July 3, 1964, p. 1; Barbee Papers, box 13, folders 10 and 11.

26. *Milwaukee Star,* June 6, 1964, p. 1; *Milwaukee Star,* June 13, 1964, p. 3; Barbee interview; Barbee campaign flyers quoted in Dougherty, *More Than One Struggle,* p. 128.

27. *Milwaukee Star,* March 20, 1965, p. 5; Fr. Matthew Gottschalk, interview with Patrick Jones, April 15, 1999; Patrick Flood, interview with Patrick Jones, March 13, 2000; Ionia Champion, interview with Patrick Jones, January 24, 2000.

28. The NAACP report was detailed in *Milwaukee Star,* September 11, 1965, p. 1. See also *Milwaukee Star,* September 18, 1965, p. 5.

29. *Milwaukee Courier,* May 22, 1965, p. 1; *Milwaukee Journal,* May 18, 1965, pt. 2, p. 12.

30. *Milwaukee Journal,* June 17, 1965, pt. 2, p. 1; *Milwaukee Journal,* May 28, 1965, p. 18; WTMJ-TV editorial (print form), May 25, 1965, Henry Maier Papers, box 44, folder 11, State Historical Society of Wisconsin, Madison; WITI-TV editorial (print form), June 23, 1965, Henry Maier Papers, box 44, folder 11.

31. *Milwaukee Journal,* June 19, 1965, p. 1; *Milwaukee Sentinel,* June 19, 1965, p. 1; *Milwaukee Star,* June 16, 1965, p. 3; Barbee interview. For an exhaustive breakdown of the court case, see the Barbee Papers.

32. *Milwaukee Journal,* August 29, 1965, p. 1; *Milwaukee Sentinel,* August 29, 1965, p. 1.

33. Text of Henry Maier's "Address to the Milwaukee Commission on Community Relations," October 13, 1965, Maier Papers, box 44, folder 11; *Milwaukee Journal,* November 10, 1965, pt. 2, p. 10; *Milwaukee Journal,* November 12, 1965, p. 1.

34. See news coverage in the *Journal* and *Sentinel* from October 18, 1965, through October 22, 1965. In addition, see coverage in the *Courier* and *Star* on October 23, 1965, and October 25, 1965.

35. MUSIC Press Release, December 4, 1965, MUSIC Papers, box 1, folder 6.

36. *Milwaukee Journal,* December 18, 1965, p. 1; *Milwaukee Sentinel,* December 18, 1965, p. 1.

37. James Scott, *Domination and the Arts of Resistance: Hidden Transcripts* (New Haven, CT: Yale University Press, 1990).

4. Father Groppi's Civil Rights Awakening

1. See David Garrow, *Protest at Selma: Martin Luther King, Jr., and the Voting Rights Act of 1965* (New Haven, CT: Yale University Press, 1978).

2. Frank Aukofer, *City with a Chance* (Milwaukee: Bruce Publishing Company, 1968), p. 94.

3. Aukofer, *City with a Chance,* p. 60; see also Patrick Flood, interview with Patrick Jones, March 13, 2000; Matthew Gottschalk, interview with Patrick Jones, April 15, 1999.

4. Flood interview; Aukofer, *City with a Chance,* pp. 92–94.

5. Flood interview; Gottschalk interview; Aukofer, *City with a Chance,* p. 93.

6. Aukofer, *City with a Chance,* pp. 91–95; Flood interview; Gottschalk interview; *Milwaukee Journal,* March 13, 1965, p. 1. On February 15, 1984, one year before Groppi's death, East Library in Milwaukee hosted a slide show presentation and YC/Commandos reunion. Groppi attended and shared his recollections of the movement. This event was tape recorded and can be found at East Library, Milwaukee, Wisconsin, and is hereafter referred to as "Groppi lecture at East Library."

7. Martin Luther King Jr., "Our God Is Marching on," March 25, 1965, http://www.stanford.edu/group/King/publications/speeches/Our_God_is_marching_on.html (accessed December 12, 2007); Garrow, *Protest at Selma.*

8. John McGreevy, *Parish Boundaries: The Catholic Encounter with Race in the Twentieth-Century Urban North* (Chicago: University of Chicago Press, 1996), p. 197.

9. Gerald Gamm, *Urban Exodus: Why the Jews Left Boston and the Catholics Stayed* (Cambridge, MA: Harvard University Press, 1999), p. 60.

10. Eugene Bleidorn, interview with Patrick Jones, November 21, 1998. See also Gottschalk interview; Flood interview.

11. For a full overview of this early history of the Catholic Church in Milwaukee's inner core, see Steven Avella, "Milwaukee Catholicism, 1945–1960: Seed Time for Change," in *Milwaukee Catholicism: Essays on Church and Community,* ed. Steven Avella (Milwaukee: Knights of Columbus, 1991), pp. 151–172. On the Capuchins, see the Gottschalk interview.

12. Gottschalk interview.

13. See Avella, "Milwaukee Catholicism, 1945–1960"; Gamm, *Urban Exodus.*

14. Comedian Redd Foxx and future Chicago mayor Harold Washington attended school at St. Benedict.

15. *Milwaukee Journal,* September 10, 1963, pt. 2, p. 1; *Milwaukee Journal,* September 4, 1965, p. 11; Michael Neuberger, interview with Patrick Jones, February 20, 2000; Bleidorn interview; Gottschalk interview.

16. Quoted in McGreevy, *Parish Boundaries,* p. 197; Rosemary Thielke, "Muddled Like Me," *Ave Maria* 101 (April 3, 1963), pp. 5–7; "Milwaukee Vindicates Griffin in a Public Show of Fairness," *National Catholic Reporter,* no. 1 (February 17, 1963), p. 2. See also relevant news coverage of the incident in the *Milwaukee Journal, Sentinel,* and *Star* in January and February of 1963.

17. Office for Social Justice, Archdiocese of St. Paul and Minneapolis, http://www .osjspm.org/cst/themes.htm (accessed May 13, 2006).

18. Some of the deeper roots of Catholic social teaching can be traced back to Thomas Aquinas's writing against private property and for the common good; Pope Paul III's sixteenth-century encyclical, *Sublimis Deus,* which condemned the treatment of native peoples by European explorers; and Pope Gregory XVI's 1839 encyclical, *Supremo Apostolatis,* condemning the slave trade.

19. Another well-known effort to put Catholic social teaching into action was the Catholic Worker Movement, founded in 1933 by journalist-activist Dorothy Day and philosopher-intellectual Peter Maurin. In general, the Catholic Worker Movement was not as influential as Catholic Action formations in Milwaukee. See Casa Maria House of Hospitality (Milwaukee, WI) Records, 1966–, found in the Catholic Worker Community Papers, Marquette University, Milwaukee.

20. For a more extensive overview of Catholic Action, see Jay Dolan, *The American Catholic Experience* (New York: Doubleday, 1985), pp. 408–409, 415–416; Bleidorn interview; Flood interview.

21. For a more lengthy exploration of the Cardijn movement as it evolved in Milwaukee, see Avella, "Milwaukee Catholicism, 1945–1960," pp. 154–159; John Dahlk, "The Black Educational Reform Movement in Milwaukee, 1963–1975" (master's thesis, University of Wisconsin–Milwaukee, 1990), p. 58; Bleidorn interview.

22. For an overview of the Second Vatican Council, see Dolan, *The American Catholic Experience,* pp. 424–426; McGreevy, *Parish Boundaries,* pp. 155–173. See also Bleidorn interview; Neuberger interview; Flood interview; Gottschalk interview.

23. Flood interview. Fathers Bleidorn, Gottschalk, and Neuberger expressed similar sentiments in their interviews.

24. See "Father Groppi," typescript of the first chapter of an autobiographical sketch, undated, ca. 1971, James Groppi Papers, box 14, folder 7, p. 6–7, State Historical Society of Wisconsin, Madison. Hereafter referred to as "Groppi Autobiography."

25. "Groppi Autobiography," pp. 7–8. See also James Groppi, interview with Frank Aukofer, October 13, 1967, in Aukofer Papers, State Historical Society of Wisconsin, Madison. In addition, Groppi's friction with the local church may help explain, in part, the foundations of his later criticism of the church.

26. Aukofer, *City with a Chance*, pp. 89–90.

27. Ibid.

28. Groppi interview with Aukofer.

29. Flood interview; Gottschalk interview; Dennis McDowell, interview with Patrick Jones, August 11, 2005; Rozga, quoted in David Chang, "White Priest, Black Power: Civil and Religious Disobedience in the Activism of Father James Groppi," unpublished graduate paper, in author's possession; Flood interview; "Groppi Autobiography," pp. 14–15.

30. According to Margaret Rozga, "[Groppi] was really a great hit at St. Veronica's [with the students], a young enthusiastic priest. So they got a lot of carry-over effect, you know a lot of people who got interested in civil rights because they knew him, a lot of former parishioners." See Rozga, interview with Patrick Jones, July 19, 2005; Aukofer, *City with a Chance*, p. 91.

31. Father Austin Schlaefer took careful notes throughout this trip and organized them into a twenty-three-page report titled "Southbound," which he submitted to provincial superiors afterward. In 2005, Father Matthew duplicated the report for the author, who maintains a copy in his possession. See also Gottschalk interview.

32. Groppi autobiography, pp. 19–20; Gottschalk interview; Flood interview.

33. Father Groppi may have taken other trips south as well. During the East Library lecture, he alluded to a trip south with DeWayne Tolliver, but no details were provided. It is unclear whether this was the same trip that Nathanial Harwell participated in, or separate. See Groppi lecture at East Library. Margaret Rozga, in her interview, estimated that Father Groppi had taken three trips south before the Alverno trip.

34. See Groppi lecture at East Library; Rozga interview; Flood interview.

35. Groppi lecture at East Library.

36. Aukofer, *City with a Chance*, p. 94; Flood interview.

37. Flood interview; *Milwaukee Journal*, April 4, 1965, p. 2; Aukofer, *City with a Chance*, pp. 94–95.

38. The University of Cincinnati *News Record*, January 21, 1969, p. 2; Rozga interview.

39. Jeffrey Burns, *Disturbing the Peace: A History of the Christian Family Movement, 1949–1974* (South Bend, IN: University of Notre Dame Press, 1999), p. 205.

40. Flood interview; Rozga interview.

41. Groppi lecture at East Library; *Milwaukee Courier*, March 27, 1965, p. 1.

42. Martin Luther King Jr., *Why We Can't Wait* (New York: Harper and Row, 1964). p. 81.

43. *Milwaukee Courier,* March 27, 1965, p. 1.

44. *Milwaukee Courier,* May 22, 1965, p. 1; *Milwaukee Journal,* May 18, 1965, pt. 2, p. 12.

45. *Milwaukee Journal,* August 29, 1965, p. 1; *Milwaukee Sentinel,* August 29, 1965, p. 1; Flood interview; Rozga interview.

46. There were several white liberal Protestant churches and reformed Jewish synagogues in Milwaukee that also reached out to inner core African Americans and supported civil rights and, later, the activism of Groppi, the YC and the Commandos. For instance, Grand Avenue Congregational, First Methodist, Friedens Evangelical and Reformed, Calvary Presbyterian, First Baptist, and St. Paul's Lutheran admitted African Americans as members and participated in Milwaukee NAACP and Milwaukee Urban League programs and activities. Similarly, Temple Emanu-El B'ne Jeshurun and Congregation Shalom were particularly outspoken civil rights advocates, and Rabbi Dudley Weinberg, of Temple Emanu-El, played a particularly notable public role during the mid-1960s demonstrations. See Kevin Smith, " 'In God We Trust': Religion, the Cold War and Civil Rights in Milwaukee, 1947–1963" (PhD diss., University of Wisconsin–Madison, 1999), pp. 281–287.

47. *Milwaukee Courier,* March 20, 1965, p. 1.

48. Priests' Statement, September 28, 1965, Bleidorn Papers, box 7, folder 4, Cousins Catholic Center, Milwaukee; Press Release, October 7, 1965, Bleidorn Papers, box 7, folder 4; Eugene Bleidorn, *In My Time* (self-published memoir, 1994), p. 68.

49. Edmund Goebel to Reverend Father, October 14, 1965, Bleidorn Papers, box 7, folder 4.

50. Roman Atkielski to Eugene Bleidorn, October 15, 1965, Bleidorn Papers, box 7, folder 4; Bleidorn, *In My Time,* p. 69. See also Flood interview; *Milwaukee Journal,* October 16, 1965, p. 1.

51. Father Bleidorn kept a list of statements on the controversy. See Bleidorn Papers, box 4, folder 7; Priests' Press Release, October 16, 1965, Bleidorn Papers, box 4, folder 7; *Milwaukee Journal,* October 17, 1965, p. 1; *Milwaukee Sentinel,* October 17, 1965, p. 1.

52. Pastors' Press Release, October 17, 1965, Bleidorn Papers, box 4, folder 7; Print Version of ad, October 17, 1965, Bleidorn Papers, box 4, folder 7.

53. Among the various freedom songs sung by the protesters that day was a twist on a classic: "Ain't Gonna Let No Bishop Turn Me Around." See *Milwaukee Journal,* October 18, 1965, p. 1; *Milwaukee Journal,* October 19, 1965, p. 1; Roman Atkielski to Eugene Bleidorn, October 19, 1965, Bleidorn Papers, box 4, folder 7; Bleidorn to Atkielski, October 19, 1965, Bleidorn Papers, box 4, folder 7. See also Pastors' Press Release, October 19, 1965, Bleidorn Papers,

box 4, folder 7; "Catholic Controversy Chronology," Bleidorn Papers, box 4, folder 7.

54. Bleidorn Papers, box 4, folder 7; *Milwaukee Journal*, October 18, 1965, p. 12; Rozga interview.

5. The Youth Council and Commandos

1. The following overview of the YC march to Wauwatosa was culled from local and national newspaper coverage. See *Time*, September 9, 1966, pp. 23–24; *Milwaukee Journal*, August 24, 1966, pt. 2, p. 10; *Milwaukee Journal*, August 29, 1966, p. 1; *Milwaukee Sentinel*, August 29, 1966, p. 1; *Milwaukee Star*, September 3, 1966, p. 1; Frank Aukofer, *City with a Chance* (Milwaukee: Bruce Publishing Company, 1968), p. 101.

2. Alberta Harris, interview with Patrick Jones, August 27, 2005; Thomas Jacobson, interview with Patrick Jones, November 1, 1999; John Givens, interview with Patrick Jones, October 17, 1999; *Milwaukee Sentinel*, March 26, 1963, p. 8; *Milwaukee Journal*, March 26, 1963, p. 14; "Why We Demonstrate," Milwaukee NAACP Youth Council flyer, ca. March 1963, Milwaukee NAACP Papers, State Historical Society of Wisconsin, Madison; *Milwaukee Sentinel*, March 28, 1963, pt. 2, p. 1; *Milwaukee Journal*, March 28, 1963, pt. 2, p. 2; *Milwaukee Star*, April 6, 1963, p. 2.

3. Harris interview; Givens interview; Jacobson interview.

4. Harris interview. Other early YC members corroborated this story, including Dennis McDowell, Velma Coggs, and Margaret Rozga.

5. Velma Coggs, interview with Patrick Jones, March 27, 1999; Paul Crawford, interview with Arlene Zakhar, April 25, 1984; Margaret Rozga, interview with Patrick Jones, July 19, 2005.

6. Aukofer, *City with a Chance*, pp. 91–92; Eugene Bleidorn, interview with Patrick Jones, November 21, 1998; Michael Neuberger, interview with Patrick Jones, February 20, 2000; Patrick Flood, interview with Patrick Jones, March 13, 2000; Prentice McKinney, interview with Patrick Jones, November 13, 1999; Joe McClain, interview with Patrick Jones, March 29, 1999; Coggs interview; Harris interview; Dennis McDowell, interview with Patrick Jones, August 11, 2005; James Groppi, interview with Frank Aukofer, October 13, 1967, in Aukofer Papers, State Historical Society of Wisconsin, Madison.

7. Pamela Jo Sargent lecture, University of Wisconsin–Milwaukee, September 29, 2007; Ed Thekan, interview with Arlene Zakhar, circa 1984, in author's possession; Groppi lecture at East Library, February 15, 1984. See also Harris interview; Rozga interview; McDowell interview.

8. Harris interview.

9. Groppi lecture at East Library.

10. YC Fund-raising Letter, April 1966, Bleidorn Papers, box 7, folder 3, Cousins Catholic Center, Milwaukee; Richard Green, interview with Arlene Zakhar, April 19, 1984; Harris interview.

11. McDowell interview; Groppi lecture at East Library; *Milwaukee Courier*, August 20, 1966, p. 1; Rozga interview.

12. Harris interview; McDowell interview. See also Rozga interview.

13. Rozga interview; Harris interview.

14. McDowell interview; Harris interview.

15. Aukofer, *City with a Chance*, pp. 97–98.

16. Rozga interview.

17. *Milwaukee Journal*, July 9, 1964, pt. 2, p. 5; *Milwaukee Journal*, July 28, 1964, p. 17.

18. *Milwaukee Journal*, January 28, 1965, pt. 2, p. 1; *Milwaukee Journal*, February 5, 1965, p. 16; Lloyd Barbee to Edward Lane, May 3, 1965, Barbee Papers, box 12, folder 6, State Historical Society of Wisconsin, Madison.

19. *Milwaukee Journal*, March 17, 1966, pt. 2, p. 1; *Milwaukee Star*, March 19, 1966, p. 1.

20. *Milwaukee Journal*, April 1, 1966, pt. 2, p. 11; Resolution printed in *Milwaukee Eagle*, March 19, 1966, p. 1. See also *Milwaukee Journal*, March 16, 1966, pt. 2, p. 1. There is a bundle of documents related to Maier's decision to maintain his membership in the EC in the Maier Papers, box 44, folder 13, State Historical Society of Wisconsin, Madison.

21. Harris interview; *Milwaukee Journal*, March 3, 1966, pt. 2, p. 1; *Milwaukee Journal*, March 24, 1966, pt. 2, p. 2.

22. John Gilman's personal papers are extensive and can be found at the Wisconsin State Historical Society archive. His story appears to merit further research; *Milwaukee Journal*, August 9, 1966, p. 1.

23. *Milwaukee Journal*, September 25, 1966, p. 1; *Milwaukee Journal*, September 26, 1966, pt. 2, p. 10; *Milwaukee Star*, October 1, 1966, p. 1; *Milwaukee Journal*, June 19, 1967, p. 1. The Milwaukee Citizens Council placed a large billboard, reading "King Is a Communist," across the street from where Martin Luther King gave his 1965 University of Wisconsin—Milwaukee speech. Newspapers also reported that the Milwaukee Citizens Council attempted to affiliate with the White Citizens' Council in Mississippi.

24. Isaac Coggs to Henry Maier, July 4, 1965, Maier Papers, box 44, folder 13; Maier to Coggs, July 6, 1965, Maier Papers, box 44, folder 13; *Milwaukee Journal*, March 10, 67, pt. 2, p. 11.

25. *Milwaukee Journal*, August 9, 1966, p. 1; Western Union Telefax from Roy Wilkins to Henry Maier, August 9, 1966, in Maier Papers, box 44, folder 13; "Statement by Mayor Henry W. Maier Regarding Bombing of NAACP Headquarters," August 9,

1966, Maier Papers, box 44, folder 13; *Milwaukee Journal,* August 10, 1966, p. 22. Various other statements condemning the bombing can be found in the Maier Papers, box 44, folder 13.

26. *Milwaukee Journal,* August 10, 1966, p. 1; *Milwaukee Journal,* August 11, 1966, pt. 2, p. 2; McDowell interview.

27. *Milwaukee Journal,* August 10, 1966, p. 2. On Black Power and armed self-defense, see Timothy Tyson, "Robert F. Williams, 'Black Power,' and the Roots of the African American Freedom Struggle," *Journal of American History* 85 (1998): 540–570; Lance Hill, *The Deacons for Defense: Armed Resistance and the Civil Rights Movement* (Chapel Hill: University of North Carolina Press, 2004); Peter Levy, *Civil War on Race Street: The Civil Rights Movement in Cambridge, Maryland* (Gainesville: University Press of Florida, 2003); Christopher Strain, *Pure Fire: Self-Defense as Activism in the Civil Rights Era* (Athens: University of Georgia Press, 2005); Simon Wendt, *The Spirit and the Shotgun: Armed Resistance and the Struggle for Civil Rights* (Gainesville: University Press of Florida, 2007); Simon Wendt, "God, Gandhi and Guns: The African American Freedom Struggle in Tuscaloosa, Alabama, 1964–1965," *Journal of African American History* 89 (2004): 36–56; Simon Wendt, "The Roots of Black Power? Armed Resistance and the Radicalization of the Civil Rights Movement," in *The Black Power Movement: Rethinking the Civil Rights-Black Power Era,* ed. Peniel Joseph (New York: Routledge, 2006), pp. 145–166; Akinyele Umoja, "The Ballot and the Bullet: A Comparative Analysis of Armed Resistance in the Civil Rights Movement," *Journal of Black Studies* 29 (1999): 558–578; Simon Wendt, " 'Urge People Not to Carry Guns': Armed Self-Defense in the Louisiana Civil Rights Movement and the Radicalization of the Congress of Racial Equality," *Louisiana History* 45 (2004): 261–286; Akinyele Umoja, " 'We Will Shoot Back': The Natchez Model and Paramilitary Organization in the Mississippi Freedom Movement," *Journal of Black Studies* 32 (2002): 271–294.

28. *Milwaukee Journal,* August 10, 1966, p. 1; Roy Wilkins to James C. Newcomb, August 15, 1966, Maier Papers, box 125, folder 5; *Milwaukee Journal,* August 11, 1966, p. 1.

29. WITI editorial, August 15, 1966, Maier Papers, box 44, folder 13; *Milwaukee Journal,* August 11, 1966, p. 20; *Milwaukee Journal,* August 12, 1966, pt. 2, p. 1; Aukofer, *City with a Cause,* p. 100.

30. Todd Michney, "Race, Violence, and Urban Territory," *Journal of Urban History* 32 (2006): 404–428; James Ralph, *Northern Protest: Martin Luther King, Jr., Chicago, and the Civil Rights Movement* (Cambridge, MA: Harvard University Press, 1993); Jeff Kelly Lowenstein, "Resisting the Dream," *The Chicago Reporter,* http://www.chicagoreporter.com/index.php/c/Inside_Stories/d/Resisting_the_Dream (accessed November 22, 2007); *Milwaukee Journal,* August 14, 1966, pt. 5, p. 1.

31. *Milwaukee Journal,* August 20, 1966, p. 9.

32. Harris interview; Rozga interview.

33. Rozga interview; Aukofer, *City with a Chance,* p. 101. See also extensive daily coverage in the *Journal, Sentinel, Star,* and *Courier,* from August 19, 1966, through the first week of September.

34. Aukofer, *City with a Chance,* p. 102; FBI report on Father James Groppi, January 10, 1968, p. 4, in Father James Groppi FBI file, part 1, obtained under the Freedom of Information Act and in the possession of the author.

35. *Milwaukee Journal,* August 29, 1966, p. 18; Undated statement by Mayor Maier, Maier Papers, box 44, folder 13; *Milwaukee Journal,* September 1, 1966, p. 1; *Milwaukee Journal,* September 9, 1966, p. 1; *Milwaukee Journal,* September 15, 1966, p. 30; *Milwaukee Eagle,* March 28, 1966, p. 1; *Milwaukee Journal,* September 2, 1966, pt. 2, p. 1.

36. *Milwaukee Star,* April 2, 1966, p. 3; *Milwaukee Journal,* September 2, 1966, p. 12.

37. "News Release: Catholic Archdiocese Council On Urban Life," August 31, 1966, Bleidorn Papers, box 8, folder 2. In addition to the Council on Urban Life, MUSIC, the *Star,* the *Courier,* the *Catholic Herald,* the Greater Milwaukee Conference on Religion and Race, the Milwaukee Committee on Equal Opportunity, Councilwoman Vel Phillips, MCORE, MNALC, the Marquette Faculty Association for Interracial Justice, the Southeastern Wisconsin Chapter of the National Association of Social Workers, St. Boniface Parish, the Wisconsin Commission on Human Rights, and the Milwaukee County Labor Council also publicly supported the YC and Groppi.

38. Print version of WTMJ-TV editorial, August 26, 1966, Maier Papers, box 44, folder 13.

39. *Milwaukee Journal,* March 13, 1966, pt. 2, p. 19; "Here Comes Whiteman" comic book, Bleidorn Papers, box 5, folder 4; Dr. Billy James Hargis, "Martin Luther King: Spokesman for the Enemy," Maier Papers, box 44, folder 17.

40. *New York Times,* August 30, 1966, p. 16; *Time,* September 9, 1966, p. 23.

41. *Milwaukee Journal,* August 27, 1966, p. 1; *Milwaukee Star,* October 15, 1966, p. 1; *Milwaukee Courier,* September 17, 1966, p. 1; *Milwaukee Journal,* August 27, 1966, p. 1; *Milwaukee Journal,* August 30, 1966, p. 1; *Milwaukee Journal,* August 31, 1966, p. 1.

42. *Milwaukee Star,* September, 10, 1966, p. 3; *Milwaukee Journal,* September 2, 1966, p. 1; *Milwaukee Journal,* September 4, 1966, p. 1; *Milwaukee Journal,* September 20, 1966, p. 16; *Milwaukee Journal,* October 2, 1966, p. 1; *Milwaukee Star,* October 8, 1966, p. 2. Although the YC agreed to halt demonstrations at the homes of prominent EC members, it did not stop the protests altogether. About sixty-five civil rights supporters marched in front of the EC on September 28 to protest a meeting held there by the Citizens for Decent Literature. On

October 13, the YC and MUSIC picketed again in opposition to an award banquet honoring outgoing school chief Harold Vincent. The next night, the YC joined Marquette students—over 300 civil rights demonstrators in all—in protest of a school dance held at the EC and attended by more than 2,700 students. The Marquette Eagles protest also marked the first appearance of the Commandos at a demonstration.

43. *Milwaukee Sentinel,* October 5, 1966, p. 1; *Milwaukee Journal,* October 5, 1966, p. 1; *Milwaukee Star,* October 15, 1966, p. 1; McClain interview; McKinney interview; Aukofer, *City with a Chance,* p. 103. Benning quoted in Julius Modlinski, "Commandos: A Study of a Black Organization's Transformation from Militant Protest to Social Service" (PhD diss., University of Wisconsin–Madison, 1978): p. 77; *Milwaukee Journal,* October 6, 1966, pt. 2, p. 1; *Milwaukee Courier,* October 8, 1966, p. 1.

44. McKinney interview. McKinney repeated a version of the same story during the Groppi lecture at East Library.

45. Harris interview.

46. Modlinski, "Commandos," pp. 75–76; Thekan interview. See also McKinney interview; McDowell interview.

47. McClain interview; Groppi lecture at East Library; McDowell interview; Harris interview.

48. Thekan interview; Jacobson interview; Harris interview. See also Groppi lecture at East Library.

49. Thekan interview; Harris interview; McDowell interview; McKinney interview; McClain interview.

50. McDowell interview; Groppi lecture at East Library. See also Modlinski, "Commandos"; McKinney interview; McClain interview; Squire Austin, interview with Patrick Jones, October 7, 1999.

51. McDowell interview; McClain interview; McKinney interview; Rozga interview; Harris interview; Coggs interview.

52. See Lance Hill, *The Deacons for Defense: Armed Resistance and the Civil Rights Movement* (Chapel Hill: University of North Carolina, 2004); *Milwaukee Journal,* October 6, 1966, pt. 2, p. 1. Later, in June 1967, Milwaukee newspapers also reported on a white-helmeted group of 150 African American youths in Tampa, Florida, which had helped police soothe tempers following two days of rioting in the city's black community. That same month, African Americans in Dayton, Ohio, followed Tampa's lead. Unlike in the other examples, police in Tampa and Dayton embraced the youth patrols and, in fact, worked with them. In Tampa, for instance, police put five of the patrollers on their payroll as a permanent part of the city's police community-relations board. In Dayton, too, African American youth rode alongside regular officers in squad cars. See *Milwaukee Journal,* June 16, 1967, p. 4; *Milwaukee Journal,* June 17, 1967, p. 8.

53. On Black Power, see Peniel Joseph, *Waiting 'til the Midnight Hour: A Narrative History of Black Power in America* (New York: Holt, 2006); Joseph, *The Black Power Movement;* Timothy Tyson, *Radio Free Dixie: Robert F. Williams and the Roots of Black Power* (Chapel Hill: University of North Carolina Press, 1999); William Van DeBerg, *New Day in Babylon: The Black Power Movement and American Culture, 1965–1975* (Chicago: University of Chicago Press, 1992); Komozi Woodard, *A Nation within A Nation: Amiri Baraka (LeRoi Jones) and Black Power Politics* (Chapel Hill: University of North Carolina Press, 1999).

54. "Groppi in Black for Yule Mass," *National Catholic Reporter,* January 3, 1967, p. 7; Karen Kelly, "The Scene—Milwaukee," *Community,* October 1967, p. 3. For a transcript of the Associate Press story, see Groppi Papers, Milwaukee County Historical Society.

55. Quoted in Aukofer, *City with a Chance,* p. 85.

56. Groppi interview; see also Aukofer, *City with a Chance,* pp. 83–84.

57. *Milwaukee Journal,* October 12, 1966, p. 24; *Milwaukee Sentinel,* October 7, 1966, p. 22; *Milwaukee Courier,* October 15, 1966, p. 1; *Milwaukee Sentinel,* October 7, 1966, p. 5; *Milwaukee Journal,* October 7, 1966, p. 1; McKinney interview.

58. McKinney interview.

59. *Milwaukee Sentinel,* October 9, 1966, p. 1; *Milwaukee Journal,* October 9, 1966, p. 1; *Milwaukee Journal,* October 20, 1966, pt. 2, p. 4.

60. Rozga interview.

61. *Milwaukee Star,* July 22, 1966, p. 1; *Milwaukee Journal,* July 14, 1966, pt. 2, p. 1. YC and Commando membership increases came in waves. After the Wauwatosa protest and the open housing protests of 1967–1968, both groups experienced a significant spike in interest. Similarly, when the YC relocated its Freedom House, the group began to attract new members from the surrounding neighborhood. See Rozga interview; McDowell interview; Harris interview.

6. Police–Community Tensions and the 1967 Riot

1. In addition to the well-known civil disorders in Newark and Detroit, major racial violence had also taken place in Nashville, Houston, Tampa Bay, Cincinnati, Buffalo, Niagara Falls, Atlanta, Boston, Cambridge, Philadelphia, and several other cities by July. In that month alone, 103 cities experienced some level of racial discord. See, Otto Kerner National Advisory Committee Staff, *The Kerner Report: The 1968 Report of the National Advisory Commission on Civil Disorders* (New York: Bantam, 1968), pp. 1–22; Henry Meyer, *The Mayor Who Made Milwaukee Famous* (Boulder, CO: Madison Books, 1993), pp. 63–92. It is important to acknowledge that the terminology for racial violence is contested.

Traditionally, social scientists, historians, politicians, and journalists have called them "riots," which places the accent on the chaotic, insurrectionary, and extralegal elements of these incidents but also implicitly places most of the blame on participants in the disorder rather than on social conditions or injustices that may have fueled that behavior. In response, some use the term "race rebellion" or "insurrection" to signify the political nature of this action and to suggest that it is not as irrational as previous analysts have suggested. I have chosen to use "civil disorder" or "civil disturbance" but sometimes use the other terms. I ascribe no political meaning to the use of these different terms in this work. Rather, it is simply an attempt to keep my prose interesting and varied.

2. *Milwaukee Journal*, July 31, 1967, p. 1; *Milwaukee Sentinel*, July 31, 1967, p. 1. For an overview of the Milwaukee civil disturbance, see Frank Aukofer, *City with a Chance* (Milwaukee: Bruce Publishing Company, 1968), pp. 7–20; Maier, *The Mayor Who Made Milwaukee Famous*, pp. 63–92. In addition, the Henry Maier Papers contain the "Mayor's Official Riot Log," which provides a detailed narrative of events from an official perspective. Maier Papers, box 43, folder 20, State Historical Society of Wisconsin, Madison.

3. Squire Austin, interview with Patrick Jones, October 7, 1999.

4. As racial violence spread from Watts to Detroit, Henry Maier studied the responses of public officials. In anticipation of a conflagration in Milwaukee, Maier had moved to consolidate authority and communication throughout his office. To that end, he set up a hotline connecting his office directly to the governor's office, authorized a plan of action, and ordered the city attorney research emergency powers. See, Maier, *The Mayor Who Made Milwaukee Famous*, pp. 63–92.

5. Four other officers were injured that night in other incidents, including twenty-five-year-old John Carter, who was left permanently blinded.

6. *Milwaukee Journal*, August 1, 1967, p. 1; *Milwaukee Sentinel*, August 1, 1967, p. 1; Milwaukee *Shepherd-Express*, August 1, 2002. See also Austin interview.

7. "Proclamation," July 31, 1967, Maier Papers, box 43, folder 20; "My Fellow Citizens," Maier Papers, box 43, folder 20; "Resolution RE Proclamation Declaring that A State of Emergency Exists in the City of Milwaukee," Milwaukee Common Council, Maier Papers, box 43, folder 6; "Riot Log," Maier Papers.

8. By midnight on Monday, roughly 4,800 total Guardsmen had poured into staging areas from around the state.

9. Fagan's help sprang, in part, from a political rivalry he had with Mayor Maier. Fagan was an ambitious Republican with designs on city hall. See *Milwaukee Journal*, August 2, 1967, p. 1; *Milwaukee Sentinel*, August 2, 1967, p. 1.

10. *Milwaukee Journal*, August 1, 1967, pt. 2, p. 1; *Milwaukee Sentinel*, August 1, 1967, p. 1; *Milwaukee Journal*, August 2, 1967, p. 1.

11. *Milwaukee Journal,* August 3, 1967, p. 1; *Milwaukee Sentinel,* August 3, 1967, p. 1; *Milwaukee Star,* August 5, 1967, p. 1; *Milwaukee Star,* August 6, 1967; "Riot Log," Maier Papers; *Milwaukee Journal,* August 7, 1967, pt. 2, p. 1; *Milwaukee Journal,* August 8, 1967, pt. 2, p. 1.

12. "Riot Log," Maier Papers. See the series of articles in the *Milwaukee Journal* and the *Milwaukee Sentinel,* July 31 through August 9, 1967. In addition, see coverage in the *Milwaukee Star* and the *Milwaukee Courier* on August 6 and 13, 1967.

13. *Milwaukee Sentinel,* February 16, 1964, p. 1; *Milwaukee Journal,* February 16, 1964, p. 1.

14. Vel Phillips, interview with Patrick Jones, April 20, 1999; Prentice McKinney, interview with Patrick Jones, November 13, 1999; Joe McClain, interview with Patrick Jones, December 3, 1998; Velma Coggs, interview with Patrick Jones, March 27, 1999; Groppi lecture at East Library, February 15, 1984. Prentice McKinney also related an even more dangerous situation. "They [Milwaukee police] made their position clear," he said. "They would arrest you and if the opportunity presented itself they would blow you away . . . I was walking down the street, by myself. The Tactical Squad pulled up. A guy leveled a shot-gun. He said, 'McKinney, one day I'm going to blow you away.' I said, 'The only thing that I can say to you is that they make two coffins, not one.' OK? That was the attitude prevailing constantly. People were intimidated."

15. *Milwaukee Journal,* May 31, 1966, p. 1; *Milwaukee Journal,* June 2, 1966, pt. 2, p. 1; *Milwaukee Journal,* July 20, 1966, p. 14; *Milwaukee Journal,* September 6, 1966, pt. 2, p. 1; *Milwaukee Journal,* September 7, 1966, p. 21; *Milwaukee Journal,* September 8, 1966, pt. 2, p. 16; *Milwaukee Journal,* August 15, 1966, pt. 2, p. 1.

16. WTMJ Film Archive, May 11, 1967, Urban Archive, University of Wisconsin–Milwaukee.

17. *Milwaukee Journal,* September 6, 1966, p. 1; *Milwaukee Sentinel,* September 6, 1966, p. 1; *Milwaukee Star,* September 10, 1966, p. 1; *Milwaukee Courier,* September 10, 1966, p. 1; *Milwaukee Sentinel,* September 30, 1966, p. 1; *Milwaukee Courier,* September 10, 1966, p. 1.

18. *Milwaukee Journal,* September 30, 1966, p. 14; *Milwaukee Sentinel,* September 30, 1966, p. 1; *Milwaukee Journal,* October 1, 1966, p. 3.

19. *Milwaukee Sentinel,* September 30, 1966, p. 1; *Milwaukee Journal,* October 1, 1966, pt. 2, p. 1; *Milwaukee Sentinel,* October 6, 1966, p. 5; *Milwaukee Journal,* October 6, 1966, pt. 2, p. 1.

20. *Milwaukee Journal,* September 10, 1966, p. 1.

21. A series of articles relating to the internal NAACP schism appeared in local newspapers between October 1966 and April 1967. See also McClain interview; McKinney interview. In July of 1967, a similar leadership struggle took place at the national NAACP convention in Boston. A group of "young turks", largely

dissatisfied with the conservative approach of the traditional leadership, attempted, unsuccessfully, to wrestle away control of the board of directors. See *Milwaukee Journal,* July 12, 1966, p. 14.

22. This challenge appears to have been mainly a tit-for-tat reaction from moderate and conservative elements within the state conference and the Milwaukee adult branch for the challenge to their leadership at the November conference. Much of the opposition to Groppi's role in the Movement came from people outside the YC or Commandos. Reportedly, a few older YC members complained that Groppi was listening too much to his white legal team during the Eagles protest. Groppi replied that the volatile circumstances necessitated the meetings and that YC members were welcome to attend meetings. Throughout this process, Groppi maintained the support of the overwhelming majority of the local YC and Commandos. The rock-throwing incident with Thomas Leubenow confirms the fierce loyalty many YC members felt for their advisor. In retrospect, the challenge does not appear to have presented a serious threat to Groppi's leadership. See WTMJ Film Archive, April 4, 1967; *Milwaukee Sentinel,* April 9, 1967, p. 1; *Milwaukee Journal,* April 9, 1967, p. 1; *Milwaukee Star,* April 15, 1967, p. 1.

23. Quoted in Jules Modlinski, "Commandos: A Study of a Black Organization's Transformation from Militant Protest to Social Service" (PhD diss., University of Wisconsin–Madison, 1978), p. 81. See also McKinney interview; McClain interview; Austin interview.

24. *Milwaukee Journal,* May 19, 1967, p. 1; *Milwaukee Sentinel,* May 19, 1967, p. 1; *Milwaukee Journal,* May 20, 1967, pt. 2, p. 1; *Milwaukee Journal,* May 25, 1967, pt. 2, p. 1.

25. *Milwaukee Journal,* April 19, 1967, pt. 2, p. 1; *Milwaukee Journal,* April 21, 1967, p. 1; *Milwaukee Journal,* April 4, 1967, pt. 2, p. 1.

26. Associated Press, "Angry Priest," May 18, 1967, found in Groppi Papers, box 15, folder 10, Milwaukee County Historical Society; Groppi lecture at East Library; *Milwaukee Journal,* May 19, 1967, p. 1.

27. *Milwaukee Sentinel,* May 11, 1967, p. 1; *Milwaukee Journal,* May 11, 1967, p. 1; According to news accounts, Sprague had been recently named chairman of a John Birch–related group called the Committee on Police Support. See *Milwaukee Journal,* May 12, 1967, pt. 2, p. 1.

28. *Milwaukee Journal,* May 12, 1967, pt. 2, p. 1; Reverend E.R. Eschweiler, et. al., to Mayor Henry Maier, May 13, 1967, Maier Papers, box 43, folder 7; *Milwaukee Journal,* May 16, 1967, p. 13; *Milwaukee Journal,* May 23, 1967, pt. 2, p. 4; *Milwaukee Star,* July 1, 1967, p. 3; *Milwaukee Star,* May 13, 1967, p. 6.

29. *Milwaukee Journal,* May 14, 1967, pt. 2, p. 1; *Milwaukee Sentinel,* May 14, 1967, p. 5; *Milwaukee Star,* May 15, 1967, p. 1.

30. *Milwaukee Journal,* May 8, 1967, pt. 2, p. 1.

31. *Milwaukee Journal,* June 22, 1967, pt. 2, p. 1; *Milwaukee Journal,* July 23, 1967, p. 16; *Milwaukee Journal,* July 26, 1967, pt. 2, p. 1; *Milwaukee Journal,* July 29, 1967, p. 1; *Milwaukee Journal,* July 29, 1967, p. 1.

32. McKinney interview; Dennis McDowell, interview with Patrick Jones, August 11, 2005; McClain interview.

33. McClain interview.

34. McDowell interview. See also McKinney interview; Margaret Rozga, interview with Patrick Jones, July 19, 2005; McClain interview; Alberta Harris, interview with Patrick Jones, August 27, 2005.

35. *Milwaukee Journal,* May 1, 1967, p. 1; *Milwaukee Star,* March 11, 1967, p. 3.

36. Otto Kerner National Advisory Committee Staff, *The Kerner Report,* pp. 84–107.

37. *Milwaukee Journal,* September 11, 1966, pt. 2, p. 1.

38. "Riot Log," Maier Papers; *Milwaukee Sentinel,* August 4, 1967, copy in Maier Paper, box 43, folder 7; Ray Hinz to Mayor Maier, August 4, 1967, Maier Papers, box 43, folder 26; Groppi, quoted in Maier, *The Mayor Who Made Milwaukee Famous,* p. 89; *Milwaukee Journal,* August 10, 1967, p. 22.

39. See Karl Flaming, "The 1967 Milwaukee Riot: A Historical and Comparative Analysis" (PhD diss., Syracuse University, 1970); Karl Flaming, *Who Riots and Why? Black and White Perspectives in Milwaukee* (Milwaukee: Milwaukee Urban League, 1968).

40. Otto Kerner National Advisory Committee Staff, *The Kerner Report,* pp. 1, 2, and 10.

41. Douglas Pollack to Mayor Henry Maier, July 31, 1967, Maier Papers, box 43, folder 22. There are literally dozens of letters contained in Maier's papers that express a similar view to Pollack's.

42. For an overview of statewide editorial commentary, see *Milwaukee Journal,* August 6, 1967, p. 18.

43. *Milwaukee Journal,* August 6, 1967, pt. 2, p. 1; Maier, *The Mayor Who Made Milwaukee Famous,* pp. 67–80; Father James Groppi FBI file, obtained under the Freedom of Information Act and in the possession of the author.

44. The Kerner Commission ranked Milwaukee's civil disturbance the eighth biggest of the 164 total disorders reported nationwide in 1967. Yet, despite this high ranking, the Milwaukee conflict paled in comparison to the more well-known eruptions in Newark and Detroit. See Aukofer, *City with a Chance,* p. 7; *Report of the National Advisory Commission on Civil Disorders,* pp. 56–68, 84–107; Maier, *The Mayor Who Made Milwaukee Famous.*

45. Interestingly, over the years a number of Milwaukee residents have told me, formally and informally, that during the riot, groups of whites, fueled by a fear of marauding black "hoodlums" spilling out of segregated inner core neighborhoods into more orderly and affluent suburban white areas, organized and armed themselves. The most common story I heard claimed that a small group

of men on a particular street held a meeting in someone's living room to discuss the threat and how to best protect their families and property.

46. "Mayor Maier's Remarks—Meeting with Businessmen on Crusade for Resources," August 3, 1967, Maier Papers, box 43, folder 8. Other similar speeches from that time period can be found in the same location. See also *Milwaukee Journal,* August 3, 1967, p. 1. A transcript of the *New York Times* ad, titled, "A Statement of Concern about the Crisis of Our Cities," can be found in the Maier Papers, box 43, folder 8.

47. "No Place to Run—to Hide—to Escape from Central City Responsibilities," WITI-TV editorial, August 4, 1967, Maier Papers, box 43, folder 8.

48. Common View Group, "Statement to the Milwaukee Community," August 4, 1967, Frank Aukofer Papers, box 2, State Historical Society of Wisconsin, Madison. See also *Milwaukee Journal,* August 5, 1967, p. 1; *Milwaukee Sentinel,* August 5, 1967, p. 1.

49. "Comments by Lucius Walker in Pewaukee on Sunday," August 9, 1967, Maier Papers, box 43, folder 20. Text of Maier's remarks to African American community members can be found in the Maier Papers, box 43, folder 20. See also Aukofer, *City with a Chance,* pp. 17–19; Maier, *The Mayor Who Made Milwaukee Famous,* p. 80.

50. Richard Green, interview with Arlene Zakhar, April 19, 1984; McKinney interview; "Statement by Mayor Maier," August 5, 1967, Maier Papers, box 43, folder 20; "Statement of How (Milwaukee's Marshall Plan)," Maier Papers, box 43, folder 20; Aukofer, *City with a Chance,* pp. 18–19. See also *Milwaukee Sentinel,* August 5, 1967, p. 5; *Milwaukee Journal,* August 7, 1967, pt. 2, p. 1.

7. The Struggle for Open Housing

1. WTMJ-TV Film Archive, August 13, 1967. Urban Archive, University of Wisconsin–Milwaukee.

2. *Milwaukee Courier,* August 26, 1967, p. 1.

3. *Milwaukee Sentinel,* August 29, 1967, p. 1.

4. See Stephen Grant Meyer, *As Long as They Don't Move Next Door: Segregation and Racial Conflict in American Neighborhoods* (Lanham, MD: Rowman & Littlefield, 2000); Kenneth Jackson, *Crabgrass Frontier: The Suburbanization of the United States* (New York: Oxford University Press, 1987).

5. Meyer, *As Long as They Don't Move Next Door,* pp. 79–97; Ira Katznelson, *When Affirmative Action Was White: An Untold Story of Racial Inequality in Twentieth-Century America* (New York: W. W. Norton, 2006); Thomas Sugrue, "Crabgrass-Roots Politics: Race, Rights, and the Reaction against Liberalism in the Urban North, 1940–1964," *Journal of American History* 82 (1995): 566; *New York Times,* March 17, 2007, p. A1.

6. Declining property values were usually the result of panicked selling by fearful white homeowners who undersold their property in order to flee the area. For one detailed report on this phenomenon, see "Racial Land Value Fear Refuted," March 11, 1960, Barbee Papers, box 10, folder 4, State Historical Society of Wisconsin, Madison.

7. Quoted in *Milwaukee Reader,* April 17–23, 1961, p. 5. See Milwaukee NAACP Papers, box 3, folder 11, State Historical Society of Wisconsin, Madison.

8. For an overview, see Meyer, *As Long as They Don't Move Next Door,* esp. chapters 10 and 11.

9. Ibid., p. 7.

10. *Milwaukee Journal,* March 26, 1965, pt. 2, p. 8.

11. For an overview of the entire Greenfield Trailer Camp incident, see William Thompson, *The History of Wisconsin,* vol. 6: *Continuity and Change, 1940–1965* (Madison: State Historical Society of Wisconsin, 1988), pp. 334–335; *Milwaukee Star,* May 25, 1963, p. 1; *Milwaukee Star,* June 22, 1963, p. 3.

12. "Program: Annual Meeting of Wisconsin Conference, NAACP," May 28, 1960, Milwaukee NAACP Papers, box 10, folder 4; "Citizens Committee for Fair Housing Practices," January 19, 1961, Milwaukee NAACP Papers, box 3, folder 11. Examples of "forced housing" cards can be found in Barbee Papers, box 34, folder 3; John Carroll, "On the Matter of Open Occupancy Legislation," WITI-TV editorial, November 2, 1963, Henry Maier Papers, box 44, folder 9, State Historical Society of Wisconsin, Madison; *Milwaukee Journal,* November 1, 1963, p. 23; *Milwaukee Journal,* February 13, 1964, p. 1; *Milwaukee Sentinel,* February 13, 1964, p. 1.

13. *Milwaukee Journal,* April 23, 1965, p. 13; *Milwaukee Journal,* May 15, 1965, p. 7; *Milwaukee Journal,* April 30, 1965, pt. 2, p. 5.

14. "WTMJ-TV Editorial," November 4, 1965, Maier Papers, box 44, folder 12.

15. Vel Phillips, interview with Patrick Jones, April 20, 1999.

16. Phillips interview; Michael Timm, "The Fight for Fairness," *Shepherd Express,* September 27, 2007.

17. Timm, "The Fight for Fairness".

18. See *Milwaukee Journal,* March, 29, 1966, p. 1; *Milwaukee Journal,* April 14, 1966, pt. 2, p. 2.

19. *Milwaukee Journal,* July 1, 1966, pt. 2, p. 1.

20. Quoted in Meyer, *As Long as They Don't Move Next Door,* p. 204.

21. Ibid., pp. 183–188. For an overview of the civil rights insurgency in Chicago, particularly the SCLC campaign, see James Ralph, *Northern Protest: Martin Luther King, Jr., Chicago, and the Civil Rights Movement* (Cambridge, MA: Harvard University Press, 1993).

22. *Milwaukee Journal,* October 15, 1966, p. 8.

23. Margaret Rozga, interview with Patrick Jones, July 19, 2005; Margaret Rozga, "March on Milwaukee," *Wisconsin Magazine of History* 90 (2007): 28–39. See also WTMJ-TV News Archive, August 29–September 3, 1967.

24. Phillips interview; Squire Austin, interview with Patrick Jones, October 7, 1999.

25. Phillips interview; *Milwaukee Journal,* September 1, 1967, pt. 2, p. 1.

26. *Milwaukee Journal,* March 9, 1967, pt. 2, p. 1; *New York Times,* September 13, 1967.

27. *Milwaukee Journal,* June 20, 1967, pt. 2, p. 1; *Milwaukee Star,* June 24, 1967, p. 3; *Milwaukee Star,* July 1, 1967, p. 3; *Milwaukee Journal,* July 6, 1967, pt. 2, p. 1; *Milwaukee Journal,* July 7, 1967, pt. 2, p. 7; *Milwaukee Star,* July 24, 1967, p. 1; *Milwaukee Journal,* July 20, 1967, p. 17; *Milwaukee Star,* July 29, 1967, p. 1.

28. *Milwaukee Star,* July 1, 1967, p. 4; *Milwaukee Journal,* July 11, 1967, pt. 2, p. 7; *Milwaukee Journal,* July 20, 1967, p. 17; *Milwaukee Journal,* July 11, 1967, pt. 2, p. 7.

29. *Milwaukee Journal,* June 22, 1967, pt. 2, p. 1.

30. WTMJ-TV Film Archive, August 23, 1967.

31. *Milwaukee Star,* July 6, 1963, p. 12.

32. Rozga interview; Prentice McKinney, interview with Patrick Jones, November 13, 1999; Jesse Wade, interview with Arlene Zakhar, May 1, 1984.

33. *Milwaukee Journal,* September 30, 1967, p. 22; WITI-TV editorial, August 30, 1967, Maier Papers, box 43, folder 9; *Catholic Herald,* September 2, 1967, p. 4.

34. Austin interview; Dennis McDowell, interview with Patrick Jones, August 11, 2005; Wade interview; Timm, "The Fight for Fairness."

35. *Catholic Herald,* September 2, 1967, p. 5; WTMJ-TV News Archive, August 30, 1967.

36. Phillips interview; *Milwaukee Journal,* September 1, 1967, pt. 2, p. 1.

37. *Milwaukee Journal,* August 30, 1967, p. 22; *Milwaukee Sentinel,* August 30 1967, copy in Maier Papers, box 43, folder 9; WTMJ-TV Film Archive, August 30, 1967.

38. *Milwaukee Journal,* August 31, 1967, pt. 2, p. 1.

39. Henry Maier, *The Mayor Who Made Milwaukee Famous: An Autobiography* (Lanham, MD: Madison Books, 1993), p. 94; "Mayor's Statement to TV and Press," September 1967, Maier Papers, box 43, folder 20.

40. *Milwaukee Journal,* September 16, 1967, p. 1; *Milwaukee Journal,* September 13, 1967, p. 1; McKinney interview; "MCEO Press Release," September 8, 1967, James Barrett Papers, series 3, box 1, folder 1, Marquette University.

41. "Proclamation," Maier Papers, box 43, folder 20; "Press Statement," August 31, 1967, Maier Papers, p. 2; "Journal Clips," Frank Aukofer Papers, box 2, State Historical Society of Wisconsin; WTMJ-TV News Archive, August 29–September 3, 1967; See also Maier, *The Mayor Who Made Milwaukee Famous,* p. 98.

42. WTMJ-TV News Archive, August 29–September 3, 1967.

43. *Milwaukee Journal,* August 31, 1967, p. 1; *Milwaukee Sentinel,* August 31, 1967, p. 1; *Milwaukee Star,* September 4, 1967, p. 1; *Milwaukee Courier,* September 2, 1967; Press Release by MCORE, August 31, 1967, Maier Papers, box 43, folder 9.

44. WTMJ-TV News Archive, August 29–September 3, 1967.

45. *Milwaukee Journal,* September 1, 1967, p. 13; *Milwaukee Sentinel,* September 1, 1967, p. 1.

46. *Milwaukee Journal,* September 1, 1967, p. 1; *Milwaukee Sentinel,* September 1, 1967, p. 1; *Milwaukee Star,* September 2, 1967, p. 1.

47. *Milwaukee Journal,* September 2, 1967, p. 1; *Milwaukee Sentinel,* September 2, 1967, p. 2; *Milwaukee Star,* September 9, 1967, p. 1; Maier, *The Mayor Who Made Milwaukee Famous,* p. 99; Eugene Bleidorn, interview with Patrick Jones, November 21, 1998.

48. *Milwaukee Journal,* September 3, 1967, p. 1; *Milwaukee Sentinel,* September 3, 1967, p. 1; *Milwaukee Star,* September 9, 1967, p. 1.

49. *Milwaukee Courier,* September 9, 1967, p. 1.

50. *Milwaukee Journal,* September 7, 1967, pt. 2, p. 1; *Milwaukee Journal,* September 8, 1967, p. 16.

51. *Milwaukee Journal,* September 8, 1967, p. 16.

52. Ibid.; *Milwaukee Star,* September 9, 1967, p. 1; McKinney interview.

53. *Milwaukee Journal,* September 8, 1967, p. 16.

54. Henry Maier to Roy Wilkins, September 7, 1967, Maier Papers, box 125, folder 5; *Milwaukee Journal,* September 8, 1967, p. 1.

55. *Milwaukee Journal,* September 8, 1967, p. 1; WTMJ-TV editorial, September 8, 1967, Maier Papers, box 43, folder 11; *Sentinel* quote in Maier, *The Mayor Who Made Milwaukee Famous,* p. 110; "It Was Not Civil Rights—But the Deliberate Lawlessness of Hoodlums," WITI-TV editorial, September 8, 1967, James Groppi Papers, box 15, folder 11, State Historical Society of Wisconsin, Madison; *New York Times,* September 13, 1967, p. 12; "Statement by James C. Newcomb on NAACP Youth Council Sit-In," September 7, 1967, Maier Papers, box 43, folder 15; "Statement by Henry Maier," September 7, 1967, Maier Papers, box 43, folder 11.

56. *Concern,* October 15, 1967, p. 6; telegram from Dr. Martin Luther King Jr. to Father James Groppi, September 4, 1967, Groppi Papers, Manuscript EX, box 2, folder 3 (the original telegram was not punctuated); Groppi Papers, box 11, folders 2 and 6.

57. *Milwaukee Journal,* September 8, 1967, pp. 1, 16; *Milwaukee Sentinel,* September 8, 1967, p. 1.

58. "March on Milwaukee," Groppi Papers, box 1, folder 38; *Milwaukee Journal,* September 11, 1967, p. 1; *Milwaukee Sentinel,* September 11, 1967, p. 1; *Milwaukee Star,* September 16, 1967, p. 1; *Catholic Herald Citizen,* September 16, 1967, p. 7.

59. *U.S. News and World Report,* September 25, 1967, p. 24.

60. *Milwaukee Journal,* September 18, 1967, pt. 2, p. 1.

61. WTMJ-TV News Archive, August 29–September 3, 1967.

62. *Milwaukee Journal,* October 17, 1967, p. 1.

63. Meyer, *As Long as They Don't Move Next Door,* p. 182; Maier, *The Mayor Who Made Milwaukee Famous,* p. 105; *Milwaukee Journal,* September 23, 1967, p. 10.

64. Jeffrey Bartell and Edward Stege, "The Mediation of Civil Rights Disputes: Open Housing in Milwaukee," *Wisconsin Law Review* (1968): 1129–1191.

65. *Milwaukee Journal,* December 13, 1967, p. 4.

66. "MCEO Newsletter," December 1967, Milwaukee Citizens for Equal Opportunity Papers, "Micro Collection 16," Milwaukee County Historical Society, Milwaukee.

67. In St. Louis, where Father Groppi and several YC and Commando leaders attended an open housing conference, the priest caused a minor national media stir when he used the word "fuck" on live television while describing the harassment he and other civil rights advocates had faced on Milwaukee's South Side.

68. *U.S. News and World Report,* September 11, 1967, and September 25, 1967; *Time,* September 15, 1967, and September 22, 1967; *Newsweek,* October 2, 1967, and November 20, 1967; *Esquire,* November 1967; *New York Times,* September 13, 1967; *U.S. News and World Report,* September 25, 1967; *Milwaukee Journal,* November 7, 1967, p. 3; *Milwaukee Journal,* September 21, 1967, p. 1.

69. *Newsweek,* October 2, 1967; Maier, *The Mayor Who Made Milwaukee Famous,* p. 122; *Catholic Herald Citizen,* January 13, 1968, p. 37; *Esquire,* November 1967, p. 133.

70. *Marquette Tribune,* December 13, 1967, p. 4; *Catholic Herald Citizen,* September 23, 1967, p. 6.

71. Austin interview. The burned-out Freedom House was also a significant site for open housing activists. Across the door, someone had scrawled, "The police burned it down." It was a favorite destination during North Side marches and a source of inspiration to many YC and Commando leaders.

72. *Milwaukee Journal,* September 5, 1967, pt. 2, p. 1; Austin interview; Ben Barkin, interview with Patrick Jones, November 4, 1999.

73. McClain interview; McKinney interview; Austin interview; Fred Reed lecture, Milwaukee, Wisconsin, September 29, 2007, tape recording in author's possession.

74. McKinney interview; Rozga interview.

75. McKinney interview; McClain interview; Wade interview; Richard Green, interview with Arlene Zakhar, 1984; McDowell interview; Austin interview; Phillips interview; Rozga interview; Alberta Harris, interview with Patrick Jones, August 27, 2005; Lloyd Barbee, interview with Patrick Jones, January 30, 1999.

76. The boycott emerged as an off-the-cuff suggestion, at first, and evolved into a formal campaign. Some questioned the choice of Schlitz. According to Frank Aukofer, Schlitz "was a leading force for civic betterment and had, in fact, contributed money to civil rights causes and programs to alleviate the problems of Milwaukee's black ghetto." Ben Barkin, who worked as a public relations executive for the company, said that Schlitz was the first Milwaukee brewery to hire African Americans in significant numbers. Aukofer suggested that Gregory probably did not know this history and probably chose the brewery because, with its slogan "The beer that made Milwaukee famous," it symbolized the city. See Barkin interview; Frank Aukofer, *City with a Chance* (Milwaukee: Bruce Publishing Company, 1968), pp. 131–132.

77. *Wall Street Journal,* November 12, 1967, p. 1; *Milwaukee Journal,* September 13, 1967, p. 1; *Milwaukee Journal,* September 26, 1967, p. 1.

78. *Wall Street Journal,* November 12, 1967, p. 1; *Milwaukee Courier,* November 18, 1967, p. 2; John Givens, interview with Patrick Jones, October 17, 1999.

79. *Milwaukee Journal,* December 19, 1967, p. 22.

80. *Wall Street Journal,* November 12, 1967, p. 1; *Milwaukee Journal,* November 9, 1967, pt. 2, p. 1; *Milwaukee Journal,* December 18, 1967, pt. 2, p. 2.

81. Aukofer, *City with a Chance,* pp. 132–134.

82. *Marquette Tribune,* January 5, 1968, p. 3; *Milwaukee Journal,* December 21, 1967, p. 4; *Milwaukee Journal,* December 26, 1967, pt. 2, p. 4.

83. *Milwaukee Journal,* March 5, 1968, p. 1; *Milwaukee Sentinel,* March 5, 1968, p. 1; *Milwaukee Courier,* March 9, 1968, p. 1; Aukofer, *City with a Chance,* p. 135.

84. *Milwaukee Journal,* March 15, 1968, p. 1; *Milwaukee Sentinel,* March 15, 1968, p. 1; *Milwaukee Journal,* March 16, 1968, p. 14; Rozga, "March on Milwaukee," p. 38.

85. Quoted in Aukofer, *City with a Chance,* p. 142.

86. *Milwaukee Sentinel,* April 8, 1968, p. 1; *Milwaukee Journal,* April 8, 1968, p. 1; Aukofer, *City with a Chance,* pp. 142–143.

87. Barkin interview.

88. *Milwaukee Courier,* May 4, 1968, p. 1; *Milwaukee Courier,* May 11, 1968, p. 2; Aukofer, *City with a Chance,* pp. 143–144; Bartell and Stege, "The Mediation of Civil Rights Disputes"; Timm, "The Fight for Fairness."

8. Black Power Politics

1. In addition to Groppi, the delegation included five Commandos—Richard Green, Lawrence Friend, Jerry Sims, Raymond Blathers, and Charles Harper—Father Patrick Flood of the Council on Urban Affairs, and Reverend David Owen of the Milwaukee Methodist Church.

2. *Milwaukee Journal,* October 1, 1967, p. 12; *Concern,* October 15, 1967, p. 8; *Milwaukee Journal,* September 29, 1967, p. 1; *Milwaukee Journal,* October 1, 1967, p. 1.

3. *Milwaukee Journal,* October 1, 1967, pp. 1 and 12; *Concern,* October 15, 1967, p. 8.

4. *Concern,* October 15, 1967, pp. 9–10; *Milwaukee Journal,* October 1, 1967, pt. 2, p. 1; *Catholic Herald Citizen,* September 23, 1967, p. 6; *Catholic Herald Citizen,* October, 7, 1967, p. 5; *Milwaukee Journal,* October 9, 1967, pt. 2, p. 1.

5. Squire Austin, interview with Patrick Jones, October 7, 1999; Prentice McKinney, interview with Patrick Jones November 13, 1999; Margaret Rozga, interview with Patrick Jones, July 19, 2005; Frank Aukofer, *City with a Chance* (Milwaukee: Bruce Publishing Company, 1968), pp. 137–138; Jack Dougherty, *More Than One Struggle: The Evolution of Black School Reform in Milwaukee* (Chapel Hill: University of North Carolina Press, 2003), p. 120; Dennis McDowell, interview with Patrick Jones, August 11, 2005.

6. McDowell interview.

7. McKinney interview.

8. A group of World War II and Korean War veterans in Jonesboro, Louisiana, formed the original Deacons for Defense and Justice in 1964 to protect nonviolent civil rights demonstrators from Ku Klux Klan violence. Unlike the Milwaukee group by the same name, the Louisiana Deacons worked in tandem with nonviolent activists, not in opposition to them. In fact, there was no formal link between the Louisiana group and the Milwaukee group. For more on the original Deacons for Defense and Justice, see Lance Hill, *The Deacons for Defense: Armed Resistance and the Civil Rights Movement* (Chapel Hill: University of North Carolina Press, 2004). Insightful work on the Deacons can also be found in Simon Wendt, *The Spirit and the Shotgun: Armed Resistance and the Struggle for Civil Rights* (Gainesville: University Press of Florida, 2007) and Christopher Strain, *Pure Fire: Self-Defense as Activism in the Civil Rights Era* (Athens: University of Georgia Press, 2005).

9. *Milwaukee Journal,* September 20, 1967, p. 6.

10. Groppi testimony before the National Advisory Commission on Civil Disorders, James Groppi Papers, box 15, folder 5, State Historical Society of Wisconsin, Madison.

11. Quoted in FBI report on James Groppi, January 10, 1968, Father James Groppi FBI file, part 1, obtained under the Freedom of Information Act and in the possession of the author.

12. Groppi testimony before the National Advisory Commission on Civil Disorders, Groppi Papers, box 15, folder 5; Groppi FBI file, parts 1 and 2.

13. Richard Green, interview with Arlene Zakhar, April 19, 1984; McKinney interview; Austin interview.

14. The fact that the anti–open housing advocates sang "The Battle Hymn of the Republic" contained a certain irony that escaped most commentators at the time. The song was published during the Civil War by Julia Ward Howe—an abolitionist—in 1862 and was based on a popular marching song, "John Brown's Body." The original commemorated the failed raid on Harper's Ferry by the radical white abolitionist John Brown. Over time, this racialized history has been largely forgotten, and the tune has come to symbolize a more general patriotism and nationalism.

15. *Milwaukee Sentinel,* October 9, 1967, p. 1; *Milwaukee Journal,* October 9, 1967, p. 1; *Milwaukee Star,* October 14, 1967, p. 1; *Milwaukee Courier,* October 16, 1967, p. 1.

16. Quoted in Jules Modlinski, "Commandos: A Study of a Black Organization's Transformation from Militant Protest to Social Service" (PhD diss., University of Wisconsin–Madison, 1978), p. 91.

17. Ibid., p. 92.

18. *Milwaukee Journal,* October 10, 1967, pt. 2, p. 2.

19. *Milwaukee Journal,* October 10, 1967, p. 1; *Milwaukee Sentinel,* October 10, 1967, p. 1; *Milwaukee Star,* October 14, 1967, p. 1; Modlinski, "Commandos," pp. 90–94.

20. *Milwaukee Courier,* September 9, 1967, p. 3; *Milwaukee Journal,* September 2, 1967, p. 1; *Milwaukee Journal,* September 15, 1967, p. 1; *Milwaukee Journal,* September 25, 1967, p. 1; *Milwaukee Journal,* October 11, 1967, p. 1.

21. McKinney interview.

22. Green interview.

23. "Confidential Memo: Bert to Mayor," November 17, 1967, Henry Maier Papers, box 43, folder 12, State Historical Society of Wisconsin, Madison; *Milwaukee Journal,* October 20, 1967, pt. 2, p. 2.

24. Steve Estes, *I Am a Man: Race, Manhood, and the Civil Rights Movement* (Chapel Hill: University of North Carolina Press, 2005), p. 2; Groppi lecture at East Library, February 15, 1984; Ed Thekan, interview with Arlene Zakhar, February 2, 1984; McDowell interview; Rozga interview. See also Joe McClain, interview with Patrick Jones, December 3, 1998; McKinney interview; Austin interview; Alberta Harris, interview with Patrick Jones, August 27, 2005; Betty Martin public lecture, "March on Milwaukee" conference, Milwaukee, September 29, 2007, tape recording in the possession of the author. See also Peter Ling and Sharon Monteith, *Gender and the Civil Rights Movement* (New Brunswick, NJ: Rutgers University Press, 2004).

25. Estes, *I Am a Man,* pp. 131–151.

26. McDowell interview.

27. Harris interview; Rozga interview; Betty Martin public lecture.

28. Harris interview; Martin talk; Rozga interview.

29. Martin talk.

30. Rozga interview; Dick Gregory public lecture, "March on Milwaukee" conference, Milwaukee, September 29, 2007, tape recording in the possession of the author.

31. See George Lipsitz, *The Possessive Investment in Whiteness: How White People Profit from Identity Politics* (Philadelphia: Temple University Press, 1998).

32. *Milwaukee Sentinel,* September 11, 1967, p. 1; *Milwaukee Journal,* September 11, 1967, p. 1.

33. Henry Maier to Irwin Maier, September 12, 1967, Maier Papers, box 45, folder 5; *Milwaukee Courier,* September 16, 1967, p. 2; *Catholic Herald Citizen,* September 16, 1967, p. 3; *Milwaukee Journal,* September 12, 1967, p. 1.

34. *Milwaukee Journal,* September 13, 1967, p. 1. See also, "Correspondance, Hate, 1967," Groppi Papers, box 9, folders 1–6.

35. *Milwaukee Journal,* September 13, 1967, p. 1; *Milwaukee Sentinel,* September 13, 1967, p. 1.

36. Aukofer, *City with a Chance,* p. 126; *Texas Catholic Herald,* November 17, 1967, p. 1; *Catholic Herald Citizen,* October 14, 1967, p. 8; *Milwaukee Journal,* September 27, 1967, pt. 2, p. 2. At least thirty-two stores boarded up their windows after the South Side violence out of fear over continued property destruction. See *Milwaukee Journal,* September 15, 1967, p. 11; *Milwaukee Journal,* September 14, 1967, p. 1; *Milwaukee Journal,* September 14, 1967, p. 1; *Milwaukee Sentinel,* September 14, 1967, p. 1; *Milwaukee Star,* September 16, 1967, p. 1; *Catholic Herald Citizen,* September 16, 1967, p. 1; *Time,* September 22, 1967, p. 4; *U.S. News and World Report,* September 25, 1967, p. 24.

37. *Catholic Herald Citizen,* September 16, 1967, p. 4.

38. *Milwaukee Journal,* September 23, 1967, p. 4.

39. Steve Leahy at the University of Wisconsin–Fox Valley has been using GPS technology to map letters from the civil rights era. Although still a work in progress, the clear indication from Leahy's preliminary results is that white opposition did not simply emanate from working-class South Side neighborhoods or from Polish Americans, primarily, but came from every section of the city and from all classes.

40. Thousands of letters can be found in the Groppi Papers. Although most came from Milwaukee or outlying areas, hundreds came from outside the city and state. A sampling of locations includes New York, Los Angeles, San Francisco, Boston, Cleveland, Chicago, St. Louis, Tulsa, Mississippi, Atlanta, Detroit, Buffalo, Cincinnati, Madison, Minneapolis, Philadelphia, Durham, Anchorage, Pittsburgh, Roanoke, Houston, Appleton, and Birmingham. In addition, the Eugene Bleidorn Papers and Henry Maier Papers also include similar, but smaller, samples.

41. Groppi Papers. See also Maier Papers, Bleidorn Papers, and Clemente Zablocki Papers, all at the State Historical Society of Wisconsin.

42. Steve Meyer, "Rough Manhood: The Aggressive and Confrontational Shop Culture of U.S. Auto Workers during World War II," *Journal of Social History* 36 (2002): 125–147.
43. Telegram from Dr. Martin Luther King Jr. to Father James Groppi, September 4, 1967, Groppi Papers, Manuscript EX, box 2, folder 3. (The original telegram was not punctuated.)

9. The Decline of Direct Action

1. *Milwaukee Courier,* September 20, 1969, p. 1; *Milwaukee Journal,* September 23,1969, pt. 2, p. 1; *Milwaukee Journal,* September 24, 1969, pt. 2, p. 8; *Madison Capital Times,* September 25,1969, p. 2; *Milwaukee Journal,* September 25, 1969, pt. 2, p. 12; *Madison Capital Times,* September 26, 1969, p. 2; *Milwaukee Journal,* September 27, 1969, pt. 2, p. 3; *Madison Capital Times,* September 27, 1969, p. 1; *Wisconsin State Journal,* September 28, 1969, sec. 3, p. 3.
2. *Milwaukee Journal,* September 29, 1969, pt. 2, p. 1; *Wisconsin State Journal,* September 28, 1969, sec. 3, p. 3; *Milwaukee Sentinel,* September 29, 1969, pp. 1, 12. See also Dismas Becker, interview with Patrick Jones, November 19, 1998 and January 27, 1999.
3. *Madison Capital Times,* September 30, 1969, p. 1; *Wisconsin State Journal,* September 30, 1969, p. 1; *Milwaukee Journal,* September 30, 1969, p. 1; *Milwaukee Sentinel,* September 30, 1969, p. 1; Becker interview.
4. Ibid.
5. See *Milwaukee Journal,* October 2, 1969, p. 1; *Milwaukee Sentinel,* October 2, 1969, p. 3; *Milwaukee Sentinel,* October 3, 1969, p. 1; Becker interview.
6. Becker interview.
7. Gerald McKnight, *The Last Crusade: Martin Luther King, Jr., the FBI, and the Poor People's Campaign* (Boulder, CO: Westview Press, 1998).
8. Unacknowledged May 1968 news clipping in Father James Groppi FBI file, part 2, obtained under the Freedom of Information Act and in the possession of the author.
9. McKnight, *The Last Crusade,* p. 103.
10. Ibid., p. 119; FBI, "Supplemental Correlational Summary," September 30, 1970, p. 7, Groppi FBI file, part 2.
11. For a full overview of the development of the Commandos, Inc., and the Commando Project I, see Julius Modlinski, "Commandos: A Study of a Black Organization's Transformation from Militant Protest to Social Service" (PhD diss., University of Wisconsin–Madison, 1978). See also Jesse Wade, interview with Arlene Zakhar, May 1, 1984.
12. Prentice McKinney, interview with Patrick Jones, November 13, 1999.
13. Becker interview.

14. Paul Crawford, interview with Arlene Zakhar, April 25, 1984.

15. "The Milwaukee 14," University of Wisconsin–Milwaukee online archive, http://www.uwm.edu/Libraries/arch/nhd2005/htm/vietnam.htm (accessed October 27, 2004).

16. Zach Schwartz, "The 1971 Yale Strike: Imperial Power, Workers' Struggle and Urban Renewal in the Globalization of the University," April 16, 2004, http://problemofleisure.blogspot.com (accessed January 11, 2008).

17. *Milwaukee Courier,* March 23, 1968, p. 1; James Jones, interview with Patrick Jones, March 16, 1997.

18. Jones interview.

19. Ibid.; *New York Times,* May 25, 1968, p. 70.

20. *IUE News,* August 11, 1968, p. 1, International Union of Electronic, Electrical, Technical, Salaried & Machine Workers, AFL-CIO, Local 1131 Records, box 9, folder 1, Urban Archive, University of Wisconsin–Milwaukee; *Milwaukee Journal,* August 11, 1968, p. 1; *Milwaukee Sentinel,* August 15, 1968, p. 1; "Rumors-Confusion," *IUE News,* August 26, 1968, International Union of Electronic, Electrical, Technical, Salaried & Machine Workers, AFL-CIO, Local 1131 Records, box 9, folder 1.

21. *Milwaukee Courier,* August 10, 1968, p. 4. Similar statements appear in materials located in the James Groppi Papers, boxes 14 and 15, State Historical Society of Wisconsin, Madison; *New York Times,* August 11, 1968, p. 41; *Milwaukee Sentinel,* August 12, 1968, p. 1; *Milwaukee Journal,* August 14, 1968, p. 1.

22. *Milwaukee Courier,* October 17, 1968, p. 1.

23. The *Milwaukee Journal* ran articles on August 11, 13, 14, 15, 16, 17, 18, 19, 20, and 21, and the *Milwaukee Sentinel* published pieces on August 12, 15, 16, 17, 21, 22, and 23. See also *New York Times,* August 11, 1968, p. 41; Jones interview.

24. *Milwaukee Journal,* August 19, 1969, p. 1; *Milwaukee Journal,* August 22, 1969, p. 1.

25. *Business Week,* January 11, 1969, p. 90; Jones interview.

26. Felicia Kornbluh, *The Battle for Welfare Rights: Politics and Poverty in Modern America* (Philadelphia: University of Pennsylvania Press, 2007); Annelise Orleck, *Storming Caesar's Palace: How Black Mothers Fought Their Own War on Poverty* (Boston: Beacon Press, 2006); Premill Nadasen, *Welfare Warriors: The Welfare Rights Movement in the United States* (New York: Routledge, 2004); Francis Fox Piven and Richard Cloward, *Poor People's Movements: How They Succeed and Why They Fail* (New York: Random House, 1979); Becker interview.

27. Becker interview.

28. Ibid.

29. Vel Phillips jokingly asserted that Pitts's election to the Common Council created an instantaneous "Black Caucus" in city government. In fact, as the only two African Americans on the council, the two representatives did often consult

one another about issues of concern to inner core residents; Vel Phillips, interview with Patrick Jones, April 20, 1999.

30. For a full overview of the Black Panther Party in Milwaukee, see Andrew Witt, "Self-Help and Self-Defense: A Revaluation of the Black Panther Party with Emphasis on the Milwaukee Chapter" (master's thesis, University of Wisconsin–Milwaukee, 1999).

Conclusion

1. Jonathan Coleman, *Long Way to Go: Black and White in America* (New York: Atlantic Monthly Press, 1998).

2. Ibid., pp. 6–23.

3. Telegram from Dr. Martin Luther King Jr. to Father James Groppi, September 4, 1967, James Groppi Papers, Manuscript EX, box 2, folder 3, State Historical Society of Wisconsin, Madison.

4. Quoted in John McGreevy, *Parish Boundaries: The Catholic Encounter with Race in the Twentieth-Century Urban North* (Chicago: University of Chicago Press, 1996), p. 202.

5. Margaret Rozga, interview with Patrick Jones, September 19, 2005.

6. Coleman, *Long Way to Go,* p. 6.

7. William Thompson, *The History of Wisconsin,* vol. 6: *Continuity and Change, 1940–1965* (Madison: State Historical Society of Wisconsin, 1988), p. 395.

8. See http://www.jsonline.com/news/census2000 (accessed December 12, 2007).

9. *Madison Insurgent,* February 2002, p. 1.

Sources

Manuscript Collections

Atkielski, Roman. Papers. Cousins Catholic Center, Milwaukee.

Barbee, Lloyd. Papers. State Historical Society of Wisconsin, Madison.

Barrett, James. Papers. Marquette University, Milwaukee.

Becker, Dismas. Papers. State Historical Society of Wisconsin, Madison.

Bleidorn, Eugene. Papers. Cousins Catholic Center, Milwaukee.

Bleidorn, Eugene. Papers. State Historical Society of Wisconsin, Madison.

Casa Maria Catholic Worker Community. Records. Marquette University, Milwaukee.

Christian Family Movement, Milwaukee Chapter. Records. Notre Dame University, South Bend, Indiana.

Congress of Racial Equality. Papers. State Historical Society of Wisconsin, Madison.

Cullen, Michael Denis. Papers. Marquette University, Milwaukee.

Dorothy Day Catholic Worker. Papers. Marquette University, Milwaukee.

Fisher, Cecil. Papers. University of Wisconsin–Milwaukee.

Freedom School. Papers. Cousins Catholic Center, Milwaukee.

Friend, Henry C. Papers. Milwaukee County Historical Society, Milwaukee.

Groppi, Father James. Papers. Milwaukee County Historical Society, Milwaukee.

Groppi, Father James. Papers. State Historical Society of Wisconsin, Madison.

Jacobson, Thomas. Papers. Milwaukee County Historical Society, Milwaukee.

Johansen, Marilyn and Walter. Papers. University of Wisconsin–Milwaukee.

Maier, Henry. Papers. State Historical Society of Wisconsin, Madison.

Milwaukee City Attorney. Papers. Legislative Reference Bureau, Milwaukee.

Milwaukee Commission on Community Relations. Papers. Legislative Reference Bureau, Milwaukee.

Milwaukee Common Council. Papers. Legislative Reference Bureau, Milwaukee.

Milwaukee Congress of Racial Equality. Papers. State Historical Society of Wisconsin, Madison.

Milwaukee County Welfare Rights Organization. Papers. State Historical Society of Wisconsin, Madison.

Milwaukee Journal Stations. 1922–1969. Milwaukee Transcript Collection 203. Wisconsin Historical Society. Milwaukee Area Research Center. University of Wisconsin–Milwaukee.

Milwaukee National Association for the Advancement of Colored People (MNAACP). Papers. State Historical Society of Wisconsin, Madison.

Milwaukee United School Integration Committee (MUSIC). Papers. State Historical Society of Wisconsin, Madison.

Milwaukee Urban League. Papers. State Historical Society of Wisconsin, Madison.

National Association for the Advancement of Colored People (NAACP). Papers. Library of Congress, Washington, DC.

National Catholic Conference for Interracial Justice. Collection. Marquette University, Milwaukee.

Radtke, Lorraine. Papers. University of Wisconsin–Milwaukee.

St. Boniface Church. Papers. Cousins Catholic Center, Milwaukee.

United Community Services of Greater Milwaukee. Papers. University of Wisconsin–Milwaukee.

Zeidler, Frank and Carl. Papers. State Historical Society of Wisconsin, Madison.

Newspapers and Magazines

America

Business Week

Catholic Herald Citizen

Catholic World

Chicago Tribune

Christian Century

Ebony

Economist

Kaleidoscope

Look

Marquette Tribune

Milwaukee Courier

Milwaukee Defender

Milwaukee Journal

Milwaukee Magazine

Milwaukee Sentinel

Milwaukee Star

The Nation

The National Review

The New Republic
Newsweek
New York Times
Time
U.S. News and World Report
Wall Street Journal

Interviews by the Author

Cleo Adams
Squire Austin
Lloyd Barbee
Ben Barkin
Dismas Becker
Sylvia Bell-White
Clayborn Benson
Eugene Bleidorn
Mary Agnes Blonien
Richard Budelman
James Cameron
Reverend Inonia Champion
Velma Coggs
Marianne Epstein
Patrick Flood
John Gilman
John Givens
Grant and Lucinda Gordon
Father Mathew Gottschalk
Reverend B. S. Gregg
Reuben Harpole
Alberta Harris
Thomas Jacobson
Conrad Kaminski
Myrtle Kastner
Betty Martin
Joe McClain
Dennis McDowell
Prentice McKinney
Michael Neuberger
Vel Phillips
Fred Reed

Margaret Rozga
Wesley Scott
Calvin Sherard

Other Interviews Used

Special thanks to Professor Walter "Bud" Weare at the University of Wisconsin–Milwaukee, who generously donated a number of interview tapes and transcripts that a graduate assistant, Arlene Zakhar, conducted for him in 1984. Here is a list of the interviewees:

Eugene Bleidorn
Velma Coggs
Mike Connors
Paul Crawford
Tyrone Daniels
Patrick Flood
George Gerhorz
Richard Green
James Groppi and Vel Phillips (television interview)
James Groppi (lecture at East Side Library)
Loretta Jones
Anthony Maggiore
Betty Martin
Marilyn Clark Mindimoye
Kathleen Moylan and Flo Seefeldt
Cynthia Pitts
Juanita Renteria
Reverend Kenneth Smith
Ed Thekan
Jesse Wade
Loretta Webster

Acknowledgments

I have come to understand that no book is the work of a single author. There are many people who contributed to this project and deserve my heartfelt thanks. First and foremost, this project was a collaborative effort between a young, aspiring historian, concerned with the state of race relations in the United States and interested in telling a story of the northern civil rights movement, and the Milwaukee African American community, which was gracious enough to trust me with their experiences, their stories, and their aspirations. Over the many hours I spent with this diverse cross-section of people, their courage, conviction, and dignity in the pursuit of racial justice endlessly inspired me. I have labored long in their honor, for the sacrifices many of them made to help the United States live up to its most noble ideals. It is they who deserve credit for anything that seems worthwhile in these pages. I take sole responsibility for any shortcomings.

As my mentor, colleague, and friend, Tim Tyson, more than any other person, has helped me understand the "subversive joy" of African American history and culture. He taught me to be a rigorous historian, but also to consider history a "creative art." Tim's imprint on this project and in my development as a professional historian is profound.

As a graduate student at the University of Wisconsin–Madison, I was fortunate to learn from an amazing group of scholars, including Paul Boyer, Bill Cronon, Linda Gordon, Herbert Hill, Steve Kantrowitz, Stanley Kutler, Alfred McCoy, Nellie McKay, Brenda Gayle Plummer, Joel Rogers, William Van de Berg, and Craig Werner. I am also deeply indebted to a circle of friends and fellow graduate students for both their scholarly and personal support, including Charles Hughes, Hiroshi Kitamura, Lisa Levenstein, Jennifer Mandel, Danielle McGuire, T. J. Mertz, Lisa Tetrault, and Simon Wendt.

As a scholar, you fall in love with ideas and books, and they affect you. I want to acknowledge some of the many thinkers and writers in my field who have made their mark on me over the years: Carol Anderson, Curtis Austin, Davarian Baldwin,

James Baldwin, Derrick Bell, Ira Berlin, Martha Biondi, Taylor Branch, Clayborn Carson, Dan Carter, William Chafe, Jeff Chang, Matthew Countryman. Emilye Crosby, Harold Cruse, John Dittmer, Jack Dougherty, W. E. B. Du Bois, Mary Dudziak, Steve Estes, Adam Fairclough, Eric Foner, Glenda Gilmore, Robert Gordon, Jacquelyn Dowd Hall, Vincent Harding, Lance Hill, Darlene Clark Hine, Michael Honey, Thomas Jackson, Kenneth Jolly, Jacqueline Jones, Will Jones, Peniel Joseph, Robin Kelley, Jonathan Kozol, Chana Kai Lee, Lawrence Levine, Peter Levy, David Levering Lewis, Greil Marcus, Nell Painter, Orlando Patterson, Charles Payne, Barbara Ransby, David Roediger, Scott Saul, Robert Self, Thomas Sugrue, Patricia Sullivan, Jeanne Theoharis, Joe Trotter, Cornel West, Rhonda Williams, Yohuru Williams, Komozi Woodard, Nan Woodruff, Cynthia Young, and Howard Zinn.

I would be remiss if I did not recognize the trailblazing work on the history of Black Milwaukee by Frank Aukofer, Jack Dougherty, and Joe Trotter. My work stands on their shoulders.

The University of Nebraska–Lincoln (UNL) generously supported research for this book through a grant and a one-semester leave. A number of UNL faculty and staff have helped along the way: Waskar Ari, Tim Borstelmann, Andy Graybill, Lisa Gustafson, Cindy Hilsabeck, Nancy Knapp, Jill Mustard, Sandra Pershing, Doug Seefeldt, Will Thomas, and Ken Winkle.

A special thanks to all of the library and archives workers who have helped me find what I was looking for, particularly Jim Danky at the State Historical Society of Wisconsin, Ed Duesterhoeft and Karla Klein in the Memorial Library microfilm room, Lori Bessler in the State Historical Society of Wisconsin microfilm room, Harry Miller and Dee Grimsrud in the State Historical Society of Wisconsin archive, and Tim Carey at the Cousins Catholic Center in Milwaukee. Their work is too often overlooked yet indispensable to our success as historians.

I am fortunate to work with Harvard University Press and their stellar editorial staff, particularly Kathleen McDermott and her assistant, Kathleen Drummy, as well as John Donohue and the staff at Westchester Book Services. This work is better because of their efforts.

One of the most meaningful gifts this project gave me was the opportunity to conduct oral histories with so many fascinating people. All of the folks I spoke with enriched my understanding of race relations and civil rights insurgency in Milwaukee, but a few warrant special mention: Margaret Rozga trusted me enough to share the story of her life with Father Groppi, and that has made all the difference in the world to this book. Joe McClain and Dennis McDowell took me inside the Commandos. Lloyd Barbee offered not only his rich experience as a freedom fighter but also his love of Nina Simone. And Vel Phillips, a bona fide Milwaukee civil rights legend and an indefatigable spirit, was kind enough to let me into her world, share her stories, and, in the process, become my dear friend.

I would also like to extend a hearty thanks to Jasmine Alinder and Aims McGuinness at the University of Wisconsin–Milwaukee. Jasmine played a lead organizing role in the "March on Milwaukee" fortieth anniversary commemoration of the open housing campaign that took place on September 29, 2007. Both Jasmine and Aims have been enthusiastic supporters of my research throughout the process.

Anyone who knows me understands my love affair with coffeehouses. In a society with few public spaces that bring us together to talk and share, I have long appreciated the fascinating collection of writers, thinkers, poets, musicians, athletes, activists, philosophers, freaks, and folks that you find at cafés across the country. A large portion of this project was written with light conversation, clanking glasses, and the occasional acoustic guitar humming in the background. In Madison: Ground Zero, Mother Fools, and Café Zoma. In Cleveland: Cravings and Arabica. In Milwaukee: Rochambo and Fuel. In Meadeville: Artist's Cup. In Lincoln: The Mill, MoJava, Jones Coffee, Kopeli, Thé Cup, and The Coffee House.

I thank all of my good friends who believed in my vision and extended a hand when necessary, particularly Blair and Stacy Williams, Wick Pancoast and Carrie Wilson, James and Jenny Garza, Chris DeVine, Bill Elliott, T. J. Mertz and Karin Schmidt, Amanda Jones and Bennett Salber, Joe Germuska, Les Murphy, Rachel Steury, David Klagsbrun, Bob and Jody LePage, Katie Sisco, David and Jill Baum, Tous Teamore, Don and Elizabeth Hanigan, Petra Kleinlein, and the entire Freedom Ride 2001 community.

My family has provided unending support and love throughout this journey. As anyone who writes knows, it is your personal relationships that get you through the rough spots. My brothers and sisters-in-law—Chris, Jeff, Ruth, and Jodi—have consistently encouraged me and have been there to lend an ear, offer advice, or give a pep talk when necessary. My nieces and nephews—Nathan, Noel, Sophia, Emily, and Lauren—are a source of unending joy. They provided extra inspiration by being thrilled that "Uncle Patrick" was writing a book; they think this is cool, and I do, too. I thank Dennis and Regina Wilson, who have opened their hearts and their home to me and invited me to be a part of their family; and Kaya Phoenix Jones, the little furry monster that lay on my feet over the final six months of this project.

There are three people who have been so spectacularly significant during the completion of this manuscript that no words can possibly convey my debt. Andréa Wilson, the love of my life, has been an unending source of inspiration, kindness, and compassion. She has picked up so much slack during the last year of this effort, that I'll be cooking dinner, washing dishes, and doing laundry for the next ten years to make up for it. She is my everything, and I am deeply grateful to have her in my life.

The fierce loyalty, support, pride, and love of my parents, Betty and Ray Jones, have never faltered for a moment. They are the source from which I spring and to which I consistently return for renewal and wisdom. This project truly could not have happened without them. My dad deserves an extra helping of praise for serving as my personal editor and chief counsel on this project.

Finally, I am deeply indebted to all of the people, ordinary and extraordinary, across the country and around the world, who have courageously participated in one of the greatest social movements in our nation's history: the black freedom movement. I am particularly moved by the example of Ella Baker and the Student Nonviolent Coordinating Committee. The profound respect and dignity for all people, regardless of caste or class, that lay at the heart of their approach to social change has been one of the single most transformative influences in my life. It is their example that I strive to emulate in my work as a teacher, scholar, and citizen.

Index

Acculturation model, 26, 29–30, 39, 41, 49, 57, 76, 85, 87, 231

African Americans: early history in Milwaukee, 11–14, 18–23, 267n4; middle-class, 14, 20, 21–22, 26, 29, 30, 36, 37, 38, 41–42, 45, 54, 56, 57, 153, 171, 175, 180, 226; post–World War II population growth, 19, 23–26, 269n28; and segregation, 19, 21, 24, 25, 27, 40, 50, 59–79; migration, 23–24; political leadership, 25–26, 56–57, 269n33, 301n29; and Milwaukee police, 36–37; and Catholic Church, 86–88; and housing, 171–172; and post–civil rights era, 252–259

Allen-Bradley Corporation: and John Birch Society, 129; protest, 243–248; "friends and family" policy, 244

Anwar, Ali, 43, 44, 46

Atkielski, Roman, 104, 105

Aukofer, Frank, 3, 60, 81, 82, 93, 114, 126, 127, 139, 166, 205, 208

Austin, Squire, 144, 179, 184, 200, 201, 213, 218

Barbee, Lloyd: background, 25, 30, 60–61; Fred Lins protest, 53; and MUSIC protest, 59–60, 63–64, 67–78, 101–102, 103, 253, 256; leadership style, 61–62; and *Brown v. Board of Education* decision, 62; opposition, 63–64; and EC protest, 120; and MNAACP bombing, 122; and police–community relations, 150, 156;

and open housing campaign, 174, 181; and Welfare Mothers March, 237, 238; as legislator, 249, 250, 253

Barrett, Tom, 258

Barry, Marion, 210

Battle, Melvin, 38

Bay View, Wisconsin, 17, 93

Beauchamp, Louis, 68, 222

Becker, Dismas, 239, 241, 247–248

Bell, Daniel: murder, 32–33, 270nn1, 2; inquest, 34; protest, 36–39, 41, 43, 47, 48, 54, 55, 57, 103

Bell, Sylvia, 33, 39

Big Boy protest, 112

Biondi, Martha, 6

Birmingham, Alabama, 49–51

"Black Christmas" protest, 204–205, 213

Black Panther Party, 132, 136, 137, 243, 249, 252, 253

Black Power: and open housing campaign, 1, 180, 182, 192, 204, 210–215, 219, 221, 254; historiography, 4, 6, 7, 123; and Father Groppi, 4, 138, 154, 216, 217; in Milwaukee, 7, 148, 212–223, 234–235, 255; and EC protest, 110; and armed self-defense, 123–124, 297n8; and "not-violence," 133–135, 285n52; and the YC, 137–140, 153; and the Commandos, 137–140, 141; nationally, 137–138, 143; and Henry Maier, 165; and Washington, D.C., incident, 210–213, 296n1; and police–community relations, 218–221; and violence, 219–221; and class tensions,

North Division High School, 77, 95, 190, 258
"Not-violence," 133–134, 140, 215, 216, 222, 223, 224, 234, 254, 285n52

Ochs, Phil, 243
Oliver, Joe, 12
Ono, Yoko, 243
Open housing campaign: demonstrations, 1–4, 169–170, 180–206; role of police, 1–4, 8, 170, 179, 184, 188–189, 190, 192, 193, 195, 196, 201, 203, 206, 208, 213, 215, 218–221, 226, 228, 229, 230; role of YC, 1–4, 7, 11, 34, 95, 158, 168, 169–170, 179–217, 219, 220, 232, 235, 254, 255; role of Father Groppi, 1–4, 11, 158, 168, 169–170, 179–214, 216–217, 219, 220, 222, 223, 225–250, 254; white reaction, 1–4, 170, 172, 173–174, 177, 179, 183–185, 195–196, 204–205, 215, 218, 227–234, 235, 255, 290n45, 299n36; role of Commandos, 2, 4, 11, 168, 169–170, 180–191, 195, 196, 200–203, 205–208, 210–227, 232, 245, 254, 255; residential segregation, 19–20, 177; state law, 52, 174–175; and St. Boniface, 138, 194, 200–201, 213, 215, 222, 227; role of Vel Phillips, 150, 175–179, 180, 181, 183, 185, 188, 189, 190, 196, 197, 198, 207, 208, 209, 212; role of Common Council, 150, 158, 169, 170, 176, 183, 185, 191, 195, 196–198, 199, 205, 206, 208, 222, 230, 255; picketing aldermens' homes, 158; role of Henry Maier, 165, 166, 177, 180, 181, 182, 184, 186–187, 188, 191, 192, 193, 194, 195, 196, 198, 199, 206, 208, 224, 228; background, 170–175; as a national crusade, 178, 183, 189–196, 197, 199, 200–203, 206, 207, 210–213, 217, 231, 254, 255; Ronald Britton incident, 179; and beer boycott, 191, 194, 203, 204, 296n76; and "Black Christmas" campaign, 204–206, 213; assessment of, 255–258
Orellana, Armando, 245–246
Organization of Organizations, 157
Osofsky, Gilbert, 19

Phillip, E. B., 38
Phillips, Dale, 175, 179

Phillips, Vel: background, 26, 30, 103, 175; and Daniel Bell protest, 38; and Maier's "go slow" approach, 51; and Fred Lins protest, 55; and school boycott, 76; and EC protest, 130; and police–community relations 150, 157; and open housing campaign, 175–181, 183, 185, 188, 189–190, 196–197, 198, 207, 208, 209, 212; election of 1956, 176; and alliance with YC and Father Groppi, 179–180; after open housing campaign, 249, 250, 258. See also Open housing campaign: role of Vel Phillips
Pierce, Jimmy, 180, 241
Pitts, Orville, 249
Pitts, Terence, 153
Police–community relations: Daniel Bell case, 32–41; during the 1950s, 35–36, 42–43; Chief Harold Breier, 148–149; Tactical Squad, 149–150, 288n14; conflict with YC and Commandos, 150–153, 155–157, 218–221; and Black Power, 218–221. See also Open housing campaign: role of police
Poor People's Campaign, 206, 238–240
Pratt, Marvin, 257
Pride, Inc., 210–211, 222

Randolph, A. Philip, 41, 44, 61, 250
Richardson, Gloria, 6
Riots. See Civil disturbance
Robinson, Bill, 245
Rozga, Margaret, 84, 94, 97, 98, 100, 102, 107, 114, 118, 119, 126, 142, 183, 202, 207, 213, 223, 225, 226, 227, 250, 255, 258
Rubin, Jerry, 243

Sargent, Pamela Jo, 115, 184, 226, 258
Schlaefer, Austin, 80, 83, 96
Scott, Wesley, 51, 164, 206
Seale, Bobby, 136, 243
Seefeldt, Flo, 68
Segregation: early history, 13–14; white ethnic neighborhoods, 16–17; in housing, 19–20, 292n6; in social life, 20; in education, 63–64; in post–civil rights era, 257–258
Self, Robert, 6